# Internal exile in Fascist Italy

MANCHEStER
1824

Manchester University Press

# Internal exile in Fascist Italy

*History and representations of* confino

Piero Garofalo, Elizabeth Leake and Dana Renga

Manchester University Press

Published by Manchester University Press
Oxford Road, Manchester M13 9PL
www.manchesteruniversitypress.co.uk

British Library Cataloguing-in-Publication Data
A catalogue record for this book is available from the British Library


ISBN 978 0 7190 9059 2 hardback
ISBN 978 1 5261 6387 5 paperback

First published 2019
Paperback published 2022

Typeset by Newgen Publishing UK

# Contents

# Acknowledgements

We are indebted to the staff of the Archivio Centrale dello Stato in Rome, the Biblioteca Nazionale Centrale di Roma, the Biblioteca Nazionale Centrale di Firenze, the Istituto Storico della Resistenza in Toscana, the Centro Studi e Ricerche di Storia e Problemi Eoliani, and the Istituto Provinciale per la Storia del Movimento di Liberazione nelle Marche e nell'Età Contemporanea Ascoli Piceno for the assistance they have given us. A portion of Chapter 4 appeared as 'Screening Confino: Male Melodrama, Trauma, Exile Cinema,' in the *Journal of Italian Cinema and Media Studies* 5.1 (2017): 23–46, published by Intellect Ltd, Bristol. We thank the *Journal of Italian Cinema and Media Studies* for their permission to republish. We extend our gratitude to Elio Girlanda, Paul Rowley, Debora Inguglia, and Gabriella Romano for sharing their films with us and to Manlio Todeschini for sharing his film archive. Many thanks also to Maria Coletti, Viridiana Rotondi and Valeria Dalle Donne for granting access to the film archives in Rome and Bologna.

Dana Renga thanks Amy Boylan, Danielle Hipkins, Catherine O'Rawe, Elena Past, Kevin Regan-Maglione and Sergio Rigoletto for helpful comments on early drafts, The Division of Arts and Humanities at Ohio State University and the Coca-Cola Critical Difference for Women Program for their generous assistance, and Richard Samuels for intellectual and amorous support. Elizabeth Leake thanks Irene Bulla, Alessia Palanti, and Jennifer Rhodes for their insightful comments. Piero Garofalo thanks Mauro Canali, Andrea Di Stefano, Giuseppe La Greca, Cristian Muscelli, Paula Salvio, and Daniela Selisca for their invaluable assistance, the University of New Hampshire's Center for the Humanities for its generosity, and Karen, Matteo, Alessia, and Alessandro for their infinite support and patience.

# Abbreviations

| | |
|---|---|
| ACS | *Archivio Centrale dello Stato* (State Central Archive) |
| b. | *Busta* (Envelope) |
| CPC | *Casellario Politico Centrale* (Central Political Registry) |
| DAGR | *Divisione Affari Generali e Riservati* (Division of General and Confidential Affairs) |
| DGPS | *Direzione Generale della Pubblica Sicurezza* (General Directorate of Public Security) |
| f. | *Fascicolo* (File) |
| GOI | *Grande Oriente d'Italia* (Grand Orient of Italy) |
| ICRC | International Committee of the Red Cross |
| IRC | Italian Red Cross |
| MI | *Ministero dell'Interno* (Ministry of the Interior) |
| MVSN | *Milizia Volontaria per la Sicurezza Nazionale* (Voluntary militia for national security or Blackshirts) |
| PCI | *Partito Comunista Italiano* (Italian Communist Party) |
| PNF | *Partito Nazionale Fascista* (National Fascist Party) |
| OVRA | secret police |
| RD | *Regio Decreto* (Royal Decree) |
| RDL | *Regio Decreto Legge* (Royal Legislative Decree) |
| TULPS | *Testo Unico delle leggi di pubblica sicurezza* (consolidated acts on public security) |
| UCI | *Ufficio Centrale di Investigazione* (Investigations Central Office) |
| UCP | *Ufficio Confino Politico* (Political Confinement Office) |

# Introduction

                    Richard Lovelace, 'To Althea, from Prison' lines 25–6.

Writing from London's Gatehouse in 1642, Lovelace idealises the spiritual transcendence of corporeal incarceration to celebrate the freedom of conscience. Contrast this cavalier indifference to material restraints with that of Black Arts Movement poet Etheridge Knight who, writing from Indiana State Prison, argues 'that physical brutality is as nothing compared to the brutality of the soul incurred by years and years of cancerous prison life'.[1] These two competing narratives of freedom and torment are recurring motifs in the memories of Italians sentenced to *confino* (internal exile) under Fascism. Confined to prisons without walls (remote islands and villages) far from their Altheas, thousands of men and women suffered this punitive practice, which the Regime had adopted as a political means to discipline dissidents.[2] To pre-empt public criticism of the measure, Mussolini spun these detention sites as more akin to island getaways than to isolated penitentiaries.

Fast-forward to 2003, when, in an interview with conservative columnists and apparent Berlusconi enthusiasts Boris Johnson and Nicholas Farrell, Italy's premier parroted these Fascist platitudes when favourably contrasting *Il Duce* to deposed Iraqi president Saddam Hussein: 'Mussolini did not murder anyone. Mussolini sent people on holiday to confine them'.[3] Berlusconi's flippant assessment was more mainstream than fringe: today's global war on terrorism, stoked by the global refugee crisis, has led democracies to enact legislation that restricts due process to enhance national security.[4] Pre-emptive detention (devoid, however, of consolatory aesthetics) is once again rationalised as a necessary measure to prevent violence. Current national security policies as exemplified by the United States Department of Homeland Security's 'If You See Something, Say Something™' campaign adjures citizens to report suspicious behaviour to law enforcement. With such vague parameters, the authorities have broad discretionary leeway to determine whether a complaint warrants investigation. This mobilisation of the public for the public good may or may not be effective, but Fascism evinces its potentials for abuse:

> Alle volte, bastava una parola, un gesto, un'imprecazione mormorata a denti stretti ... Bastava questo, per meritarsi il confino durante il fascismo. Perché da qualche parte c'era sempre un solerte cittadino che per paura, o per cieca fede nel regime, cambiava strada e infilava la porta di un commissariato per fare delazione ... E la formidabile rete spionistica, affidata pure a cittadini comuni, non limitava le sue attenzioni ai comportamenti politici o alle dichiarazioni pubbliche: non erano consentite critiche al fascismo neppure se contenute in diari chiusi nei cassetti delle scrivanie o affidate a lettere private.[5]

> (Sometimes a word, a gesture, a curse muttered between gritted teeth sufficed ... This was enough to earn *confino* under Fascism. Because somewhere there was always a diligent citizen who, out of fear or blind faith in the Regime, would change directions and sneak into a police station to inform ... And this formidable spy network, entrusted also to ordinary citizens, did not limit its concerns to political behaviour or to public statements: criticisms of Fascism were not allowed even if held in diaries locked in drawers or confided in private letters.)

The Regime was unrepentant in its need to control, restrict, document, and discipline those who questioned any aspect of Fascism because to question a part was to challenge the whole.

Contemporary practices of *a priori* confinement are constrictive variants of an exile tradition that crosses cultures and far-pre-dates Fascism.[6] In China the seventh-century Tang Code lists exile among the five forms of corporal punishment. In feudal Japan, political offenders were banished to small islands under a punishment known as *Shimanagashi*. Both Imperial Russia and the Soviet Union utilised political and administrative exile to tragic effect. The practice of ὀστρακισμός (ostracism) in fifth-century BCE Athenian democracy was a pre-emptive measure to neutralise perceived threats to the state by exiling citizens from the polis. Under this procedure, which operated outside the judiciary, no charges were filed and no defence could be mounted.[7]

To limit the discussion to the Italian territory, ancient Syracuse practised Petalism, which allowed for the banishing of suspect citizens. In Republican Rome, exile was generally not a formal legal penalty, but rather a long-standing practice adopted as both a defence and a punishment.[8] Imperial Rome maintained the tradition of forced resettlement with high profile evictions such as Augustus' inscrutable removal of Ovid to Tomis and Claudius' salacious expulsion of Seneca to Corsica. The end of Roman rule in the peninsula hardly ended the practice: the Ostrogoth Theodoric the Great banished Boethius to the *Ager Calventianus*, a country estate in the environs of Pavia, in the sixth century CE. Subsequently, such illustrious figures as Dante and Machiavelli suffered exile – the former external and the latter internal. In short, throughout history, those in power have utilised exile as an expeditious instrument to vacate political challenges. In this sense then, the Regime's implementation of the measure could be considered another manifestation of Fascist *Romanitas*. Because *confino* expanded upon a familiar historical sanction, people could be lulled into complacency rather than roused to outrage at exile's incarnation under Fascism. Indeed, to become inured to the commonplace was precisely the public response that Mussolini sought by stressing environment over individuals.

For seventeen years, from 1926 to 1943, the Regime relocated political and social undesirables to the desolate margins of the nation. Well-known dissidents and future leaders of the Republic such as Giorgio Amendola, Amadeo Bordiga, Francesco Fancello, Leone Ginzburg, Antonio Gramsci, Pietro Nenni, Randolfo Pacciardi, Ferruccio Parri, Sandro Pertini, Giuseppe Romita, Carlo Rosselli, Nello Rosselli, Pietro Secchia, Altiero Spinelli, Umberto Terracini, and Tito Zaniboni suffered internal exile along with thousands of men and women whose names history has neglected. As a precautionary measure dispensed administratively, this punishment was not subject to judiciary review. Moreover, it could be applied (and was) to prevent people who had completed their prison sentences from re-entering society. In addition, a *confinato* (person sentenced to *confino*) charged with violating a regulation, could be brought before a court or the Special Tribunal for Defense of the State to stand trial thereby making 'recidivism' a desired outcome for the Regime. Thus, internal exile was less a preventive act than a means to assert political and social control.

Although memoirs of the *confino* experience circulated after the war, critical reassessments of this disciplinary strategy did not begin in earnest until the 1970s, catalysed by the pioneering work of Celso Ghini and Adriano Dal Pont, *Gli antifascisti al confino*.[9] This historical reconstruction received an infusion of data in 1983, when Dal Pont and Simonetta Carolini produced the monumental four-volume *L'Italia al confino 1926–1943*, which documented the sentencing records of 12,330 political detainees.[10] Following this data-driven lead, Salvatore Carbone took, in what has now become the series *Il popolo al confino*, a regional approach to organising archival materials on detainees.[11] In these studies as well, the emphasis is on cataloguing information on the prisoners and on identifying the detention sites. These initial enquiries into *confino* reflected the dominant historiography on Fascism of the post-war period, one that treated the dictatorship as an anomaly: a violent minority that had imposed its will by force upon Italians, who were essentially *brava gente* (good people) and never identified with the Regime.[12] Hence, the story goes, this silent majority then fought back against totalitarianism under the banner of the Resistance to claim the moral authority for post-war reconstruction. Renzo De Felice, among other historians, challenged this foundational narrative by underscoring consensus as an integral aspect of the Regime's sustainability.[13] This revisionist approach has informed subsequent studies, which have processed these data to address other aspects of confinement. Enlightening in this respect is Silverio Corvisieri's impassioned critique, *La villeggiatura di*

*Mussolini*, which emphasises the human toll and suffering that raw numbers fail to convey.[14] Taking a comparative approach, Camilla Poesio's synthetic review of *confino* contextualises the practice in relation to Nazism's *Schutzhaft*.[15] Opting to focus on a particular aspect of the experience, Ilaria Poerio sheds light on an unintended consequence of internal exile: raising the prisoners' political consciousness and fomenting anti-Fascist sentiment.[16] Anna Foa's *Andare per i luoghi di confino*, in the series 'Ritrovare l'Italia' (Discovering Italy), takes the discussion to the general public by presenting *confino* as a neglected aspect of Italians' collective memory.[17] In English, the most comprehensive and insightful analysis is Michael R. Ebner's *Ordinary Violence in Mussolini's Italy*, which exposes the violence that the Regime instrumentalised to control and define everyday life for all Italians.

In the wake of these foundational studies, *Internal Exile in Fascist Italy* adopts a culturalist approach that considers *confino* from both historical and cultural perspectives to establish how the Regime suppressed dissent and to evince the diverse representations of the exile experience. This treatment of self-representation acknowledges the varied, fluid, and ambivalent moral and political positionings of those exiled. The historiographic research on this disciplinary practice is primarily in Italian and has, to date, either ignored or treated peripherally cultural representations of *confino*. This phenomenon also merits consideration because it contributes to Italians' historical memory. The birth of the Republic, indeed, the initiative of the European Union, trace their origins to the ideals, the relationships, the experiences, the writings of those people who suffered confinement so that *confinati* are, by definition, anti-Fascists, and exile becomes a preparatory prelude to the Resistance. As John Foot has argued, however, the collective memory is a divided one, which contests events and experiences thereby resisting consensus.[18] The memoirs of detainees confirm Foot's thesis. Historical revisionism, at its best, challenges this foundational mythology by arguing for a nuanced perspective that recognises degrees of responsibility rather than the post-war historiography that exculpates Italians of participation in Fascism.[19] Historical revisionism, however, has also facilitated the rehabilitation and the legitimisation of the New Right by reclaiming and redefining aspects of this political heritage. Berlusconi's electoral victory in 1994, and the reconfiguration of *Movimento Sociale Italiano* (Italian Social Movement) into *Alleanza Nazionale* (National Alliance), under Gianfranco Fini in 1995, mark the New Right's success in the political sphere. By employing a relativist strategy, these revisionists morally equate Fascists and anti-Fascists as patriotic actors who defended different aspects of the nation. The journalist Giampaolo Pansa's writings on the Resistance and Carlo Mazzantini's novel, *A cercar la bella morte*, which counters the Resistance legacy in its unapologetic humanisation of those youths who fought for Mussolini, are popular manifestations of this moral levelling.[20]

This study contributes to the former critique by evincing both the scope of *confino* and the diverse responses to it, and it refutes the latter critique by documenting both the practice of *confino* and the impact of internal exile on people's lives. Part I, 'Context and history of internal exile', provides historical contexualisation for *confino* by examining the Lipari colony's administration and population as a concrete example of how the Regime implemented the practice and how the prisoners experienced it and by reviewing the political and legislative policies that led to the establishment of internal exile as an administrative means to suppress dissent. Drawing on archival and non-archival materials from primary sources (e.g., detainees' personal files and ministerial files from the State Central Archive in Rome, prisoners' memoirs, Savoy Code, Zanardelli Code, Rocco Code), these initial chapters reconstruct in detail *confino*'s history (including its historical antecedents in both pre-unification and pre-Fascist Italy). The study's emphasis is on 'political' confinement although it also treats 'common' confinement, a sentence applied liberally to those people suspected of various criminal or anti-social behaviours. Thus, this enquiry concentrates on the political colonies, which the Ministry of the Interior established on small sparsely inhabited islands, rather than on the detention sites on the peninsula.

Part II, 'Representations of internal exile in literature and film', addresses an aspect of *confino* that has been neglected: its cultural manifestations. These chapters focus on cultural production by exploring prisoners' self-expression (e.g., memoirs, personal correspondence, dedicated literary works) and by investigating cinematic texts (i.e., feature films, documentaries, and made-for-television-movies) that reflect on the practice of *confino*. They give voice and vision to a diverse array of experiences, the everyday life of Italian exiles, in all its ambivalent contradictions. *Alltagsgeschichte*, the history of everyday life, provides a conceptual framework through which to consider interpersonal relationships, community formation, and varied responses to internal exile.[21] The concern in this section is not with historical facticity, but rather with representational strategies. In examining how these texts express the internal exile experience, new literary and filmic subgenres and themes emerge.

Literary texts that foreground their fictional status (e.g., Cesare Pavese's *Terra d'esilio* and *Il carcere*, Giorgio Bassani's *Gli occhiali d'oro*, Carlo Lucarelli's *L'isola dell'angelo caduto*) present complex relationships between self and the other, which may be expressed, among other ways, through gender dynamics, sexual preference, class conflict, religious beliefs, geographic diversity, or political affiliation. By blurring distinctions between historical narrative, life writing, and literary convention, these fictional texts adopt representational strategies similar to those of what might be termed 'foundational' texts (e.g., Emilio Lussu's *La catena*, Francesco Fausto Nitti's *Le nostre prigioni e la nostra evasione*, Carlo Rosselli's *Fuga in quattro tempi*), which established thematic parameters of confinement narratives. Internal exile was not a homogenous experience, so some writings (e.g., Giovanni Ansaldo's *L'antifascista riluttante*, Camilla Ravera's *Vita in carcere e al confino*) offer a counter-narrative, a response to these foundational texts by relating different representations both of *confino* and of self. Certainly, historical experiences are contradictory, ambiguous, and ambivalent. A significant aspect of these diverse literary expressions is their tendency to reveal people's complicated relationship to the Regime: relationships that cannot be reduced to facile moral oppositions. In considering this large body of literature, preference has been given to relatively unknown *confinati* (e.g., Emma Turchi, Cesira Fiori) over familiar figures (e.g., Gramsci, Ginzburg) to introduce new perspectives and to acknowledge differences in privilege.

Similarly, cinematic treatments of *confino* have received scant critical attention. When addressed at all, the examples referenced invariably tend to be Ettore Scola's *Una giornata particolare* (*A Special Day*, 1977) and Francesco Rosi's *Cristo si è fermato a Eboli* (*Christ Stopped at Eboli*, 1979). These concluding chapters expand the cinematic corpus to twenty-two films that address the exile experience of *mafiosi*, of gender nonconforming people, and of those deemed by the Regime to be politically suspect. Melodrama, trauma, mourning, memory, and the exile-as-holiday motif are recurring elements in these films, which frequently critique both political systems and gender policies. While the feature films tend to adopt melodrama as the preferred means of expression, the documentaries project private memories that engage with and become part of the collective memory.

A final motivation for this study is the continued presence of *confino*-like practices in societies. Confinement's legacy is visible throughout the world in politically sanctioned extrajudicial detentions. Remembering and understanding how Fascism suppressed dissent is necessary not because historical memory is short, but because those experiences continue to define how society develops and defines itself. The past is present, but it need not be the future.

## Notes

1    Etheridge Knight, 'Inside These Walls', in Etheridge Knight (ed.), *Black Voices from Prison* (New York: Pathfinder Press, 1970), p. 129. First published two years earlier in Italy as *Voce negre dal carcere* (Bari: Laterza, 1968).

2    The Regime distinguished between two types of confinement: 'political' and 'common'. The roughly 15,000 Italians sentenced for political reasons generally served their time on designated island colonies while the 25,000 to 50,000 Italians sentenced for non-political reasons were usually sent to remote villages. See Michael R. Ebner, *Ordinary Violence in Mussolini's Italy* (Cambridge: Cambridge University Press, 2011), p. 2. The *Casellario Politico Centrale* (CPC) holds 152,589 files on anti-Fascists (147,584 men and 5,005 women). Some files have been lost, several are incomplete or contain errors, while still others apply different classification criteria – all factors that make arriving at definitive numbers a Sisyphean labour.

3    Silvio Berlusconi interviewed on 4 September 2003 by Boris Johnson and Nicholas Farrell for the *Spectator* and *La voce di Rimini*. Published in *La voce di Rimini* on 11 September 2003; and in the column 'Diary', in the *Spectator* (11 September 2003), p. 9.

4    Due process is enshrined by the fifth and fourteenth Amendments to the United States Constitution and draws on clause 39 of Magna Carta. Critics contend that legislation such as the USA PATRIOT Act (26 October 2001) erode civil liberties. See Dave Cole and James X. Dempsey, *Terrorism and the Constitution: Sacrificing Civil Liberties in the Name of National Security* (New York: W. W. Norton & Co., 2002); and Susan N. Herman, *Taking Liberties: The War on Terror and the Erosion of American Democracy* (Oxford: Oxford University Press, 2011).

5   Marcello Sorgi, 'Quando Lussu, Rosselli e Nitti andavano in "vacanza" a Lipari', in *La Stampa* (7 August 2014), p. 29. Unless otherwise stated, all translations are the authors'.

6   For a general survey of exile from the earliest written records to the modern era, see Paul Tabori, *The Anatomy of Exile: A Semantic and Historical Study* (London: Harrap, 1972).

7   Aristotle, *Athenaion Politeia*, 22, and Aristotle, *Politics*, 3, 1284a. Jakob Seibert's *Die politischen Flüchtlinge und Verbannten in der griechischen Geschichte: von d. Anfängen bis zur Unterwerfung durch d. Römer* (Darmstadt: Wissenschaftliche Buchgesellschaft, [Abt. Verl.], 1979) provides a comprehensive study of exile in ancient Greece. See also Sara Forsdyke, *Exile, Ostracism, and Democracy* (Princeton: Princeton University Press, 2005).

8   The term *exsilium* referred to three forms of exile (*aquae et ignis interdictio, deportatio*, and *relegatio*). For exile in the Roman world, see Jo-Marie Claassen, *Displaced Persons: The Literature of Exile from Cicero to Boethius* (Madison: University of Wisconsin Press, 1999); and Gordon P. Kelly, *A History of Exile in the Roman Republic* (Cambridge: Cambridge University Press, 2006).

9   Celso Ghini and Adriano Dal Pont, *Gli antifascisti al confino: 1926–1943* (Rome: Editori Riuniti, 1971). Dal Pont followed up with *I lager di Mussolini: l'altra faccia del confino nei documenti della polizia fascista* (Milan: La Pietra, 1975) and five years later, with co-author Simonetta Carolini, *L'Italia dissidente e antifascista* (Milan: La Pietra, 1980). Leopoldo Zagami's *Confinati politici e relegati comuni a Lipari* (Messina: Tipografia Ditta D'Amico, 1970) is one of the earliest studies to focus on a specific colony.

10  Adriano Dal Pont and Simonetta Carolini, *L'Italia al confino: le ordinanze di assegnazione al confino emesse dalle Commissioni provinciali dal novembre 1926 al luglio 1943*. 4 vols (Milan: La Pietra, 1983). In volume one, Leonardo Musci's introduction, 'Il confino fascista di polizia. L'apparato statale di fronte al dissenso politico e sociale' (pp. xxi–ci) is a fundamental reference.

11  The series is organised by region: Donatella Carbone, *Il popolo al confino: la persecuzione fascista in Basilicata* (Rome: Ministero per i beni culturali e ambientali, 1994); Katia Massara, *Il popolo al confino: la persecuzione fascista in Puglia*, 2 vols (Rome: Ufficio centrale per i beni archivistici, 1991); Rosa Spadafora, *Il popolo al confino: la persecuzione fascista in Campania*, 2 vols (Naples: Athena, 1989); Salvatore Carbone and Laura Grimaldi, *Il popolo al confino: la persecuzione fascista in Sicilia* (Rome: Ministero per i beni culturali e ambientali, 1989); and Salvatore Carbone, *Il popolo al confino: la persecuzione fascista in Calabria* (Cosenza: Lerici, 1977). This last volume was reissued in 1989. Though distinct from the series, Salvatore Pirastu has published a volume on Sardinia, *I confinati antifascisti in Sardegna: 1926–1943* (Cagliari: Anippia, 1997).

12  For an authoritative discussion on the meaning and the impact of Italian Fascism, see Richard J. B. Bosworth, *The Italian Dictatorship: Problems and Perspectives in the Interpretation of Mussolini and Fascism* (New York: Oxford University Press, 1998).

13  See, for example, Renzo De Felice, *Mussolini il duce. Gli anni del consenso 1929–1936*, Vol. 3.1 (Turin: Einaudi, 1996); Bordon W. Painter, 'Renzo De Felice and the Historiography of Italian Fascism', *American Historical Review* 95:1 (1990), 391–405; and Giulia Albanese and Roberta Pergher (eds), *In the Society of Fascists: Acclamation, Acquiescence, and Agency in Mussolini's Italy* (New York: Palgrave Macmillan, 2012).

14  Silverio Corvisieri, *La villeggiatura di Mussolini: il confino da Bocchini a Berlusconi* (Milan: Baldini Castoldi Dalai, 2004).

15  Camilla Poesio, *Il confino fascista: l'arma silenziosa del regime* (Bari: Laterza, 2011).

16  Ilaria Poerio, *A scuola di dissenso: storie di resistenza al confino di polizia (1926–1943)* (Rome: Carocci, 2016).

17  Anna Foa, *Andare per i luoghi di confino* (Bologna: Il Mulino, 2018).

18    John Foot, *Italy's Divided Memory* (New York: Palgrave Macmillan, 2009).

19    See by way of example, Claudio Fogu, '*Italiani brava gente*: The Legacy of Fascist Historical Cultures on Italian Politics and Memory', in Richard Ned Lebow, Wulf Kansteiner, and Claudio Fogu (eds), *The Politics of Memory in Postwar Europe* (Durham and London: Duke University Press, 2006), pp. 147–76.

20    Of Giampaolo Pansa's histories, see, in particular, *Il sangue dei vinti* (Milan: Sperling & Kupfer, 2003), and Carlo Mazzantini, *A cercar la bella morte* (Milan: Mondadori, 1986).

21    The German historians, Alf Lüedtke, Detlev Peukert, and Hans Medick popularised the microhistorical approach of *Alltagsgeschischte* in the 1980s. By way of introduction, see Alf Lüedtke (ed.), *The History of Everyday Life: Reconstructing Historical Experiences and Ways of Life* (Princeton: Princeton University Press, 1995). In the Italian context, see Joshua Arthurs, Michael Ebner, and Kate Ferris (eds), *The Politics of Everyday Life in Fascist Italy* (New York: Palgrave Macmillan, 2017).

# PART I

# Context and history
# of internal exile

# 1

# The Lipari colony: *paradiso/inferno*

## Lipari

Lipari. To Sicilianise Compton Mackenzie's Highlands, 'inadequate indeed would be the guidebook or traveller's tale that did not accord to Lipari a place of honour in the very forefront of Italian scenery and romance'.[1] Benito Mussolini and his Chief of Police, Arturo Bocchini, professed similarly grandiose sentiments to dismiss denunciations of *confino*, Fascism's extrajudiciary practice of internal exile. In fact, Bocchini went so far as to argue that bucolic settings were necessary to confinement because their very beauty served to 'sfatare la leggenda tanto cara ai fuoriusciti italiani e alla stampa estera ostile al Regime, circa il presunto inumano trattamento ai confinati politici'.[2] ([D]ebunk the legend so dear to exiled Italians and to the foreign press hostile to the Regime, that the political exiles are supposedly ill-treated.) They countered political outrage with feigned naiveté: how could such Mediterranean wonders be sites of human despair? Rather than address the material conditions of sequestration, these apologists engaged in an axiological short con that rhetorically conflated the island's stirring landscape with the detention experiences of its prisoners.[3]

For those stripped of their civil liberties and confined to a liminal legal state in a secluded colony, the stark contrast between the beauty of the setting and the brutality of the conditions permitted no such delusive conflation. The juxtaposition between weal and woe is a constant in narratives that relate the *confino* experience. For example, Ettore Franceschini, one of Lipari's first detainees, has a double take reaction:

> Entrando a Lipari ci parve di entrare in un paradiso. Piante di rose si notavano a profusione e l'aria era profumata di zagare. Aspetto del paese come quello di una cittadina del continente sia pure piccolissima. Vedevamo qualche 'politico' parlare con i paesani, mentre a Favignana non era possibile conversare con nessuno del luogo, perché le donne stavano quasi sempre chiuse in casa, gli uomini, quasi tutti pescatori, non erano in paese nelle ore della nostra libertà. Poco dopo incominciammo a scoprire

i rovesci della medaglia. Un paese infestato di spie, fatte venire appositamente per questo concentramento di coatti politici, spesso sotto spoglie di condannati politici, di finti fascisti dissidenti.[4]

(Entering Lipari it seemed as though we were entering paradise. Rose plants abounded and the scent of orange blossoms filled the air. The town was similar to little cities on the continent, even if quite small. We saw some 'political prisoners' talking to villagers, whereas in Favignana we couldn't speak with any of the locals because the women were almost always shuttered in their homes and the men, almost all of them fishermen, weren't in town during the hours we could circulate. Shortly thereafter we began to see the flip side of the coin: a town infested with spies, expressly brought among the political detainees, often under the guise of being political prisoners, of fake Fascist dissidents.)

Franceschini's rapturous impression of Lipari soon ruptures as the imaginary *paradiso* succumbs to the reality of the *inferno*. The shattered illusions he describes are recurring motifs in the memoirs of these political prisoners.

The Regime sought to stifle such laments by classifying the colonies as essentially extraterritorial areas, shadow zones beyond the jurisdiction of national and international laws and to negate complaints by propagating its own idyllic narrative of island paradise. An improbable event, however, brought Lipari and *confino* to the attention of the world: Carlo Rosselli, Emilio Lussu, and Francesco Fausto Nitti's audacious escape from the colony, on 27 July 1929.[5] Thanks to the fugitives' stirring accounts of both the oppressive conditions and their intrepid flight, the foreign press dubbed Lipari the 'Devil's Island' or 'Mussolini's Siberia'.[6] Stoking the outrage, Nitti's American publisher, the future Mr Amelia Earhart, George Putnam, claimed to have received, on Fascist letterhead no less, death threats should he proceed with the book's release. Even though it was a promotional ruse, this publicity stunt reinforced Anglo-Americans' negative perceptions of both Mussolini and *confino*.[7] Ultimately, such unwelcome scrutiny of the government's detention practices contributed to the Ministry of the Interior's decision to shutter the political colony after six years of operation.[8] Closure was not immediate: bureaucratic morass and administrative exigencies sustained the site until 10 January 1933. During its period of activity, however, the Lipari colony held over 1,400 political prisoners: approximately 9 per cent of the national total. Its organisational and financial logistics made it the most complex colony of the *confino* system. Although each internal exile experience was unique, Lipari's comparatively well-documented history elucidates the implementation and conditions of this extrajudiciary punishment as it was conceived and enacted.

## The lay of the island

When the Interior Ministry began to sentence political undesirables, *confinati politici*, to Lipari in December 1926, the Regime was reintroducing a tradition dating back millennia to when Republican Rome had neatly coupled pleasure and penitence by utilising the isle as both a therapeutic retreat and an exile site. Largest of the Aeolian Islands both as land mass (37.29 km²) and population (14,276),⁹ Lipari's proximity to the Sicilian shores (some 30 km north) ensured both separation from and accessibility to *terra firma*: an isolation that facilitated the Ministry's ability to control access to the colony.

Throughout its history of continual invasions and rampant piracy, Lipari subsisted on agriculture, fishing, and pumice mining. Annexation by the Kingdom of Italy limited rather than expanded any efforts to diversify the local economy because the nascent national government designated the island as a detention site for criminals. The relegation to colonial penitentiary resulted from the promulgation of the 1863 Pica law, which imposed *domicilio coatto*, a policy of forced residence, on those deemed undesirable by the State.[10] For the inhabitants, the presence of *coatti* was onerous both physically and financially. Moreover, as the scope of security legislation became increasingly aggressive in its clampdown on dissidents, the number of those interned swelled. By the turn of the century, the inefficacy and brutality of the practice led critics to launch a campaign to end it.[11] The political activist Ettore Croce wrote two books criticising *domicilio coatto* while serving his sentence on Lipari.[12] Inspired by Croce's exposé, the writer Irma Melany Scodnik followed up with her own denunciation of detention on the Aeolian Islands.[13] Eight years later, the living conditions for *coatti* had not improved as evinced by Zina Centa Tartarini's account published in the *Corriere della Sera*'s monthly *La Lettura* in 1908.[14]

Although the colony officially closed in 1916, Lipari continued to serve as an internment site for political dissidents during the Great War. Following the Paris Peace Conference, however, the opportunity to refashion the island into a tourist destination seemed both desirable and possible. City councillor Francesco De Mauro emphasised this point on 11 October 1920:

> [L]a nostra città murata potrebbe essere il sito per ospitarvi altri ospiti da noi ben voluti e da noi molto più cari. Tutto lo spazio della città murata ben sistemato, dopo sgombrate di tutte quelle vecchie cadenti luride casupole, potrebbe essere destinato a costruzione di nuove case, di qualche bello albergo e perciò utile per stimolare qui in Lipari il movimento dei forestieri.[15]

> (Our walled city could be a place to host other guests, more welcome and important to us. After clearing out the old dirty broken down hovels, the entire walled city area, all fixed up, could be used for new houses and some nice hotels to encourage visitors here to Lipari.)

Tourism was an untapped revenue stream of which the island was in dire need. The Great War had strapped the municipality's finances. Its nearly exclusive reliance on pumice as a funding source led to fiscal insolvency when budgetary expenses almost quadrupled while tax revenues decreased by over 70 per cent – from pre-war levels of £300,000 to post-war levels of £80,000.[16] Thus De Mauro's proposal was as much an economic development effort to diversify the tax base as it was a civic impetus to improve the living conditions on Lipari. Moreover, the *de facto* collapse of the Latin Monetary Union exacerbated the economic crisis, which in turn fostered civil discontent.[17] Rather than address the needs and demands of the populace, the political response was an unwavering commitment to sustaining the status quo by stymying efforts to effect change. New administrative reforms, such as transferring control from local officials to a *podestà*, an external appointment in lieu of an elected mayor, effectively suppressed grassroots initiatives.[18] In the spring of 1926, instead of the construction projects De Mauro had envisioned, the new administration began to expand the castle's barracks and its environs (in the space that the Archaeological Museum occupies today) for discouragingly familiar purposes well before the enactment of the so-called *Leggi eccezionali del fascismo*. In July, a citizens' committee sought to prevent the rehabilitation of the colony. It launched a campaign, which included soliciting the support of public figures.[19] Amongst these was consummate self-aggrandiser Gabriele D'Annunzio, who sent a telegram expressing a singular solidarity with the population: 'Siate sicuro che sosterrò col più alto fervore l'aspirazione della più bella fra le isole eolie dove io vorrei essere felicemente relegato per polire con la pomice cutulliana [sic] il mio ultimo libro'.[20] (Be assured that I support with the greatest fervour the aspiration of the most beautiful of the Aeoliean islands where I would happily like to be confined to polish my latest book with Catullian pumice.) Such ambivalent empathy failed to dissuade the authorities. Tensions continued to escalate culminating in a violent anti-colony protest that caused significant property damage. In response to the civil unrest, the Commissioner of Public Security, Attilio Stagni, called for military reinforcements from Messina on 29 August 1926. Stagni had Francesco De Mauro as well as other civic leaders and protestors arrested, but Lipari's resistance perhaps did have some effect: rather than intern criminals, the island became a political colony.[21] The Prefect of Messina spun this strategic modification by reassuring the population that 'coloro che arriveranno non sono criminali comuni né persone pericolose, ma sono persone rispettabilissime: professori, avvocati, professionisti, che anzi daranno lustro alla cittadina'[22] (those who will be arriving are neither common criminals nor dangerous people, rather they are extremely respectable people: professors, lawyers, professionals, who in fact will bring honour to the town). The determination to shunt criminal offenders for political suspects makes clear that the Regime had already vetted the provisions and programmed the implementation of *confino* well before the ratification of the *Leggi eccezionali* under the legislative bill *Testo Unico delle leggi di pubblica sicurezza* (TULPS: consolidated acts on public security).[23] The Ministry of the Interior activated the Lipari political colony between December 1926 and January 1927, and by the end of 1927, some 250 respectable *confinati* graced Lipari's shores.[24]

### Portrait of a *confinato*

Who were these prisoners? In her rich and detailed study, Alessandra Pagano examined the personal data cards of 1,401 *confinati* sentenced to Lipari.[25] Of these, she determined that roughly 30.5 per cent came from northern Italy, 53 per cent from central Italy, 15 per cent from the South, and 1.5 per cent from other areas (e.g., colonies and territories).[26] Five regions accounted for almost two-thirds of the detainees: Lazio (18.4 per cent), Emilia-Romagna (17.4 per cent), Tuscany (10 per cent), Lombardy (9.6 per cent) and Veneto (7.8 per cent). By sequestering its opponents to colonies, the Regime, unintentionally, forged relationships among political dissidents who would otherwise never have had occasion to meet.

In terms of socio-economic standing, Pagano determined that the distribution was heavily weighted towards the petite bourgeoisie, approximately 59 per cent, followed by the working class (29 per cent) and the bourgeoisie (6.5 per cent). Predominantly students and elected government officials comprised the remaining 5.5 per cent.

Politically, the vast majority of prisoners identified as Communists (60.9 per cent), with the Anarchists (14 per cent) and Socialists (9.5 per cent) trailing substantially. The next largest group, generically designated as anti-Fascist, tallied at 7.5 per cent. Representation of other parties amongst the detainees was rather limited: Republicans (3 per cent), Subversives (2 per cent), with Apoliticals, Slavophiles, and Fascists/ex-Fascists each at 1 per cent. Six additional political affiliations counted a total of ten adherents: Freemasons (Lelio D'Alessandris, Francesco Leti, Ermanno Solimene, and Domizio Torrigiani[27]), Anti-nationalists (Giovanni Kralj and Santo Mausich), Popularists (Antonio Bazzan), Liberals (Riccardo Bauer[28]), Pan-Germanists (Josef Noldin[29]), and Sardists (Emilio Lussu[30]). Provenance, political orientation, and professional affiliations all served as organising principles for *confinati* in regulating their social lives in the colony.[31]

Physical proximity led to an unintended consequence of confinement: fostering relationships between political activists from different areas of Italy. Much like the draft imposed a national identity on recruits from disparate backgrounds, *confino* made manifest the shared concerns and aspirations of the exiled. Thus, individual isolation and political communion co-existed for the interned as totems of subservience and subversiveness.

For women, however, *confino* presented additional challenges. Beyond exile, they also had to confront and mediate social taboos that the men did not experience. Sixteen women suffered confinement in Lipari for anti-Fascist activities. Given that at least 343 women were sent to the political colonies, this number is quite small.[32] Moreover, of these sixteen, four were sent to Lipari after the Ministry of the Interior had decided to close the colony so, for these prisoners, the island served principally as a transfer station to the political colony on the island of Ponza. Certainly one reason Lipari received few women detainees is that the majority of *confinati* were sentenced after its closure in 1933. Still, this explanation does not suffice. From an administrative standpoint guarding women created logistical and financial complications so to house such a small population was inefficient. The Ministry of the Interior's motivations remain inscrutable, but for these women this decision greatly accentuated their isolation. To remember their names is to recognise the violence they endured:

1. Luigia Berto, an Anarchist homemaker from Adria (Rovigo), was sentenced on 27 January 1932.
2. Agata Bertollini, a Republican peasant from Monterotondo (Rome), was sentenced on 29 August 1927.
3. Maria Ciarravano, an Anarchist seamstress from Bologna, received a five-year sentence on 11 October 1927.
4. Palmira Ciccolerio, an Apolitical homemaker from Rome, was sentenced on 31 October 1927.
5. Lea Giaccaglia, a resident of Bologna, was a teacher. While in police custody, she learned of her daughter's death. After serving a prison term (6 June 1929–27 October 1931) for Communist propaganda, she was immediately sentenced to *confino* for five years (18 November 1931). Transferred to Ponza on 5 January 1933, her sentence was commuted to a two-year probation thanks to an amnesty (11 July 1934). The probation restrictions were lifted a few months early (1 June 1936) to celebrate the military victory in Ethiopia. Giaccaglia died forty days later in Bologna on 10 July 1936.[33]
6. Paola Giannella, a Communist homemaker from Monza (Milan), was sentenced on 23 December 1929.
7. Teresa Meroni, a Communist office worker from Milan, was sentenced on 16 September 1932.
8. Miselena Michelangeli, a peasant from Monterotondo (Rome), was sentenced for subversive activities on 12 August 1927.
9. Zelmira Peroni, an Anarchist homemaker from Caprigliola (Massa and Carrara), was sentenced on 19 November 1926.
10. Vittoria Polo was a prostitute in Rome. She was accused of insulting Mussolini and sentenced on 28 July 1929.
11. Florinda Salvatelli, a Communist peasant from Monterotondo (Rome), was sentenced on 24 October 1927.
12. Vera Santoni was a Communist-anarchist from Florence. Arrested for lighting a candle and laying flowers at the tomb of the Communist Spartaco Lavagnini, she was sentenced on 1 July 1927.[34]
13. Ida Scarselli, an Anarchist seamstress from Rome, was sentenced on 30 September 1929.
14. Ermenegilda Villa, an Anarchist homemaker from Milan, was sentenced on 23 December 1929.
15. Irma Zanella, a Communist from Adria (Rovigo), was sentenced on 12 July 1928.
16. Margherita Zocchi, a Communist office worker from Trieste, was sentenced on 30 May 1932.

These prisoners represent a sociological cross-section of the detainee population. Geographically, they hail from northern and central Italy, including six from Rome and its environs. Politically, they are overwhelmingly Communists or

Anarchists (with Vera Santoni pulling double duty). Professionally, they encompass seven different occupations with five identified as homemakers. These sixteen women share no common profile: what unites them is that they each offended the State.

Lea Giaccaglia's experience exposes the hidden sacrifices and sufferings that women, in particular, endured in *confino*. Torn from their families, separated from male *confinati*, treated with suspicion and derision by both the security forces and the local inhabitants, subject to the judgemental gaze of the State, the populace, and their male counterparts, they endured an emotional, intellectual, and physical isolation that far exceeded that of the men.[35]

## Colony regulations and administrative organisation

The 1926 TULPS established the general parameters of internal exile, but its implementation required modifications.[36] This supplemental legislation (21 January 1929) stipulated the regulations governing the treatment of *confinati*.[37] The most significant directives were in seven articles (340–4 and 347–8). Two of these concerned securing housing and employment: at the colony director's discretion, and at the prisoners' expense, *confinati* could secure private lodging. Similarly, *confinati* could request to have family members reside with them (Art. 340); those ones not of independent means were required to work to cover the cost of their detention. Should they fail to secure adequate employment then they would pay nothing and would instead receive a *mazzetta* (daily allowance) as determined by the Minister of the Interior (Art. 341). Two articles addressed housing requirements and furnishings. Assigned lodgings should conform to the prescribed sanitary standards: have adequate lighting at night, provide a minimum of twenty cubic metres per person, have an odourless outhouse and urinal per twenty people, and have access to sufficient water for ordinary needs (Art. 342). As for furnishings, each prisoner in assigned housing would receive a metal cot and mattress, two sheets and a pillowcase, two woollen blankets, a chair and metal night table, a metal coat rack, a jug, a washbowl and a metal washbowl carrier, a bottle and a glass, and two towels – with a change of linens on the first and fifteenth of each month. Moreover, prisoners without means would receive annually a suit and a pair of shoes (Art. 343). Article 344 allowed for free medical assistance and medicine to impoverished *confinati*. The last two articles expounded on the proscriptions concerning behaviour and lifestyle (detailed in articles 189–90 of the TULPS). The first, Article 347, specified that prisoners could not: (1) gamble (2) charge interest for lending money (3) sell, trade, or confiscate items provided by the administration (4) engage in commerce without the approval of the colony's director (5) make noise during quiet hours (6) damage walls, furniture, clothing and other objects provided by the administration (7) discuss politics or engage in political propaganda, and (8) go boating. The second, Article 348, established curfews.[38] These regulations sought to emulate military rigour and discipline by imposing material conditions. Authorities surveilled and scrutinised the prisoners' comportment with any infraction resulting in swift punishments.

Three distinct units oversaw security on the island: the *Carabinieri* (national gendarmerie), the MVSN (*Milizia Volontaria per la Sicurezza Nazionale* – voluntary militia for national security or Blackshirts) and the Ministry of the Interior's Public Security agents. Both the *Carabinieri* and the militia patrolled Lipari's perimeter, while the former also oversaw the transport of prisoners. The Public Security agents, under the supervision of the colony director, managed the administrative functions including dispensing the *mazzetta*, checking mail, overseeing the *cameroni* (prisoners' barracks) inspections, and interactions with *confinati*.[39]

Poor Sicilians, for whom a daily wage of twenty lira plus room and board was a marked improvement over a labourer's pay, comprised the MVSN. Whether to combat boredom or to justify their presence those in the militia tended to enforce rigorously the regulations.[40]

Magistrates assigned to the Aeolian Islands also held jurisdictional authority over the colony though the director would usually participate in any proceedings concerning *confinati*. Serious crimes, however, were invariably advanced to Messina's trial court. Prior to the passage of RD 62 (21 January 1929), which delineated the disciplinary responsibilities of the colonial administrations, the colony's director held broad discretional authority. The militia or the Public Security agents initiated legal proceedings and detained those prisoners accused of crimes or infractions. The director then reviewed the evidence to decide whether to go through the court or to dispense justice on his own. The new legislation established a formal procedure for addressing infractions while advancing all serious charges to court.[41] For minor offences, the director issued a reprimand. A disciplinary commission, consisting of the colony's director, the medical examiner and the chaplain, adjudicated repeated transgressors. The range of measures at the commission's disposal consisted of confinement (from one to thirty days), reduction of the allowance (to no less than 50 per cent), replacement of the cot with a plank-bed, and restricting meals to two daily rations of bread and broth. Moreover, the offender could not communicate with others and was confined to quarters bar a single daily outing for fresh air. The commission favoured isolation and confiscation of the *mazzetta* as punishment, perhaps because these actions imposed visible and lasting hardships.[42]

### A day in the life of a *confinato*

Arrival on the Aeolian isle concluded a protracted transit: the transfer from sentencing to internment site could take days, weeks, or even months.[43] Handcuffed, chained, and loaded down with what belongings they could carry, the prisoners suffered extreme physical hardships as they were transported from one way station to the next. Landing in Lipari presented its own particular challenges. Since the harbour was too shallow to accommodate the steamships (the *Adele* and the *Etna*

maintained daily transport between Milazzo and Lipari), they were ferried in
*schiavettoni* (iron handcuffs padlocked to a heavy chain tethering four prisoners) to
the shore.[44] After experiencing arrest, imprisonment, sentencing, and shackled transport, they may well have greeted disembarkation at Marina Corta with a sense of
relief. Wide-open spaces and curious onlookers lining Piazza Ugo di Sant'Onofrio
were a sharp and welcome contrast to the confinement and solitude to which they
had never become accustomed.[45] From the quay, they shuffled, fettered and guarded
by *Carabinieri*, up to the colony's administrative offices in the castle where, following
inspection, the director allowed them to shed their manacles.

At the castle, they received their *carta di permanenza* (sojourn permit), which
enumerated the regulations governing movement (e.g., curfew and prohibited
areas) and behaviour (e.g., political engagement and fraternisation) on the
colony.[46] The director confiscated any suspicious items including monies deemed
excessive, which he deposited in frozen accounts that could only be accessed with
his permission. Regulations restricted their movements to the centre of the town.
A crude wire fence, patrolled by armed guards, formed the perimeter of this zone
and reinforced the visual impression that Lipari was under siege.

The arrival experience of Flavio Fornasiero, an eighteen-year-old Anarchist
from Adria (Rovigo), was relatively typical:

Appena sbarcati a Marina Corta, eravamo stati condotti alla presenza del commissario
che, dopo una minacciosa prolusione, ci aveva ben spiegato che non eravamo gente
libera, bensì reclusi cui veniva magnanimamente concessa la facoltà di muoversi entro
un certo perimetro. Quindi non dovevamo abusare della sua tolleranza o deludere
la generosità dimostrata verso di noi dal governo … Ci disse infine che era nostro
preciso dovere ripulire le menti da ogni pregiudiziale ideologica che non coincideva
con il fascismo. Dopo di ciò venne consegnato a ognuno di noi il 'Libretto personale
di permanenza' elencante le norme, i divieti e le prescrizioni cui dovevamo sottostare,
pena il carcere. Consultandolo, non ci parve idoneo a modificare i nostri punti di
vista, ma anzi a ribadirli. Proprio per questo il confino servì a migliaia di italiani come
un momento fondamentale di riflessione e di scelta politica. Bastava passare da lì, per
convincersi che il fascismo non era altro che violenza, stupidità e brutalità poliziesca.[47]

(As soon as we disembarked at Marina Corta, we were led before the director who,
after an ominous introduction, explained to us that we were not free, but rather
prisoners to whom had been given magnanimously the privilege to circulate within
a limited area. We were not to test his patience or betray the generosity that the government had shown us … He then told us that it was our duty to cleanse our minds
of all ideological prejudices that were not compatible with Fascism. After which, each
of us received a 'Registration and Sojourn Booklet' listing the norms, prohibitions,
and rules to obey or face imprisonment. After consulting it, we thought it best not to
change our views, but instead to reaffirm them. This is precisely why, for thousands of
Italians, *confino* served as a fundamental time of reflection and of political choices. One
only had to go through that to be convinced that Fascism was just violence, stupidity,
and police brutality.)

Fornasiero's subsequent fighting in both the Spanish Civil War (as part of the Italian Column) and the Resistance (*nom de guerre* Ribelle) supports the assertion that *confino* served to solidify his own anti-Fascist convictions, but his certainty as to its political impact on other detainees amounts to wilful projection. Certainly many *confinati* shared Fornasiero's vituperative reaction, but others sought clemency by appealing directly to Mussolini. Although the government did not engage actively in ideological rehabilitation, the practice of what Michael R. Ebner appropriately underscores as ordinary violence could achieve a similar political result.[48]

Such was the case of the Genoese journalist Giovanni Ansaldo who received a five-year sentence to Lipari, on 30 May 1927, for anti-Fascist activities. He repented immediately, repulsed at the prospect of sullying himself amongst the *hoi polloi*. Ansaldo described himself as 'severo osservatore dei miei colleghi di confino, e molto lontano spiritualmente da loro'[49] (strict observer of my *confino* colleagues, and spiritually very far from them), but he also abhorred the militia that policed the island:

> V'erano le prescrizioni che bisognava assolutamente osservare, e di cui le principali erano: non oltrepassare i confini dell'abitato … e ritirarci all'ora prescritta. Chi infrangeva queste regole, correva davvero rischio di essere arrestato, rinchiuso in prigione … la milizia era particolarmente accanita a cogliere in flagrante i contravventori, con ronde istituite tanto per giustificare la presenza e la paga. Conveniva dunque ottemperare a quelle regole, ed era facile il farlo; per conto mio, non solo per timore di guai, ma per il ribrezzo, quasi fisico, che mi inspirava la possibilità di contestazione e di contatto con gli scherani, anticipai sempre di un quarto d'ora la mia ritirata … Ma tanti altri! Erano un bellissimo esempio della cocciutaggine umana: stavano a contestare l'ultimo minuto; son le nove, no, non sono le nove; e parecchi, così, finirono 'dentro'.[50]

> (The regulations had to be strictly obeyed. The principal ones were: not to leave the town limits … and to be home by curfew. Whoever broke these rules ran the real risk of being arrested, locked in prison … the militia was especially driven to catching violators in the act. It set up patrols to justify its presence and pay. Thus, it behooved one to obey those rules, which was easy to do. For my part, not only for fear of trouble, but also for an almost physical disgust that I felt at the possibility of protesting and engaging with those thugs, I would always return home a quarter of an hour early … But so many others! They were a wonderful example of human pig-headedness: they would stay out to challenge the final minute: it's nine; no, it's not nine. Many ended up 'inside'.)

Ansaldo's self-absorbed posturing and disparaging assessment of his fellow internees resulted in social and political isolation; however, it also convinced the colony's director, Francesco Cannata, of Ansaldo's rehabilitation. Mussolini promptly rewarded the journalist's solicitousness with a pardon on 8 September 1927, after which, Ansaldo began a new life as an apologist of Fascism. He faced no reckoning for in 1946, he again enjoyed the largesse of the State: the 'Togliatti

Amnesty', a Presidential Decree, allowed him to abscond responsibility for his actions.[51]

Ansaldo's circumstances were atypical:[52] for the majority of *confinati*, sentences lasted far longer than a few months so living arrangements were a high priority. Those who could afford independent housing spent the first few nights in guesthouses as they sought appropriate lodging.[53] Those who could not afford private quarters resided in the *cameroni*, which were quite squalid and, most onerously, under strict surveillance. The colony's director had foreseen this need as the castle lacked sufficient space to billet all *confinati*.[54] For the island's residents, this arrangement proved both convenient and profitable.

Yet, even for those with extramural accommodations, the castle heights were a daily purgatory. An imposing presence, the castle wrested conflicting emotions of promise and despair from the detainees. Perched above the quay, it cast an oppressive shadow across land and sea, but it was also the symbolic dispenser of solace. As the postal drop box, the castle was the stoic gatekeeper to the outside world. Moreover, every day at 8.00 a.m., the prisoners trudged up the rock to receive their ten-lira allowance, the dispensation of which doubled as morning roll call.[55] Their economic security was inextricably shackled to the security measures of the colony.

To survive on the risible *mazzetta* required ingenuity and solidarity. Adopting an economy of scales approach to reduce costs, the internees established and managed a cooperative under the supervision of the authorities. For meals, they received authorisation to organise a canteen of sorts at a fixed price of five lira, which was half their daily allowance. The colony rules prohibited all types of visitations so that eating at the mess required a permission slip from the director. These passes were allotted in one-hour blocks: 12.00–13.00 for lunch and 18.00–19.00 for dinner.[56] Even eating together required the director's approval. Ansaldo, with his dismissive insouciance, detailed the lack of local cuisine:

> Quei siciliani ignorano veramente cos'è la cucina: non v'era trattoria, perché laggiù non si mangia; dico non si mangia nel significato un po' raffinato che noi diamo alle parole, e all'azione che essa esprime. Povero, povero Mezzogiorno! In tutto il resto di Europa, da Roma in su, esiste in ogni casa, in ogni abitazione umana, più o meno provveduta, un locale, un angolo, un fornello, adibito alla preparazione del cibo: e quando son le sette di sera, da Roma in su, per tutta Europa, si nota in quel locale, in quell'angolo, attorno a quel fornello, una certa agitazione, una certa animazione, foriera del desinare. A Lipari, niente di tutto questo. Come cenasse la gente non mi è riuscito di approfondirlo.[57]

> (Those Sicilians truly do not know what cuisine is: there were no restaurants, because down there they don't eat. I say don't eat in the slightly refined sense that we give the word and the action it expresses. Poor, poor South! In the rest of Europe, from Rome on up, there exists in every home, in every human habitation, more or less furnished, a place, a corner, a burner, designated for food preparation. And when it's seven p.m., from Rome on up, in all of Europe, one can see in that space, in that corner, around

that burner, a certain excitement, a certain liveliness, heralding supper. On Lipari, none of this. I was not able to determine how people dined.)

Ansaldo's aspersion of the local populace articulates a clear divide between North and South. In quaint Lombrosian fashion, he considers the islanders to be entirely of criminal stock and directly descended from the boors of yesteryear.[58] He postulates their ignorance and asserts such mores are irremediable.

Ansaldo's financial independence also distinguished him from the other prisoners who relied on the *mazzetta* for subsistence living. Despite the work requirement (Article 189 of the TULPS), the vast majority of *confinati* were unable to find jobs within the restricted zone.[59] Many had already expended their savings while under arrest and imprisonment to support their families. Unemployment was rampant among Lipari's inhabitants as well, but they could and did emigrate. Among *confinati*, a few found work in the trades or as labourers, but professional opportunities verged on the nonexistent. A notable exception was dentistry, which two prisoners, Pacifico Prosperi and, later, Teodoro Sardoc, practised to the benefit of both detainees and locals. On occasion prisoners were able to ply their actual trades (e.g., tailor, cobbler, painter, blacksmith, mechanic, barber), but, for the most part, they had to adapt to the demands of the environment. Service positions such as operating the canteen, working in restaurants/hotels, or providing assistance to prisoners of means were common occupations.[60] The freelance professionals (e.g., lawyers), deprived of their clientele, struggled financially and had to rely on savings or the kindness of comrades to support themselves. Francesco Fausto Nitti claimed that economic duress was extreme:

> We soon found that it was impossible to keep body and soul together on the island with our allowance of ten liras a day. Rents were very high; hovels of two or three rooms cost two or three hundred liras a month. The inhabitants were growing rich on the deportees ... the natives laboured under the delusion that we were all wealthy and that they were justified in exploiting us ... In reality, the majority of the deportees were practically without private means and many of them almost starved to death on their pitiful allowance.[61]

The fiscal impossibility of maintaining two households forced many *confinati* to have their families move to Lipari: rather than a luxury, it was an economic necessity. Antonia Abbiati lays out the plight of those left behind in her appeal to Brescia's police commissioner on 4 January 1928:

> [I]o sottoscritta, moglie di Abbiati Luigi confinato politico mi permetto di farle presente le condizioni in cui sono stata lasciata da mio marito dopo il suo arresto [4 dicembre 1927]. Rimasi sola con due bimbi, uno di due anni e un'altra di mesi otto, senza casa, senza pane, senza fuoco, col crudo inverno. Come posso provvedere al sostentamento delle mie creature, io che non trovo lavoro? Eppure esse vogliono

mangiare e piangono se non c'è pane. Ed io, che per loro farei di tutto, no so quello che sarà di me domani.[62]

(I, the undersigned, wife of political *confinato* Luigi Abbiati, would like to bring to your attention the conditions in which I have been left following my husband's arrest [4 December 1927]. I was left alone with two children, a two-year-old and an eight-month-old, without a home, without bread, without heat, in the raw of winter. How can I provide for the sustenance of my children when I cannot find work? And yet, they want to eat and they cry if there is no bread. And I, who would do anything for them, don't know what will become of me tomorrow.)

Luigi Abbiati was fortunate to find employment as a mechanic in Lipari so consolidating the costs of the household was essential for the family's economic well-being. Such precarious conditions wrenched families from their communities, where displays of solidarity could lead to charges of collaboration, and forced them to seek permission to relocate in the colonies. Frequently, they leased the very homes of those islanders who had emigrated. Of course, the locals welcomed this familial presence, which along with that of the bureaucratic infrastructure of the colony (i.e., police, militia, customs officials, soldiers, administrators) provided a stimulus to the local economy through increased demand for goods and services.

For the unemployed, the monotony of indolence could prove a complacent siren. After collecting the dole, they usually spent the remainder of the morning at the beach (a restricted stretch of rocky shore), walking, or waiting for the arrival of steamship *Adele*, which carried the mail, the newspaper, and the new *confinati*. After lunch, it was either back to the beach, a game of chess (cards were prohibited), or back to the citadel until dusk. Two trumpet blares announced the re-entry time. Within thirty minutes, the nightly patrols began verifying presence: anyone caught violating curfew was subject to arrest and prosecution. For those residing in the *cameroni*, the evening roll call commenced at 21.00, after which the guards locked the doors for the night.

To stave off boredom, idleness, and isolation, *confinati* established a library and organised primary and continuing education programmes. The increased presence of families and, therefore, of children, necessitated a different educational space because their numbers exceeded the local school's capacity.[63] For both the authorities and the interned, integrating the children, for whom schooling was obligatory until the age of fourteen, with the local population presented problems. The compromise solution was to allow the prisoners to rent the facilities during off hours for educational purposes. For adults, the continuing education programme provided learning opportunities and countered *taedium vitae*. For the colony's administrators, the school was preferable to the devil's workshop.

Director Francesco Cannata, apparently approved these scholastic arrangements on his own authority and soon received pushback from his superiors. Ernesto Vitetti, Messina's Prefect, expressed his concerns to both Cannata and Rome.[64] Moreover, according to Jaurès Busoni, the *confinato* Antonio Filippo Cocco denounced the schools as fronts for subversive propaganda. Busoni speculates that Cocco did so to have his sentence commuted.[65] Regardless, Bocchini telegraphed the immediate suppression of the schools on 21 November 1927:

> [R]ivelato che in Lipari con autorizzazione direzione colonia sono state istituite scuole regolari e che insegnamento è stato affidato confinati politici medesimi dei quali è nota invincibile ostilità regime, invita provvedere affinché predetti corsi scolastici cessino immediatamente o quanto meno disponga siano tolti confinati per confidarli a personale di sicura fede regime.[66]

> (Having been made aware that in Lipari, with the authorisation of the Colony Director, regular schools have been instituted and that teaching is assigned to political *confinati* whose resolute hostility to the Regime is known, you are asked to ensure that these courses cease immediately or that at least the teaching be reassigned to personnel loyal to the Regime.)

Bocchini was exceeding his authority and jurisdiction: the Undersecretary of the Interior, not Bocchini, was the Prefect's immediate superior. So Bocchini sought to bypass the prefecture and to exert pressure through the *questura* (police headquarters). Although he did offer an alternative to shuttering the schools, the logistical and fiscal challenges of hiring the appropriate staff alongside the scepticism of the students towards these instructors made the proposal appear all the more disingenuous. Cannata responded to Bocchini on 27 November 1927: 'Assicurarsi aver provveduto confermare disposizioni date revoca incarichi e cessazione insegnamento confinati Lipari et famiglie'.[67] (Rest assured. Have made arrangements and am able to confirm the revocation of teaching assignments and termination of instruction to *confinati* and their families on Lipari.)

Thus, after this brief experiment, education reverted to private lessons and clandestine encounters.[68] Following the episode, which perhaps Bocchini interpreted as evidence of subversion, *Carabinieri* reinforcements arrived on 11 December 1927. A dragnet of 250 arrests ensued alarming both *confinati* and locals with its violence and inexplicable cause. Such displays of coercive power enforced a general psychological strategy to keep the interned on edge and mindful that their lives were not their own.

With the schools' closure, the library proved essential for the education of both children and adults. Relatively well-furnished across genres, the library reached 2,384 volumes. The colony's director reviewed acquisition requests, and the prisoners' dues paid for the purchases.[69] Each director applied different criteria in determining the appropriateness of certain authors and titles: books that one director found acceptable another might sequester so that periodic purges culled the collection.[70] Moreover this discretionary approach led to inconsistencies across detention sites since what was forbidden in Lipari might be available in another colony.

Despite censorship controls, banned books frequently made it to the island through gifts and visitors. The majority of objectionable texts presented obvious historical, social, or political challenges to Fascism though the rationale, as Mino Maccari commented, could be difficult to discern:

> Segretario della biblioteca [Iffrido Scaffidi] è un comunista siciliano … È furibondo anche perché la Direzione della colonia ha ritirato centonovantacinque libri, ritenendo non essere opportuno che fossero dati in lettura ai confinati … – Andreieff – comincia – Ambrosini Gaspare, Ambrosini Vittorio … Come, come? Anche Claudel, Paul Claudel, ambasciatore di Francia a Washington? Il libro interdetto è *Crisi meridiana*. Rimango un po' perplesso. L'ho letto: è pura letteratura, senza ombra di politica. E allora? Dò un'altra occhiata al titolo, e mi vien subito un dubbio orribile. Che abbiano letto *Crisi meridionale*? … Il bibliotecario lascia nelle mie mani l'elenco. Come sempre, come tutti, anch'egli attribuisce i fatti, che ritiene penosi o ingiusti, a particolari vedute d'organi esecutivi. – Se il Duce sapesse! – in questa frase c'è una confessione, che vale molto più di tanti piccoli malumori.[71]

> (The library's administrator [Iffrido Scaffidi] is a Sicilian communist … He is also furious because the Colony's directorate has removed 195 books, maintaining that they were not appropriate readings for *confinati* … – [Leonid] Andreyev – he begins – Gaspare Ambrosini, Vittorio Ambrosini … What? How? Even Claudel, Paul Claudel, French ambassador to Washington? The banned book is *Crisi meridiana* [*Partage de Midi*. 'Break at Noon']. I've read it: it's pure literature, without a hint of politics. So? I look at the title again and am assailed by a horrible doubt. Could they have read *Crisi meridionale* ['Southern Crisis']? … The librarian leaves the list in my hands. As always, as everyone, he attributes the facts, those that he considers distressing or unjust, to the particular mentalities of executive authorities. – If the Duce only knew! – in this phrase there is a confession that is worth far more than many little irritations.)

A perusal of the sequestered volumes suggests that *confinati's* reading interests extended well beyond their stated personal political affiliations and that they sought to inform themselves of other political currents. The list contains, alongside the expected Marxist and anarchist texts, influential works by German social democrats (e.g., Karl Kautsky, August Bebel, Franz Mehring, and Eduard Bernstein), French socialists (e.g., Jean Jaurès and Benoît Malon), and American and English utopian socialists (Edward Bellamy and William Morris).[72] These books provided the theoretical underpinnings for the maturation of the detainees' political philosophies and contributed to the formation of what Ilaria Poerio characterises as a 'school of dissent'.[73] In addition to these partisan political studies, authorities confiscated Friedrich Nietzsche's writings (e.g., *Thus Spoke Zarathustra*, *Twilight of the Idols*, and *Beyond Good and Evil*) – perhaps because aspects of his work appealed across the political spectrum.[74] The banning of Giuseppe Mazzini's writings is even more puzzling given the Regime's ideological appropriation of 'The Beating Heart of Italy' as a precursor to Fascism.[75]

Socially engaged fiction also succumbed to the wrath of the censors: Russian literature, with Maxim Gorky at the forefront (though Chekhov, Dostoyevsky, Pushkin, Tolstoy, and Turgenev figure prominently as well), English literature (e.g.,

Charles Dickens's *A Christmas Carol*), and even Norwegian literature (i.e., Knut Hamsun's novels *Hunger, Pan, Victoria,* and *Under the Autumn Star*) fell afoul of accept-able readings. Among the many Italian writers, the anti-Fascist Mario Mariani, although rather neglected today, authored eleven books on the censor's list. As for American literature, authorities bristled at the social justice novels of Upton Sinclair and Jack London. In particular, the latter's dystopian *The Iron Heel*, with its socialist critique of American capitalist democracy succumbing to oligarchic tyranny, found no favour with the colony's administrators. Its confiscation is not surprising given that this soft science fiction novel is also a political primer on socialism.

In a sense, by prohibiting these books, the directors were compiling an anti-Fascist compendium. That so many books should be confiscated, many of them repeatedly, also suggests that, alongside, the library's official holdings, the detainees maintained a clandestine collection of suspect texts.[76] Communist *confinati*, in particular, conceived of the library as a pedagogical project to train detainees for future socio-political struggles.[77] Whether walking, swimming, eating, or playing chess, every occasion was an opportunity to discuss, to debate, and to engage with both the texts and each other. Divorcing politics from pleasure proved impos-sible: reading was as much an individual diversion as an act of group solidarity through which the prisoners could find common cause.[78] For pragmatists like Mario Magri,[79] however, this abstract political consciousness-raising fell short of praxis:

> Sono anni che mi trovo confinato ed ho conosciuto centinaia di rivoluzionari; però, questi rivoluzionari li ho visti sempre, o sopra i libri, o con i libri sotto il braccio. Mai nessuno che si sia rivolto a me per avere le nozioni militari che sono necessarie in una rivoluzione. Vuol dire che questa guerra rivoluzionaria sarà fatta scagliando i libri. Può darsi che ciò abbia la sua efficacia, ma fa parte di una strategia a me sconosciuta.[80]

> (I have been exiled for years and have met hundreds of revolutionaries, but I have always seen these revolutionaries either reading books or toting books. Never did anyone turn to me for the type of military knowledge necessary for a revolution. It must mean that this revolution will be waged by hurling books. Perhaps such a strategy will be effective, but it is one unknown to me.)

This droll provocation ignores that reading was not merely escapism and passive; it was also educational and practical. The desperate clinging to texts that he observes was a means of engaging intellectually with one's self and with others to resist the numbing tedium and complacence of isolation.[81] Although sharing nothing temperamentally or politically with Giovanni Ansaldo, like the journalist, Magri is an atypical prisoner.[82] Indeed, his gibe aside, for many *confinati* studying did serve a concrete purpose: preparation for building a new socio-political order. This optimism proved prescient for from their ranks emerged leaders of both the Resistance and post-Fascist Italy.

## The Regime's response to international criticism

Mario Magri's critique of the contemplative life, however, did not go unheeded. The midnight flight of Rosselli, Lussu, and Nitti ruptured the detainees' isolation and drew international attention to Lipari.[83] News of their escape was not made public until 8 August 1929. The *Agenzia Stefani*, Italy's leading press agency, released the following terse statement: 'Nella notte dal 27 al 28 luglio sono evasi da Lipari i confinati ex-deputato Emilio Lussu, prof. Carlo Rosselli e Francesco Fausto Nitti'.[84] (On the night of 27–28 July, the *confinati* ex-deputy Emilio Lussu, Prof. Carlo Rosselli and Francesco Fausto Nitti escaped from Lipari.) Although buried on page seven, this attempt to downplay the incident was unsuccessful.

*The Times* of London picked up the story on the same day: 'It is reported that three political exiles, the former Deputy Signor Emilio Lussu, Professor Carlo Rosselli, and Signor Francesco Fausto Nitti, escaped from the island of Lipari during the night of July 27–28. From the fact that the announcement is only made now and in such a form, it must be presumed that the three men have not been recaptured'.[85] The article goes on to provide biographical information on the escapees. In the ensuing days, the news spread across the globe and brought, for the Regime, unwelcome international scrutiny to the practice of *confino*.[86]

In an effort to quell the public uproar over the revelations of Lipari's fugitives, Mussolini acquiesced to international criticism by granting a correspondent of the Turin daily *La Stampa* limited access to the colonies of Ponza and Lipari. The Regime's recourse to transparency, an administrative placebo, utilised the media to convey a representation of *confino* that conformed to the government's rhetoric. The honour of palliation fell to Curzio Malaparte, né Kurt Erich Suckert, who was then editor of *La Stampa*. Since he was on assignment in the USSR, Malaparte advanced Mino Maccari, the paper's managing editor, to report on the conditions on the islands.

In September 1930, Maccari's eleven-piece exposé appeared in *La Stampa*. Despite the prominent byline 'Dal nostro inviato' (From our correspondent), Maccari had completed the assignment in November of the preceding year. Each 'dispatch' appeared on the daily's third page – the one dedicated to cultural issues – nestled with a literary article or an original fiction.[87] Maccari split time equally between the two colonies. He presented the first five articles from Ponza, the last five from Lipari, and related the passage between the two islands in the sixth instalment.

Unsurprisingly, the results of Maccari's investigation complemented the Regime's narrative. He describes the punishment on Lipari as a 'holiday' for those whom the commissions, perhaps mistakenly, categorised as political when they were also guilty of criminal acts:

Nei loro confronti, il confino è veramente un provvedimento di una generosità e, direi, di una dolcezza senza pari. Per essi è davvero da usarsi la definizione di 'villeggiatura';

e non è a dirsi come di tale situazione siano scandalizzati i confinati politici sul serio, che si riducono presso a poco a tre o quattrocento in tutto, tra Ponza e Lipari.[88]

(Towards them, *confino* is truly a generous, and, I would say, a kind measure without equals. For them, one should indeed define it as 'holiday'; needless to say, such arrangements scandalised the real political *confinati*, who number in total some three or four hundred between Ponza and Lipari.)

Maccari repeatedly extolled the island's beauty and tourism potential thereby reinforcing implicitly the association of *confino* with holiday: 'Non avevano torto, i Liparesi, a coltivare la speranza che nella loro ridente isoletta si potesse formare un centro di villeggiatura estiva; né ebbero torto a lamentarsi, quando appresero che una colonia di confinati avrebbe frustrata quella speranza'.[89] (Lipari's inhabitants were not wrong to cultivate the hope that their delightful little island could be a summer vacation destination; nor were they wrong to complain when they realised that a colony of *confinati* would crush that hope.) In other words, Lipari was ideally suited for tourism, but the prisoners were usurping the chaise longues.

Maccari was not alone to report from the isles. Mussolini had also granted Thomas B. Morgan, United Press's Rome correspondent, access to Lipari. Mussolini's courting of the foreign press along with the correspondents' compliant reliance on the Regime for entry and information ensured favourable coverage. Indeed, Morgan did not disappoint. While hardly comparable to Maccari's exposé either in breadth or in depth, Morgan's perfunctory analysis did 'scoop' *La Stampa* by four months and gift the Regime an ingratiating portrayal of *confino*.[90]

An editor's note introduced the subject matter of the article and emphasised its exclusivity: 'The secrets of the Lipari Islands, where anti-Fascist exiles are sent, have been explored by Thomas B. Morgan, Rome manager of the United Press, who visited the islands with the permission of the Italian government, and is the first American newspaperman ever to have done so. The results of Morgan's observations are set forth in the following article'. Despite Morgan's extraordinary access, the brevity and superficiality of his assessment amounts to a nothing-to-see-here-move-along defence of the status quo:

ISLAND OF LIPARI. (UP) – The Lipari Islands, dreaded place of exile for those who run afoul of the Fascist regime, do not look foreboding to the visitor approaching them from Sicily. Set in the blue of the Mediterranean, the 'Aeolian Islands' of the Greeks and Romans present a charming picture – their volcanic slopes covered with luxuriant foliage, and their cliffs and peaks presenting a spectacle of scenic beauty. They are not hard to reach, with the proper credentials – although those exiled there have found them hard enough to leave. No restrictions were placed on this correspondent, and I was able to roam at will through the exile colony, talking to anyone and investigating any aspect of the lives of the deportees. Life for the political offenders seems to be what they make it. They are not imprisoned and from 6 a.m. until 9 p.m. can wander at will and use their time as they please, provided they stay within the territorial limits of the town. Patrols, armed with rifles, are at [p. 12] the wharves and guard the town limits. There is a force of 200 Fascist militia. The deportees are obliged to be in quarters at 9 p.m. Patrols make visits to various houses during the night, and the occupants must come to the window and answer 'present' when called. There are 250 deportees, all political. Sixty live in barracks provided by the government, which I found modern and comfortable. The remainder, of more means, live either in houses or in rooms which they rent. Fifty have their families with them. Since the colony was established three years ago, thirty have married girls from among the regular civilian population of the island. The deportees are given ten lira a day by the government for living expenses. Ten lira amounts to about 50 cents, and it is distributed every morning at roll call. On the whole my investigation of the island disclosed tolerable healthy conditions with little sickness and almost no discomforts. Dr. Carol [sic] Silvestri, former Milan political editor and irreconcilable foe of Fascism, said: 'I must say in all fairness that life here is not infernal and that this is not the Devil's island it has been portrayed'.[91]

Morgan's rhetorical opening regurgitates the *confino*-as-vacation motif expounded by the Regime. He then goes on to contradict the editor's note by downplaying the constraints on press coverage. Indeed, he rather improbably suggests that he toured Lipari without any restrictions when even Maccari acknowledges a basic tenet of penal security.[92] The Carlo Silvestri to whom Morgan referred was a life-long friend of Mussolini's. They had known each other since 1910, but fell out when Silvestri became an early and vociferous critic of Fascism. In 1924, Silvestri, then lead editor in the Rome office of the daily *Corriere della Sera*, accused Mussolini of involvement in the kidnapping and murder of Giacomo Matteotti. The result was exile in 1926: first to Ustica, then Ponza, and finally Lipari. He was released and returned to journalism in 1932. Although a critic of Fascism, he remained a confidant of Mussolini's to the end.[93]

Every point in Morgan's article finds an expansive equivalent in Maccari's eleven articles, including an interview with Silvestri, in which the latter confesses that 'egli ha voluto, né più né meno, dimostrare e riconoscere giusto il provvedimento della sua assegnazione al confino' (he wanted to show and acknowledge, no more no less, the justness of the measure sentencing him to *confino*).[94] Moreover, the con-veniently round numbers (i.e., '200 Fascist milita', '250 deportees', 'Sixty live in barracks', 'Fifty have their families', and 'thirty have married') cited by Morgan suggest that the information conveyed is proximate rather than precise: a veneer of specificity that glosses over reality. Rather than stridently defend *confino*, this pococurante reporting dismissed concerns over the practice by ignoring them.

Similar to Morgan's piece, though far more explicit in its effort to persuade, the *New York Times* ran an article by Arnaldo Cortesi[95] describing the living conditions on the island as a counter to international criticism. The dispatch's oxymoronic headline, 'Prisoners are free on island of Lipari. Men confined by Italy for political crimes live and work as they please', anticipates the sympathetic presentation:

Rome, Aug. 15. – The Escape of Ex-deputy Lussu, Professor Carlo Rosselli and Francesco Nitti from the island of Lipari focused a certain amount of public attention on the conditions of those condemned to political prison for crimes against the Fascist State. Interviews were printed abroad with some of them describing the islands in which those guilty of political crimes were confined as 'Fascist Siberia.' This made many people wonder whether their fate was as terrible as some would have us believe. I may say right at the start I have never been to either Lipari or Ponza where persons found guilty of plotting to overthrow the Fascist State serve their sentences. I have, therefore, no first-hand information. On the other hand, I have spoken to several persons who have been there and I can therefore talk with a fair knowledge of my subject. Having made this point clear, my readers will be able to judge my remarks for what they are worth. All sentences for political crimes are served on the two islands of Lipara [sic] and Ponza while the common criminals are sent to the islands of Tremiti, Lapdeusa [sic], Pantelleria and Ustica. The two classes are kept completely separate, the first two islands being reserved exclusively for those found guilty of political crimes. Lepari [sic] is a small island off the northern coast of Sicily, to the northeast of Messina. Ponza is a small island off Gaeta, almost due west of Naples. Both are described in guide books as holiday resorts. Numerous visitors go to Lipari owing to the springs of medicinal water existing there. Both islands have mild climates, fruitful soil and considerable scenic beauty. Perhaps the description of these islands may sound too idyllic. I myself should hate to be sent there to serve a term of political confinement. I can, however, think of many worse places to be sent to if the above descriptions tally with the truth.

Although declaring that he has no first-hand knowledge, Cortesi goes on to proclaim that those serving terms have complete freedom on the islands and live in relative comfort. He concludes with a quantitative analysis:

The question has often been asked just how many persons have been condemned to political confinement. According to official figures they, at the present moment, number about 600. It should be noticed, however, that they include about 100 who, though officially classed as serving sentence for political reasons, are responsible for crimes which should be more appropriately termed of a social rather than a political nature. They include usurers, extortioners, medical practitioners, &c. The number of those serving sentences for true political reasons are, therefore, about 500. The government has used its powers of grace with considerable liberality. Following personal appeals to Premier Mussolini, 396 condemned to political confinement have been pardoned and 190 had their sentence converted to an admonition and 35 to a warning. Thus it is seen that those who have been pardoned or who have obtained lighter sentences in consequence of appeals are more numerous than the total number at present serving sentences.[96]

Cortesi's rationalisation fails to persuade in part because his argument contains factual errors and in part because it reads as a press release. A year later, Cortesi reiterates the munificence of the Regime to counter mounting international criticism against the practice of *confino*. He marshals the testimony of the rather disreputable lawyer Vittorio Ambrosini as *prima facie* evidence of the reasonable conditions on the islands:

> Rome, Nov. 28. About conditions of life of Fascismo's political prisoners confined on the islands of Lipari and Ponza much has been recently written abroad and most of it has described these conditions as bad. Considerable interest, therefore, attaches to a long letter printed by the Lovoro [sic] Fascista of Rome giving a picture of these two islands by one who has been there for three years. The writer is Vittorio Ambrosini, a lawyer of some repute, who was condemned to three years' exile on the islands for political reasons. Perhaps the fact that the letter was intended to be published by a Fascist newspaper led him to dwell more on the pleasant than the unpleasant aspects of the life of the political prisoners and his descriptions of its delights must be taken with a grain of salt. Nevertheless it contains several statements which may be presumed to be correct.[97]

Cortesi paraphrases Ambrosini's statement, which ingeminates the descriptions in Cortesi's previous article. Given that Ambrosini informed on anti-Fascists for the Regime, the reliability of his testimony is suspect.[98] Duplicitous behaviour aside, Ambrosini does introduce a new element into the depiction of the colonies when he discusses the political sympathies of *confinati*:

> The number of those who rather admire the social policies of Fascismo are greater than might be imagined, he says. In particular, he asserts, there are several former exponents of proletariatism [sic], who, if given the opportunity, would make declarations which would have the most favorable effect on the Italian working masses.[99]

Ambrosini implies that many prisoners have realised that they erred, but that a vocal minority distracts from the silent majority.

Morgan's innocuous depiction of life on the isle and Cortesi's impassioned defence of the Regime lost credence to rather more damning portrayals of misery and cruelty. For example, Padraic King, relying heavily on Nitti's and other exiles' exposés, outlines an absolute condemnation of the 'Hell on earth of Mussolini'. He concludes:

> As a result of the barbaric cruelties of the militia there are frequent clashes between the exiles and these underlings of Mussolini. Should a prisoner be so bold as to resent the indignities to which he is subjected, he would incur the wrath of officialdom. This means either death or insanity. Exiles have a mysterious way of disappearing on the 'Devil's Island' of Italy. The 'missing men' just drop out of sight for all time. … None of the political exiles have been tried before a properly constituted court. While many of the internees are avowed anti-Fascists, there are, without doubt, others who have been deported on the flimsiest of evidence. But guilty or not guilty, these Italian exiles

> all have to drag out a life of living death, because of their opposition, real or imaginary, to the rule and sway of Signor Mussolini.[100]

King's alarmist description counters Morgan's feigned objectivity though its assertions are more anecdotal than evidentiary. Pagano has documented eighteen deaths among the detainees:[101] five (Luigi Amoroso, Luigi Campomori, Giuseppe Cassano, Egidio Fratini, and Vittorio Repulus) died in hospitals; four (Isso Del Moro, Antonio Mottino, Antonio Raina, and Costanzo Raina) committed suicide (Del Moro allegedly hanged himself in the psychiatric ward where he was being treated); two (Giovanni Caputi and Amedeo Cinti) died in a psychiatric ward; Giuseppe Filippich died following a beating by milita; Oreste Solazzi was killed by Pietro Alessi (a fellow prisoner); Antonio Camerini fell from scaffolding; no cause given for Egidio Cobianchi; for three of the deceased, Domenico Calducci, Amedeo Sarattini, and Duie Urdoliach, no information is available as to when, where or how they died – they just disappeared.

Whether these deaths arose to the level of King's condemnations remains moot. His assertions of death, insanity, and disappearance are correct, but perhaps not at quite the quantitative level he suggests. Nevertheless, despite the occasional apologia, the 'Devil's Island' narrative emerged as the dominant representation of *confino* in the American press.

In addition to courting the domestic and foreign press, the Regime also sought to deflect Anglo-American and French criticisms by discreetly soliciting an inspection by the International Committee of the Red Cross (ICRC).[102]

In April 1931, Étienne Clouzot, the ICRC's Head of Secretariat, met in Rome with Senator Filippo Cremonesi, President of the Italian Red Cross (IRC), to discuss the logistics of the mission, which was to include visiting Ponza, Lipari, and the Tremiti Islands.[103] Mussolini accepted the ICRC's request, and Cremonesi, accompanied by the police commissioner Armando Carcaterra, embarked on a tour of the colonies. Cremonesi conducted a two-day inspection of Lipari on 4–5 May 1931, and submitted his report to the ICRC on 11 May 1931.[104]

Their first stop was Ponza, where they spent two days. In his report to Geneva, Cremonesi explained that he would not travel to the Tremiti Islands because formally they were not a political colony. Nor, he rationalised without being asked, would he examine mainland sites because the situations of these persons could hardly be considered *confino*: 'Qualche altro cittadino è confinato in vari luoghi della Penisola, ma questa loro stessa condizione dà la certezza assoluta che trattasi non già di un confino, ma di un comodo soggiorno'[105] (A few other citizens are internally exiled in various places in the Peninsula, but their very situation provides the absolute certainty that it is not *confino*, but rather a comfortable stay). Cremonesi's insouciance to the conditions of *confinati* on *terra firma* betrays the Red Cross's dependence upon local and national governments. Objectivity is a pretence to which all parties necessarily subscribe. The ICRC had not requested that he investigate those sites so the 'comodo soggiorno' description appears gratuitous.

## Closing of the colony

Bad publicity was a factor, but hardly the sole one, prompting the decision to close the colony. At least six considerations figured into Lipari's shuttering. First, the Nitti-Rosselli-Lussu escape had generated negative international publicity and scrutiny. Second, the island's relatively large territory and varied transportation connections to Sicily presented serious difficulties for maintaining security. Third, limiting contact between transient civilian populations and *confinati* proved challenging. Fourth, the large-scale amnesty, granted on 4 November 1932, to celebrate Fascism's tenth year in power, reduced both the detainee population and the quantitative demand for space. Fifth, the spectacle of exile had shifted from public admonition to private detention: its usefulness as an overt political instrument was diminishing. Sixth, though perhaps the single deciding factor, the financial costs of sustaining the colony did not justify its political purposes. On 10 January 1933, the authorities shut down the Lipari colony and transferred all *confinati* to Ponza.

Given Lipari's notoriety, the decision to downsize garnered international interest. The Associated Press ran an article announcing the closure:

> The prison island of Lipari will be abandoned on Jan. 10 as a place of confinement and the few remaining anti-Fascists living in exile there will be moved elsewhere. This is a consequence of Premier Mussolini's declaration of amnesty celebrating the tenth year of fascism, by which 20,000 detainees were released. Many of those amnestied had been sent to *confino* for attacks upon or conspiracy against fascism. Less than 400 political *confinati* were left on the various penal islands, and all these are to be concentrated elsewhere.[106]

Here the rationale is reduced to a pragmatic factor: too few prisoners to justify maintaining the site. A memo from Vice Chief of Police Carmine Senise to Arturo Bocchini summarises the motivations behind the Ministry of the Interior's decision to close the colony after six years of operation:

> In dipendenza della recente amnistia e dei numerosi successivi atti di clemenza di S.E. il Capo del Governo, il numero dei confinati politici si è ridotto di due terzi. Tale riduzione coincide con le economie che la Finanza ha deciso di apportare al bilancio di questo Ministero per l'esercizio in corso. E poiché le tre colonie di confino politico ora esistenti (Lipari, Ponza e Ventotene) sono esuberanti ai bisogni, lo scrivente ritiene doveroso proporre all'E.V. la soppressione della colonia di Lipari. Resterebbe così la colonia di Ponza affidata per la vigilanza alla MVSN, pei confinati più pericolosi; quella di Ventotene, pei meno pericolosi. La proposta riduzione, che offrirebbe anche il vantaggio di concentrare tutti i confinati politici sotto un'unica Autorità provinciale di PS, importerebbe un'annua economia di oltre tre milioni di lire.[107]

(As a result of the recent amnesty and of the numerous additional acts of clemency of His Excellency, the Prime Minister, the number of *confinati* has been reduced by two thirds. Such a reduction coincides with the cuts that the Finance Ministry has decided to apply to this Ministry for the current budget. And since the three colonies for political internment now in operation (Lipari, Ponza and Ventotene) exceed our needs, I deem it necessary to propose to Your Excellency the suppression of the Lipari colony. Thus we would have the Ponza colony entrusted to the MVSN to guard the most dangerous *confinati* and Ventotene for the less dangerous. The proposed reduction, which would also offer the additional advantage of concentrating political *confinati* under a single provincial authority of Public Security, would provide an annual savings of over three million lira.)

Whereas the MVSN counted some 300 Blackshirts, the amnesty had reduced the number of *confinati* on Lipari to 120.[108] Because Ponza and Ventotene had experienced a similar exodus, these colonies had ample resources to accommodate additional detainees. In fact, the transfer of political prisoners from Lipari to the Pontine Islands had already begun in December 1931, so the actual decision to close the Lipari colony predates Senise's memorandum. Given the state of government finances, the opportunity to consolidate made economic sense. Moreover, these two islands' relative proximity to Rome facilitated Bocchini's oversight of political prisoners while Lipari's closure, in the service of public relations, mollified international critiques.

Those political detainees denied amnesty were transferred to Ponza and Ventotene in three successive waves so that, by 6 January 1933, administrators and security forces were left with but thirteen *confinati* to supervise.[109] No longer a political colony, Lipari became a detention site similar to those on the mainland.

In other words, it continued to exist and, in its post-colonial capacity, was the confinement destination for the same Curzio Malaparte who had overseen Maccari's reportage of Lipari. His fall from grace came three years after the journalistic coup. In a clash of egos and pettiness with Italo Balbo, the Marshal of the Air Force, Malaparte presumed too much and suffered Mussolini's peremptory justice.[110] Although taken into custody on 7 October 1933, his arrest was not made public until three days later when newspapers, including *La Stampa*, published the *Agenzia Stefani*'s generic notice: 'Roma, martedì sera. In seguito a manifestazioni di antifascismo da lui compiute all'estero è stato arrestato in questi giorni e tradotto a Regina Coeli, Curzio Erick [sic] Suckert'[111] (Rome, Tuesday Evening. Following demonstrations of anti-Fascism committed abroad, Curzio Erick [sic] Suckert, has been arrested and taken to Regina Coeli prison).

Balbo had accused Malaparte of engaging in anti-Fascist activities abroad, but this charge was political escamotage to avoid an internecine spectacle. Instead, Malaparte was condemned for defamation of a minister, for which he received the maximum sentence on 13 November 1933: 'Roma martedì sera. La Commissione provinciale del confino di Roma, riunitasi in data 13 corrente, previo interrogatoria di Curzio Erick [sic] Suckert, detto Malaparte, gli ha inflitto cinque anni di confino a Lipari'[112] (Rome, Tuesday Evening. Rome's Provincial Commission for *confino*, having deliberated on the thirteenth of this month, upon questioning Curzio Erick [sic] Suckert, also known as Malaparte, has imposed upon him five years of *confino* in Lipari). Compared to other *confinati*, his transfer was relatively quick: he disembarked on 30 November 1933, and spent a scant seven months on the island before departing for Ischia on 27 June 1934. Thanks to Galeazzo Ciano's intercession, Mussolini acquitted Malaparte the following year on 12 June 1935.

Despite Lipari's closure as a political colony, it served, in Pasquale Iuso's words, as 'a false *confino*' for some 450 Ustaše Croatian nationalists, whom the Regime deemed political liabilities in the wake the assassinations of King Alexander I of Yugoslavia and French foreign minister Louis Barthou in Marseille on 9 October 1934.[113] Six years later, in 1940, authorities converted Lipari's facilities into an internment camp. This false *confino* continued until a United States naval expedition landed troops on Lipari and liberated the last prisoners on 17 August 1943.

## Notes

1    Compton Mackenzie, *The Monarch of the Glen* (London: Chatto & Windus, 1967), p. 9. Mackenzie's 1941 comic novel depicts the Scottish Highlands through the fictional laird and estate of Glenbogle.

2    Corvisieri, *La villeggiatura di Mussolini*, 20.

3    Corvisieri, *La villeggiatura di Mussolini*, 7–8.

4    Hector France S. (pseudonym of Ettore Franceschini), *'Il domicilio coatto' (il cosiddetto 'Confino di polizia'): come l'ò visto io* (Rome: L. Morara, tip. Ed., 1956), pp. 50–1. Franceschini (30 August 1889–89 December 1960) served as Perugia's first Socialist mayor from 28 October 1920 to 4 May 1921 – a term cut short by violent Fascist opposition. In 1926, the Special Tribunal sentenced him to five years of *confino*, first to the island of Favignana off Sicily's western coast and then to Lipari.

5    'Fugitive to bare Fascist prisons: Putnam will publish book by Nitti, Ex-Premier's nephew, who fled Lipari islands. Uncle pens introduction. Revelations of inner workings of Regime promised – Editions to appear in five languages', *New York Times* (16 December 1929), p. 7. Cf. Robert Sage, 'Exiles of Duce escape guards on Italian Elba', *Chicago Daily Tribune* (8 August 1929), p. 3; Robert Sage, 'Escaped exiles of Duce allege life of horrors. Lipari hangs as sword over Italians, they say', *Chicago Daily Tribune* (9 August 1929), p. 7; 'Prisoners of the Fascists. How they are treated', *Manchester Guardian* (4 December 1929), p. 5; 'Fascist delirium of patriotism. Mussolini dreams of empire', *Manchester Guardian* (6 December 1929), p. 17; 'The Lipari Islands. Fascism's Siberia', *Sun* (8 September 1929); 'Foes of Fascism beaten in prison, Nitti says', *Atlanta Constitution* (1 September 1929), p. A6; 'Escape from Fascist prison described by Italian noble', *Atlanta Constitution* (2 September 1929), p. 3; 'Risks life to escape Fascist penal colony', *Boston Globe* (8 September 1929), p. B15; and 'Italians oppose Fascism, says Prof. Rosselli', *Christian Science Monitor* (4 December 1929), p. 4.

6    See Emilio Lussu, *La catena* (Paris: Respublica, 1930); Carlo Rosselli, 'Fuga in quattro tempi', in *Almanacco socialista 1931* (Paris: PSI, 1931), pp. 76–89; Francesco Fausto Nitti's account appeared in 1930, in French, English, Spanish, German, Japanese, and Swedish: *Nos prisons et notre évasion* (Paris: Librarie Valois, 1930); *Escape: The*

*personal narrative of a political prisoner who was rescued from Lipari, the Fascist 'Devil's Island'* (New York and London: G. P. Putnam's Sons, 1930); *Fugados del infierno fascista* (Madrid: Oriente, 1930); *Flucht: die persönlichen Erlebnisse eines politischen Gefangenen, der von der faschistichen Teufelsinsel Lipari befreit wurde* (Potsdam: Müller & Kiepenheuer, 1930); *Mussoriini kyōfu seiji to itaria dasshutsuki* (Tokyo: Senkōsha, Shōwa 5, 1930); and *Flykten: Mina upplevelser som politisk fånge och vår flykt från Lipari, fascisternas 'djävulsö'* (Stockholm: Natur och Kultur, 1930). The Italian edition came out after the war: *Le nostre prigioni e la nostra evasione* (Naples: Edizioni scientifiche italiane, 1946). *Die Rote Fahne*, the newspaper co-founded by Rosa Luxemburg and the central organ of the Communist Party of Germany, adopted the Siberian identification even prior to Nitti's revelations: *Die Rote Fahne* 280 (14 December 1926).

7    Putnam claimed to have received two letters with the date line Paris, 29 December 1929, and signed 'the Fascists of Paris'. The first letter, written in Italian, stated: 'We have read in the newspapers here that you will publish a work by Francesco Fausto Nitti about his escape from Lipari. But this must not be done. Fascism will not tolerate such an offense. We and our New York correspondents will know what to do. All the wretched police of New York will not be able to prevent your establishment from being blown into the air with two bombs. We have already warned the Fascisti in New York. For your own safety and security you must not publish Nitti's book. We know how to gain our objectives'. The second letter, written in English, called the book the propaganda of a traitor. Special Cable to the *New York Times* (31 December 1929), p. 6. In January, Putnam said that he had received two more letters (one in French and the other in Italian, always from Paris): 'One contained the sketch of a black hand decorated with fasces, a dagger, a pistol and a coffin with the inscription: "Warning to the pig who publishes the book of the other pig, Francesco Nitti, against Italy and the great man Mussolini,"' *New York Times* (18 January 1930), p. 12. Later, Putnam revealed that it had all been a publicity ploy. See Mary Lovell, *The Sound of Wings: The Life of Amelia Earhart* (New York: St Martin's Press, 1989), pp. 157–8.

8    Giuseppe La Greca, under the auspices of the *Centro Studi e Ricerche di Storia e Problemi Eoliani* is preparing a *I Quaderni del Confino* six-volume anthology of testimonials documenting *confino* on Lipari. The first volumes are *Voci dal Confino. Antifascisti a Lipari: anno 1926 – L'arrivo* (Lipari: Edizioni del Centro Studi Eoliano, 2014) and *Voci dal Confi no. Antifascisti a Lipari: 1927 – Il Primo Anno* (Lipari: Edizioni del Centro Studi Eoliano, 2016).

9    The population figure is from the census of 1931, see Istituto Nazionale di Statistica, *Popolazione residente dei comuni: censimenti dal 1861 al 1991* (Rome: Istat, 1994), p. 394.

10   Named after its sponsor the Deputy from Abruzzo, Giuseppe Pica, Law 1409 (15 August 1863) *Procedura per la repressione del brigantaggio e dei camorristi nelle Provincie infette* was enacted to counter brigandage and organised crime. See 'Liberal Italy's *domicilio coatto*' in Chapter 2 of this study.

11   The Socialist Deputy Andrea Costa denounced the practice in the Chamber of Deputies on 20 February 1899. The speech is reproduced in Giuseppe La Greca, *La lunga notte di Lipari* (Lipari: Edizioni del Centro Studi Eoliano, 2010), pp. 116–27.

12   Ettore Croce, *A domicilio coatto: appunti di un relegato politico* (Lipari: Tipografia Pasquale Conti, 1899); and Ettore Croce, *Nel domicilio coatto: notarelle di un relegato* (Lipari: Tipografia Pasquale Conti, 1900). Cf. Lipari's magistrate, Felice D'Aniello, *Intorno al domicilio coatto* (Lipari: Tip. Carlo Accattatis, 1908).

13   Irma Melany Scodnik, *Nelle isole eolie* (Naples: Stab.Tip. Di G. Cozzolino e C., 1900).

14   'La vita dei coatti alle Isole di Lipari', in *Corriere della Sera. La Lettura. La rivista mensile del Corriere della Sera* 8:3 (March 1908), 228–32. The article is signed 'Rossana', which

was a pseudonym used by the feminist and prison reform advocate Zina Centa Tartarini.

15  Cited in La Greca, *La lunga notte di Lipari*, 156. Tourism from Sicily had existed since the nineteenth century, but interest in Lipari expanded to Europe following the publication of Archduke Ludwig Salvator's eight-volume chronicle, *Die Liparischen Inseln* (Prague: Druck und Verlag von Heinrich Mercy, 1893–96).

16  Lipari's mayor, Felice Ferlazzo (elected 23 December 1919) discussed the financial impact of declining revenues from the pumice tax in the town council meeting minutes of 14 April 1923. www.archiviostoricoeoliano.it/wiki/il-comune-rischio-di-collasso-poi-ripresa-e-rilancio (accessed 13 February 2018).

17  See Kee-Hong Bae and Warren Bailey, 'The Latin Monetary Union: Some Evidence on Europe's Failed Common Currency', *Review of Development Finance*, 1:2 (April–June 2011), 131–49; Gianni Toniolo, Leandro Conte, and Giovanni Vecchi, 'Monetary Union, Institutions and Financial Market Integration: Italy, 1862–1905', *Explorations in Economic History*, 40:4 (October 2003), 443–61; Paolo Pecorari, *La lira debole: l'Italia, l'unione montaria latina e il «Bimetallismo zoppo»* (Padua: CEDAM, 1999); and Michele Fratianni and Franco Spinelli, *A Monetary History of Italy* (Cambridge: Cambridge University Press, 1997).

18  Law 237 (4 February 1926), *Istituzione del Podestà e della Consulta municipale nei Comuni con popolazione non eccedente i 5000 abitanti*, published in *Gazzetta Ufficiale del Regno d'Italia*, 40 (18 February 1926), 806–7; and RD 1910 (3 September 1926), *Estensione dell'ordinamento podestarile a tutti i comuni del regno*, published in *Gazzetta Ufficiale del Regno d'Italia*, 257 (19 November 1926), 5050–1. See Loreto Di Nucci, 'Podestà', in Victoria De Grazia and Sergio Luzzatto (eds), *Dizionario del fascismo. II: L-Z* (Turin: Einaudi, 2003), pp. 395–8, and 'Il podestà fascista. Un momento della costruzione dello stato totalitario', *Ricerche di Storia Politica*, 1:1 (1998), 12–21. Cf. Federico Lucarini, 'Breve viaggio attraverso una presunta continuità? Per un riesame dell'assetto istituzionale e amministrativo del comune italiano durante il fascismo (1926–1941)', *Quaderni fiorentini per la storia del pensiero giuridico moderno*, 39 (2010), 437–64.

19  For a historical reconstruction of the protests, the demonstrations, and the letter-writing campaign against the re-establishment of a colony on Lipari, see La Greca, *La lunga notte di Lipari*, 174–87.

20  Cited in La Greca, *La lunga notte di Lipari*, 181.

21  On 16 October 1929, the Messina court absolved the 48 defendants of crimes directly related to the events of 28 August 1926, see La Greca, *La lunga notte di Lipari*, 187.

22  Cited in La Greca, *Voci dal Confino* (2014), 28. Ettore Porro served as Prefect of Messina from 1 August 1924 to 16 December 1926.

23  In Italian legal parlance, *Testo Unico* is a descriptive phrase used to reference a collection of laws that pertain to a common issue. The TULPS was approved as RD 1848 (6 November 1926). Published in the *Gazzetta Ufficiale del Regno d'Italia*, 257 (8 November 1926), the new law replaced the TULPS of 30 June 1889. See 'The exceptional laws' in Chapter 2 of this study.

24  The records in the *Confinati Politici* files of the ACS contain references to both December 1926 and January 1927 as the inauguration of the colony. A communication from the DGPS to the DAGR, *Spese per l'impiego della MVSN componente i reparti autonomi per la vigilanza dei confinati (23/12/32)* (ACS, MI, DGPS, DAGR, UCP, 710/32, b. 16, 1933) indicates the suppression of the colony. The Provincial Commission submitted work requisitions on 22 November 1926. See La Greca, *Voci dal Confino* (2014), 29. The documentation concerning the directorship of the colony is limited. The first director may have been the police commissioner Giacomo Provenzale, who

received the title of *Cavaliere* in 1931 (as per the *Gazzetta Ufficiale del Regno d'Italia*, 220 (23 September 1931), 4662). After six months, Francesco Cannata replaced Provenzale and served as Director until the end of the summer of 1929. The Rosselli-Lussu-Nitti escape cost him his post.

25    In listing each *confinato*, Pagano provides personal data, political affiliation, and date of sentencing. See Alessandra Pagano, *Il confino politico a Lipari 1926–1933* (Milan: Franco Angeli, 2003), pp. 205–68.

26    This analysis draws on data in Pagano, *Il confino politico a Lipari*, 117–27.

27    D'Alessandris, Leti, and Solimene all received the maximum five-year sentence (along with five other Freemasons) for engaging in masonic activities on 25 May 1929. For Torrigiani, Grand Master of the *Grande Oriente d'Italia*, and the Freemasons in general, see 'From domicilio coatto to confino' in Chapter 2 of this study.

28    Bauer was an active cultural and political proponent of democratic ideals. He collaborated with Piero Gobetti on the journal *La Rivoluzione liberale* and was one of the founders, along with Ferruccio Parri, of the weekly *Il Caffè*. For anti-Fascist activities, he was sentenced to Ustica and Lipari on 5 May 1927. Later, he joined the movement *Giustizia e Libertà*, but was betrayed by Carlo Del Re, arrested, and sentenced to twenty years incarceration in 1931. In 1939, he was transferred from prison to *confino* in Ventotene where he remained until 1943. He then fought in the Resistance as a leader of the Action Party. See Arturo Colombi, *Riccardo Bauer e le radici dell'antifascismo democratico* (Bologna: Forni, 1979); and Ernesto Rossi, *Una spia del regime: Carlo Del Re e la provocazione contro Giustizia e Libertà* (Turin: Bollati Boringhieri, 2000).

29    Josef (Giuseppe) Noldin was sentenced to Lipari for five years on 25 January 1927, for promoting and teaching German. Although legal in other parts of Italy, teaching German was banned in the South Tyrol to facilitate Italianisation: the so-called Tolomei Programme (see Article 17 of the law *Ordinamento dei gradi scolastici e dei programmi didattici dell'istruzione elementare*, RD 2185 (1 October 1923); published in the *Gazzetta Ufficiale del Regno d'Italia*, 250 (24 October 1923), 6506–7). In response, Noldin and others organised *Katakombenschule* (schools in the catacombs) also known as *Geheimschulen* (secret schools). See Thomas Benedikter (ed.), '*Ich will nicht Gnade, sondern Recht' – Josef Noldin 1888–1929: Vorkämpfer für die deutsche Schule Südtirols. Sein Leben, seine Zeit, sein Tagebuch auf Lipari* (Bolzano: Athesia, 2000); and Christoph von Hartungen and Alois Sparber (eds), *Josef Noldin: Sein Einsatz – sein Opfermut – sein Nachwirken* (Bolzano: Athesia, 2009).

30    Lussu co-founded the Sardinian Action Party and was elected to Parliament in 1921. Vocally anti-Fascist, he withdrew from Parliament (the so-called Aventine Secession) after the murder of Giacomo Matteotti in 1924. He was sentenced to Lipari for five years on 27 October 1927, but famously escaped from there with Carlo Rosselli and Francesco Fausto Nitti on the night of 27 July 1929. He later co-founded and led the *Giustizia e Libertà* movement. See Giuseppe Fiori, *Il cavaliere dei rossomori: vita di Emilio Lussu* (Turin: Einaudi, 1978).

31    For a detailed explication of the detainees' socio-political profile, see Pagano, *Il confino politico a Lipari*, 117–55.

32    The case listings in Dal Pont and Carolini, *L'Italia dissidente e antifascista* indicate that the Regime sentenced at least 343 women to political *confino*, see Alessandra Gissi, 'Un percorso a ritroso: le donne al confino politico 1926–1943', *Italia contemporanea*, 226 (March 2002), 32. Pagano, *Il confino politico a Lipari*, 135 placed the number at 145, but this calculation appears to be based on incomplete data in Ghini and Dal Pont, *Gli antifascisti al confino*.

33  Giaccaglia's husband, Paolo Betti was incarcerated from 1927 to 1934. See Alessandro Albertazzi, Luigi Arbizzani, and Nazario Sauro Onofri (eds), *Gli antifascisti, i partigiani e le vittime del fascismo nel bolognese (1919–1945). Vol. III. Dizionario biografico: D-L* (Bologna: Istituto per la Storia di Bologna, 1986), pp. 359–60; and *Annali Istituto Gramsci Emilia Romagna*, 1 (1997) (Bologna: CLUEB, 1998), which is devoted in its entirety to the correspondence between Paolo Betti and Lea Giaccaglia.

34  Pagano, *Il confino politico a Lipari*, 136. Spartaco Lavagnini, a militant Socialist turned Communist, was murdered by a Fascist squad on 27 February 1921.

35  See Giovanni De Luna, *Donne in oggetto. L'antifascismo nella società italiana, 1922–1939* (Turin: Bollati Boringhieri, 1995) and Laura Mariani, *Quelle dell'idea. Storia di detenute politiche, 1927–1948* (Bari: De Donato, 1982).

36  See 'The exceptional laws' in Chapter 2 of this study.

37  § 37 *Del trattamento dei confinati e della disciplina del confino* of RD 62 (21 January 1929), *Approvazione del regolamento per l'esecuzione del testo unico delle leggi di pubblica sicurezza, 6 novembre 1926, n. 1848.* The section consists of Articles 340–54. See RD 62 (21 January 1929), *Supplemento ordinario alla Gazzetta Ufficiale*, 26 (31 January 1929), 32–3.

38  Curfew varied according to the season: from 1 November to 28 February it was 19.00–7.00; from 1 March to 30 April and from 1 September to 31 October it was 20.00–7.00; and from 1 May to 31 August it was 21.00–6.00. See Article 348 in RD 62 (21 January 1929), *Supplemento ordinario alla Gazzetta Ufficiale*, 26 (31 January 1929), 33.

39  Following Rosselli's, Nitti's, and Lussu's escape in July 1929, Rome clamped down on the colony by removing its director, Francesco Cannata, and reorganising security. The Ministerial circular 710-II489 (3 November 1929) increased the authority of the MVSN at the expense of the director and *Carabinieri*. By 1 December 1929, the MVSN militia had increased to 260 men while the *Carabinieri* forces had decreased to 16. See Pagano, *Il confino politico a Lipari*, 89. From 1929 until the colony's closure, administrative tensions over jurisdictional enforcement remained constant.

40  Jaurès Busoni, *Confinati a Lipari* (Milan: Vangelista editore, 1980), pp. 46–50.

41  Articles 351–2 of RD 62 (21 January 1929).

42  A prisoner's family suffered as well if it were financially dependent on the *mazzetta*. Physical detention enhanced social isolation, but also generally precluded working for those who had managed to find employment. The commission appears to have rarely applied the plank or dietary restrictions as punishments. See Pagano, *Il confino politico a Lipari*, 100.

43  Nitti, *Escape*, 55–73 details his twelve-day transfer journey from Rome's Regina Coeli prison to the island of Lampedusa.

44  *Schiavettoni* were 'Bagno' handcuffs used to transport prisoners. Shaped like a trident with a threaded centre tyne, these 625-gram cuffs used an adjustable horizontal bar to secure prisoners. With arms crossed, the hands slid into the cuffs, essentially a wrist vice, that were tightened by a wing nut fastened beneath the bar at the point of the middle tyne. A hammered ring then locked the wing nut and horizontal bar.

45  For first-hand testimonies of the arrival experience, see La Greca, *Voci dal Confino* (2014), 31–43.

46  The *carta di permanenza* differed slightly from colony to colony and from director to director. For example, Giacinto Bressan's, signed by the director Francesco Cannata on 3 July 1928, consists of 23 regulations including a detailed description of the circulation zone: 'Si rende noto che la zona ordinaria dei confinati è il centro urbano di Lipari e Chiesa di S. Anna e della Maddalena, imboccatura del Vallone Ponte, stretto Diana, di S. Lucia, Vico Barrone e Chiesa di Porto Salvo' (Note that the permitted

area for *confinati* consists of Lipari's town centre to the Churches of S. Anna and della Maddalena, the entrance of Vallone Ponte, Diana way, S. Lucia, Barone road, and the church of Porto Salvo). Whereas Armando Di Grisogano's *carta di permanenza*, signed by the director Giovanni Consoli and dated 31 August 1930, listed 26 prescriptions regulating colonial life and described generically the circulation limits: 'Non allontanarsi dalla Colonia che è costituita dalla zona urbana delimitata, discontinuamente, con sentinelle fornite dalla MVSN' (Do not leave the colony, which consists of the urban zone, marked, at intervals, with Blackshirt guards). The additional regulations in Di Grisogano's papers prohibit the possession or use of motorised vehicles, of radios, transmitters, or telephones, and of printing materials or cameras. Both documents are reproduced in Pagano, *Il confino politico a Lipari*, 295–8. Armando Di Grisogano's papers appear to contain orthographic errors. An engineer, Armando's birth name was Ljubo (De) Grisogono and he was born in Knin (not Kuin) as recorded in the *carta*.

47    La Greca, *Voci dal Confino* (2014), 48. For resisting a public official and instigating disobedience, Fornasiero was sentenced to Lipari for five years on 27 January 1932. He benefited from the 1932 amnesty and went to France. He then joined the *Colonna Rosselli* in the Spanish Civil War defending the Spanish Republic. Arrested in France and sent to Ventotene, he later fought in the Resistance.

48    Ebner, *Ordinary Violence in Mussolini's Italy*, 39–65.

49    Giovanni Ansaldo, *L'antifascista riluttante: memorie del carcere e del confino 1926–1927* (Bologna: Il Mulino, 1992), p. 323. He presents his taxonomic analysis of the *confinato* population in pp. 298–321.

50    Ansaldo, *L'antifascista riluttante*, 295–6.

51    *Decreto Presidenziale, Amnistia e indulto per reati comuni, politici e militari*, 4 (22 June 1946) in the *Gazzetta Ufficiale*, 137 (23 June 1946). On 22 July 1946, Sandro Pertini addressed the Constituent Assembly to condemn, among others, Ansaldo, who benefited from the amnesty: '[N]oi abbiamo visto uscire non soltanto coloro che dell'amnistia erano meritevoli, cioè coloro che avevano commesso reati politici di lieve importanza, ma anche gerarchi: Sansanelli, Suvich, Pala; abbiamo visto uscire propagandisti e giornalisti, che si chiamano Giovanni Ansaldo, Spampanato, Amicucci, Concetto Pettinato, Gray. Costoro, per noi, sono più responsabili di quei giovani che, cresciuti e nati nel clima politico pestifero creato da questi propagandisti, si sono arruolati nelle brigate nere ed in lotta aperta hanno affrontato i partigiani e ne hanno anche uccisi'. (We have seen released not only those who were deserving of amnesty, that is to say, those who had committed political crimes of slight significance, but also leaders: Sansanelli, Suvich, Pala. We have seen propagandists and journalists called Giovanni Ansaldo, Spampanato, Amicucci, Concetto Pettinato, Gray. These, for us, are more responsible than those youths, born and raised in the vile political climate created by these propagandists, enrolled in the black brigades and in open battle engaged and even killed partisans.) *Assemblea Costituente, X. Seduta di lunedì 22 luglio 1946* (22 July 1946), p. 209. Cf. Michele Battini, *The Missing Italian Nuremberg: Cultural Amnesia and Postwar Politics* (New York: Palgrave Macmillan, 2007).

52    See 'The diarist' in Chapter 3 of this study.

53    The cost of private rooms varied. For example, the journalist Giovanni Ansaldo rented his room at a monthly rate of 150 lira: a prohibitive expense for someone dependent on the dole. See Ansaldo, *L'antifascista riluttante*, 345. Cf. Nitti, *Escape*, 146.

54    A report dated 15 November 1927, from the Inspector General of Public Security Biagio Ranalli, lists a total of 217 colony-owned or contracted beds. Furthermore, the report indicates that of the colony's 357 *confinati*, 305 secured private housing. ACS MI DGPS DAGR UCP, 710/30, 1926–30, b. 4.

55  The purchasing power of the *mazzetta* corresponds to a value of 7 USD or 5 GBP in 2018. Following the economic crisis of 1929, the government reduced the subsidy to five lira both to save money and to increase hardship on *confinati*. A supplement was provided for those with families: one lira for the spouse and half a lira per child.

56  Busoni, *Confinati a Lipari*, 46.

57  Ansaldo, *L'antifascista riluttante*, 297.

58  'La popolazione, tutta di sangue coatto – da secoli, Lipari è luogo di deportazione: munziosamente spopolata dai saraceni, è stata ripopolata coi deportati di tutti i regimi' (The population is all of *coatto* blood – for centuries, Lipari is a deportation site: completely wiped out by the Saracens, it has been repopulated with the deportees of all the regimes), Ansaldo, *L'antifascista riluttante*, 296.

59  Giovanni Battista Canepa (1896–1994) received a special dispensation to live and work in Canneto for the pumice exporter Ninì Ferlazzo, see La Greca, *Voci dal Confino* (2014), 54–5. For other descriptions of employment, see Busoni, *Confinati a Lipari*, 23–6 and 53–4. Canepa met his future wife, Maria Vitiello, while internally exiled. He returned to Liguria and, adopting the *nom-de-guerre* 'Marzo', fought in the Resistance. He related the experiences of Ligurian partisans in *La Repubblica di Torriglia* (Genoa: Di Stefano Editore, 1975).

60  For a detailed analysis of the economic conditions of *confinati*, see Pagano, *Il confino politico a Lipari*, 157–64.

61  Nitti, *Escape*, 146–7.

62  Cited in La Greca, *Voci dal Confino* (2014), 62.

63  By 1929, 120 children of *confinati* resided in Lipari. See Poerio, *A scuola di dissenso*, 152).

64  Law 660 *Estensione delle attribuzioni dei Prefetti* (3 April 1926) expanded the authority of prefects. The Lipari colony fell under the jurisdiction of the Prefect of Messina. The strengthening of the prefectures, at the expense of the PNF, served to centralise the executive authority of the government. See Claudio Meoli, *Il prefetto nell'ordinamento italiano* (Florence: R. Noccioli, 1984). Law 660 was published in the *Gazzetta Ufficiale del Regno d'Italia*, 97 (27 April 1926), 1750.

65  Busoni, *Confinati a Lipari*, 57.

66  The telegram is cited in Busoni, *Confinati a Lipari*, 58.

67  *Ibid.*

68  Shuttering the schools led to informal study groups that Rosselli seems to have utilised as a cover to communicate with Nitti and Lussu, see Stanislao Pugliese, *Carlo Rosselli: Socialist Heretic and Antifascist Exile* (Cambridge, MA: Harvard University Press, 1999), p. 93.

69  Pagano, *Il confino politico a Lipari*, 180. The library's holdings at the time of its closing are listed in ACS, MI, DGPS, DAGR, UCP, 710/1, 1932, b. 1, *Elenco delle opere e pubblicazioni nella biblioteca dei confinati politici (4/1/1933)*. In 1932, the library counted 210 members who paid a two lira monthly fee to finance the initiative. See Patrizia Gabrielli, *Mondi di carta: lettere, autobiografie, memorie* (Siena: Protagon, 2000), p. 145. For a general discussion of how reading materials circulated in the colonies, see Silvia Vecchini, 'Leggere al confino di polizia. Fonti e studi', *TECA. Testimonianze, editoria, cultura, arte* 0 (September 2011), 1–19.

70  A reproduction of the list of 241 books sequestered from *confinati* is in Pagano, *Il confino politico a Lipari*, 281–5.

71  Mino Maccari, 'Un mese a Ponza e a Lipari. Fra le quinte del "confino"', *La Stampa* 224 (23 September 1930), p. 3.

72  For the influence of these works on Italian socialism, see Pagano, *Il confino politico a Lipari*, 182–3.

73   See Poerio, *A scuola di dissenso*, 113–65.

74   For example, the Socialist Jack London, whose works were also subjected to censorship, wrote 'I have been more stimulated by Nietzsche than by any other writer in the world' in *The Letters of Jack London. Vol. 3. 1913–1916* (Stanford: Stanford University Press, 1988), p. 1485.

75   Paolo Benedetti, 'Mazzini in "camicia nera"', *Annali della Fondazione Ugo La Malfa* XXII (2007), 163–206; and XXIII (2008), 159–84. See also Simon Levis Sullam, *Giuseppe Mazzini and the origins of Fascism* (New York: Palgrave Macmillan, 2015).

76   For example, authorities confiscated some ten copies of London's *The Iron Heel*, see Pagano, *Il confino politico a Lipari*, 183.

77   Poerio, *A scuola di dissenso*, 156–7.

78   Vecchini, 'Leggere al confino di polizia', 6.

79   Mario Magri (1897–1944) was a decorated WWI major and irredentist who helped coordinate with Gabriele D'Annunzio the taking of Fiume on 12 September 1919. Following the murder of Giacomo Matteotti, he sought support for a unity government and was sentenced without a trial to *confino*. Internally exiled for a record seventeen years, he was murdered by the SS at the Fosse Ardeatine massacre on 24 March 1944. See, published posthumously, Mario Magri, *Una vita per la libertà: diciassette anni di confino politico di un martire delle Fosse Ardeatine* (Rome: Editore Ludovico Puglielli, 1956) and Enzo Gradassi, *Il Capitano Magro: l'avventura di un giovane aretino da Fiume alle Fosse Ardeatine* (Arezzo: Fuorionda, 2014).

80   Cited by Mario Pianesi in Ghini and Dal Pont, *Gli antifascisti al confino*, 323.

81   The idea that meditating on readings is an act that both connects us to humanity and provides a respite to the de-humanisation of imprisonment is expressed most eloquently and tragically not by *confinati*, but by Primo Levi in *Se questo è un uomo* (Turin: Einaudi, 1947).

82   See 'Foundational texts' in Chapter 3 of this study.

83   For an exhaustive treatment of their famous flight, see Luca Di Vito and Michele Gialdroni, *Lipari 1929. Fuga dal confino* (Bari: Editori Laterza, 2009). For a succinct account, see Gianfranco Porta, 'L'evasione da Lipari', in Mario Isnenghi (ed.), *Gli italiani in guerra: conflitti, identità, memorie dal Risorgimento ai giorni nostri. Vol. IV. Il Ventennio fascista. T. 1. Dall'impresa di Fiume alla Seconda guerra mondiale (1919–1940)* (Turin: UTET, 2008), pp. 572–7.

84   'Evasione da Lipari di tre confinati', *La Stampa* 190 (9 August 1929), p. 7.

85   'Italian political exiles', *The Times* (9 August 1929), p. 11.

86   For international reactions to the escape, see the newspaper articles in Note 5 of this chapter.

87   Since the nineteenth century, the *Terza pagina* (third page) was a prestigious feature in Italian newspapers indicating intellectual cachet. By the end of the twentieth century, the majority of papers had abolished the distinctive page (including *La Stampa* in 1989) and had transferred the cultural content to other sections. Maccari's eleven articles were: 'A Ponza e a Lipari tra i "confinati"', *La Stampa* 210 (4 September 1930), p. 3; 'Un mese a Ponza e a Lipari. Come vivono i "confinati"', *La Stampa* 212 (6 September 1930), p. 3; 'Un mese a Ponza e a Lipari. Che cosa dicono i "confinati"', *La Stampa* 214 (9 September 1930), p. 3; 'Un mese a Ponza e a Lipari tra i "confinati". Tipi fatti e discorsi di tutti i giorni', *La Stampa* 216 (11 September 1930), p. 3; 'Un mese a Ponza e a Lipari. Scene della vita al "confino"', *La Stampa* 218 (13 September 1930), p. 3; 'Un mese a Ponza e a Lipari. Primo bilancio di un'inchiesta al "confino"', *La Stampa* 220 (16 September 1930), p. 3; 'Un mese a Ponza e a Lipari. Tra i "confinati" di Lipari', *La Stampa* 222 (18 September 1930), p. 3; 'Un mese a Ponza e a Lipari. Discussioni e vita familiare al "confino"', *La Stampa* 224 (20 September

1930), p. 3; 'Un mese a Ponza e a Lipari. Fra le quinte del "confino"', *La Stampa* 226 (23 September 1930), p. 3 (perhaps not ironically nestled in the pit of Mario Praz's article, 'Keats e la Bellezza'); 'Un mese a Ponza e a Lipari. Un comizio di "confinati"', *La Stampa* 228 (25 September 1930), p. 3; and 'Un mese a Ponza e a Lipari. Ultimo capitolo', *La Stampa* 231 (28 September 1930), p. 3. The eleven articles have been compiled and reissued in Mino Maccari, *Visita al confino (a Ponza e a Lipari nel 1929)* (Marina di Belvedere: Cultura Calabrese Editrice, 1985).

88  Maccari, 'Un mese a Ponza e a Lipari. Fra le quinte del "confino"', 3.

89  *Ibid.*

90  Mussolini personally reviewed Maccari's reportage: a ten-month vetting. See Maccari, *Visita al confino*, 22.

91  Thomas B. Morgan, 'Anti-Fascist exiles living comfortably. Press correspondent visits island by permission', *Ames Daily Tribune-Times* (15 May 1930), pp. 1 and 12.

92  'Ogni mio colloquio e ogni mia visita sono scrupolosamente controllati' (Every one of my conversations, every one of my meetings are scrupulously watched) in Maccari, 'Un mese a Ponza e a Lipari. Fra le quinte del "confino"', 3.

93  Antonio Pitamitz, 'Silvestri: L'ultimo amico di Mussolini', *Storia Illustrata* 271 (June 1980), 13. See also Gloria Gabrielli, *Carlo Silvestri socialista, antifascista, mussoliniano* (Milan: Franco Angeli, 1992) and Stefano Fabei, *I neri e i rossi: tentativi di conciliazione tra fascisti e socialisti nella Repubblica di Mussolini* (Milan: Mursia, 2011).

94  Maccari, 'Un mese a Ponza e a Lipari. Discussioni e vita familiare al "confino"', 3.

95  Arnaldo Cortesi served as the *New York Times* correspondent in Italy for seventeen years (1922–39) and as the paper's foreign correspondent until 1963. He received a Pulitzer Prize for Correspondence in 1946 for his dispatches from Buenos Aires. A profile of the reporter in *Time* magazine, 'The Press: Mr. Cortesi Gets Mad' (8 June 1945), suggests that he was too cosy with Mussolini's Regime while also providing readers with creative pronunciation tips: 'Cortesi managed to get along with Fascist officials while many another newsman was kicked out of the country. Cortesi (rhymes with more-lazy) had to get along: he was an Italian citizen'.

96  Arnaldo Cortesi, 'Prisoners are free on island of Lipari. Men confined by Italy for political crimes live and work as they please', *New York Times* (18 August 1929), p. E3.

97  Arnaldo Cortesi, 'Writes of exiles on Italian islands. Lawyer released after three years calls life on Lipari and Ponza not unpleasant. Prisoners virtually free', *New York Times* (30 November 1930), p. E3.

98  ACS, SIS (Divisione servizi informativi e speciali), Alto commissariato per i reati fascisti, Ricorsi confidenti OVRA, b. 16, fasc. Ambrosini Vittorio. See Mauro Canali, *Le spie del regime* (Bologna: Il Mulino, 2004), p. 374.

99  Cortesi, 'Writes of exiles on Italian islands', E3.

100  Padraic King, 'Would American civilization stand for a penal colony modelled after French prison of horror, Devil's Island?', *Syracuse Herald* (15 February 1931), Features Fiction: Magazine Section, pp. 1 and 10.

101  Pagano, *Il confino politico a Lipari*, 166–7.

102  See Filippo Mazzonis' reconstruction of the ICRI's investigation in 'Confinati politici a Lipari nei documenti inediti del Presidente generale della CRI 1', *Trimestre*, 9:3–4 (July–December 1976), 463–96; and continued in 'Confinati politici a Lipari nei documenti inediti del Presidente generale della CRI 1', *Trimestre*, 10:1–2 (January–June 1977), 320–61.

103  Filippo Cremonesi (22 August 1872–19 May 1942) served as Rome's mayor when Mussolini seized power. Following a two-year (1927–28) stint as President of the Instituto Luce, he held the presidency of the IRC from 20 August 1928 to 1 May 1940. Prior to visiting Lipari, he reported on Ponza, where he spent two days (18–19

April 1931). Cremonesi did not inspect the Islands because the archipelago was not, as of yet, a political colony – it would become one in 1936.

104 Reprinted in Mazzonis, 'Confinati politici a Lipari' (1976), 474–95.

105 Mazzonis, 'Confinati politici a Lipari' (1976), 473. Cremonesi spent two days (18–19 April 1931) on Ponza and sent his report to the ICRC on 29 April 1931.

106 'Italy to shut Lipari prison, shifting exiles from island', *New York Times* (30 December 1932), p. 5.

107 ACS, MI, DGPS, UCP, Affari Generali, 710/32, 1933, b. 16, Appunto del MI per S.E. il Capo della Polizia: *Motivazione della soppressione della colonia di Lipari (17/12/ 32)*. Cited in Pagano, *Il confino politico a Lipari*, 107.

108 Pagano indicates that 167 detainees benefited from the amnesty though some studies suggest that as many as 250 *confinati* may have been released. See Pagano, *Il confino politico a Lipari*, 106–8.

109 The first transfer, 31 *confinati* to Ponza occurred on 29 December 1931; the second transfer, 36 *confinati* to Ventotene, occurred on 2 January 1932; and the third transfer brought another 27 to Ponza and 9 to Ventotene. For medical or disciplinary reasons 13 detainees did not participate in the transfer. ACS DGPS DAGR UCP 710/32, 1933, b. 16, *Soppressione della colonia dei confinati politici (28/12/32), Allegato*. Cited in Pagano, *Il confino politico a Lipari*, 112–14.

110 For a detailed analysis of Malaparte's *confino* experience, see Giuseppe La Greca, *Curzio Malaparte alle Isole Eolie* (Lipari: Edizioni del Centro-Studi Lipari, 2012), and Giordano Bruno Guerri, *L'arcitaliano* (Milan: Mondadori, 2000), pp. 139–87.

111 'Curzio Suckert tradotto a Regina Coeli per antifascismo all'estero', *La Stampa della Sera* 240 (10–11 October 1933), p. 1.

112 'Cinque anni di confino a Curzio Malaparte', *La Stampa della Sera* 270 (14–15 November 1933), p. 1.

113 Italian police arrested Ante Pavelić on 17 October 1934, and he was subsequently incarcerated in Turin until March 1936. See Carlo Spartaco Capogreco, *I campi del duce: l'internamento civile nell'Italia fascista (1940–43)* (Turin: Einaudi, 2004), p. 22. See also Teodoro Sala, 'Le basi italiane del separatismo croato (1929–1941)', in Massimo Pacetti (ed.), *L'imperialismo italiano e la Jugoslavia: atti del convegno Ancona 14–16 ottobre 1977* (Urbino: Argalía Editore, 1981), pp. 283–350; Pasquale Iuso, *Il fascismo e gli ustascia, 1929–1941: il separatismo croato in Italia* (Rome: Gengini Editore, 1998), 81–105; and Pasquale Iuso, 'Un falso confino: gli ustascia in Italia (1934–1941)', in Costantino Di Sante (ed.), *I campi di concentramento in Italia: dall'internamento alla deportazione (1940–1945)* (Milan: Franco Angeli, 2001), 228–49.

# 2

# *Confino* in historical perspective

## A prison without walls

'[U]na grande cella senza muri, tutto cielo e mare. Funzionano da muri le pattuglie dei militi. Muri di carne e ossa, non di calce e pietra',[1] (A giant cell without walls: all sky and sea. The patrols are walls: walls of flesh and bone, not of mortar and stone), so Carlo Rosselli, sentenced to the Lipari colony, described *confino* in 1928. For *Liberal Socialism*'s author, the open island, to which nature and nation bound the unfettered prisoner, mocked the semblance of freedom. In 2003, political philosopher Massimo Cacciari seized on this illusory liberty as the locus of *confino* punishment:

> La prigione impone isolamento, separatezza. È una violenza che può distruggere, ma anche suscitare resistenza, reazione. La tortura del confino, invece, nell'immaginario del persecutore, è ancora più dura, anche se forse egli non se lo confessa e può credere, anzi, di essere più 'benigno' nell'infliggerla. Al confino tu sei vicino agli altri – e solo. La prossimità con gli altri rende la solitudine ancora più dolorosa … Là dove si vive e si parla sei escluso dalla vita comune e dai colloqui. L'esclusione appare così in tutta la sua violenza, proprio perché si riflette nello specchio della comunità che ti ospita negandoti l'ospitalità.[2]

> (Prison imposes isolation, separation. It is a violence that can destroy, but also engender resistance, reaction. The torture of *confino*, however, is harsher still in the imagination of the persecutor, even if he does not acknowledge it and may even believe that he is 'compassionate' by inflicting it. In *confino* you are near others – and alone. The proximity to others renders the solitude all the more painful … There where they live and speak you are excluded from everyday life and conversations. The exclusion appears in all of its violence because it is reflected in the mirror of the community that hosts you denying you hospitality.)

Estrangement, segregation, exclusion defined a perpetual state of being in which the torment of physical proximity denied the possibility of emotional solidarity.

A prison without walls inflicts torments without end. Fascism's adoption of *confino* occurred in November 1926, when the Chamber of Deputies and the Senate promulgated the consolidated bill *Testo Unico delle leggi di pubblica sicurezza* (TULPS: consolidated acts on public security). Although denoted *Leggi eccezionali* (exceptional laws), their application was anything but that throughout the remainder of Mussolini's Regime.

### Liberal Italy's *domicilio coatto*

*Confino* was new, but hardly original. The State had instituted forced residence confinements (*domicilio coatto*) since its political inception.[3] The Pica law, under the guise of deterring rampant banditry in the meridional regions, legitimised military over civilian authority to subjugate the South.[4] This law also targeted sympathisers of brigandage as political subversives. Such a legal strategy suggested colonial subjugation more than restoration of public order.[5] Pica's legislation obfuscated the distinction between adopting necessary measures to protect society from criminality and institutionalising partisan governance to target political opponents. Beyond designating military tribunals to try brigands, the law also called for up to a year of forced residence for vagrants, the unemployed, and those suspected of abetting criminals. The ambiguity of offending categories expanded government's discretionary powers. Applied retroactively, the Pica law established Inquisitorial Councils in so-called infected areas to identify suspect individuals.[6] Rumour, insinuation, and false accusations bridged the gap between suspicion and charge. Tribunals applied the law expansively to shirkers of the call-up: not only evaders of conscription, but their relatives could face prosecution and their home towns could suffer repercussions as well. Hence, the measure suspended constitutional rights by transferring judiciary authority from civilian to military tribunals and, in homage to collective responsibility, punished communities based on the actions of individuals.[7]

Piqued by the policy, Sicilian Deputy Vito d'Ondes Reggio sought to modify what he described as 'profilassi di tipo coloniale'[8] (a colonial-type prophylaxis). In solidarity, Florentine Senator Ubaldino Peruzzi warned that it would 'deny political freedom', but such objections failed to persuade the majority.[9] Moreover, military censorship in the southern regions meant that neither journalists nor government officials could enter active military areas.[10] The body count was over 2,000 people killed and some 12,000 arrested between August 1863 and December 1865.[11]

The following year, in the midst of Italy's Third War of Independence, another exceptional law extended *domicilio coatto* to *camorristi* and 'persone indiziate di voler restaurare l'antico ordine di cose e nuocere in qualunque modo all'unità dell'Italia'[12] (people under investigation for seeking to restore the old political order or to harm in some way Italy's unity). By 1871, sixteen sites had been designated for *domicilio coatto*.[13] The repressive and unconstitutional aspects of these measures, however, did not go unchallenged. For example, the Socialist Vittorio Lollini published a treatise denouncing the practice:

[Il domicilio coatto] è l'apoteosi dell'arbitrio, è la negazione d'ogni giustizia, è la sanzione dell'onnipotenza ministeriale, è la violazione dello Statuto e di tutti i più inconcussi canoni del giure costituzionale … [S]i molestia … il cittadino, che avendo già scontato il debito suo verso la società, più nulla le deve, lo si priva di ogni garanzia, … si confonde il potere esecutivo con il potere giudiziario, anzi il primo al secondo sostituisce. L'art. 71 dello Statuto dice che 'niuno può essere distolto dai suoi giudici naturali' e che 'non potranno perciò essere creati Tribunali o Commissioni straordinarie'. Orbene, qui non solo si crea un tribunale straordinario, quello del ministero dell'Interno, ma si fa peggio ancora; si condanna un cittadino che non ha commesso alcun reato … [è] un'enormità che rende il paese nostro indegno del nome di libero e civile.[14]

(Forced residence confinement is the apotheosis of arbitrariness. It is the negation of justice and the sanctioning of ministerial omnipotence. It is a violation of the Statute and of the firmest canons of law … It strikes … the citizen, who having paid his debt to society owes nothing more. It deprives him of all protections … It blurs executive power with judicial power and replaces the latter with the former. Article 71 of the Statute states that 'no one may be removed from his ordinary legal jurisdiction' and that, therefore, 'no tribunals or extraordinary commissions may be created'. Well then, not only does this create an extraordinary tribunal, that of the Ministry of the Interior, but it does even worse. It condemns a citizen who has not committed any crime … It is an abomination that makes our country unworthy of being called free and civilised.)

Similar objections could and would be levied against *confino di polizia*, but these protestations went unheeded.[15] Not everyone endorsed the seizure of power, but too few dissented. Ensuing iterations of *domicilio coatto* even glossed over the appeal to public security to stress the safeguards of public morality. The regulations of 1881 included sentencing for whomever:

sia trovato a girovagare le osterie o gli altri esercizi pubblici, o darsi bel tempo nei teatri o in altri divertimenti, o altrimenti far spese eccedenti le proprie risorse, oppure cambiare spesso di abiti e vestire in modo non confacente ai propri mezzi economici, o mantenere donne pubbliche o in altro modo tenere condotta viziosa, o frequentare la compagnia di persone soggette e pregiudicate.[16]

(is found to be loitering about pubs or other public establishments, or loafing about in theatres or other diversions, or otherwise spending beyond one's means, or frequently changing clothes or dressing in ways inappropriate for one's economic resources, or maintaining public women, or in any other way demonstrating depraved behaviour, or associating with persons of interest.)

Throughout the remainder of the nineteenth century, royal decrees and legislation reaffirmed the practice of internal exile.[17] In those rare instances when political opposition explicitly defeated such efforts (e.g., the establishment of a colony of *coatti* – those provisionally released – in the Eritrean port city of Assab), the results did not change.[18] What ended the relocations was a moderate reaction to excessive demands. When President of the Council, Luigi Pelloux proposed a draconian Public Security Bill, the Socialist Party, along with other politicians and public opinion, united in opposition. The Bill's defeat forced Pelloux's resignation, thereby effectively terminating *domicilio coatto*.[19]

The respite was brief. With the Great War, Salandra's and Boselli's governments reinstituted forced residence confinements to address an array of security concerns.[20] Criticisms failed to rescind the severe Sacchi Decree, which called for a five-year imprisonment for actions, even if not illegal, deemed detrimental to the public morale.[21] Because military tribunals oversaw sentencing, such security measures lacked the formal imprimatur of the judiciary. Once again, a political crisis prompted the suppression of constitutional rights. For Mussolini, this 60-year *domicilio coatto* experience presented a historical rationale for internment. In its new iteration as *confino*, intraterritorial exile provided the political security that Fascism sought to ensure its primacy.[22]

### From *domicilio coatto* to *confino*

When in the aftermath of Giacomo Matteotti's murder Mussolini truculently addressed the Chamber of Deputies with a self-serving *je m'accuse*, he publicly proclaimed the transformation of institutional power relations: 'L'Italia, o signori, vuole la pace, vuole la tranquillità, vuole la calma laboriosa. Noi, questa tranquillità, questa calma laboriosa gliela daremo con l'amore, se è possibile, e con la forza, se sarà necessario'.[23] (Gentlemen, Italy wants peace; it wants tranquillity; it wants laborious calm. We will give it this tranquillity, this laborious calm, with love, if possible, and by force, if necessary.) Presumably, guaranteeing two out of three sufficed.

Nine days later, on 12 January 1925, Mussolini returned before the Chamber to present, with Alfredo Rocco, a bill banning public employment to those with questionable affiliations. Protesting against the law's intent, Antonio Gramsci addressed the Deputies:

> Il disegno di legge contro le società segrete è stato presentato alla Camera come un disegno di legge contro la massoneria; esso è il primo atto reale del fascismo per affermare quella che il Partito fascista chiama la sua rivoluzione. Noi, come Partito comunista, vogliamo ricercare non solo il perché della presentazione del disegno di legge contro le organizzazioni in generale, ma anche il significato del perché il Partito fascista ha presentato questa legge rivolta prevalentemente contro la massoneria.[24]

(The bill against secret societies has been presented to the Chamber as a bill against Masonry. It is Fascism's first real act to affirm that which the Fascist Party calls its revolution. We, as a Communist Party, want to understand not only why this bill has been presented against organisations in general, but also why the Fascist Party has presented the law primarily against Masonry.)

Although Freemasonry had supported Fascism's ascent, the Fascist Party (PNF) had severed ties with it by 1923.[25] While the legislation targeted Freemasons, Gramsci decried the dangerous import of the law for all organisations:

> *Gramsci.* In realtà l'apparecchio poliziesco dello Stato considera già il partito comunista come un'organizzazione segreta.
> *Mussolini.* Non è vero!
> *Gramsci.* Intanto si arresta senza nessuna imputazione specifica chiunque sia trovato in una riunione di tre persone, soltanto perché comunista, e lo si butta in carcere.
> *Mussolini.* Ma vengono presto scarcerati. Quanti sono in carcere? Li peschiamo semplicemente per conoscerli!
> *Gramsci.* È una forma di persecuzione sistematica che anticipa e giustificherà l'applicazione della nuova legge. Il fascismo adotta gli stessi sistemi del governo di Giolitti. Fate come facevano nel Mezzogiorno i mazzieri giolittiani che arrestavano gli elettori di opposizione … per conoscerli.
> *Una voce.* Ce ne è stato un caso solo. Lei non conosce il meridione.
> *Gramsci.* Sono meridionale![26]
> (*Gramsci.* Actually, the State's police apparatus already considers the Communist Party to be a secret organisation.
> *Mussolini.* That's not true!
> *Gramsci.* Meanwhile anyone meeting in groups of three is arrested and thrown in jail without charges only for being a Communist.
> *Mussolini.* But they are quickly released. How many are in jail? We nab them just to get to know them!
> *Gramsci.* It's a form of systemic persecution that anticipates and justifies the application of the new law. Fascism is adopting the same systems as Giolitti's government. You are all doing the same thing that Giolitti's goon squads did in the South when they arrested the opposition voters … to get to know them.
> *A voice.* That only happened once. You don't know the South.
> *Gramsci.* I am a Southerner!)

Gramsci argued that the PNF's political strategies represented continuity with rather than revolutionary departure from Giolitti's Liberal State. This spirited exchange underscored that the legislation was merely codifying an established practice.

Gramsci's concerns proved prescient. On 22 November 1925, in anticipation of the bill's passage, Domizio Torrigiani, Grand Master of the *Grande Oriente d'Italia*

(GOI: Grand Orient of Italy), dissolved the lodges and shuttered the association's journal, *Rivista Massonica*. Increased Fascist violence against Freemasons and lodges prompted Torrigiani's expeditious response.[27] The GOI's dissolution freed its membership from the repercussions of the 'law of association'.[28] Torrigiani tendered his resignation and the GOI went into exile.[29] This repressive legislation, which also resulted in the seizure and destruction of goods, was a precursor to both the TULPS of 1926 and the totalitarian racial laws of 1938.

Contemporaneous to suppressing the GOI, Mussolini launched an anti-Mafia campaign. Like Freemasonry, the Mafia was an organisation over which the PNF held little sway.[30] Luigi Federzoni, then Minister of the Interior, anticipated both the government's strategy in Sicily and the rationale for the exceptional laws:

> The affirmation of police authority [is] distinct and autonomous from penal authority, … and this criterion shall be applied to the institutions that deliver the cautioning and those that give *confino*, and also regards the setting up of the organization called on to carry them out; the police are to enforce administrative injunctions; … the interests of public morality are to be preeminent over all private interests.[31]

Federzoni was simply reiterating a sentiment that Alfredo Rocco, recently appointed Minister of Justice, had expressed four months earlier before the Chamber. Namely, that the State apparatus is entrusted with an ethical imperative to secure Italians' fortitude: '[L]o Stato non è solamente un organismo giuridico, è anche e deve essere un organismo etico … Lo Stato deve farsi tutore della morale pubblica e rivendicare questa morale; deve curare anche l'animo, oltre che il corpo dei cittadini'.[32] (The State is not just a legal entity; it is also, and indeed must be, an ethical one … The State must serve as guardian of public morality and lay claim to this morality; it must nurture both the soul and the body of its citizenry.) Indeed, Rocco espoused that this mystical communion could only be achieved if the State aggressively exercised its responsibility to enforce morality: 'È in nome di questo altissimo dovere, che lo Stato deve intervenire e reprimere la menzogna, la corruzione, tutte le forme di deviazione e di degenerazione della morale pubblica e privata'.[33] (It is in the name of this highest of duties that the State must intervene and repress lies, corruption, and all forms of deviation and degeneration of public and private morality.) Rocco argued that before the needs and obligations of the nation, distinctions between public and private spheres dissolved.

While the Mafia may not have posed a moral threat to the State's authority, its suppression served propagandistic and political purposes. An integral aspect of this strategy drew on the Pica law, but introduced *confino* in place of the historically charged *domicilio coatto* for the Sicilian Mafia.[34] The law's five articles provided both a blueprint and a field test for the subsequent overhaul of public security measures:

> Art. 1. Le persone designate dalla pubblica voce come capeggiatori partecipi, complici o favoreggiatori di associazioni aventi carattere criminoso o comunque pericolose

alla sicurezza pubblica possono essere, dal capo dell'ufficio di pubblica sicurezza del circondario, con rapporto scritto, denunziate, in stato di arresto, per essere assegnate al confino di polizia.

Art. 2. L'assegnazione al confino è pronunziata da una Commissione provinciale composta dal Prefetto, che la convoca e la presiede, dal procuratore del Re e da un consigliere di Prefettura.

Le decisioni della Commissione sono definitive, e possono soltanto essere revocate, dietro istanza o di ufficio, per errore di fatto.

Art. 3. Il confino di polizia dura da 1 a 5 anni, e si sconta in una Colonia o in un Comune del Regno diverso dalla residenza del confinato, designato dal Ministro per l'interno.

Art. 4. Sono applicabili agli assegnati al confino di polizia le disposizioni contenute negli articoli 117, 118, 119, 120 e 121 della legge di pubblica sicurezza testo unico 30 giugno 1880, n. 6144.

Art. 5. Il presente decreto vale soltanto per le provincie di Catania, Caltanissetta, Girgenti, Messina, Palermo, Siracusa e Trapani.[35]

(Art. 1. Those persons designated by public opinion to be ringleaders, accomplices or abettors of associations having a criminal character or at any rate posing a danger to public security may be, with a written report by the district head of public security, declared under arrest to be sentenced to *confino*.

Art. 2. Sentencing to *confino* is emitted by a Provincial Commission consisting of the Prefect, who convenes and presides over it, the King's procurator, and an adviser from the Prefecture. The Commission's decisions are final, and may only be revoked on appeal or official reasons due to factual errors.

Art. 3. *Confino* lasts from one to five years and is served in a Colony or in a Township of the Realm different from the *confinato*'s residency as designated by the Minister of the Interior.

Art. 4. The Articles 117 through 121 of the TULPS Law 6144 (30 June 1880) are applicable to those assigned to *confino*.

Art. 5. This decree applies solely to the provinces of Catania, Caltanissetta, Agrigento, Messina, Palermo, Syracuse, and Trapani.)

To enforce this decree, Mussolini sent Prefect Cesare Mori to Palermo with explicit instructions: 'vostra Eccellenza ha carta bianca, l'autorità dello Stato deve essere assolutamente, ripeto assolutamente, ristabilita in Sicilia. Se le leggi attualmente in vigore la ostacoleranno, non costituirà problema, noi faremo nuove leggi'.[36] (Your Excellency has *carte blanche*. The State's authority must absolutely, I repeat, absolutely be re-established in Sicily. If the current laws hinder you, this will not be a problem. We will enact new laws.) Judge Luigi Giampietro's appointment to Palermo reinforced Mori's authority because their relationship was one of collusion rather than checks and balances. The results were swift: within eighteen months, over 11,000 arrests.[37] Such decisive actions earned Mussolini and Fascism the accolades of the American press.[38] Of course, the suppression of civil rights coupled with a flagrant abuse of legal authority facilitated the criminal cleansing and political Fascistising of the island. While such excesses did not garner forceful objections, the Regime did face new challenges. Repeated threats on Mussolini's life called into question both the safety of his person and the stability of the government.

## (Sic) *semper tyrannis*

In the span of a tropical year, Mussolini survived four assassination attempts. Although the Interior Ministry was already preparing new public security direct- ives, these attacks provided an *ex post facto* rationalisation for repressive legislation.[39]

The police thwarted the first plot on 4 November 1925. Tito Zaniboni, Deputy for the United Socialist Party, allegedly planned the attack, though inciting agents may well have staged it.[40] Co-conspirator Carlo Quaglia apprised police commissioner Giuseppe Dosi of the plan so the arrests ensued without incident.[41]

The second attempt occurred on 7 April 1926. In Rome's Piazza del Campidoglio, Anglo-Irish aristocrat Violet Gibson fired twice at point-blank range, but just managed to graze the bridge of Mussolini's nose.[42] In a display of diplomatic largesse, Mussolini released her to British authorities.

On 11 September 1926, the Anarchist Gino Lucetti launched a bomb at Mussolini's car in Rome's Porta Pia Square. The explosion failed to breach the vehicle, but it did wound eight people. The price of failure was a 30-year sentence.[43]

Shortly afterwards, on 31 October 1926, fifteen-year-old Anteo Zamboni shot at Mussolini in Bologna. Officer Carlo Alberto Pasolini, father of poly- math Pier Paolo Pasolini, subdued Zamboni, whom Blackshirts then killed on site. Questions as to whether the Regime orchestrated the event or if Zamboni was even the perpetrator remain unanswered.[44] Mussolini's unequivocal response, however, was a clampdown:

> He now took the brakes off state repression, on 6 November stripping the moderate Federzoni of the Ministry of the Interior, which returned to his own hands, and pressing forward with other legal challenges … [I]t was now that … Italy became a one-party state. The Aventine secessionists … were finally deprived of their seats in parliament. The death penalty, the abolition of which the Grand Duchy of Tuscany and then United Italy had pioneered in Europe, was re-instated for political crimes. On 25 November a Special Tribunal for the Defence of the State … was instituted and given a party gloss, since most of the judges who served it were drawn from the MVSN. Clandestine emigration was blocked with greater energy … Italy was to be converted into a Fascist fortress.[45]

Intimations of Mussolini's mortality rationalised the impetus for the TULPS. As Federzoni's affirmations of police authority indicated, the legislation had been carefully prepared over the preceding year. The heavily publicised security breaches fed the rhetoric of permanent crisis calling for a strong government. In adopting a primitive strategy of tension, the Regime implemented new protections against perceived threats to fortify the Fascist order. Clearly, since the current security measures had not protected the Liberal State from Fascism, such measures were inadequate to protect Fascism from its enemies. A mere six days after Zamboni's death, Mussolini replaced Federzoni as Interior Minister and presented the Public Security Bill, which introduced *confino*.

## The bureaucracy of public security

The application of *confino* in lieu of *domicilio coatto* as a discretionary punishment reflected the authoritarian transformation of Liberal institutions under Fascism.[46] Rather than simply addressing delinquency, now this disciplinary action repressed political opposition through preventative measures.

The new legislation also necessitated an expansion of the forces of public order, which Mussolini cavalierly declaimed in his extollment of Italy's Fascistisation:

> Gentlemen, it is time to say that the police must be not only respected, but honored [applause]. Gentlemen, it is time to say that man, before feeling the need of culture, felt the need for orderliness. It can be said that, the policeman preceded the professor in history [laughter], because if there are not hands armed with handcuffs, laws become dead letters.[47]

The call for elevating the police glosses over their politicisation. Since 1880, the Liberal governments had expanded the institution of law enforcement, in part to control political adversaries. Beginning with the Political Office housed in the *Direzione Generale della Pubblica Sicurezza* (DGPS: General Directorate of Public Security) and followed by the *Casellario Politico Centrale* (CPC: Central Political Registry), policing evolved rapidly with the Great War to include the *Ufficio Centrale di Investigazione* (UCI: Investigations Central Office).[48] The war's end, however, brought a complete overhaul to the antiquated Piedmont-Bourbon public security bureaucracy including the reorganisation of the DGPS, the formation of both the Border Police Office and the Inspector Generals, and the expanded use of paid informants.[49] Hence, Mussolini inherited a vast internal security apparatus, albeit an inefficient one, through which to consolidate political power.

Presumably those forces did not suffice because in December 1922 new legislation sanctioned the establishment of the MVSN.[50] Significantly, it swore loyalty to the President of the Council, rendering the Blackshirts an instrument of the PNF.[51] A month later, the MVSN's General Command designated a political office to provide Mussolini with reports on individuals: even though, as an extrainstitutional entity, its activities were illegal.[52] Enhancing the police chief's administrative status and expanding the DGPS's discretionary powers further constrained the ability of the judiciary and legislative agencies to oversee the actions of the police.[53] In 1925, this totalitarian drive accelerated with the creation of Milan's *Ufficio Speciale Politico* (Special Political Office), which served as a model for the secret police force OVRA.[54]

This bureaucratic expansion of the state apparatus coincided with reliance on another instrument of social control in use since the early 1890s: telephonic surveillance.[55] Although extensive under Giolitti, the practice had remained relatively discreet. Under Fascism, such eavesdropping, while technologically sophisticated, provided limited results because its aggressive use was an open secret.[56] Nevertheless, in telephone tapping, police had a powerful tool through which to monitor the population.

Bureaucratic expansion and amassment of personal data are general tendencies of modernity that facilitate states' abilities to instrumentalise crises. Rather than target criminality, governments subject the entire population to surveillance and omnipresent suspicion. This penchant for social control is evident in Fascist Italy where several agencies compiled dossiers on individuals. The *Divisione Affari Generali e Riservati* (DAGR: Division of General and Confidential Affairs), an intelligence gathering and political police agency under the Chief of Police, oversaw the *Ufficio Confino Politico* (UCP: Political Confinement Office), the CPC, and the OVRA.[57] The DAGR also coordinated the surveillance efforts of the prefects and *questori* (provincial police chiefs).[58] Adapting and broadening the public security measures inherited from the Liberal State, led, with Arturo Bocchini's appointment to Chief of Police, to restructuring the security apparatus. In this administrative reassessment, bureaucracy itself became an instrument of totalitarian oppression. As Chiara Fonio argues:

> [T]he growing numbers of 'suspects' seemed to justify the reliance on widespread networks of informers both inside and outside Italy. Besides, the orchestrated institutional measures to maintain control over the country were facilitated thanks to denunciatory practices made by common citizens who betrayed one another to the police. Each stage reveals unprecedented levels of surveillance and epitomises the fascist vision of a totalitarian state. In two decades repression and control shifted from being anti-communist to an approach that encompassed all ranks and aspects of society through a powerful policing system.[59]

The ever-expanding repression leading to the racial laws and concentration camps became inextricably enmeshed in the social control efforts of the preceding years.

## The exceptional laws

Central to this bureaucratic reorganisation was the promulgation of the TULPS. In her study on Bocchini, Paola Carucci argues that the 1926 legislation redefines the relationship between the State and society through the innovative adaptation of phrases such as 'public order,' 'state security,' 'public morality', and 'decency'. Moreover, Carucci contends that the laws' expansive interpretation of 'subversive' and 'political suspect' along with the politicisation of the private sphere allowed authorities to strip those so classified of basic legal protections.[60] The use of vague terminology that referenced national interests and public morals compromised legal standards by blurring the distinction between the objectivity of the law and the subjectivity of the judicial agent. Such a rhetorical strategy facilitated the reclassification of licit behaviours as illicit.

In concrete terms, the legislation outlawed other political parties, suppressed opposition to the PNF, legalised the death penalty, established a Special Tribunal for political crimes, and introduced *confino*.[61] The TULPS expanded the discretionary authority of the police to the point of obfuscating the limits of individual rights. Bocchini adopted a tripartite expansion of public security: protecting Mussolini's person, establishing the *Divisione di Polizia di Frontiera e dei Trasporti* (Border and Transportation Police Division), and instituting the *Divisione Polizia Politica* (Polpol: Political Police Division). This third initiative was central to fostering a network of information-gathering agencies throughout the country that would report directly to him.[62] The Polpol maintained detailed dossiers on citizens 'that included information about education, skills, moods, moral tendencies (i.e., social attitudes, vices, sexual tendencies, weaknesses), psychological characteristics, criminal records, movements within the country and outside the national borders'.[63] As Michael R. Ebner argues, this form of documentation underscored the personalisation of the political:

> The centrality of gathering personal information on political suspects (broadly defined) fed the very personalised nature of Fascist political repression … [P]olice reports focused less on the offense, evidence, or the veracity of the accusations, and more on background information considered relevant to an individual's political, social, and moral character. These factors often determined the nature of their punishment, as did the economic status and character of the detainee's family.[64]

The political made personal. This arbitrary aspect of enforcement extended to *confino* where the individual ethics and morals of those policing determined the conditions of those sentenced.

Bocchini recognised *confino*'s utility in addressing potential threats to State authority. Such prescience derived from the knowledge that the forthcoming TULPS had Mussolini's imprimatur:

> Mussolini s'è compiaciuto di rivelare in un discorso alla Camera, che la inspirazione gli venne in automobile, così all'improvviso, e volle fissarla sulla carta, subito, con pochi appunti scritti a lapis. Non diversamente, per i piani geniali, i grandi strateghi: al Capo di Stato Maggiore poi il compito di sviluppare i dettagli. Fu il canto del cigno dell'on. Federzoni; dopo di che, egli accolse l'invito di ritirarsi dal fascismo guerriero.[65]

> (Mussolini was pleased to reveal in a speech to the Chamber that the inspiration came to him suddenly while driving, and he wanted to put it down on paper immediately, just a few notes in pencil. The great military leaders are no different with

brilliant plans: to the chief of staff the task of working out the details. It was the Hon. Federzoni's swan song: after which, he accepted the invitation to withdraw from Fascism's front line.)

Federzoni consigned the bill and then resigned as Minister of the Interior on 6 November 1926. Adding that ministry to his portfolio, Mussolini attained complete control over *confino*, which Articles 184–93 of the TULPS defined and governed:[66]

*Del confino di polizia*

Art. 184. Possono essere assegnati al confino di polizia, con l'obbligo del lavoro, qualora siano pericolosi alla sicurezza pubblica:

1° gli ammoniti;

2° coloro che abbiano commesso o manifestato il deliberato proposito di commettere atti diretti a sovvertire violentemente gli ordinamenti nazionali, sociali o economici costituiti nello Stato o a menomarne la sicurezza ovvero a contrastare od ostacolare l'azione dei poteri dello Stato, per modo da recare comunque nocimento agli interessi nazionali, in relazione alla situazione, interna od internazionale, dello Stato.

Art. 185. Il confino di polizia dura da uno a cinque anni, e si sconta in una Colonia o in un Comune del Regno diverso dalla residenza del confinato.

Art. 186. L'assegnazione al confino di polizia e la durata di questo sono pronunziate dalla Commissione provinciale di cui all'art. 168.

La Commissione può ordinare l'immediato arresto delle persone proposte per l'assegnazione al confino.

Art. 187. Le ordinanze della Commissione sono trasmesse al Ministero dell'interno per la designazione del luogo di confino e per la traduzione del confinando.

Art. 188. Contro l'ordinanza di assegnazione è ammesso ricorso ad una Commissione d'appello, che risiede presso il Ministero dell'interno, ed è composta dal Sottosegretario di Stato al Ministero dell'interno, che la convoca e la presiede, dall'avvocato generale presso la Corte di appello di Roma, dal capo della polizia, da un ufficiale generale dell'arma dei Reali carabinieri e da un ufficiale generale della Milizia volontaria per la sicurezza nazionale, designati dai rispettivi Comandi generali.

Il ricorso deve essere presentato nel termine di giorni dieci dalla comunicazione dell'ordinanza della Commissione provinciale e non sospende l'esecuzione di essa.

Anche le deliberazioni della Commissione di appello sono comunicate al Ministro per la esecuzione.

Art. 189. Tanto nel caso di confino in un Comune del Regno, quanto nel caso di confino in una Colonia, il confinato ha l'obbligo di darsi a stabile occupazione nei modi che saranno stabiliti dall'autorità di pubblica sicurezza preposta alla sorveglianza dei confinati.

La detta autorità, nel fare al confinato la prescrizione di dedicarsi a stabile lavoro, avrà riguardo alle necessità del luogo e dei lavori pubblici da eseguire, giusta le determinazioni delle competenti autorità.

L'assegnato al confino deve, inoltre, uniformarsi a tutte le altre prescrizioni che l'autorità di pubblica sicurezza riterrà di fare.

Le prescrizioni stesse sono trascritte sopra una carta di permanenza che è consegnata al confinato, redigendone verbale.

Art. 190. All'assegnato al confino può essere, tra l'altro, prescritto:

1° di non allontanarsi dall'abitazione scelta, senza preventivo avviso all'autorità preposta alla sorveglianza;

2° di non ritirarsi alla sera più tardi e di non uscire al mattino più presto di una data ora;

3° di non detenere nè portare armi proprie od altri strumenti atti ad offendere;

4° di non frequentare postriboli, nè osterie od altri esercizi pubblici;

5° di non frequentare pubbliche riunioni, spettacoli o trattenimenti pubblici;

6° di tenere buona condotta e di non dar luogo a sospetti;

7° di presentarsi all'autorità di pubblica sicurezza preposta alla sorveglianza nei giorni che saranno indicati, e ad ogni chiamata della medesima;

8° di portar sempre indosso la carta di permanenza e di esibirla ad ogni richiesta degli ufficiali o agenti di pubblica sicurezza.

Art. 191. Qualora il confinato tenga buona condotta, il Ministro per l'interno può liberarlo condizionalmente, prima del termine stabilito nell'ordinanza di assegnazione.

Art. 192. Se il confinato prosciolto condizionalmente tiene cattiva condotta, il Ministro per l'interno potrà rinviarlo al confino sino al compimento del termine, non computato il tempo passato in libertà condizionale o in espiazione di pena.

Art. 193. Il confinato non può allontanarsi dalla Colonia o dal Comune assegnatogli.

In caso di contravvenzione, il confinato è punito con l'arresto da tre mesi ad un anno, e il tempo trascorso in espiazione di pena non è computato in quello che rimane di confino.

(*On Police Confino*

Art. 184. The following, if deemed a threat to public security, may be assigned to *confino*:

    (1)   censured individuals;

    (2)   those that have committed or demonstrated the intent to commit acts aimed at violently subverting the national, social or economic order of the State or to weaken security or to hinder or to block the powers of

the State or at any rate to harm national interests in relation to the State's internal or international situation.

Art. 185. *Confino* sentencing is for one to five years and is served in a Colony or a Township of the Kingdom different from that of the *confinato*'s residency.

Art. 186. Sentencing to *confino* and its duration are determined by the Provincial Commission (Art. 168). The Commission may order the immediate arrest of those persons proposed for sentencing to *confino*.

Art. 187. The rulings of the Commission are sent to the Ministry of the Interior for the designation of the *confino* site and for the transfer of the internee.

Art. 188. A sentence may be appealed through the Appeals Commission, which is housed within the Ministry of the Interior, and which consists of the Undersecretary of State at the Ministry of the Interior, who convenes and chairs it, the attorney general of Rome's Appeals Court, the Chief of Police, an official of the *Carabinieri*, and an official of the MVSN, designated by their respective general commands.

The appeal must be presented within ten days of receipt of the Provincial Commission's sentencing and does not suspend its execution.

The deliberations of the Appeals Commission are also communicated to the Ministry for execution.

Art. 189. Whether in the case of *confino* to a Township of the Kingdom or that of a Colony, the *confinato* is required to engage in a regular occupation as will be determined by the public security authority charged with policing the *confinati*.

Said authority, in requiring the *confinato* to take on a steady job, will consider the needs of the place and of the public works to be carried out, in conformity with the decision of the competent authorities.

In addition, those sentenced to *confino* must abide by all the other regulations that the public security authority decides are necessary.

These same regulations, drawn up from the minutes, are recorded on the sojourn card that is given to the *confinato*.

Art. 190. To those sentenced to *confino*, the following may also be prescribed:

(1) not to leave the chosen residence without notifying in advance the authority in charge of surveillance;

(2) not to return home later than a given hour and not to leave the house in the morning before a given hour;

(3) not to possess or to bear weapons or other instruments capable of harming;

(4) not to frequent brothels, or taverns, or other public establishments;

(5) not to attend public gatherings, performances, or public entertainments;

(6) to be on good behaviour and not to give cause for concerns;

(7) to report to the public security authorities charged with surveillance on the days so designated and at any request by said authorities;

(8) to carry at all times the sojourn card and to present it upon request to public security officials or agents.

Art. 191. Should the *confinato's* good behaviour warrant, the Minister of the Interior may grant conditional release prior to the expiration of the sentence.

Art. 192. Should the conditionally acquitted *confinato* misbehave, the Minister of the Interior may return the detainee to *confino* for the remainder of the sentence, not counting the time spent in conditional release or in expiation of the sentence.

Art. 193. The *confinato* is not permitted to leave the Colony or Township to which he has been assigned.

Should this condition be violated, the punishment for the *confinato* is detention for a period of three months to one year, and time spent in expiation of the sentence is not counted toward the time remaining in *confino*.)

The Provincial Commission, referenced in Article 186, was under the direction of the Prefect and consisted of the prosecuting magistrate, the police commissioner, the provincial commander of the *Carabinieri*, and a senior official of the MVSN.[67] The Commission's inclusive composition suggested a broad-based management of the process, but in practice the Prefect and Chief of Police determined the outcomes. Since Article 184 effectively erased the distinction between intention and action, the Commission's power stemmed from its discretionary authority to define incriminating behaviour. Also, because it was not subject to judicial oversight, the Commission increased its own overseer capacities through the expansion of what constituted illegal activities.

Although Article 185 established sentencing guidelines of one to five years, the term could be extended for misbehaviour and could be renewed (and frequently was) at the discretion of the Ministry of the Interior, which also determined (as per Article 187) where the *confinato* would serve.[68] While the sole criterion governing location was that it not be the accused's municipality of residence, the Ministry usually opted for banishment from the mainland. An underlying rationale for *confino* was to remove potential subversives from a familiar environment where their presence could have a deleterious effect on others – hence the recurring metaphor of the communicable disease in the Regime's rhetoric. To isolate and politically quarantine these perceived threats meant, as a practical matter, establishing the vast majority of *confino* locations in southern rural communities and small islands.

As a form of preventive care, *confino* addressed potential problems before they could metastasise. To be effective, however, it required far reaching diagnostic capabilities and, therefore, enlisted the assistance of the citizenry. Anyone could go to the local police commissioner to file a complaint against someone they suspected of being detrimental to the public good. The police accepted anonymous charges as well. The commissioner would then pass on the complaint to the Prefect, who in turn would submit the accusation to the Provincial Commission. The

Commission would determine the sentence and then send the judgement to the Ministry of the Interior to establish where the sentence would be served. Once notified of the sentence (and arrested), the defendant could file an appeal through the Appeals Commission in Rome.

In composition, the Appeals Commission (Article 188) mirrored that of the Provincial Commission though the Chief of Police and Undersecretary wielded the deciding votes.[69] Decisions were swift. In part, the system's efficacy resided in its ability to bypass legal and juridical wrangling, which would prolong the process and could produce undesirable (from the Regime's perspective) outcomes. The final determination resided in Mussolini because appeals provided a self-promotional opportunity to display clemency.[70]

The process effectively suppressed citizens' guarantees against the arbitrary exercise of police power. Rocco's presentation of the TULPS both proclaimed the necessity of a police state and erased the distinction between the nation and the government:

> The function of public security is no longer to be considered as something exceptional, in conflict with the dogma of individual liberty as the foundation and aim of society. It is, on the contrary, to be judged as one of the primary functions of the activity of the State … It is therefore an activity whose exercise cannot be obstructed by absurd preconceptions.[71]

If the State's prime directive is self-preservation, then individual rights must be subordinate to the State's needs. *Confino* illustrated this conceit. Its application as a preventive measure in defence of the State stripped the accused of legal protections:

> The accused could be arrested at once, before their appeal was heard, and they were not allowed either to employ a lawyer or to summon witnesses in their defense. The jurisdiction of the magistracy was entirely excluded. Moreover these unpredictable and arbitrary procedures gave an opportunity for the party to interfere. It was usually the party which denounced suspects, and on occasion local leaders … used the mechanism of confino to deal with their personal enemies.[72]

Article 166 identified six types of offenders (loiterers, vagrants, pimps, drug dealers, addicts, and anti-Fascists) whose activities were to be reported to the Prefect. Such categorical precision belied the reality that anyone could be sentenced to *confino* because the inclusive wording of the law allowed for generous applications. While at first blush, anti-Fascism might appear as a distinct activity, the law equated these six criminal types, as moral offences against the State. Indeed, Article 166 defined anti-Fascists not by their activities, but by how the public perceived them: anti-Fascists were 'those designated by public opinion as dangerous to the national order of the State'. A malicious rumour sufficed to level charges against an individual, and those same charges were then evidence to demonstrate guilt since 'public opinion' had already tried the case. Though less restrictive measures than *confino* could be applied, they could also be bypassed:

> Primo provvedimento è la diffida. Specie di sermone morale che il capo della polizia rivolge agli interessati. In Italia son pochi gli oppositori che non hanno subìto la diffida. Il Questore, o chi per lui, si fa comparire dinanzi l'antifascista e lo invita in parole povere, a non occuparsi di politica, neppure per svago letterario.
>
> Alla diffida s'accompagna sempre il pedinamento della polizia, le perquisizioni personali e domiciliari, l'obbligo di non destare sospetti.
>
> Secondo provvedimento è l'ammonizione. Può essere inflitta per due anni, salvo, naturalmente, a ricominciare da capo, finiti i primi due. Il sottoposto all'ammonizione non può uscire dalla città o dal villaggio in cui ha il proprio domicilio; non può uscire di casa, la mattina, prima d'un'ora fissata e, la sera, deve rientrarvi al coprifuoco; non deve frequentare riunioni pubbliche. Pena l'arresto da 3 mesi ad un anno.[73]

(The first provision is the notice: a sort of moral sermon that the Chief of Police preaches to the interested parties. In Italy, few are the opponents who have not received a notice. The Police Commissioner, or another official acting on his behalf, has the anti-Fascist brought in and tells him bluntly to stay out of politics – not even as a literary distraction.

Along with the notice always come the police tail, searches of home and person, and the obligation not to raise suspicions.

The second provision is the caution. It can be imposed for two years, though, naturally, at the end of the sentence it can be renewed all over again. Those under caution may not leave the city or town of residence; they cannot leave their homes in the morning before a certain hour and must return before curfew; they may not attend public gatherings. Otherwise they risk arrest for three months to one year.)

The preventive measures of *diffida* (warning) and *ammonizione* (probation) date back to the 1865 TULPS. While the former restricted activities, the latter restricted movement. Such limitations resulted frequently in people losing their livelihoods since a job that was too far or that began too early or that ran too late was a job lost. Moreover, fear of guilt by association meant fiscal and physical ostracisation. The punishment resided precisely in these collateral effects that contrasted the perceived permanence and stability of the State with the precariousness and instability of the opposition. These measures had served as preliminary warnings leading, if deemed necessary, up to *domicilio coatto*, but under Fascism, they were frequently bypassed in favour of immediate sentencing to *confino*: 'È il capolavoro del Regime: il pericolo di esservi mandati sovrasta su tutti. Esso rende al fascismo molto più che non la stessa pena inflitta. La pena è per pochi, la minaccia è per tutti'.[74] (It is the Regime's masterpiece: the danger of being sent away hangs over everyone. It provides far more to Fascism than the punishment inflicted. The punishment is for a few; the threat is for all.) This repressive provision served as a political fail-safe because it could be applied to acquitted individuals and therefore, from the Regime's perspective, rectify the failures of the judiciary.[75] The efficacy of *confino* as a political instrument was not lost on Mussolini's critics.

The foreign press immediately recognised the extremity of the measures. In the United States, dispatches from the Associated Press and other media outlets ran the day Mussolini announced the TULPS.[76] The slew of arrests that followed the enactment of the legislation fuelled the public's negative perception of *confino*. To stem the domestic and foreign criticisms, Mussolini publicly responded to the various charges levelled against his Regime when he addressed the Chamber of Deputies in what is commonly referred to as the *Discorso dell'Ascensione* (Ascension Day Speech of 26 May 1927).[77] Although promoting a demographic policy that reflected Fascism's ideals, Mussolini concluded the address with an exposition on *confino*:

> How many are these men who have been sent to forced domicile in the islands? It is time to say to tell the world, because it has been said abroad that they amount to 200,000. (Laughter.) It has been said that in Milan alone 26,000 persons have been sent to forced domicile. All this is stupid, even more than it is cowardly. Let us in the first place note that there are two categories of people sent to forced domicile. They are the common sort and political prisoners.
>
> No sympathy need be spent on the first category. They are all thorough rascals, thieves, dope peddlers, usurers, wife-beaters, &c., who, the sooner they are withdrawn from circulation, the better. (Applause.) Perhaps the list of offenses for which one can be liable to forced domicile will be increased by some. In any case this class of persons in the Italian penal settlement now amount to 1,527.
>
> Now for those guilty of political offenses. One thousand, five hundred and forty-one individuals have been warned, 1,959 have been admonished, 698 have been sent to forced domicile. I defy anyone to deny the absolute correctness of these figures.
>
> As you see they are very small. But it is curious that none of those who have been sent to forced domicile wishes to be mistaken for an anti-Fascist; some, indeed, profess to be Fascists. In fact on May 21 last year sixty-one declared they had never participated in any political activity, 268 declared they had long previously given up all political activities, 185 that they never had been subversives, 182 that they had long previously given up all subversive activities, 59 that they belonged to no political party, 69 that they long previously severed all ties with political parties and 26 made acts of submission to the Fascist regime. Only twenty-one confirmed political ideas, while fifty-two made no statement of political tenor.
>
> I have here an interesting set of documents from a human viewpoint. I shall not tell you the names of those who have sent me these letters which are often very interesting. The fact that all these deported persons have appealed direct to me must be considered one of the greatest victories of the Fascist régime. First, because none of them wished to remain under suspicion of being anti-Fascist, and secondly because they all, despite their anti-Fascist leaning, knew that they could freely apply to me if they felt that they had not received justice.
>
> 'I believe', says one of them, 'that the fact of having held the Maximalist idea and of having been a Maximalist Deputy without ever breaking existing laws cannot

be considered sufficient reasons for the grave measures which have been taken against me'.

'I belonged', says another, 'to the Communist Party up to yesterday, but as this party has now ceased to be recognized as part of the political organism of the country, I resign'. (Laughter.)

Mr. X declares 'he is [sic] decided to abandon all political activities'. Mr. Y writes that 'the fact of having been in unorthodox political ideas is not sufficient reason for the measures taken against me'.

Another promise [sic] 'to abandon all political activities and retire to Santa Margherita Ligure'. He has chosen a good place. 'I preached Marxism', says yet another 'according to the law of evolution dialectically understood'. (Laughter.)

'It is only recently when a new corporate organization of the State was announced that my ideas cleared', says another. (Laughter.)

Yet another promises to suspend all political activities for as long as the Fascist Party remains in power. (Loud laughter.)

These documents have great human interests. Now, these deported persons certainly do not find themselves in a very brilliant position, but do not let us exaggerate. They receive ten revalued lire every day (laughter), they do not live with common deportees and they have been concentrated on only two islands.

Some people talk of amnesty. No, gentlemen, there will be no amnesty. There will not be any amnesty before 1932, and then one will talk of it only if, as I sincerely hope, it will not be necessary to extend the life of our special laws for the defense of the State. But the fact that I refuse to grant collective amnesty does not prevent me from issuing pardons in certain individual cases, especially if the individuals in question are recommended to me by some high Fascist, or, as has happened in certain cases, by entire Fascist directorates. (Lively comments.)

What plan do I follow when I pardon somebody? First I examine his war record. Evidently, if he is maimed or has won medals or passed several years in the trenches he has higher chances for clemency than one who has not. Then I examine the state of his health and his family. Finally I examine what the deportee himself has to say for himself.

Is this terror, gentlemen? No! It is hardly even severity. Is it terrorism? No! These measures are measures of social hygiene, of national prophylactics. I remove certain individuals from contact with their fellow men, as a doctor would segregate one affected with infectious disease.[78]

This five-point defence mounted for *confino* did nothing to counter the concerns voiced in the foreign press. First, Mussolini minimised the extent of the practice while ignoring the fact that the policy had been in effect for a mere six months.[79] Second, he cited letters from *confinati* as testimonials that he should be trusted. Third, he clarified that he would not consider any collective amnesties until 1932, but that living conditions were really quite good and that he would consider individual pardons. Fourth, he laid out the criteria for individual pardons. Fifth, he countered with a physiological defence of the suspension of civil liberties. Mussolini argued that *confino* was a form of social hygiene – a best practice preventive treatment to secure the health of the social body. Framing internal exile as a prescriptive measure, he implied that political dissent arose out of existing conditions and that its expansion was dependent upon those conditions. The Regime's application of *confino* continued unabated due less perhaps to rhetorical efficacy than to lack of either international pressure or internal opposition.

The distinction that Mussolini drew between common criminals and political detainees was not a legal but rather an administrative one.[80] While imbrication was inevitable, the UCP, which was under Section I of the DAGR, administered *confino politico* whereas Section II of the *Divisione Polizia Amministrativa e Sociale* (Administrative and Social Police Division) directed *confino comune*.[81] Tribunals applied *confino comune* as an efficient punitory practice:

1. to supplement the sentencing of habitual criminals (including the Mafia);
2. to mete out expeditiously criminal justice in cases where a lack of sufficient evidence or procedural challenges prevented a conviction;[82]
3. to remove from society and public view those whom the Regime deemed to be undesirable (i.e., transients, mendicants, alcoholics, sex workers, persons with mental illnesses).

In addition, the TULPS empowered tribunals to discipline social categories not specified in the penal code (e.g., gender nonconforming persons, Jehovah's Witnesses, Pentecostals, Roma, Sinti, and Camminanti). The administrative distinction had disciplinary repercussions: in January 1927, legislation conferred to the Ministry of the Interior the authority to utilise the MVSN in the *confino* colonies.[83] Nevertheless, presuming that a common criminal would develop antigovernment sentiments, officials tended to treat the two categories as one.[84]

Although Mussolini did not mention women, at least 343 were assigned to *confino politico* where they experienced isolation and alienation in male-dominated colonies that made few concessions to their needs and circumstances.[85] While men of means might have their families join them in exile, women were either alone or forced to bring their children without any familial support. Police arrested Alda Costa, perhaps the first woman sentenced to confinement, for Socialist activities on 24 November 1926, while on the other end of the temporal and political spectrum, Edda Ciano Mussolini was sent to Lipari for Fascist collaboration in September 1945.[86] Historical silence continues to marginalise women's *confino* experience.

As for amnesty, low risk *confinati* received it in commemoration of Fascism's tenth anniversary.[87] The Regime's largesse was a demonstration of its power. *Confino* was both a punishment and a mediatory measure in Fascism's disciplinary trajectory that reached its nadir in the concentration camp.[88] What had begun as a temporary suspension of civil rights instead established permanent sequestration spaces beyond the rule of law. *Confinati* were defined by the exceptional laws and, therefore, beyond the boundaries of the legal system. In essence, they were citizens deprived of citizenship. Bereft of their basic rights, they lost agency over their lives.

As such, *confino* was a manifestation of Fascism's biopolitics, in which the deprivation of citizens' political rights created a liminal space to administer extrajuridical sanctions. Discretionary authority perpetuated a political process based on the personal. Internal exile revealed the brutal efficiency with which the Regime defined and deprived citizens of their rights. Beyond the jurisdiction of criminal law, the political-juridical structure of *confino* constituted a permanent stable spatial arrangement of exception governed exclusively by the dictates of the Regime.

The lack of transparency created a public relations challenge. For the American public, Mussolini cheekily portrayed *confino* as a geographic enema that purged the constipated body politic: 'Il provvedimento è come una purga sociale che tende a sbarazzare il paese da numerose e perniciose influenze'[89] (The provision is like a social laxative that clears the country of numerous and harmful influences). This salutary portrayal did little to alleviate international concerns about a totalitarian turn in Italian politics. Eight months after the Ascension Day speech, renowned foreign correspondent, Vincent Sheean, published a four-article exposé on Italy's 'Siberias'.[90] Despite requests from foreign and domestic journalists, authorities denied access to the colonies.[91] Mino Maccari's articles for Turin's daily *La Stampa* were a notable exception to this prohibition. Maccari visited Lipari and Ponza in November 1929, and published an eleven-article reportage in September 1930. Whether because of political pressures, his artistic sensibilities, his 'idee poche ma confuse' (few, but confused, ideas), or because his objective view was such, his representation of the colonies, essentially portraying *confino* as *villeggiatura*, served as an apologia for the practice.[92] Although heavily redacted, the articles did provide insight into colonial life.[93] Neither rehabilitation nor indoctrination factored into the punishment: 'interessa che per un determinato periodo vengano eliminati i motivi o possibili motivi di perturbamento dell'ordine, non interessa, che l'individuo modifichi le proprie idee politiche o tanto meno che abiuri la propria fede e i propri convincimenti'[94] (what matters is eliminating, for a certain amount of time, the reasons or possible reasons for disrupting order, what is of no interest is that individuals modify their political ideas or, least of all, that they abjure their beliefs and convictions). What mattered was removing subversive elements from society. Since sentencing could be renewed repeatedly, for authorities reintegration of *confinati* was of little concern. Thus, rehabilitation tacitly relied on prisoners' objectivist self-interest trumping political principles.

Although the *Leggi eccezionali* contained a five-year sunset provision, the exceptions had become the norm. The 1931 TULPS renewed the provisions governing *confino* with the following clarifications:[95]

1. the expansion of eligibility to *confino* to include those people whose public reputation was defamatory as defined by Article 165;
2. the clarification that the state of admonition ceased when sentenced to *confino*;
3. sentencing to *confino* was not possible when the judiciary was already prosecuting the same charge;

4. the time spent in remand did not constitute time served toward the sentencing to *confino*;
5. probation could not be served concurrently with *confino*, but began once the sentence had expired.

In addition, Articles 177–9 restored the minimum age for sentencing to *confino* from sixteen to eighteen. The stated rationale for this adjustment was to reflect the government's practice in addressing delinquency of minors as one that seeks: 'through educational means, even if rigorous, rather than through means that may produce the opposite result, which is to say, to render antisocial those elements susceptible to reform'.[96]

The net result of these legislative efforts was a nexus between preventive measures and detention measures by empowering the Provincial Commissions to arrest anyone deemed suspect and by holding defendants acquitted by the Special Tribunal until the Public Security Authority could decide whether or not to subject them to *confino*. The repressive aspects of internal exile were enhanced by detaining people in prison for extensive periods of time without formal charges and by sentencing acquitted defendants in protective custody to *confino*. Alongside the 1931 TULPS, the promulgation of the new penal code, prepared by Alfredo Rocco, and the contemporaneous prison reform reinforced internal exile's instrumentalisation as a means to suppress political dissidence.[97]

### Uncommon *confino*

Despite having effectively suppressed internal political opposition by 1934, the Regime's use of *confino politico* escalated annually through 1943.[98] The reasons for this increase were twofold: first, the definition of 'political' expanded to encompass behaviours deemed detrimental to the State, and, second, space availability impacted sentencing so anyone assigned to a 'political' colony would be classified as 'political'. Beyond politics (e.g., Communists, Socialists, and Anarchists), authorities selectively targeted other affiliations and ethnicities (e.g., Jehovah's Witnesses, Pentecostals, Freemasons, defeatists, prostitutes, abortionists, gender nonconformists, Roma, Sinti, Camminanti, Mafia, Slovenians, Croatians) on the basis of antisocial and anticonformist comportment.[99]

Mussolini had targeted the Mafia and Freemasonry prior to 1926, but the demographic campaign promoted in the Ascension Day speech resulted in *confino* for up to 300 midwives and doctors charged with performing abortions.[100] These arrests exacerbated access to health care in communities while doing little to reduce the number of abortions performed.[101] Religious minorities, Jehovah's Witnesses and Pentecostals in particular, also came under scrutiny prior to the TULPS.[102] As early as 22 March 1924, police confiscated Watch Tower Society literature on the charge that it offended the Regime.[103] Following the Lateran Concordat, the Catholic Church supported the State's clampdown on evangelical denominations.[104] The perception that these groups claimed conscientious objection to military service, assumed political neutrality, or engaged in evangelical proselytising led to surveillance, harassment, and arrests. A directive from Undersecretary of the Interior Ministry Guido Buffarini-Guidi effectively suppressed Pentecostalism:

> Esistono in alcune Province del Regno semplici associazioni di fatto che, sotto la denominazione di Pentecostali o Pentecostieri o Neumatici o Tremolanti, attendono a pratiche di culto in riunioni generalmente presiedute da 'anziani'.
>
> Il culto professato dalle anzi dette associazioni, non riconosciute a norma dell'articolo 2 della legge 24 giugno 1929, n. 1159, non può ulteriormente essere ammesso nel Regno, agli effetti dell'articolo 1 della citata legge, essendo risultato che esso si estrinseca e concreta in pratiche religiose contrarie all'ordine sociale e nocive all'integrità fisica e psichica della razza.
>
> Pertanto le LL. EE. provvederanno subito per lo scioglimento, dovunque esistano, delle associazioni in parola; e per la chiusura dei relativi oratori e sale di riunione; disponendo conseguentemente anche per una opportuna vigilanza, allo scopo di evitare che ulteriori riunioni e manifestazioni di attività religiosa da parte degli adepti possano avere luogo in qualsiasi altro modo o forma.
>
> Si gradirà sollecita assicurazione dell'adempimento.[105]
>
> (In some provinces of the Kingdom there are simple associations that, under the denomination of *Pentecostali*, *Pentecostieri*, *Neumatici*, or *Tremolanti* attend religious services overseen generally by 'elders'.
>
> The religion professed by the aforementioned associations, not recognised according to Article 2 of Law 1159 (24 June 1929), cannot be permitted any longer in the Kingdom as per Article 1 of said law, because it expresses and realises religious practices contrary to the social order and harmful to the physical and psychic integrity of the race.
>
> Therefore, Your Excellencies will attend immediately to the disbandment of said associations wherever they might exist; and for the closing of oratories and meeting halls; and establishing appropriate surveillance to ensure that no future meetings or manifestations of religious activities by the followers take place in any other way or shape.
>
> A prompt confirmation of execution is requested.)

The directive was absolute in its suppression of Pentecostalism, which it treated as a dangerous association similar to Freemasonry. The prohibition, however, now stemmed from the need to defend the social order and the integrity of the race – the latter a rhetoric increasingly invoked by the Regime. If the judiciary failed to convict, then *confino* provided an expeditious means to address the matter. Increasingly aggressive policing, especially after 1939, led to the almost total suppression of Pentecostals and Jehovah's Witnesses in Italy.[106]

The persecution of ethnic minorities was similarly rationalised. Although the official call for the internment of Roma, Sinti and Camminanti began with the 11 September 1940 Ministry of the Interior's circular (signed by Arturo Bocchini) to prefects and police chiefs, their legislative persecution under Fascism dates to Mussolini's consolidation of power.[107] On 19 February 1926, a ministerial circular specified that they should be denied entry into the country 'che siano immediatamente respinti da qualsiasi provenienza gli zingari, saltimbanchi e somiglianti che cercassero in carovana o isolatamente di penetrare in Italia, anche se muniti di regolare passaporto'[108] (refuse entry to gypsies, charlatans, and similar people, regardless of provenance, who seek as a group or individually to penetrate Italy, even if in possession of a proper passport). On 8 August of that same year, the Ministry reiterated this need 'epurare il territorio nazionale della presenza di carovane di Zingari stranieri, di cui è superfluo ricordare la pericolosità nei riguardi della sicurezza e dell'igiene pubblica per le caratteristiche abitudini di vita'[109] (to purge the national territory of the presence of gypsy caravans, of which it is superfluous to mention the dangers posed to security and public hygiene by their distinctive way of life). Police responded to these circulars by launching raids on families in north-eastern Italy, Abruzzo, Calabria, and Sardinia. Those Roma, Sinti and Camminanti holding Italian citizenship were placed under police surveillance and subject to *confino* whereas foreigners were expelled from the national territory.[110] The 11 September 1940 circular ceased to distinguish citizenship and, instead, considered these peoples to constitute a single ethnic entity deemed dangerous. Although the legislation did not identify Romani as a distinct race, the characterisations conformed to Cesare Lombroso's study on anthropological criminality in which he delineated a profile that established racial parameters for Roma, Sinti and Camminanti:

> [S]ono l'imagine viva di una razza intera di delinquenti, e ne riproducono tutte le passioni e i vizj. Hanno in orrore … tutto ciò che richiede il minimo grado di applicazione; e sopportano la fame e la miseria piuttosto che sottoporsi ad un piccolo lavoro continuato; … ingrati, vili e al tempo stesso crudeli … Amanti dell'orgia, del rumore, nei mercati fanno grandi schiamazzi; feroci, assassinano senza rimorso, a scopo di lucro; si sospettarono, anni sono, di cannibalismo.[111]

> (They are the living image of an entire criminal race with all the passions and vices. They abhor … all that requires the slightest effort; and prefer to suffer hunger and poverty rather than subject themselves to a small steady job … ungrateful, cowardly, and, at the same time, cruel … Lovers of orgies, of noise, in the markets they make a racket; ferocious, they kill without remorse, for profit. For years they were suspected of cannibalism.)

The behaviour of an individual is not at issue, but rather all are guilty by association to a specific ethnic category as defined in the court of public opinion. Biotypology, as elaborated by Nicola Pende, underscored the 'racial inferiority' of Romani since they were found to be lacking in moral psyche: 'Le qualità psico-morali razziali degli zingari noi le definiamo "mutazioni psicologiche regressive razziali"' (We define the racial psycho-moral qualities of gypsies as 'regressive racial psychological mutations').[112] The 1926 TULPS proved an able instrument for the persecution of these peoples precisely because it ascribed to a similar rationale.[113] Salvatore Ottolenghi, student of Cesare Lombroso and founder of the Scuola Superiore di Polizia, advocated the importance of the government's discretionary authority:

> [E]sistono casi in cui persone pericolose non potrebbero essere assoggettate alle misure di sicurezza, perché non hanno riportato condanna per fatti costituenti reato, ma che non di meno sono pericolose per essere designate dalla voce pubblica come abitualmente colpevoli dei reati per i quali sono stati prosciolti ... è pure necessario conservare questo provvedimento per quelle forme di attività socialmente pericolose che non sono considerati come reati nella legge penale.[114]

> (There are situations where dangerous persons might not be subject to security measures because they have not been found guilty of a crime, but who are nonetheless dangerous because public opinion considers them habitually guilty of offences for which they have not been acquitted ... it is also necessary to preserve this provision for those forms of socially dangerous activities that are not treated as crimes in the penal code.)

Thus, the TULPS's generic language empowered the police to target groups based on beliefs or behaviours that were contrary to the perceived mores of the general public. Rather than a right to association, individuals risked guilt by association.[115]

This political subordination of individual rights to the authority of the State blurred distinctions between legality and morality. Such a premise facilitated the targeting of gay men. The rhetoric of masculinity that permeated Fascist discourse connoted both policy and policing. Hence, while homosexuality was not illegal per se, the State exercised at its discretion the self-bestowed prerogative to persecute individuals whose behaviour was deemed incompatible with Fascism's ideal of public morality.[116] Similarly, criminologists treated homosexuality not as a crime, but rather as an indicator of potential criminal behaviour. The psychoanalyst Cesare Musatti authored the *Dictionary of Criminology*'s entry:

> I rapporti omosessuali costituiscono di per sè un reato presso alcune delle legislazioni moderne (ad esempio Inghilterra e Germania). Presso altri paesi (ad esempio l'Italia) l'attività omosessuale non riveste un tale carattere, anche se, in quanto offende la coscienza morale della società, può essere soggetta a provvedimenti di polizia quando viene esercitata in forma notoria.
>
> Indipendentemente da ciò sussistono alcuni legami fra omosessualità e criminalità generica: questo non perchè vi sia naturalmente una correlazione fra omosessualità ed asocialità, ma in base a fattori d'ordine estrinseco.
>
> L'impulso omosessuale può condurre a reati sessuali analoghi a quelli che possono esser determinati dall'istinto sessuale normalmente orientato. Tuttavia le stesse difficoltà che l'omosessuale incontra nell'ambiente sociale per appagare le sue tendenze, lo pongono nella condizione di incorrere assai più facilmente in quei reati.

Inoltre queste stesse difficoltà, e insieme la notevole diffusione dell'omosessualità fra gli uomini, determinano, specialmente nei grandi centri urbani, la formazione di una prostituzione maschile. Questa naturalmente si costituisce a mezzo di individui, che nella prostituzione trovano una soluzione alla loro incapacità di inserirsi con una attività produttiva proficua nella vita sociale, e che sono per questa loro incapacità (non per la loro omosessualità) particolarmente predisposti al delitto.

Tuttavia anche a prescindere da fenomeni di questo genere, l'omosessuale, per lo stesso fatto di dover nascondere alla società il suo segreto, è più esposto a commettere atti criminosi. Egli infatti non solo si sente isolato nell'ambiente sociale, ma soprattutto è praticamente privo della tutela della legge, in tutte quelle forme della sua attività e in tutte le relazioni coi terzi che anche in modo indiretto derivano dalla sua condizione anormale; ma è inevitabile che colui il quale sente di non poter contare sulla tutela della legge sia facilmente portato – per la difesa propria e dei propri interessi – a violare egli stesso la legge.[117]

(Homosexual relations constitute a crime in and of themselves in some modern legislatures (for example, England and Germany). In other countries (for example, Italy), homosexual activity does not hold such a charge, even if, in that it offends society's moral conscience, it may be subject to police measures when practised openly.

Independently of this, there exist valid connections between homosexuality and generic criminality: not because of a correlation between homosexuality and asociality, but based on extrinsic factors.

The homosexual impulse may lead to sexual crimes analogous to those that might be driven by normal sexual orientation. Nevertheless, the very difficulties the homosexual faces in the social environment to satisfy his tendencies also greatly facilitate his susceptibility to commit those crimes.

Furthermore, these same difficulties combined with the noticeable diffusion of homosexuality among men, establishes, especially in large urban centres, the development of male prostitution. Naturally, this is established by individuals who find in prostitution a solution to their inability to adapt to social life through a useful and productive activity; and it is for this inability (not for their homosexuality), that they are particularly disposed towards crime.

Nevertheless, even setting aside cases of this kind, the homosexual, for the same reasons that he must hide his secret from society, is more at risk to engaging in criminal behaviour. For not only does he feel isolated in the social environment, but above all he is practically bereft of the law's protection in all manners of his activities and in all relations with others that derive, even indirectly from his abnormal condition. It is inevitable, however, that someone who feels that he cannot rely on the law's protection should be quite susceptible – in self-defence and out of self-interest – to breaking the law.)

Musatti adopted a social perspective that favoured psychoanalytic explanations over endocrinological or somatic ones. In essence, he argued that the sole feature distinguishing heterosexuals and homosexuals was sexual orientation.[118] While a lack of discretion could lead to police action, the perceived tendency towards criminality derived from social marginalisation. Thus, while homosexuality was not criminalised, gays were by default always people of interest subject to harassment and coercion.

Of course, the persecution of sexuality long preceded the Fascist era. In the Liberal period, the tribunals sentenced people to *domicilio coatto* for sexual behaviour even though the Pica law did not specify homosexuality. Under Fascism, punitive practices continued, but were now imbued with the rhetoric of salubrity. By treating different sexual practices as disease, the authorities pursued a strategy of containment (through institutionalisation, incarceration, or *confino*) to quarantine offenders as a form of social purification and to limit the risk of contagion.

Lorenzo Benadusi estimates that the Special Tribunals sentenced some 300 people to *confino comune* and 88 to *confino politico* on the charge of pederasty as a threat to national interests.[119] Following a similar rationale, lesbians were also assigned to *confino*.[120] Fascism's repression of homosexuality was less an extrapolation of racial purity than an anthropological impetus to redefine Italian identity. Concurrent to this regeneration of Italian character was the appropriation of sexuality as a political weapon in the PNF's internal power struggles. Nevertheless, the Regime did not treat homosexuality as a political crime when emitting rulings. As Benadusi has argued, classification as 'political' often resulted merely from serving a sentence in a political colony.[121] In 1939, the Regime designated the Tremiti island of San Domino as an exile site for gender nonconformists thereby inadvertently sanctioning the first openly gay community in Italy.[122] Tremiti was a political colony.

## The colonies

To facilitate controlling the exile populations, the Regime established nine political colonies. In selecting these sites, the Ministry of the Interior drew on historical precedents. The eight islands of Favignana, Lampedusa, Lipari, Pantelleria, Ponza, Tremiti (San Nicola and San Domino), Ustica, and Ventotene had served as relocation colonies for those sentenced to *domicilio coatto* since 1874, and half of them were still in use in 1922.[123] Many of these islands had long histories as detention and exile sites. For example, the Tremiti Islands, an archipelago that is now part of the Gargano National Park, hosted Julia the Younger, exiled by her grandfather Augustus for adultery and possible treasonous acts in 8 CE.[124] The tradition continued with Charlemagne, who exiled Paulus Diaconus to the island of San Nicola in the late eighth century. Another dynasty founder, Ferdinand IV of Naples, established a penal colony there in 1792. In 1911, Giovanni Giolitti's government deported approximately 1,300 Libyans to the Tremiti Islands for resisting in the Italo-Turkish War.[125] Because of colonial internment and *domicilio coatto*, the islands already possessed facilities to separate *confinati* from the general population when, with the exception of Ponza and Ventotene, they became political colonies in 1926.[126] By 1930, however, the Ministry of the Interior had vacated the majority of these colonies preferring to concentrate political prisoners on the Pontine Islands.[127]

Balancing financial costs with the need for secure sites to accommodate the growing population of dissidents proved difficult. In June 1932, the Interior

Ministry proposed an extraterritorial *confino* colony in Libya at Gasr Bu Hadi – the site of the 1915 military defeat, but implementation proved too costly.[128] As a cost-saving measure Carmine Senise, head of the DAGR and newly named Prefect, recommended to Bocchini shuttering Lipari on 17 December 1932.[129] Closed as a political colony, Lipari then became the detention site for 450 of Ante Pavelić's Ustaše Croatian nationalists.[130]

The mainland presented an economic alternative, but tended to be reserved for low-risk *confinati*, whose movements and activities the *Carabinieri* monitored. The Provincial Commission would select isolated villages, usually in the south, where *confinati* would have little or no contact with each other. Calabria alone hosted at least 139 *confino* sites, and in the national territory over 600 sites have been identified.[131] In 1937, however, Mussolini approved the establishment of an agricultural labour colony for *confinati politici* at Pisticci in the province of Matera. The camp was supposed to provide the opportunity for rehabilitation through work. The first labourers arrived in April 1939 and reached a maximum of 200 detainees.[132] The blending of public and private – Eugenio Parrini's firm managed the facilities, except for the actual policing, and profited from the labour – did provide gainful employment and land reclamation, but failed to produce political rehabilitation. British armed forces transformed Pisticci into a displaced persons camp on 13 September 1943.[133] With Italy's entrance into the war in 1940, the Ministry of the Interior opted to reutilise Favignana, Lampedusa, Pantelleria, and Ustica as detention sites. The political colonies would remain operational until the summer of 1943, when the Allies' advance and Mussolini's fall brought liberation.

### *Confino*'s aftermath

On 25 July 1943, following the 187th and final Grand Council meeting, Mussolini found himself stripped of power. The King and the newly named President of the Council of Ministers Pietro Badoglio now found themselves with a political liability. What to do? What had been done for seventeen years: *confino*. On 27 July, Admiral Franco Maugeri and Police Inspector Saverio Polito escorted Mussolini to Ponza. The stay was short. On 7 August, Mussolini was transferred to La Maddalena and finally to Campo Imperatore, where atop Gran Sasso, Otto Skorzeny freed him on 12 September 1943.[134] Mussolini was the first *confinato* sentenced under the new government.

Prior to his arrest, Mussolini had implemented new forms of detention between 1940 and 1943. *Confino* continued, but now the Regime established internment camps and concentration camps because exceptional circumstances called for exceptional measures.[135] The coalescence of these exceptions into a perverse normalcy facilitated the deportations to death camps in the final years of the war.

*Confino* violated a basic moral principal of criminal law: *nullum crimen, nulla poena sine praevia lege poenali* (there is no crime and, therefore, no punishment without a pre-existing penal law), and yet its abolishment was not automatic. The 1931 TULPS along with the 1940 Enforcement Regulations remain in effect to this day albeit with significant modifications.[136] In 1957, Italy's Constitutional Court rendered null and void Articles 180–9 (those governing *confino*) of the 1931 TULPS.[137] A 1965 law containing a provision for intraterritorial relocation for criminal association (i.e., Mafia) was expanded ten years later to include political elements (i.e., neofascism and terrorism).[138] Moreover, with the expansion of clandestine immigration, a 1998 legislative decree authorised detention measures all too reminiscent of *coatti* colonies.[139] Today, in the first quarter of the twenty-first century, international terrorism provides the exceptional circumstance in which to impose exception as the rule.[140]

## Notes

1   Cited in Luca Di Vito and Michele Gialdroni, *Lipari 1929: fuga dal confino* (Rome-Bari: Editori Laterza, 2009), p. 65.

2   Massimo Cacciari as cited in Nello Ajello, 'Il confino', *La Repubblica* (13 September 2003), p. 39.

3   *Domicilio coatto* was a public security measure applied to people presumed dangerous because of antisocial behaviour. Those sentenced were relocated (as determined by the Minister of the Interior) for a specified period of time and under specific disciplinary conditions. Introduced as an extraordinary measure in 1863, *domicilio coatto* remained in effect for over sixty years until *confino di polizia* replaced it in 1926. For a history of the measure, see Daniela Fozzi, *Tra prevenzione e repressione: il domicilio coatto nell'Italia liberale* (Rome: Carocci, 2011). Prior to 1861, similar measures existed in the peninsula. For example, Ferdinand II designated the islands of Ponza and Ventotene as forced residence sites, see Decree 3567 (Naples, 17 November 1856) *Decreto che approva il regolamento de' relegati e de' confinati sulle isole, e per la Compagnia di punizione in Ponza* in *Collezione delle leggi e dei Decreti Reali del Regno delle Due Sicilie. Anno 1856. Semestre II. Da luglio a tutto dicembre* (Naples: Dalla Stamperia Reale, 1856), pp. 404–44. The Zanardelli Penal Code allowed for *confino*, but as a judicial sentencing (RD 6133 of 30 June 1889 and RD 316 of 19 July 1894) rather than as a police provision. The Rocco Penal Code repealed this judiciary *confino* in 1930.

4   Law 1409 (15 August 1863) *Procedura per la repressione del brigantaggio e dei camorristi nelle Provincie infette*, is named after its sponsor, the deputy from Abruzzo Giuseppe Pica. Although enacted as a temporary measure, the law was not abrogated until 31 December 1865, at which point it had already been incorporated within the consolidated public security bill (Attachment B of Law 2248, known informally as the 'Lanza Law', for the administrative unification of the Kingdom of Italy of 20 March 1865). See Giovanni De Matteo, *Brigantaggio e Risorgimento: legittimisti e briganti tra Borbone e i Savoia* (Naples: Guida, 2000); Italo Mereu, 'Cenni storici sulle misure di prevenzione nell'Italia "liberale" (1852–1894)', *Le misure di prevenzione: atti del convegno* (Milan: Giuffrè, 1975), pp. 197–212; Luciano Violante, 'La repressione del dissenso politico nell'Italia liberale: stati d'assedio e giustizia militare', *Rivista di storia contemporanea*, 5:4 (1976), 481–524; and Giovanna Tosatti, 'La repressione del dissenso politico tra l'età liberale e il fascismo. L'organizzazione della polizia', *Studi storici*, 38:1 (1997), 217–55.

5   For a cogent critique of the war on banditry, see Angelo Del Boca, *Italiani, brava gente? Un mito duro a morire* (Vicenza: Neri Pozza Editore, 2005), pp. 57–72.

6    See Roberto Martucci, *Emergenza e tutela dell'ordine pubblico nell'Italia liberale* (Bologna: Il Mulino, 1980), pp. 79–91 and pp. 240–4, Salvatore Lupo, *L'unificazione italiana: mezzogiorno, rivoluzione, guerra civile* (Rome: Donzelli editore, 2011), pp. 129–35. Cf. Umberto Allegretti, who argues for explicit continuity between Liberal and Fascist Italy in 'Dissenso, opposizione politica, disordine sociale: le risposte dello stato liberale', in Luciano Violante (ed.), *Storia d'Italia. Annali 12. La criminalità* (Turin: Einaudi, 1997), pp. 719–56.

7    The law violated the *Statuto Albertino* of 1848.

8    Roberto Martucci, 'Un Parlamento introvabile? Sulle tracce del sistema rappresentativo sardo–italiano in regime statutario 1848–1915', in Anna Gianna Manca and Luigi Lacchè (eds), *Parlamento e costituzione nei sistemi costituzionali ottocenteschi – Parlament und Verfassung in den konstitutionellen Verfassungssystemen Europas*. Vol. 13. Annali dell'Istituto storico italo-germanico in Trento – Jahrbuch des Italienisch-Deutschen Historischen Instituts in Trient (Bologna and Berlin: Il Mulino and Duncker & Humblot, 2003), p. 130.

9    Carlo Belviglieri, *Storia d'Italia dal 1814 al 1866*, 5 vols (Milan: Corona e Caimi Editori, 1868), pp. 93–4.

10    See Martucci, 'Un Parlamento introvabile?'.

11    Mario Iaquinta, *Mezzogiorno, emigrazione di massa e sottosviluppo* (Cosenza: Luigi Pellegrini Editore, 2002), p. 63.

12    Article 3 of Law 2907 (17 May 1866). Francesco Crispi, the old guard of what had once been the Young Turks, proposed the extension. See Fozzi, *Tra prevenzione e repressione*, 77–85.

13    Three sites were on the mainland (Cuneo, Fossano and Sondrio) while the remaining thirteen were on islands (Cagliari, Elba, Favignana, Giglio, Ischia, Lampedusa, Lipari, Pantelleria, Ponza, Sassari, Tremiti, Ustica, and Ventotene). Among its provisions, Law 294 (6 July 1871) doubled sentencing to two years (including a minimum of six months for first time offenders and five years for repeat offenders). Daniela Fozzi has calculated that those sites housed 268 detainees in 1871. As capacity expanded so did the sentencing. The number of those serving time grew to 1,297 in 1872, 3,622 in 1874, and, in 1894, reached a maximum of 5,043 (Fozzi, *Tra prevenzione e repressione*, 304–06). See also Dal Pont, *I lager di Mussolini*, 20.

14    Vittorio Lollini, *L'ammonizione e il domicilio coatto* (Bologna: Fratelli Treves, 1882), pp. 129–30.

15    The renowned economist Vilfredo Pareto was a vocal critic of the practice. In a letter dated 22 October 1874, to Emilia Peruzzi, he described it thusly: 'La nostra legge sul domicilio coatto è tale che sino allo czar parrebbe troppo dispotica … Vorrei conoscere un altro paese in cui vi sia una legge simile a questa. Dracone l'avrebbe avuta per troppo severa' (Our law on *domicilio coatto* is such that even the Tsar would consider it to be too despotic … I would like to know of another country that has a law similar to this one. Draco would have found it too harsh). Vilfredo Pareto, *Lettere ai Peruzzi Vol. 1 (1872–1877)* (Rome: Edizioni di Storia e Letteratura, 1968), pp. 441–2.

16    Article 38 of the *Regolamento pel servizio di sorveglianza sulle persone pregiudicate e sospette e pel domicilio coatto* (10 December 1881).

17    Crispi proved prominent in subsequent legislation as well: as President of the Council of Ministers he advanced Law 6144 (30 June 1889) *La legge di pubblica sicurezza pel Regno d'Italia* and Law 316 (19 July 1894) *La legge sui provvedimenti eccezionali di pubblica sicurezza*, both of which expanded the provisions for *domicilio coatto*. Law 316 targeted political adversaries (i.e., Anarchists and Socialists) and provided a template for the TULPS of 1926. For a contemporaneous critique of *domicilio coatto*, see Jessie White Mario's five-part exposé, 'Il sistema penitenziario e il domicilio coatto in Italia', *Nuova*

*Antologia* 64 (1 July 1896), 16–35; *Nuova Antologia* 65 (16 September 1896), 313–35; *Nuova Antologia* 68 (16 April 1897), 680–707; *Nuova Antologia* 70 (1 August 1897), 503–19; and *Nuova Antologia* 71 (1 September 1897), 121–42.

18    In July 1896, following the Battle of Adwa, the Socialist Deputy Enrico Ferri denounced before the Chamber the illegal existence of a *coatti* colony at Assab. Antonio Starabba di Rudinì, then President of the Council, conceded Ferri's point, but then proceeded to legalise it *ex post facto*. See Dal Pont, *I lager di Mussolini*, 32. For a contemporary description of the camp in Assab, see Francesco Borsoni's letter, 'Una lettera dalla Caienna italiana. Come muoiono i coatti ad Assab', published in the socialist newspaper *Avanti!* (13 October 1898), p. 1.

19    Pelloux resigned on 24 June 1900. See Christopher Seton-Watson, *Italy from Liberalism to Fascism, 1870–1925* (London: Metheun, 1967), pp. 193–5.

20    In particular, the restrictions applied to citizens of enemy powers residing in Italy, to Italians suspected of harbouring sympathy for the enemy, and to those people engaged in antigovernment activities (e.g., pacifists).

21    Decreto luogotenenziale 1561 (4 October 1917). For an in-depth analysis of civilian internment during the Great War, see Giovanna Procacci, 'L'internamento di civili in Italia durante la prima guerra mondiale. Normativa e conflitti di competenza', *DEP: Deportate, esuli, profughe. Rivista telematica di studi sulla memoria femminile*, 5–6 (2006), 33–66.

22    On 5 November 1926, Luigi Federzoni proposed substituting *domicilio coatto* with *confino* as a punishment for both criminal acts and political offences. His proposal, along with other repressive measures, was incorporated into the TULPS of 6 November 1926 (RD 1848). Articles 184–93 of the TULPS established the new category of *confino*, which held the expansive view of applying the measure to anyone considered to be a risk to either the State or the public order

23    Speech delivered to the Chamber of Deputies on 3 January 1925.

24    Antonio Gramsci, speaking before the Chamber of Deputies on 16 May 1925. The new law, RDL 2029 (26 November 1925), appeared in the *Gazzetta Ufficiale del Regno d'Italia*, 277 (28 November 1925), 4714–15. Published in *Unità* (23 May 1923) and reprinted in Antonio Gramsci, *Sul fascismo* (Rome: Editori Riuniti, 1973), pp. 136–42. The Chamber approved the bill on 19 May 1925; and the Senate passed it on 20 November 1925. See, Fabio Venzi, *Massoneria e fascismo: dall'intesa cordiale alla distruzione delle logge: come nasce una 'guerra di religione', 1921–1925* (Rome: Castelvecchi Editore, 2008), p. 60. See also Aldo Mola, *Storia della massoneria italiana dalle origini ai giorni nostri* (Milan: Bompiani, 2001); Santi Fedele, *La massoneria nell'esilio e nella clandestinità, 1927–1939* (Milan: Franco Angeli, 2005); and Marco Francini and Gian Paolo Balli, *Il gran maestro Domizio Torrigiani (1876–1932)* (Pistoia: CRT Il Tempio, 2004).

25    Alfredo Rocco estimates the number of Italian Freemasons to be 20,000. See Rocco, *Scritti e discorsi politici di Alfredo Rocco. Vol. 3. La formazione dello Stato fascista (1925–1934)* (Milan: Giuffrè editore, 1938), p. 794.

26    Gramsci, *Sul fascismo*, 140.

27    Even Palazzo Giustiniani, which had served as the GOI's seat since 21 April 1901, came under attack. Following the repression of Freemasonry, the government purchased the building as property of the State and granted its use to the Senate. After the war, Palazzo Giustiniani continued to enjoy shared use by both the GOI and the Senate until 1985, when the GOI then transferred to Villa Vascello on the Janiculum. See Domizio Torrigiani's archive (*Archivio Domizio Torrigiani*) held in the *Istituto Storico della Resistenza in Toscana*.

28    In Florence, between 25 September and 5 October 1925, *Squadristi* (semi-autonomous fascist squads) launched an anti-masonic assault, which included, on the night of 3

October, the murders of Giovanni Becciolini, Gaetano Pilati and Gustavo Console. Vasco Pratolini's choral novel, *Cronache di poveri amanti* (Florence: Vallecchi, 1947), which is set in Florence's working-class Via del Corno, dramatically recreates the tension and events of this period. Pratolini himself served as an informant to the OVRA (secret police) between December 1939 and February 1940, see Mauro Canali, *Le spie del regime* (Bologna: Il Mulino, 2004), pp. 401–4.

29   While politically astute, Torrigiani's stratagem failed to protect his person. In April of 1927, police arrested Torrigiani while he was returning from France, where he had met with exiled Freemasons. His sentence was five years of *confino* (first to Lipari then to Ponza) on charges of abetting the Zaniboni-Capello conspiracy. Released in April of 1932, and suffering from poor health due to the strenuous conditions on the islands, he died in his birthplace, Lamporecchio, on 31 August 1932.

30   The anti-Mafia campaign began in July 1925. The inciting incident allegedly occurred when Mussolini toured Sicily in May 1924. Piqued by the suggestion that the Mafia's authority exceeded his own, Mussolini asserted his power. See John Dickie, *Cosa Nostra: A History of the Sicilian Mafia* (New York: Palgrave Macmillan, 2005), p. 153; and Arrigo Petacco, *L'uomo della provvidenza: Mussolini, ascesa e caduta di un mito* (Milan: Mondadori, 2004), pp. 94–104.

31   Dated 25 September 1925. ACS, MI, DGPS, *Divisione Polizia Amministrativa e Sociale 1919–1926*, Miscellanea, b. 2, f. 5 'Riforma legge P.S. – 1925'. Cited in Lorenzo Benadusi, *The Enemy of the New Man: Homosexuality in Fascist Italy* (Madison: University of Wisconsin Press, 2012), pp. 344–5 n. 25.

32   Rocco appeared before the Chamber on 16 May 1925. See Rocco, *Scritti e discorsi politici*, 798.

33   *Ibid.*

34   RDL 1254 (15 July 1926) *Provvedimenti per la tutela della sicurezza pubblica nelle Provincie siciliane* was published in the *Gazzetta Ufficiale del Regno d'Italia*, 172 (27 July 1926), 3334–5. RD 776 (11 July 1941) repealed the measure. For Fascism's suppression of the Mafia, see in particular, Dickie, *Cosa Nostra*, 131–60; Christopher Duggan, *Fascism and the Mafia* (New Haven: Yale University Press, 1989); and Salvatore Lupo, *History of the Mafia* (New York: Columbia University Press, 2009), pp. 167–87.

35   *Gazzetta Ufficiale del Regno d'Italia*, 172 (27 luglio 1926), 3334–5. The decree applied to all of Sicily – Enna and Ragusa were not listed because these provinces were established in 1927 (RDL 1, 2 January 1927, *Riordinamento delle circoscrizioni provinciali*, which became law on 7 June 1927).

36   Petacco, *L'uomo della provvidenza*, 101.

37   A number, which, as General Antonino Di Giorgio clarified to Mussolini in a letter (19 March 1928), did not include *confinati*. See Lupo, *History of the Mafia*, 174 and 302. As Lupo argues, in a Machiavellian ends–means sense, Fascism succeeded: 'Amidst terroristic excesses, the conviction of innocent defendants, and political persecutions, the policeman Mori and the inquisitor Giampietro met and soundly beat the Mafia', Lupo, *History of the Mafia*, 187. See also Gina Antoniani Persichilli, 'Le misure di pubblica sicurezza. Dal domicilio coatto al confino di polizia', *Temi ciociaria*, 5:4 (1978), 107–21.

38   See, for example, *Time* magazine's coverage: 'Foreign News: Mafia Trial', *Time* 10:17 (24 October 1927) and 'Italy: Mafia Scotched', *Time* 11:4 (23 January 1928). The *Washington Post* published a special cable dispatch declaring that 'The Sicilian Mafia, which for years has terrorized the fair island, has practically ceased to exist in the last three months' in 'Fascisti put end to Mafia of Sicily' (17 February 1926), p. 11. See also '600 Sicilian Mafia are taken by ruse in final round-up', *Washington Post* (1 March 1926), p. 4.

39  In particular, Law 2318 (31 December 1925), *Delega al Governo del Re della facoltà di arrecare emendamenti alle leggi di pubblica sicurezza*, authorised the government to modify the public security provisions of the 1889 code in anticipation of what would become the 1926 TULPS. RD 2318 appeared in *Gazzetta Ufficiale del Regno d'Italia*, 4 (7 January 1926), 34.

40  Adrian Lyttelton, *The Seizure of Power: Fascism in Italy, 1919–1929* (Princeton: Princeton University Press, 1987), p. 267.

41  Hans Woller, *I conti con il fascismo* (Bologna: Il Mulino, 1997), pp. 141–4.

42  Violet Gibson was the daughter of Edward Gibson (Lord Ashbourne, former Lord Chancellor of Ireland). See 'Italy: Mussolini trionfante', *Time* 7:16 (19 April 1926), 14–17; Enrico Ferri and Mary Flint Cassola (trans.), 'A character study and life history of Violet Gibson who attempted the life of Benito Mussolini on the 7th of April, 1926', *Journal of the American Institute of Criminal Law and Criminology*, 19:2 (1928–29), 211–19; and Frances Stonor Saunders, *The Woman Who Shot Mussolini* (London: Faber & Faber, 2010).

43  See Riccardo Lucetti, *Gino Lucetti, l'attentato contro il Duce, 11 settembre 1926* (Carrara: Edizioni della Cooperativa Tipolitografica di Carrara, 2000) and Marina Marini, *Gino Lucetti. Lettere dal carcere dell'attentatore di Mussolini (1930–1943)* (Salerno: Galzerano Editore, 2010).

44  See Brunella Dalla Casa, *Attentato al Duce: le molte storie del caso Zamboni* (Bologna: Il Mulino, 2000).

45  Richard J. B. Bosworth, *Mussolini* (London: Arnold Publishers, 2002), pp. 219–20.

46  A similar suppression of rights ensued in Nazi Germany with the exceptional laws of *Schutzhaft*, which exploited the concept of protective custody to rationalise the para-legal practice of blanket arrests without judicial review. For a discussion of the affinities and differences between *confino* and *Schutzhaft*, see, Poesio, *Il confino fascista*, 102–42. See also Giorgio Agamben, *Homo Sacer: Sovereign Power and Bare Life* (Stanford: Stanford University Press, 1998), pp. 167–74.

47  'Full text of Mussolini's speech outlining his plans for a greater Italy', *New York Times* (29 May 1927a), p. 12. See also Benito Mussolini, *Discorso dell'Ascensione: il regime Fascista per la grandezza dell'Italia. Pronunciato il 26 maggio 1927 alla Camera dei Deputati* (Rome: Libreria del Littorio, 1927b), p. 34.

48  The CPC was incorporated under the DGPS in 1894: Circulars DGPS 5116 (25 May 1894) and 6329 (16 August 1894). The UCI was established within the DGPS in September 1916: RD 1713 (14 October 1917).

49  The DGPS was reorganised into five divisions: (1) cabinet and inspectorial services; (2) general and confidential affairs division; (3) judiciary police division; (4) administrative and social police division; and (5) personnel division. RD 1442 (14 August 1919) added an additional public security force to the three existing entities (i.e., *Pubblica Sicurezza*, *Carabinieri*, and *Guardia di Finanza*): the *Regia Guardia*, whose primary responsibilities were to defend the State and to ensure public order. Suspicious of its allegiance, Mussolini dissolved the unit shortly after taking power with Decree 1680 (31 December 1922). Concurrent to the dissolution of the *Regia Guardia*, Mussolini was forming the Fascist Party's militia: the MVSN. See Giuseppe De Luttis, *I servizi segreti in Italia: dal fascismo all'intelligence del XXI secolo* (Milan: Sperling & Kupfer, 2010) and Paola Carucci, 'L'organizzazione dei servizi di polizia dopo l'approvazione del Testo Unico delle leggi di PS del 1926', *Rassegna degli archivi di stato*, 26:1 (1976), 82–114. For the history of policing in Fascist Italy, see Franco Fucci, *Le polizie di Mussolini* (Milan: Mursia, 1985); Gianni Oliva, *Storia dei Carabinieri: dal 1814 a oggi* (Milan: Mondadori, 2002); Amedeo Osti Guerrazzi, *Poliziotti: i direttori dei campi di concentramento italiani 1940–1943* (Rome: Cooper, 2004); and Jonathan

Dunnage, *The Italian Police and the Rise of Fascism: A Case Study of the Province of Bologna, 1897–1925* (Westport: Praeger, 1997). For the relationship between public security forces and Fascism see Jonathan Dunnage, *Mussolini's Policemen: Behaviour, Ideology and Institutional Culture in Representation and Practice* (Manchester: Manchester University Press, 2012).

50    On 28 December 1922, the Council of Ministers sanctioned the establishment of the MVSN though the official status of the PNF's militia was enacted with RDL 31 (14 January 1923). For the history of the MVSN see, Attilio Teruzzi, *La milizia delle camicie nere* (Milan: Mondadori, 1939); Luigi Salvatorelli and Giovanni Mira, *Storia d'Italia nel periodo fascista* (Turin: Einaudi, 1964); Renzo De Felice, Ettore Lucas and Giorgio De Vecchi, *Storia delle unità combattenti della MVSN 1923–1943* (Rome: Giovanni Volpe Editore, 1976); Indro Montanelli, *L'Italia in camicia nera* (Milan: Rizzoli, 1976); Ricciotti Lazzero, *Il Partito nazionale fascista* (Milan: Rizzoli, 1985); Lucio Ceva, *Storia delle Forze Armate in Italia* (Turin: UTET Libreria, 1999); Giorgio Vecchiato, *Con romana volontà* (Venice: Marsilio, 2005); and Emilio Gentile, *Fascismo: storia e interpretazione* (Bari: Laterza, 2002). See also Piero Crociani and Pier Paolo Battistelli, *Italian Blackshirt, 1935–1945* (Oxford: Osprey Publishing, 2010).

51    In fact, the control of *confinati* fell not to the police, but to the MVSN. Renzo De Felice, *Mussolini il fascista. Vol. 1. La conquista del potere, 1921–1925* (Turin: Einaudi, 1995), p. 541.

52    Fucci, *Le polizie di Mussolini*, 54. See also Guido Leto, *OVRA: fascismo e antifascismo* (Bologna: Cappelli, 1952), p. 14. An associate of Bocchini, Leto served as Director of the *Divisione Polizia Politica* from October 1938 until 26 April 1945 (the final two years with the Italian Social Republic), when he assisted the Allied Counter Intelligence Corps.

53    For the Chief of Police, see, in particular, RD 2395 (11 November 1923), *Ordinamento gerarchico delle Amministrazioni dello Stato*, which appeared in *Gazzetta Ufficiale del Regno d'Italia. Supplemento ordinario* 270 (17 November 1923), and RD 2908 (20 December 1923), *Sostituzione della denominazione di Intendente generale di polizia con quella di Capo della polizia*, which appeared in *Gazzetta Ufficiale del Regno d'Italia* 16 (19 January 1924), 293. Fucci, *Le polizie di Mussolini*, 55 estimates that, between 1922 and 1923, the Regime enacted over 100,000 laws and decrees related to public security. For the DGPS, see, respectively, RD 762 (18 March 1923) and RD 1602 (12 July 1923).

54    See Fucci, *Le polizie di Mussolini*, 56. The OVRA's officially acknowledged existence dates from 1930 to 25 July 1943. A press release of 3 December 1930 through the *Agenzia Stefani*, Italy's leading press agency, introduces the term to the public. In this dispatch, prepared by the police chief Arturo Bocchini, Mussolini replaced the word 'Police' with 'OVRA'. According to Guido Leto, who served as Director of the Political Police Division of the Ministry of the Interior between 1938 and 1945, OVRA was not an acronym, but rather a name that Mussolini derived from *piovra* (octopus – today a term used to refer to the Mafia) to suggest the tentaculoid reach of the police. Although Leto's testimony is compromised by his self-interest, Antonio Sannino also finds little merit in various proposed acronyms, see Leto, *OVRA* and Antonio Sannino, *Il fantasma dell'OVRA* (Milan: Greco & Greco, 2011). See also Mimmo Franzinelli, *I tentacoli dell'OVRA: agenti, collaboratori e vittime della polizia politica fascista* (Turin: Bollati Boringhieri, 1999) and Canali, *Le spie del regime*. The OVRA's repressive antecedent was the extralegal secret political police force known as 'Ceka' (modelled on the Soviet Cheka), which arose from 'squadrism' and was implicated in the 1924 murder of Giacomo Matteotti, see Franzinelli, *I tentacoli dell'OVRA* and Mimmo Franzinelli, 'Squadrism', in Richard J. B. Bosworth (ed.), *The Oxford Handbook of Fascism* (Oxford: Oxford University Press, 2009), pp. 91–108.

55    See Ugo Guspini, *L'orecchio del regime: le intercettazioni telefoniche al tempo del fascismo* (Milan: Mursia, 1973). Decree 987 (27 June 1925) placed the entity known as *Servizio di vigilanza e censura dei telefoni pubblici e privati ai fini della sicurezza dello Stato* under the auspices of the Ministry of the Interior. In 1927, Mussolini assumed direct oversight over the office, which with RD 27 (10 January 1929) became the *Servizio speciale riservato presso la presidenza del Consiglio*.

56    See Guido Leto, 'Memorie', *L'Europeo*, 547 (7 April 1956). Cf. Mauro Canali has argued that Fascism both adopted and adapted instruments of the Liberal State in 'Crime and Repression', in Bosworth, *The Oxford Handbook of Fascism*, 221–38.

57    The CPC maintained files on politically subversive citizens who might constitute a threat to public order or security. The 1926 TULPS expanded the CPC's authority exponentially so that within a year the number of people being monitored grew from 30,000 to 130,000, to reach a maximum of 158,000, by 1943. See Franzinelli, *I tentacoli dell'OVRA*, 63.

58    Article 2 of the 1926 TULPS empowered the prefects with the authority to adopt the appropriate means to maintain order: 'Il Prefetto, nel caso di urgenza o per grave necessità pubblica, ha facoltà di adottare i provvedimenti indispensabili per la tutela dell'ordine pubblico e della sicurezza pubblica' (The Prefect, in the case of urgency or of grave public need, has the authority to adopt the necessary provisions to ensure public order and public security). See Paola Carucci, 'Il Ministero dell'interno: prefetti, questori e ispettori generali', in Angelo Ventura (ed.), *Sulla crisi del regime fascista, 1938–1943: la società italiana dal 'consenso' alla Resistenza* (Venice: Marsilio, 1996), pp. 21–73. As Ebner, *Ordinary Violence in Mussolini's Italy*, 54 notes, these offices engaged in active efforts of social control: 'The personnel of the *questure* censored mail, recruited informants, performed interrogations, made arrests, monitored the Fascist Party and labour syndicates, conducted surveillance on suspects and ex-political detainees, and carried out a wide array of other activities. Although a prefect and *questore* needed approval from Rome to sentence an individual to *confino di polizia*, they could arrest, detain, and assign political probation without any authorisation from a court or the Interior Ministry in Rome'.

59    Chiara Fonio, 'Surveillance under Mussolini's regime', *Surveillance & Society*, 9:1/2 (2011), 82. See also Chiara Fonio and Stefano Agnoletto, 'Surveillance, repression and the welfare state: Aspects of continuity and discontinuity in post-Fascist Italy', *Surveillance & Society*, 11:1/2 (2013), 74–86.

60    Paola Carucci, 'Arturo Bocchini', in Ferdinando Cordova (ed.), *Uomini e volti del fascismo* (Rome: Bulzoni, 1980), pp. 72–3.

61    Efficiently implemented, sentencing to *confino* began by 22 November 1926. The *Tribunale Speciale per la Difesa dello Stato* consisted of a more cumbersome bureaucratic process than *confino*. Instituted with Law 2008 (25 November 1926) and governed by the Minister of War, it became operational on 1 February 1927. Badoglio's government dissolved it on 29 July 1943 (RDL 668). See, Cesare Rossi, *Il Tribunale Speciale: storia documentata* (Milan: Ceschina, 1952); Italy, Ministero della Difesa, *Tribunale Speciale per la difesa dello stato. Decisioni emesse* [1927–43] 17 vols (Rome: Stato Maggiore dell'Esercito – Ufficio Storico, 1980–99); Adriano Dal Pont, Alfonso Leonetti, Pasquale Maiello, and Lino Zocchi, *Aula IV. Tutti i processi del Tribunale Speciale fascista* (Milan: La Pietra, 1976); and Claudio Longhitano, *Il Tribunale di Mussolini (Storia del Tribunale Speciale 1926–1943)* (Rome: ANPPIA, 1994).

62    Fucci, *Le polizie di Mussolini*, 62.

63    Fonio (2011: 83). See also Franzinelli, *I tentacoli dell'OVRA*, 64.

64    Ebner, *Ordinary Violence in Mussolini's Italy*, 57–8.

65    Emilio Lussu, *La catena* (Rome: Edizioni U, 1945), p. 72.

66    Mussolini took a direct interest in individual cases: 'In moltissimi fascicoli personali dei confinati … appaiono frasi scritte di suo pugno dal dittatore (più frequentemente si tratta di vistosi NO! seguiti dall'inconfondibile M)'. (In many *confinati* personnel files … the dictator's written notations appear (usually a grandiose NO! followed by the unmistakable M)), in Corvisieri, *La villeggiatura di Mussolini*, 15.

67    In 1942, with Law 182 (29 January 1942), *Modificazione degli articoli 166 e 184 del testo unico delle leggi di pubblica sicurezza approvato col R. decreto 18 giugno 1931-IX, n. 773*, the PNF's federal secretaries became members of the Provincial Commissions. See *Gazzetta Ufficiale del Regno d'Italia*, 67 (23 March 1942), 1122–3.

68    Residents in occupied territories could also be sentenced to *confino* though the provisions were not identical. Articles 181–90 of RD 884 (8 May 1927), *Ordinamento di polizia per la Tripolitania e la Cirenaica*, specified the application of *confino* in the North African territories. Published in *Gazzetta Ufficiale del Regno d'Italia*, 139 (17 June 1927), 2472–93. For example, Article 182 allowed for a sentencing to exceed five years with no maximum specified; also, the possibility of appeals did not exist. This legislation was modified with RD 1104 (6 July 1933) in *Gazzetta Ufficiale del Regno d'Italia*, 207 (6 September 1933), 3969–93; and RD 571 (26 February 1934) in *Gazzetta Ufficiale del Regno d'Italia*, 89 (16 April 1934), 1980–1.

69    Arturo Bocchini served as Chief of Police until his death on 22 November 1940, when Carmine Senise assumed the charge. The undersecretaries were Giacomo Suardo (November 1926–March 1928) followed by Michele Bianchi (until September 1929), then Leandro Arpinati (until May 1933), and then for ten years Guido Buffarini-Guidi (until February 1943)

70    Under Senise's leadership, the Commission was less perfunctory in its adjudications than under Bocchini; however, such discrepancies could be due to political manoeuvring in preparation for possible power shifts. On the appeals process, see Leonardo Musci in Dal Pont and Carolini, *L'Italia al confino*, lvii–lxxv. On clemency, see Ebner, *Ordinary Violence in Mussolini's Italy*, 139–65.

71    Silvio Trentin, *Les transformations récentes du Droit public Italien: de la Charte de Charles-Albert à la creation de l'État fasciste* (Paris: Marcel Giard, 1929), p. 380, as cited in Lyttelton, *The Seizure of Power*, 298.

72    Lyttelton, *The Seizure of Power*, 298. See also Alberto Aquarone, *L'organizzazione dello stato totalitario* (Turin: Einaudi, 1965), pp. 555–60; and Paolo Barile (ed.), *La pubblica sicurezza* (Vicenza: Neri Pozza, 1967), p. 26.

73    Lussu, *La catena*, 74–5.

74    Lussu, *La catena*, 77–8.

75    See Carbone and Grimaldi, *Il popolo al confino*, 48–9. See also Antonino Cordova, *Commento al Testo Unico delle leggi di Pubblica Sicurezza 6 novembre 1926 n. 1848 e al Regolamento 21 gennaio 1929 n. 62* (Palermo: Orazio Fiorenza, 1929). RD 62 (21 January 1929), *Approvazione del regolamento per l'esecuzione del testo unico delle leggi di pubblica sicurezza, 6 novembre 1926, n. 1848*, clarified ambiguities in the TULPS and appeared in *Gazzetta Ufficiale del Regno d'Italia. Supplemento ordinario*, 26 (31 January 1929).

76    See 'Agents of police to keep close eye upon all in Italy', *Washington Post* (7 November 1926), p. M16; and 'Makes it a crime to oppose Fascism', *New York Times* (7 November 1926), p. 19.

77    Mussolini, 'Full text of Mussolini's speech', 48–52. For the speech's impact on the Regime's public policies see David G. Horn, *Social Bodies: Science, Reproduction and Italian Modernity* (Princeton: Princeton University Press, 1994), pp. 66–94 and Victoria De Grazia, *How Fascism Ruled Women: Italy, 1922–1945* (Berkeley: University of California Press, 1992), pp. 41–76. See also Barbara Spackman, *Fascist Virilities: Rhetoric,*

*Ideology, and Social Fantasy in Italy* (Minneapolis: University of Minnesota Press, 1996), pp. 114–55.

78   Mussolini, *Discorso dell'Ascensione*, 12. The *New York Times*' translation contains several numerical errors: 959 admonished (not 1,959); 286 had given up political activities (not 268); 175 denied being subversives (not 185); 69 claimed no party affiliation (not 59); the '69 that they … severed all ties with political parties' is a redundancy; and 29 made acts of submission (not 26).

79   Leonardo Musci estimates the number of *confinati* at 1,200. See Dal Pont and Carolini, *L'Italia al confino*, lviii. Henry Jones Jr., reporting for the *Chicago Tribune*, ran a three-article series in December 1928, on repressive measures in Italy. In the first article, 'Fascisti forbid political foes right of defense', he suggested that both the perception and the reality of *confino* differed from Mussolini's explication: 'The exact number of people on the islands is not known. No one is ever allowed to approach the islands. Several hundred sentences this year have swelled the already large numbers of prisoners on the islands and no one knows just how many there are. Premier Mussolini said two years ago that there were fifteen hundred there under sentence for political activities. Some other estimates put the number as high as 200,000. From the rate at which the [special military] tribunal works, it does not appear that Premier Mussolini's figures are correct' in the *Chicago Tribune* (9 December 1928) Part 1, p. 27.

80   The distinction between *confino politico* and *confino comune* is important because, as of 1955, those persecuted under Fascism for political or racial reasons were entitled to reparations. See Law 96 (10 March 1955), *Provvidenze a favore dei perseguitati politici antifascisti o razziali e dei loro familiari superstiti*, in *Gazzetta Ufficiale della Repubblica Italiana, Serie Generale*, 70 (26 March 1955).

81   RDL 1254 (15 July 1926) established the division governing non-political *confino*.

82   For example, rape was a difficult crime to prosecute because the law required that a formal complaint [*querela*] be lodged and victims were reticent to do so fearing the consequences of going public. On the other hand, rumours and anonymous accusations could suffice to sentence a suspected rapist to *confino*. The *querela* requirement for rape was part of the Zanardelli Penal Code (1890) and of the Rocco Code (1930) that replaced it. For the implications of *querela* in cases of rape, see Rachel A. Van Cleave, 'Rape and the Querela in Italy: False Protection of Victim Agency', *Michigan Journal of Gender & Law* 13 (2007), 273–310.

83   Article 10 of RDL 33 (9 January 1927), *Riordinamento del personale dell'Amministrazione della pubblica sicurezza e dei servizi di polizia*. Published in the *Gazzetta Ufficiale del Regno d'Italia*, 18 (24 January 1927), 294.

84   Giacomo Suardo, Undersecretary of the Interior, informed prefects that the 'battle against those who disturb and plot against the Regime must not neglect petty delinquents, as it is not a question of two distinct battles but of two faces of a single initiative with a common aim: to ensure the peace and tranquillity of the workers and producers' in ACS, *Telegrammi ufficio cifra in partenza*, circular 28,942 (28 November 1926). Cited in Benadusi, *The Enemy of the New Man*, 120.

85   Gissi, 'Un percorso a ritroso', 32.

86   Alda Costa served a two-year sentence at Tremiti and Carleto Perticara (Potenza), see ACS, *confinati politici*, b. 290, 'Alda Costa'. Edda Ciano, elegant, candid, strong-willed, hard-drinking, and hard-playing, embodied a more complicated conception of the Fascist new woman than that of wife and mother in the service of the nation. Of international fame and interest, she appeared on the cover of *TIME Magazine* on 24 July 1939. Sentenced to two years, she served less than one thanks to an amnesty granted by Palmiro Togliatti (Presidential Decree, 4 (22 June 1946), *Amnistia e indulto per reati comuni, politici e militari*). See Marcello Sorgi, *Edda Ciano*

e il comunista: l'inconfessabile passione della figlia del Duce (Milan: Rizzoli, 2009); Edda Ciano, La mia vita (Milan: Mondadori, 2001); Antonio Spinosa, Edda: una tragedia italiana (Milan: Mondadori, 1993).

87  RD no. 1403 (5 November 1932), *Concessione di amnistia e indulto nella ricorrenza del I Decennale*, published in *Gazzetta Ufficiale del Regno d'Italia*, 256 cont. (7 November 1932).

88  Agamben has argued that concentration camps emerge when the state of exception transitions from the exceptional to the norm (*Homo Sacer*, 168–9).

89  Lussu, *La catena*, 84. Mussolini frequently employed physiological metaphors to rhetorically represent the nation as a physical body in need of diagnosis, treatment and prevention from social and cultural infirmities, see Augusto Simonini, *Il linguaggio di Mussolini* (Milan: Bompiani, 1978), pp. 142–4; Francesca Rigotti, 'Il medico-chirurgo dello Stato nel linguaggio metaforico di Mussolini', in Camillo Brezzi and Luigi Ganapini (eds), *Cultura e società negli anni del fascismo* (Milan: Cordani, 1987), pp. 501–17; Spackman, *Fascist Virilities*, 145–8; and Chiara Ferrari, *The Rhetoric of Violence and Sacrifice in Fascist Italy: Mussolini, Gadda, Vittorini* (Toronto: University of Toronto Press, 2013), pp. 24–5.

90  Vincent Sheean's articles appeared in the *Los Angeles Times*: 'Mussolini's exiles live lonely days on islets' (29 January 1928), p. 8; 'Italy grades her exiles' (30 January 1928), p. 2; 'Italy's exiles get daily dole' (31 January 1928), p. 6; and 'Italy's heroes fill jails' (1 February 1928), p. 9. In the first, he described his efforts, all in vain, to visit Mario Magri and Alfredo Morea, two political *confinati* sentenced to Lipari. In the second, Sheean examined Lipari's hierarchy of exiles. The third article explained how the *confinati* lived in terms of both physical conditions and financial resources. The concluding article focused on public figures that had been sentenced to the islands.

91  While the exact details are somewhat contradictory, apparently on 16 January 1938, Mussolini approved a photoreportage of Ponza to promote a positive image of *confino* to Americans. The assignment went to the caricaturist Paolo Garretto (1903–89) and to the photographer Stefano Bricarelli (1889–1989), both of whom were in contact with Henry Luce, editor of *LIFE* magazine. Il Luce, as he was known, rejected the submission because 'se lo pubblicassimo i nostri lettori ci chiederebbero se siamo tutt'a un tratto diventati fascisti' (if we were to publish it, our readers would wonder whether we had suddenly become Fascists). See Stefano Bricarelli, 'Fai vedere come vivevano. Dall'archivio di un grande fotografo degli anni Trenta un inedito reportage sui confinati del regime a Ponza', *Storia illustrata*, 30:359 (October 1987), pp. 24–33; and Domizia Carafòli and Gustavo Bocchini Padiglione, *Il viceduce. Storia di Arturo Bocchini capo della Polizia fascista* (Milan: Rusconi, 1987), pp. 138–40.

92  Ennio Flaiano recounts that Maccari pronounced the phrase 'Ho poche idee, ma confuse' in 'Taccuino 1946' of *Diario notturno*, see Ennio Flaiano, *Opere, 1947–1972* (Milan: Bompiani, 1990), p. 372.

93  See 'The Regime's response to international criticism' in Chapter 1 of this study; and Corvisieri, *La villeggiatura di Mussolini*, 9 and 21–8.

94  Maccari, *Visita al confino*, 92.

95  RD 773 (18 June 1931) was published in the *Gazzetta Ufficiale del Regno d'Italia. Supplemento ordinario*, 146 (26 June 1931). Articles 180–9 govern *confino*. The new TULPS both confirmed and expanded the scope of the 1926 legislation. For example, Article 121 now banned charlatanism, but what constituted charlatanism remained the purview of local authorities.

96  *Gazzetta Ufficiale del Regno d'Italia. Supplemento oridinario*, 146 (26 June 1931), 3.

97  The Rocco Code, which remains, with modifications, in effect today, replaced the Zanardelli Code of 1889. Five years in the making – RD 2260 (4 December

1925) called for a reform of the penal code – the new code was promulgated by RD 1398 (19 October 1930) and published in the *Gazzetta Ufficiale del Regno d'Italia. Straordinario*, 251 (26 October 1930). Named for Minister of Justice Alfredo Rocco, the new penal code went into effect on 1 July 1931. Prison reform was addressed in RD 787 (18 June 1931).

98   Ebner, *Ordinary Violence in Mussolini's Italy*, 167.

99   Prostitution was a licensed profession to be practised under restrictions imposed by the State. Regulations governing brothels were thorough encompassing both physical and moral health (including medical check-ups twice a week and a visit on Fridays by a priest to administer communion and to hear confession). The minimum age to practise was twenty-one, and, after 1938, women seeking employment in brothels needed to hold a PNF card. The Socialist Senator, Lina Merlin, introduced a bill to close the brothels in August 1948, but the 'Merlin law', Law 75 (20 February 1958), *Abolizione della regolamentazione della prostituzione e lotta contro lo sfruttamento della prostituzione altrui*, was not ratified until *Gazzetta Ufficiale della Repubblica Italiana*, 55 (4 March 1958).

Vagrancy was treated as criminal activity in the previous TULPS as well. See Eugenio Florian and Guido Cavaglieri, *I vagabondi: studio sociologico-giuridico*, 2 vols (Turin: Fratelli Bocca Editori, 1897), 1, 279–336. In their study, Roma are treated as a distinct race (Vol. 2, p. 44).

For anti-Slavic discrimination, see Stefano Bartolini, *Fascismo antislavo: il tentativo di «bonifica etnica» al confine nord orientale* (Pistoia: Istituto storico della Resistenza e della società contemporanea, 2006).

100   Ebner, *Ordinary Violence in Mussolini's Italy*, 172. Articles 112, 113, and 115 of the 1926 TULPS banned the publication and dissemination of information that might assist in preventing or interrupting pregnancies. See also Denise Detragiache, 'Un aspect de la politique démographique de l'Italie fasciste: la répression de l'avortement', *Mélanges de l'École française de Rome*, 92:2 (1980), 691–735. Title X (Articles 545–5) of the Penal Code (RD 1398, 19 October 1930) classified abortion as a crime against the 'integrity and health of the race'. For an overview of Fascist demographic policies see, Carl Ipsen, *Dictating Demography: The Problem of Population in Fascist Italy* (Cambridge: Cambridge University Press, 1996). See also de Grazia, *How Fascism Ruled Women*; Anna Treves, *Le nascite e la politica nell'Italia del Novecento* (Milan: LED, 2001); and Alessandra Gissi, 'Reproduction', in Arthurs, Ebner, and Ferris, *The Politics of Everyday Life in Fascist Italy*, 99–122.

101   Gissi, 'Reproduction', 114.

102   See Ebner, *Ordinary Violence in Mussolini's Italy*, 197–203; Giorgio Peyrot, *Gli evangelici nei loro rapporti con lo Stato del fascismo ad oggi* (Torre Pellice: Società di studi valdesi, 1977); Paolo Piccioli, 'I testimoni di Geova durante il regime fascista', *Studi Storici*, 41:1 (2000), 191–229; Giorgio Rochat, *Regime fascista e chiese evangeliche: direttive e articolazioni del controllo e della repressione* (Turin: Claudiana, 1990); Pietro Scoppola, *La chiesa e il fascismo: documenti e interpretazioni* (Bari: Laterza, 1973); and Giorgio Spini, *Italia di Mussolini e protestanti* (Turin: Claudiana, 2007).

103   The publication was banned by 20 November 1928, Piccioli, 'I testimoni di Geova durante il regime fascista', 192–4.

104   The Concordat (11 January 1929) also provided the basis for the Vatican's opposition to the marriage prohibition between Jews and non-Jews in the 1938 anti-Semitic legislation.

105   Circular 600/158 dated 9 April 1935. ACS, DGPS, DAGR, *Categoria G.1 1920–45*, b. 26 f. 299 1-c-z. The directive remained in effect until 16 April 1955. See Giorgio Peyrot, *La circolare Buffarini-Guidi e i Pentecostali* (Rome: Associazione Italiana per la Libertà della Cultura, 1955).

106  Throughout the 1920s and 1930s, officials failed to understand the differences between various evangelical organisations (e.g., Pentecostals, Jehovah's Witnesses, Salvation Army) and frequently treated them interchangeably. See Piccioli, 'I testimoni di Geova durante il regime fascista', 214–15.

107  Broadly speaking, the Roma crossed the Adriatic Sea to southern Italy in the fourteenth century; the Sinti migrated from the Balkans to northern Italy; and the Camminanti population is identified primarily with Sicily, see Massimo Converso, 'Rom, Sinti e Camminanti in Italia: l'identità negata', in Giovanna Boursier, Massimo Converso and Fabio Iacomini (eds), *Zigeuner: lo sterminio dimenticato* (Rome: Sinnos editrice, 1996), pp. 82–7. Although not explicitly identified in the 1938 racial laws, these minority populations were effectively treated as a distinct race. In 1940, Guido Landra, the first director of the Ministry of Popular Culture's Office of Racial Studies published an article, 'Il problema dei meticci in Europa' in the journal *La difesa della razza*, 4:1 (1940), 11–15, in which he catalogued the racial characteristics of Romani and, drawing on the case of Germany, warned of the dangers of racial mixing. See Giovanna Boursier, 'Gli zingari nell'Italia fascista', in Leonardo Piasere (ed.), *Italia romani*, Vol. 1 (Rome: CISU, 1996), pp. 7–8; and Aaron Gillette, 'Guido Landra and the Office of Racial Studies in Fascist Italy', *Holocaust Genocide Studies*, 16:3 (Winter 2002), 357–75.

108  Memorandum of Ministry of the Interior to prefects (19 February 1926), ACS, MI, DGPS, DAGR, 1926, b. 28, f. Zingari greci e altri. See Boursier, 'Gli zingari nell'Italia fascista', 5–20 and Luca Bravi, *Rom e non-zingari: vicende storiche e pratiche rieducative sotto il regime fascista* (Rome: CISU, 2007).

109  Annamaria Masserini, *Storia dei nomadi: la persecuzione degli Zingari nel XX secolo* (Padua: Edizioni GB, 1990), p. 47. See also Luca Bravi, 'Lo sterminio degli zingari', in Alessandra Chiappano and Fabio Minazzi (eds), *Il paradigma nazista dell'annientamento: la Shoah e gli altri stermini* (Florence: Editrice La Giuntina, 2006), 109–22.

110  The invasion of Yugoslavia (6 April 1941) led to a large influx of Roma into Italy, which was soon followed by the ministerial circular of 27 April 1941, calling for their internment. See. ACS, MI, DGPS, DAGR, II Guerra mondiale, b. 68.

111  Cesare Lombroso, 'Etiologia delle razze', *Rendiconti (Reale Istituto Lombardo di Scienze e Lettere)* 2:8 (1875), 133. Lombroso was emphasising race as a predictor of criminal behaviour by contrasting what he considered to be atavistic and immoral races (e.g., Romani) with Jewish people whose limited criminality he ascribed to particular economic milieus. Cf. Carlo Umberto Del Pozzo, 'Oziosi e vagabondi', in Eugenio Florian, Alfredo Niceforo, and Nicola Pende (eds), *Dizionario di criminologia* (Milan: Francesco Vallardi, 1943), p. 618: 'Tipici rappresentanti del vagabondaggio etnico sono gli zingari, veri delinquenti professionali che vivono girovagando, rubando, truffando, rapinando, ricattando. Sono tutti in un certo senso, degli "immorali etnici", in quanto tutta la loro tradizione di famiglia e di razza li sospinge a questa vita girovaga, dedita professionalmente al delitto' (Gypsies are typical representatives of ethnic vagrancy. They are true professional delinquents who live by wandering, stealing, conning, thievery, and blackmail. They are all, in a certain sense, 'ethnic immorals', in that their entire familial and racial traditions push them into this roving life professionally devoted to crime). The *Dizionario di criminologia*'s final entry, penned by Tancredi Galimberti, is 'Zingari' (pp. 1050–3). Galimberti estimates their population in Italy to be roughly 32,000 and concludes the entry (and volume) by referring the reader to the entry 'Razza' (race).

112  Roberto Semizzi, 'Gli Zingari', in *Rassegna di clinica, terapia e scienze affini*, 38:1 (1939), 70. Cf. Nicola Pende, *Trattato di biotipologia individuale e sociale: con applicazioni alla medicina preventiva, alla clinica, alla politica biologica, alla sociologia* (Milan: Francesco Vallardi, 1939).

113  Limited data makes quantifying the number of victims difficult, but the primary *confino* sites for Romani were in Basilicata and Sardinia. See Cristoforo Magistro, 'Storie di confino: gli zingari nel Materano', *Basilicata regione notizie*, 127–8 (20 October 2011), 216–25.

114  Salvatore Ottolenghi, *Trattato di polizia scientifica* (Milan: Società editrice libraria, 1932), p. 234.

115  The constitution of the Italian Republic ensures freedom of association (Article 18).

116  Under Fascism, both political and professional discourse applied several terms interchangably to describe 'homosexuality' including 'pederasty', 'sodomy', 'sexual inversion', and 'intersexuality'. See Benadusi, *The Enemy of the New Man*, 88–110 for an examination of the legal debates concerning homosexuality during the *ventennio* (the twenty years of Fascist rule in Italy).

117  Cesare Musatti, 'Omosessuali,' in Eugenio Florian, Alfredo Niceforo, and Nicola Pende (eds), *Dizionario di criminologia* (Milan: Francesco Vallardi, 1943), p. 605. Musatti also discusses women, but argues that lesbianism carries less social stigma than male homosexuality and that it is frequently transitory (p. 602).

118  Aldo Mieli, founder of the *Società italiana per lo studio delle questioni sessuali* (Italian Society for the Study of Sexual Matters) and editor of the Society's journal, the bimonthly *La Rassegna di studi sessuali* advocated a similar view to Musatti's. On the other hand, Giovanni Franceschini, author of *La vita sessuale: manuale ad uso dei medici e degli studenti di medicina* (Milan: Hoepli, 1923), considered punishment and incarceration as the proper means to purge the social body of homosexuality. For an overview of the index case literature and debates on sexuality during the *ventennio*, see Benadusi, *The Enemy of the New Man*, 31–78.

119  Benadusi, *The Enemy of the New Man*, 127. Benadusi bases his estimate on the relevant files housed in the ACS. Article 184, no. 2 of the 1926 TULPS (reaffirmed with Article 181, no. 3 of the 1931 TULPS) provided the rationale for the charge.

120  See Nerina Milletti, 'Accuse innominabili. Lesbiche e confino di polizia durante il fascismo', in Nerina Milletti and Luisa Passerini (eds), *Fuori della norma: storie lesbiche nell'Italia della prima metà del Novecento* (Turin: Rosenberg & Sellier, 2007), 135–69.

121  See Benadusi, *The Enemy of the New Man*, 131–2. For an opposing view, see Giovanni Dall'Orto, 'Il paradosso del razzismo fascista verso l'omosessualità', in Alberto Burgio (ed.) *Nel nome della razza: il razzismo nella storia d'Italia, 1870–1945* (Bologna: Il Mulino, 2000), pp. 515–28; Patrizia Dogliani, *L'Italia fascista, 1922–1940* (Milan: Sansoni, 1999), pp. 282–83; Gianfranco Goretti, 'Il periodo fascista e gli omosessuali. Il confino di polizia', in Circolo Pink, *Le ragioni di un silenzio: la persecuzione degli omosessuali durante il nazismo e il fascismo* (Verona: Ombre Corte, 2002), p. 64.

122  Gianfranco Goretti and Tommaso Giartosio's *La città e l'isola. Omosessuali al confino nell'Italia fascista* (Rome: Donzelli editore, 2006) is the first study to examine in depth this aspect of Fascist repression. Historical awareness of this memory site continues to grow. See also Luca de Santis's award-winning graphic novel (illustrated by Sara Colaone), *In Italia sono tutti maschi* (Bologna: Kappa Edizioni, 2008); Roberto Paterlini's award-winning novel, *Cani randagi* (Rome: Rai Eri, 2012); Alan Johnston, 'A Gay Island Community Created by Italy's Fascists', *BBC News Magazine* (12 June 2013) www.bbc.co.uk/news/magazine-22856586 (accessed 15 January 2019). Debora Inguglia's documentary, *Isola Nuda* (Visionaria, 2009) draws from Goretti and Giartosio's research to examine another exile site for gay men: Ustica.

123  Favignana, Lampedusa, Tremiti Islands, and Ustica still served as detention sites for *coatti* in 1922. See Fozzi, *Tra prevenzione e repressione*, 239–44.

124  Barbara Levick, 'The Fall of Julia the Younger', *Latomus*, 5.2 (April–June 1976), 301–39; Frances Norwood, 'The Riddle of Ovid's *Relegatio*', *Classical Philology*, 58.3 (July

1963), 150–63; and Andrew Pettinger, *The Republic in Danger: Drusus Libo and the Succession of Tiberius* (Oxford: Oxford University Press, 2012), pp. 123–33.

125  Angelo Del Boca estimates that between 25 and 30 October 1911 (in retribution for Sciara Sciat), General Carlo Caneva deported over 4,000 Arabs to Tremiti, Ustica, Ponza, Caserta, Gaeta, and Favignana (*Italiani, brava gente?* 112). The order stemmed from Giolitti's telegram to Caneva at 16.45 on 24 October 1911: 'Quanto a rivoltosi arrestati, che non siano fucilati costà, li manderà alle isole Tremiti, nel mare Adriatico coi domiciliati coatti, dove ella può direttamente dirigerli avvisandomi partenza. Le isole Tremiti possono ricevere oltre quattrocento detenuti. Mando colà ispettore generale della pubblica sicurezza per regolare il loro collocamento' (As for the rebels arrested, if not executed there, send them to the Tremiti Islands, in the Adriatic Sea with the confined residents, where you may send them directly alerting me of departure. The Tremiti Islands may receive over four hundred detainees. I am sending there the Inspector General for Public Security to oversee their placement) ACS, Carte Giolitti, b. 22, f. 58 telegram 27979 (24 October 1911). Within a year, approximately 400 of the prisoners died from various diseases. On 26 October 2006, Tremiti Islands' mayor Giuseppe Calabrese inaugurated in San Nicola a commemorative mausoleum. Subsequently, in 2008, DNA tests, conducted at the request of Libyan leader Muammar Gaddafi, determined that the Tremiti Islands' current inhabitants were not descended from the Libyan deportees. See Nicola Labanca, *La guerra italiana per la Libia 1911–1931* (Bologna: Il Mulino, 2012).
        After 1926, authorities applied the TULPS to colonial subjects as well. See Dal Pont, *I lager di Mussolini*, 45–8.

126  Forced residence on the mainland was reserved for *confinati* who posed a minimal risk of flight or violence. Ponza became a colony on 29 July 1928 and as such remained operational until the DGPS closed it in July 1939. Following the Rosselli-Lussu-Nitti escape from Lipari, the Ministry of the Interior designated Ventotene a colony for high-risk *confinati*.

127  Luciano Previato, *L'altra Italia: carceri, colonie di confino, campi di concentramento durante il ventennio fascista* (Bologna: Consiglio regionale dell'Emilia-Romagna, 1995), pp. 35–48; and Ebner, *Ordinary Violence in Mussolini's Italy*, 103–28.

128  Dal Pont, *I lager di Mussolini*, 133–6.

129  Mussolini approved the proposal, and the colony was cleared by 10 January 1933. The most dangerous *confinati* were transferred to Ponza, which the MVSN supervised, and the remaining to Ventotene, see Dal Pont, *I lager di Mussolini*, 46–7. After Bocchini's death, Senise became Chief of Police (22 November 1940–14 April 1943).

130  See Note 113 in Chapter 1 of this study.

131  Previato, *L'altra Italia*, 50.

132  Previato, *L'altra Italia*, 41. See also Carbone, *Il popolo al confino*; Michele Crispino, *Storie di confino in Lucania* (Venosa: Edizioni Osanna, 1990); Pirastu, *I confinati antifascisti in Sardegna*; and Pietro Mascaro (ed.), *Le ali della memoria: confinati a Cortale durante il regime fascista* (Lamezia Terme: Centro-stampa Dal Margine, 2000).

133  See Capogreco, *I campi del duce*, 26–30; Adele Rita Meneghini, 'L'antifascismo nella provincia di Matera (1926–1943)' (Thesis, Università degli Studi di Roma 'La Sapienza', 1990–91); Leonardo Sacco, *Provincia di confino: la Lucania nel ventennio fascista* (Fasano: Schena Editore, 1995); and Loris Pescarolo, *Il lungo cammino* (Suzzara: Edizioni Bottazzi, 1984).

134  For first hand accounts, see Benito Mussolini, *Il tempo del bastone e della carota. Storia di un anno (Ottobre 1942 – Settembre 1943)*, Corriere della sera (Supplement 190) (9 August 1944); and Franco Maugeri, *Mussolini mi ha detto: confessioni di Mussolini durante il confino a Ponza e alla Maddalena* (Rome: Quaderni di politica estera, 1944).

135  RD 1415 (8 July 1938), *Approvazione dei Testi della Legge di guerra della legge di neutralità*, commonly referred to as the 'War Law', introduced internment, but Law 415 (21 May 1940) *Organizzazione della Nazione per la guerra* explicated the process. Circular 442/38954 (1 June 1940) *Norme da tenersi in caso di emergenza, relative alle persone arrestate ed internate* provides an overview of internment. See also Capogreco, *I campi del duce*, 49–55.

136  TULPS Enforcement Regulations RD 635 (6 May 1940) in *Gazzetta Ufficiale del Regno d'Italia. Supplemento ordinario*, 149 (26 June 1940).

137  On 1 March 1957, Italy's Constitutional Court, having already struck Articles 165 and 166 (19 June 1956), ruled that Law 1423 (27 December 1956) along with Article thirteen of the Constitution (i.e., personal liberty is inviolable) rendered null and void Articles 180–9 of the 1931 TULPS. Article 3 of Law 1423 does carry a provision for intraterritorial relocation, but eliminates the political motivation.

138  Law 575 (31 May 1965) in *Gazzetta Ufficiale della Repubblica Italiana*, 138 (5 June 1965), and Law 152 (22 May 1975) in *Gazzetta Ufficiale della Repubblica Italiana*, 136 (24 May 1975).

139  Legislative decree 286 (25 July 1998), which took effect on 2 September 1998

140  See international terrorism legislation, Law 155 (31 July 2005) in *Gazzetta Ufficiale della Repubblica Italiana*, 177 (1 August 2005). See Giorgio Agamben, *Stato di eccezione. Homo Sacer II, 1* (Turin: Bollati Boringhieri, 2003).

# PART II

# Representations of internal exile in literature and film

# 3

# Writing internal exile

## Writing confinement

This chapter examines internal exile as it appears in literary fiction, personal correspondence, and memoirs. Unlike in the previous discussion of the history of confinement, the concern is not with the investigation and deployment of truths but rather with representational strategies; we are interested in *how* these texts convey information and how they suppress it. The questions addressed in the following sections, then, are the following: How did people write about their experiences in internal exile? What did they talk about (or omit) when they talked about it, and in what terms? And what relationship does the text impose between its form and the reading strategies contained implicitly therein? Thus, for example, we do not scan the memoirs to determine the precise motives behind Giovanni Ansaldo's request for exoneration. By the same token, we do not ask to what extent Cesare Pavese's *Il carcere* (*The Political Prisoner*, 1948) is fictional, though it is also most likely the bearer of certain kinds of truth, disguised and manipulated though these may be.

Instead, we mine the works for the ways they negotiate the conditions of their production, for the ways they create meaning out of a fairly limited set of narrative possibilities, a condition made clear when we note the homogeneity of the content of the letters of the prisoners. In the majority of texts, specific attention is almost invariably focused on arrest, the transfer from prison cell to the site of exile, including the painful ordeal of handcuffs; the difficulty of getting on the train; filthy conditions in prisons where they stop en route to the boat; the attitude of non-political detainees with respect to the political prisoners; agonising seasickness; the arrival, and first impressions of the island. More or less objective descriptions of the barracks, regulations, and geography of the site often follow, as do descriptions of reading, sunbathing, the trials and travails of surveillance, 'classes' (informal courses of study organised by and for the exiles), acts of revolt and subsequent incarceration, and anecdotes about prominent co-prisoners.

Themes recurrent in the prisoners' correspondence include health, the cost of living, the challenges and unexpected rewards of communal housing, surveillance, lack of privacy, loneliness, boredom, political activities, expressions of affection, the small change of married life, and so on.

There are, of course, exceptions, such as Ettore Franceschini's *Il domicilio coatto (Il cosiddetto 'confino di polizia')* come l'hò visto io, whose exuberance is made visible through the prolific use of italics, large-font bold typefaces, and multiple exclamation points (!!!!), and Ernesto Rossi's *Miserie e splendori del confino di polizia: lettere da Ventotene, 1939–1943*, in which Rossi discusses being covered in boils, and how he dislikes his wife's photo so much that he destroys it. Most *confino* correspondence, however, is somewhat more prosaic. Perhaps as a consequence of the relative paucity of narrative fodder, one can attend to even the smallest differences in the tone of the letters, and, after reading over the course of a prisoner's whole correspondence, can perceive a keen sense of the writerly personality of the prisoner. We must, of course, make allowances for the public nature of these letters – first, because the majority of the authors make explicit mention of the censors at one point or another, and second, because in many cases, letters addressed to one family member were intended to be circulated among other family members, friends, and party/political links (there were strict, though historically variable, limits on the number and relation to the prisoner of permissible correspondents). In both cases, letters might be written in a complicated code in order to get past the censors and to protect the recipients. Nonetheless, in spite of these conditions, the prisoner's personality emerges clearly. We note, for example, the unflagging generosity of spirit at the foundation of Camilla Ravera's lengthy correspondence. Similarly, we cannot avoid noting Pavese's peevishness and ingratitude in the many letters to his sister. In fact, the last anthologised letter (12 March 1936) of his *confino* years, addressed to his family, ends, 'Che vi venga il cancro a tutti'[1] (May you all develop cancer). We do not intend to draw conclusions about the actual character of the authors but rather to underscore the ways the works *perform* authorial character. Much like the highly restrictive formal parameters of the sonnet, which emphasise the poet's capacity for innovation with diminished means, the conditions of production of these writings, too, bring into high relief the variety of their literary qualities.

Thus we begin the discussion with those texts that most explicitly foreground their fictional status ('Confinement in fiction': Pavese, Lucarelli, Bassani, Ginzburg, Levi). Although it is an arrangement admittedly questionable from the standpoint of Ginzburg and Levi, whose works confound such neat distinctions, we do this to underscore the fact that though internal confinement as a historical phenomenon is the ostensible object of enquiry, these texts also offer the opportunity for their authors to investigate aspects of the relationship between self and the other, whether that otherness resides in gender, sexual preference, class, religion, or region of origin. The 'truth' of confinement as recounted by these authors is thus a point of entry into the wider field of self-representation.

We privilege fictional accounts of exile in terms of the space and of the position they occupy in this chapter, to drive home our convictions about the intimate relations between historical narrative, life writing, and literary convention. Lussu, Nitti, Jacometti, and Rosselli, whom we discuss in the section 'Foundational texts', have long been considered the standard bearers of the genre for the ways they established its thematic parameters, for the ways the mutual corroboration of their accounts lent them the weight of historical accuracy, and for their respective high political profiles. Also in this section, we discuss the memoir of Mario Magri, whose Rocambolesque adventures push to the extreme the dramatic potential of the flight attempts by his contemporaries, Lussu, Rosselli and Nitti. We organise the remainder of the discussion around writers who *don't* conform to the standard models, whether of the dramatic 'escape from Lipari' variety or the more prosaic handcuffs, train ride, and surveillance variety. These authors resist the received wisdom according to which Lussu, Nitti, and Rosselli teach us all we need to know about internal exile.

Reading not just *beyond* but *against* Lussu et al., both broadens our historical understanding of the genre and underscores the impossibility of disentangling historical and literary discourses, among which we identify three particularly common modalities. Though in very different ways, the intimist musings of the authors (Ravera, Ansaldo, Turchi) in 'The diarist' section suggest that internal exile poses interior challenges to do with emotions and morality as well as external or physical challenges. The poetic aspirations of the writers (Fiori, Braccialarghe) discussed in 'The poets' section confirm both the consolatory power of language, and its ability to create alternative narrative genealogies. Finally, the heroic Ecclesiastes narrative ('let us now praise famous men') of the final grouping (Gualino, Amendola, Spinelli) performs its authors' high status and reaffirms them (retroactively in the case of Amendola and Spinelli) as canonical, prophetic models of behaviour. In all of the above cases, in so far as these groupings make sense, they confirm these writers' identification of the epistemological function of literature. The alignment of their protagonists with various, pre-existing literary types suggests that these writers believed they could best achieve their ostensible goal of communicating information about their experiences through recourse not to journalistic, pedagogical, or chronicle-based models, which belong to the register of historical knowledge, but instead to those of literature, the narrative humus in which we commonly speak of ourselves. Whether or not they initially conceived of themselves in those terms, or mounted their stories on an already familiar scaffolding as a narrative expedient, is beyond our ability to determine. But the resemblances are striking nonetheless, and speak to the inseparability of history and its narration.

There is a further consideration to be made as well, and it is related to the question of the opportunity that these texts offered to their writers: where is Italy in these texts? To the question, 'how do internal exiles represent the nation?', the answer is, simply, they do not: a surprising absence considering that it is to the perception of harm to the nation that the punishment of internal exile responds. The irony of internal exile is that on the one hand, Italy itself is at once victim of a crime and its punishment, and insufficient *amor patriae* can be corrected with more *patria*: it is an example of *contrappasso* by affinity (for having already exiled themselves from the Fascist community) as well as by contrast (they are exiled from their elective anti-Fascist community). On the other hand, political exiles themselves would likely claim to have acted in the best interests of the nation and its people. What's more, it was the failure of the internationalist projects of the early twentieth century that lent pith and moment to Fascism as a nationalist movement. Lussu, Jacometti, Nitti, Rosselli, Ravera, Spinelli, Amendola and Rossi-Doria laboured and suffered in the name of the recuperation of a pacifist national referent compatible with, and not in opposition to, an internationalist vision. Consequently, here, too, we may observe how these works point towards much broader questions than the ones they apparently address; they focus on the minutiae of the very local (on Ventotene, Lipari, and so on) as a way, precisely, to discuss the nation.

Finally, this discussion is incomplete for reasons both of space and of class. The great majority of the prisoners cited here came from relatively privileged family backgrounds (Emma Turchi is an exception) and therefore their views are not remotely representative of the average prisoner's views or even of those of the average political prisoner. The institution of internal exile was radically fluid across time and highly segmented according to the class origins of its victims. Social class thus impacts upon both the confinement experience and its representation (as the recurrence of the theme of nostalgia in many of the memoirs makes clear). Thus the numerous references to, say, sunbathing, or afternoons spent reading and swimming in the sea, were by no means universal experiences: the vast majority of the hardships of the penal colony were never set down in writing by those who suffered them. The decision to devote relatively little space (e.g. Lussu, Rosselli, Jacometti) or no space (e.g. Gramsci, Ginzburg) to some of the best-known figures in favour of lesser knowns (e.g. Turchi, Fiori, Magri) is also an attempt to present to the reader the discrepancies in experience born of differences in privilege.[2]

## Confinement in fiction

Pavese's *Terra d'esilio* (*Land of Exile*), composed in 1936 and published by Einaudi in 1953, represents Cesare Pavese's first short story as well as his first attempt at writing on *confino*. Narrated in the first person by a construction engineer sent to a coastal town in southern Italy to oversee the building of a new highway (recall that Pavese served his sentence in Brancaleone), it recounts the brief acquaintance of the narrator and Otino, a *comune*, that, is, a prisoner internally exiled for non-political reasons. Otino, a worker from Turin, has been sentenced to five years of internal exile for striking a soldier who showed interest in his wife.

Otino is distraught because his wife refuses to join him and he feels certain that she is being unfaithful. He converses with the narrator when the latter is not at work, swimming, or chatting with a prostitute named Concetta. Eventually, Otino learns that his wife was violently murdered by the man with whom she had been conducting an affair for two years. Devastated and psychologically diminished, Otino is reduced to the same state as Ciccio, the local drunken beggar, whose company he will henceforth keep. The engineer leaves town when his job there is suspended.

Here we see, albeit in very shorthand form, several of the motifs that characterise Pavese's later fiction. The natural world is a constant presence: the sea and the sun, of course (hardly surprising given the setting, though the prominence of the sea is interesting in an exile narrative that is *not* set on an island, where the water functions as a prison wall), but also donkeys, agave leaves, and (inevitably, for Pavese) hills. Similarly, the twinned themes of sexual jealousy and female infidelity, coupled with the intimation of masculine sexual insufficiency, are foregrounded in the stories both of Otino and of Ciccio, whose uxoricide *manqué* proleptically anticipates the actual death of Otino's wife.[3] Of greater interest, however, is the mobilisation of a different set of Pavese's hobbyhorses to discuss internal exile: the themes of the alibi and of solitude.

By alibi, we mean Pavese's recurrent examination of the excuses for continued anti-social behaviour that are afforded by events outside of one's individual control. This concern will be prominent, as we will see, in the case of *Il carcere*, but it is also present in *Terra d'esilio*, oblique in form but significant in its position as the first sentence of the story, in which he claims that he found himself by happenstance in a place at once a punishment and a pleasure. The paradox of Pavese's fictional stance is clearly present in *Terra d'esilio* and *Il carcere*[4] in that they conform closely to the conventions of *confino* narrative (including those of other genres), even as they foreground their ultimate disinterest in the phenomenon of *confino* except as a metaphorical state, for several of the earmarks of the conventional *confino* narrative are present nonetheless. These texts share thematic elements (the strangeness of the people and customs; the sea, swimming and sunbathing, boredom, the vexations associated with sexual abstinence, distant loved ones, and so on), as well as structural elements, such as the coincidence of the termination of the sojourn with the conclusion of the narration.

But in *Terra d'esilio*, the first-person narrator is not in fact a real *confinato*, just a metaphorical one: '"E anche lei confinato?" gridò di là il giovanotto. –"Qui lo siamo un po' tutti", dissi forte'.[5] ('Are you a prisoner as well?' the young man called over. 'Here, we all are a bit', I shouted.) The narrator is an engineer working on the construction of a road, but he frames his stint in the unnamed village as the equivalent of a forced internment. In remarks that act as book-ends to the story, he makes clear his sense of powerlessness in the face of external exigencies – here, not of the law, but of his job. This occurs early on, when he asks his company to transfer him to another job, and the story ends when he is granted (at least temporary) release from duty because of the weather. Rather, internal exile is explicitly framed as a metaphorical condition, one that can apply regardless of the presence, absence, or degree of external restrictions on an individual's movement, activities, and so on. In other words, in *Terra d'esilio*, the narrator's exile is a state of mind, a fact rendered thematically evident by the role of the sea that, unlike in the many confine texts set on islands, does not demarcate the boundaries of a carceral space. Not only that, but the inhabitants of the village, too, are figured as guests, visitors, detached from their physical environment as though they were just passing through, their minds elsewhere. They, too, are in metaphorical exile.

It should be noted, however, that we have been forewarned about the risks of taking these claims too seriously. The story, told in flashback after the narrator has returned home to Turin, anticipates a motif that will reappear more than a decade later in his 1950 *La luna e i falò*, namely the appreciation for a person, place, or thing that is possible only once it is lost. The purpose of this declaration is two-fold. First, it presents a variant on the philosophy of Anguilla, a character in the 1950 novel, according to which you get what you want only once you no longer need it (in Anguilla's case, the recognition by his former *paesani* (townsfolk) of his financial stability and social status; in the case of the unnamed narrator of the story, true understanding). Second, it functions as a disclaimer or justification for the discreet disavowal of any fiduciary relationship to the reader, further emphasised by the remark that his northern origins estranged him even more from his new surroundings. Pavese's story is at once an early iteration of the psychological concerns of later writings such as *La casa in collina* and *La luna e i falò*; the initial exploration of the fictional possibilities of his personal experience in internal exile, to be continued in *Il carcere*; and, insofar as this fictional account nonetheless also adheres to the conventions of the genre of the *confino* memoir, an invitation at once to invoke and to disavow the readerly expectations that accompany that form.

As in *Terra d'esilio*, whose partial focus on an emphatically non-political *confinato* serves to articulate *confino* as an alibi for self-imposed isolation, so, too, does Pavese's *Il carcere* establish its concern with the public enforcement of private preferences. In doing so, it places the text squarely amongst Pavese's other works, most explicitly *La casa in collina* (written 1947–48).

In *Terra d'esilio*, the *confinato* and the narrator depoliticise the confinement experience to refocus the narrative on Otino's personal drama and the narrator's existential crisis. In *Il carcere*, the protagonist Stefano is, instead, a political prisoner but here, too, the prisoner's experience as it is recounted is resolutely apolitical.[6] In Pavese's works, the increasing concern with political apathy – passivity, cowardice, ethical sloth, as well as social and psychological isolation – reaches its apex in *La casa in collina*. This later novel renders explicit its protagonist's conscious avoidance of the political, until the end of the novel when political engagement (in the form of an awareness that, in turn, prompts the composition of the novel) becomes inevitable, when he literally stumbles upon the body of a dead soldier. In *Il carcere*, instead, Stefano's refusal to communicate with another internee underscores the paradox of the former's total lack of interest in engagement, whether of an ideological or personal nature. Instead, though *Il carcere* (originally entitled *Memorie di due stagioni*) does not articulate the theme of the alibi or excuse as explicitly, the emphasis is decidedly on confinement not so much as a physical carceral space as a metaphorical space, one, moreover, whose origins are equally (if not preponderantly) imposed by forces internal to the character as they are by external forces such as the Fascist penal system.

The theme and setting of *confino*, here even more than in *Terra d'esilio*, serve Pavese well as a testing ground for the later development of his thematic preoccupation with the competing needs for intimacy and for solitude. As in his later novels, that tension is organised around Stefano's relationships – one consummated, the other merely fantasised – with two very different women. While the effortlessness of Stefano's success in seducing Elena might suggest their intimacy is both emotional and erotic, it is in fact facilitated by the dispensability of conversation between the two of them. She is a devoted, consciously maternal presence (he calls her *mammina*,[7] mummy), of few words and unable to make any inroads into Stefano's affections. The 'strange red flowers' she leaves on his table anticipate Elvira's spectacularly unsuccessful seduction of Corrado in *La casa in collina*: clumsy attempts to inspire a passion of which he is constitutionally incapable.

The object of Stefano's more passionate erotic engagement, in contrast, is the servant girl Concia. Much attention is given to her desirability and yet Stefano refrains from approaching her, in part because he misconstrues her relations with another man, Giannino, but also, we might hazard, because to embark upon a relationship based on something more than the intermittent, lukewarm desire he feels for Elena poses a much greater threat to his autonomy and much vaunted solitude. And yet Stefano does manage a kind of phantasmagoric bodily union with the young servant, a union enacted through a dense series of imagistic equivalences, starting with Concia's numerous explicit comparisons to a goat. Concia's caprine qualities are prefigured in a complex series of metaphors that recall the depiction of Gisella of *Paesi tuoi* (written a few months after *Il carcere*, and published in 1941) as an animal, a fruit, and as water.[8] Here, there is a repetition and imbrication of the terms *fianchi* (flanks – both Concia's and the sides of the water pitcher, and a reference to Stefano's own *anca*); *caprigno* (goatlike – in reference to Concia and to the water); *acqua* (water – that carried by Concia, and that in Stefano's pitcher); and *gerani* (geraniums – again in reference to Concia and to the water in the pitcher) sets up a series of identifications which conclude, in essence, with Stefano's figurative ingestion of Concia:

[Stefano] si sentiva vivo e desto, e a volte gli accadeva di tastarsi l'anca con la mano. Tali appunto, magri e forti, dovevan essere i fianchi di quella donna. [...] Stefano [...] stringeva con le mani i fianchi svelte e umidicci [dell'anfora], e sollevandola di peso se la portava alle labbra. Scendeva con l'acqua un sapore terroso, aspro contro i denti, che Stefano godeva di piú dell'acqua e gli pareva il sapore stesso dell'anfora. C'era dentro qualcosa di caprigno, selvatico e insieme dolcissimo, che ricordava il colore dei gerani.[9]

([Stefano] felt alive and watchful, and sometimes he laid his hand on his hip. The girl's hips would be like that, slender yet strong. ... Stefano stroked the damp, slender side [of the pitcher] and, raising it from the ground, applied it to his lips. With the water came an earthy taste that felt harsh against his teeth; he enjoyed this more than the water; it seemed to be the taste of the vessel itself. It suggested something wild and goatlike yet smooth. It was all somehow mixed up in his mind with the colour of the geraniums.)[10]

He goes on, exaggerating the comparison (here emphasising the chromic resemblances) almost to the point of parodic excess: 'Anche la donna scalza, come tutto il paese, andava ad attinger acqua con un'anfora come quella. La portava poggiata oblique sul fianco, abbandonandosi sulle caviglie. Tutte queste anfore erano dolci e allungate, d'un colore tra il bruno e il carnicino, qualcuna piú pallida',[11] ('Like everyone else in the place, the barefoot girl went to draw water in a similar vessel. She walked along with the rim resting obliquely on her hip, putting her weight on her ankles. All these vessels were smooth and elongated in shape; their colour was midway between brown and flesh-pink, some were paler'.)[12]

We must read this virtual consumption/consummation alongside the disgust that prevents Stefano from a sexual encounter with Annetta (as well as the narrator's disgust, in *Terra d'esilio*, at the sight of two kids hanging disembowelled in a butcher's shop, which he must pass to reach the prostitute Concetta who is in residence there during her secret stay in town). For Gian-Paolo Biasin, this disgust 'teaches him renunciation'[13] but more than that, we would argue, the visceral response of disgust serves as a corporeal justification – another alibi – for the protagonist's existential policy of *noli me tangere*. It is as though Pavese's Stefano somatises the existential solitude of a (non-fictional, historical) prisoner. Both the fictional Stefano and many of the protagonists of the non-fiction texts we will examine describe confinement as the (often excruciating) vacillation between too much intimacy – whether with other prisoners or with the agents who keep them under surveillance – and too little (because the very objective of confinement is to isolate the prisoner from his or her family, friends, and political contacts). Stefano's relationship to Elena and his relationship *manqué* to Concia exemplify precisely this tension.

The contradictory impulses to flight and to intimacy evident in the doubled female foils are further bolstered, among the male characters, by the presence in *Il carcere* of a kind of *sosia* or double, Giannino. Though friendship is perhaps too strong a word to describe their fellowship, Giannino performs an important function in Stefano's psychic life. He serves as both a witness to Stefano's relationship with Elena and as a masculine presence capable of sharing and even, paradoxically, enhancing the isolation at once damaging and necessary to Stefano's well-being. After Giannino's arrest and Elena's estrangement, Stefano is alone. Refusal to meet the other political prisoners is not out of fear of the consequences (*confinati* in the interior were not permitted to have contact with each other) but stems rather from his fundamentally asocial nature. He is neither curious about the Anarchist prisoner nor sympathetic to his invitation to solidarity, however provisory.[14] In a similar vein, the obsessive thematic focus on the sea (evident, for example, in repeated references to its role as the fourth wall in his carceral landscape), to swimming, and to sunbathing, too, bring to the fore the two-pronged tensions between isolation and intimacy and within them, both their intentional and obligatory variants. Pavese's elegiac literature of reclusion is ultimately profoundly solipsistic. It is a novel of exile written by a real political prisoner who nonetheless writes as though confinement were merely a state of mind. At the same time, as we noted, he anticipates a tension that will structure many of the narratives written by actual prisoners, namely the tension between solitude and forced intimacy. In doing so, he draws our attention, through its negation, to one of the ironies of internal exile. A punishment intended to isolate prisoners from their network of contacts, it often produced the opposite effect, placing prisoners in politically promiscuous positions, as it were, such that they were able to create new alliances, temporary and contingent though they may be.

If Pavese drew on his personal experience to tell a story about exile as a state of mind, Carlo Lucarelli's *L'isola dell'angelo caduto* reduces the exile element even further, employing internal exile as an environmental expedient, as atmosphere in which to set his thriller. *L'isola dell'angelo caduto* tells the story of the discovery of a religious cult involved, depending on one's perspective, in either diabolic or Dionysian sexual rituals. The story is set in 1925 (and thus before the existence of internal exile of the sort that concerns us) on the Island of the Fallen Angel, notable mostly for its unusually strong and variable wind patterns. The penal colony, nicknamed Caienna,[15] holds an unspecified number of political prisoners, of which the most important is Doctor Valenza. Valenza and the *Commissario* team up to solve the mystery of three murders, which take place over the course of a few nights. Loosely connected to the religious cult, the murders turn out to be motivated by the pathological need of Fascist group leader Mazzarino to maintain command over the island and its prison by suppressing official orders to shut it down and to return all prisoners and personnel to the mainland. The murders take place in the very same days in which the *Commissario*, a northerner (reminiscent of Sciascia's Captain Bellodi of *Il giorno della civetta*), and his wife Hana (housebound because psychologically unstable) are informed that they are about to be transferred to a new post away from the island. The novel's moral conflict, then, is ostensibly whether the *Commissario* need remain on the island to solve the mysteries when an expeditious return to the mainland might save his wife, whose health is rapidly deteriorating.

The novel is founded on a series of shorthand references to real events and historical personages who are expected to provide enough narrative ballast to balance what is otherwise a series of cinemorphic visuals. For example, the prison, Caienna, is at once the nickname of a real prison in Sassari and the real name of the capital city (and formerly an island) of French Guiana, site of one infamous penal colony and close to another, on Devil's Island (to which the fallen angel in the island's name makes indirect reference). The frequent and assiduous references to the wind, similarly, recall descriptions of Ventotene. Aleister Crowley (1874–1947), occultist, mystic, and founder of Thelema Abbey in Cefalù, Sicily, is an absent presence and the two characters at the centre of the Dionysiac rituals – an Englishwoman and her husband, who is called the Englishman (though he is not English) – are former Thelemites, who arrive on the island after leaving the Abbey in 1923 (the year in which the historical Crowley was forced out of Italy). Other historical references are fudged, including the real date of the release of the song that obsesses Hana, and the chronology of the founding of the institution of internal confinement. A tautological *postilla* by the author is meant to justify these anachronisms: 'Del resto, l'isola in cui questo romanzo è ambientato non è un'isola come le altre, ha un realismo tutto suo, un po' magico e un po' diabolico, ed è talmente piena di strane licenze da poterne concedere qualcuna anche a me'[16] (Besides, the island on which this novel is set is not like other islands; it has a realism all its own, a bit magical and a bit diabolical, and it is so full of strange indulgences as to justify conceding me a few as well).

Lucarelli, playing fast and loose with historical data, underscores how different the role of internal exile is in his novel compared with the other we will encounter. Levi, Fiori, and even Pavese (though to a greatly limited extent) engage with the realities of *confino politico* even as they fictionalise them; confinement is the very fabric on which they embroider. Lucarelli, in contrast, uses the spatial configuration of confinement as a ready-made block with which to construct the scaffolding of a thriller narrative that could as easily be set in any quarantine situation, carceral or otherwise, or, say, a desert or jungle outpost during any war. In doing so, he identifies the contemporary narrative models that interest him, inserting his book in a genealogical line of works set in isolated cabins, on trains, on distant planets, and so on. Thus, the notion of the alibi so central to Pavese's works operates here, too. Where *Terra d'esilio* and *Il carcere* were concerned with confinement as an existential alibi, in *L'isola dell'angelo caduto* confinement is, instead, an alibi at the level of structure and of elective narrative affinity; it provides a setting that can be instrumentalised for purposes other than the exploration of confinement.

What's more, with Lucarelli, we come to understand the position of internal exile within the Italian popular historical narrative. Exile has entered into the public imagination to the extent that only a paragraph or two is necessary to remind the reader of the lay of the land, and indeed Lucarelli's foray into didacticism provides background information that is at once as factual and functional to the construction of the island setting as a world apart. As such, the novel is all the freer in its relations to the conventions of the genre, which it can adopt or disregard without remark. The fact that in 1999, internal exile could still function as a narrative expedient suggests that it continues to have meaning, though perhaps minimal, for Italian readers.

Bassani's short novel, *Gli occhiali d'oro* (*The Gold-rimmed Spectacles*, 1958) deploys confinement in order to examine the mechanisms of anti-Semitism as they emerge and become operative in 1930s Ferrara. Where in his *Il giardino dei Finzi-Contini* (*Garden of the Finzi-Continis*, 1962) mention of Alberto's homosexuality was limited to a passing reference to the art of Filippo De Pisis (referenced proleptically in *Gli occhiali d'oro* as well), here the sexual preferences of the elegant and humane physician (and wearer of the gold-rimmed spectacles) Athos Fadigati are at once widely acknowledged and generally tolerated so long as they are enacted discreetly and in a fashion consonant with class norms. Thus the first twelve chapters of the book deal with his initially successful acculturation and integration into the bourgeois society in Ferrara. But when he began openly to conduct a liaison with Eraldo Deliliers, notorious for his youth, athleticism (he was a champion at boxing, that most Fascist of sports), striking good looks and Fascist bona fides (his father was killed in action in 1918, leading a group of *Arditi*), public opinion turned against him. Important for this argument is precisely the timing of this shift, which takes place at the very moment when anti-Semitic sentiment enters public discourse in polite Ferrara society. The slippage between discourses of homophobia and anti-Semitism is marked by no other than the Duce himself, who appears on the beach at the very moment when Deliliers is expected to make his morning appearance, and thereby mortifying Fadigati, who had been labouring with some success to normalise relations with his neighbours on the beach. Mussolini's appearance causes the conversation to change course, so that the topic of racial discrimination follows directly after the homophobic insult directed at Fadigati. Soon thereafter, the novel loses track of Fadigati and focuses, instead, on events connected to the run-up to the Racial Laws of 1938. Eventually the two narratives of oppression converge, and another symbolic exchange takes place. Just as Athos Fadigati dies, a presumed suicide, in the very spot where he and the narrator were supposed to meet, it is learned that Mussolini does not intend to endorse the Racial Laws. (A further fold: in *Il giardino dei Finzi-Contini*, the narrator attributes Fadigati's suicide to an unhappy love affair, thereby depoliticising the death and declustering the two narratives of political persecution.) The temporary reprieve against anti-Semitism would seem, then, only to be possible through the suppression of homosexuality. It is not our contention that the novel celebrates this exchange in any way, shape, or form, but rather we note that its construction of homophobic bias is inseparably twinned with that of Fascist religious oppression and indeed serves as its narrative alibi.

Furthermore, for a novel ostensibly focused on a character who, historically, would have been a strong candidate for internal exile, there is only one mention of it, and it is used as a metaphor for isolation; Fadigati's disconsolate face has the look of a prisoner being transferred to Ponza or Tremiti 'per restarci chissà quanto'[17] (for who knows how long). The text recodes the political in intimate, psychological terms; no longer a historical fact, it is as though internal exile were a state of mind. Here as in the other texts mentioned above, where homosexuals go, other, ostensibly *more* oppressed subjects are sure to follow.

Forty-six years later, Giorgio Robiony and Rosaria Conte would achieve the same result precisely by representing, and not stifling, gay experiences in *confino*. Robiony and Conte's 2004 *Amori al confino*, set in the Tremiti Islands, recounts the experiences of a group of gay *confinati* ('femminielli' in the novel). It is told from the retrospective viewpoint of a journalist who has come to the islands to unravel the mystery of a sunken ship and the lethal hazing of a gay *confinato* by a group of island toughs with repressed homoerotic tendencies. The thematic questions addressed by the book have to do with gender identity and discrimination, as the *femminielli* move within and around the periphery of island culture, both that of the *confinati* and of the free inhabitants, and exhibit, alternately, interest in and aversion towards monogamy, hustling, and campy theatrical productions.

Here, the question of the alibi takes on several meanings. First, there is the question of truth-value. For in spite of the book's declaration that it is a novel, it gives the impression that it is a work of non-fiction, because of the non-fiction trappings with which it veils itself. Specifically, it contains many of the earmarks of journalistic or non-fictional writings of Nitti's and Lussu's books, lending the story an air of 'legitimacy' or truth-value, the label 'romanzo' notwithstanding. So, for example, the hub of the novel comprises the memories of a character named Trifone, a protagonist of the mystery that dates back to the *confino* years. But his recollections are framed by the story of a journalist named Yuri who goes to the Tremiti at the request of the *Arcigay*, for which he is a reporter. Yuri's story is a dispassionate description of trawling through archives, finding witnesses, conducting interviews, consulting history books, offering reportage-like descriptions of the luxurious landscape, and dropping the names of real historical personages.[18] This cool-headedness of Yuri's contributes much to the book's journalistic feel, and it is not by chance that Yuri is decidedly straight: his heterosexuality, we are led to believe, lends him greater 'objectivity' as he probes what he had initially dismissed as a 'gay' story, that is, one without broader human interest. Here we might recall the most famous literary namesake, Yuri Zhivago, protagonist of Boris Pasternak's 1957 novel, published first in Italy by Giangiacomo Feltrinelli. It is a name that invites us to inflect Robiony and Conte's character with the same qualities as Pasternak's: we are to understand our Yuri as a hybrid mix of poet and rationalist, with strong spiritual leanings and a political idealism that transcends the need for ideological conformity.

Eventually, Yuri discovers the solution to the enigmas he came to explore. He writes the exposé and submits it to *Arcigay* for publication, and in doing so, gives voice to people who had been stripped of the possibility of speaking of experiences long silenced. At the novel's conclusion, however, Yuri abandons journalism (along with life on the mainland) altogether, so that he can remain on the Tremiti with the beautiful female diver who had helped him puzzle out the mystery. Hence the second alibi: confinement, here, far from the logical setting in which to give voice to experiences otherwise unheard, is rather the setting in which to reassert normative behaviours and to cancel the traces of the past. The islands are safeguarded once again for *hetero*-sexual heroes: the documentary reverts to novel and the seas close back over the enigma of the other *confinati*, relegating them once again to silence. Robiony and Conte's analysis of *confino*, then, has not strayed too far from the path set by its illustrious predecessors. In spite of the in some ways groundbreaking contributions to *confino* studies made by this book, its adherence to the conventions of the *genre* established by its antecedents evacuate those contributions of their potential political force.

Here, then, is how we might articulate the move, performed around the traumatic node of Fascism and homosexuality, following Eric Santner's work on narrative fetishism.[19] The *Fascist* mandate was to isolate homosexuals and deny the existence of its practice(s) even as it poured money and manpower into suppressing them; the current cultural corollary is analogous – to marginalise and silence homosexuality at a *textual* level. Consider Millicent Marcus's concern with 'weak memory',[20] that is, with the idea that Italian films have 'failed to coalesce into a coherent, continuous cinematic tradition'[21] with respect to representing the experiences of Italian Jews during the *ventennio* (the twenty years of Fascist rule). This failure, though regrettable, does not necessarily follow the logic of narrative fetishism insofar as the experiences of Italian Jews under Fascism are represented at only a single remove, that is, are representations that evince a one-to-one correspondence with their objects, so that texts about Italian Jews under Fascism are effectively about Italian Jews under Fascism. This is, in other words, a case very different from that of homosexuality under Fascism because unlike the situation described by Marcus, here we can evoke an economy of narrative fetishisation. First, as we just saw in the discussion of genre, shifting readerly expectations about non-hetero-normative sexuality based on generic conventions means that discourses engaged at the level of content are evacuated of meaning at the level of structure or, if you prefer, the promise of a fungible cultural artefact is held out with one hand and disavowed with the other. And second is the question of removal or refraction – that is, the idea that a text that is only ostensibly about non-hetero-normativity-uses a surface engagement with non-hetero-normativity as an alibi or an instrument to reflect on other, perhaps larger instances of oppression or invisibility. Taken together, the trauma of Fascist oppression of homosexuality is subsumed under the narrative fetishist refusal to mourn (again following Santner), here evident in the deceptive emplotment of traumatic events, such as Yuri's abdication of a potential pluralist sexual-cultural norm in favour of a full and vigorous re-insertion into the hetero-normative economy. It is a narrative short circuit, that is, the fantasy of what Santner called a 'condition of intactness, typically by situating the site and origin of loss elsewhere'.[22]

What are the stakes? We are not arguing for Italian exceptionality; it is not our contention that this collective psychological sleight of hand is unique to the Italian corpus. Its motivations have to do with the historical moment in which much of this narrative was being written, as well as the question of who was doing the writing (for a long time, straight or apparently straight male historians in the 1950s). Nor can we fail to recognise the therapeutic potential of elisions that permit the recuperation of narrative pleasure, of the possibility of making present, after a long absence, a collective libidinal investment. Rather, the argument advanced here holds that both historically (that is, for the homosexual *confinati* depicted – or resolutely *not* depicted, if they are homosexual women) and historiographically (that is, in terms either of any attempt to trace genealogies by contemporary gay communities or to re-emplot the trauma precisely as trauma and thus to take cognisance of it), this adherence in recent works (like *Amori al confino*) to the conventions of genre established by their antecedents subverts their political aims to the point that they remain essentially gestures.

If the texts above have one common denominator, it is that they use confinement as an excuse to think about the Self. Natalia Ginzburg's 'Inverno in Abruzzo' and Carlo Levi's *Cristo si è fermato a Eboli*, in contrast, use confinement as a lens with which to investigate the Other. Unlike Pavese, Bassani, Lucarelli, and, to a lesser degree, Robiony and Conte, Ginzburg and Levi engage directly and consistently with the historical realities of confinement. Also unlike the first group of texts, which did not question their status as fiction and thus invoked unequivocal reading strategies, Ginzburg's and Levi's texts confound the distinction between fiction and non-fiction in complex ways, complicating our assumptions as readers about how to approach the information they contain. They do this, in part, through a series of references to a shared literary precedent, Ignazio Silone, that informs our readings, though in very different ways.

Natalia Ginzburg describes her experience in exile with her family in Pizzoli, Abruzzo from 1940 to 1943 in the short text, 'Inverno in Abruzzo' (in *Le piccole virtù*), written when she and her husband Leone Ginzburg returned to Rome in the fall of 1944. As much a meditation as an essay, the text begins with a line from Virgil's *Eclogues*: 'God has granted us this tranquillity'. There are two valences to this quotation. First, it is used, we assume, ironically to suggest that internal exile is a form of (compulsory) leisure, given, here, not by God but by the Fascist authorities. Second, it serves as an intertextual reference to Ignazio Silone's 1937 novel *Bread and Wine*, also set in Abruzzo and also the story of an anti-Fascist martyr. It is worth recalling that by the time of the composition of this text, Ginzburg and her family had returned to Rome, and her husband Leone had been imprisoned and killed soon thereafter. While it is not our contention that Ginzburg was drawing intentionally on any of the particulars of Silone's novel, the Virgil reference encourages reflection on the similarities between Ginzburg's experience and that of Silone's Don Benedetto (the anti-Fascist priest in whose mouth Silone places Virgil's words), and positions Ginzburg's husband Leone in the shared space of forced inactivity inhabited by Don Benedetto for the similarly perceived affronts to Fascism.

But though Silone's fiction is located in the same world as Ginzburg's and at roughly the same time, Silone's attitude towards his characters is distinctly different. Ginzburg's narrators, unlike Silone's, do not come from the world that they describe:

> 'Quando venni al paese di cui parlo, nei primi tempi tutti i volti mi parevano uguali, tutte le donne si rassomigliavano, ricche e povere, giovani e vecchie. [...] Ma poi a poco a poco cominciai a distinguere Vincenzina da Secondina, Annunziata da Addolorata'.[23]

> ('When I first arrived in that countryside all the faces looked the same to me, all the women – rich and poor, young and old – resembled one another. ... But then, gradually, I began to distinguish Vincenzina from Secondina, Annunziata from Addolorata').[24]

Ginzburg's naively ethnographic stance in these passages, visible in the tropes of the interchangeable, hard-working, impoverished, ignorant, gossiping, deeply Catholic southerner, suggests (like Pietro Spina's diary in *Vino e pane*) that foundational to the experience of exile is the encounter with another, previously unknown, Italy. She also anticipates Carlo Levi's much lengthier descriptions in *Cristo si è fermato a Eboli*, which he began to write just a few months after Ginzburg. Exile, *c'est l'autre*: both of these texts are as much about alterity as they are about internal exile. And this, of course, is the point of internal exile: the prisoner is sent away to be a stranger among his or her own people.

Like in her *Lessico famigliare* (1963), Ginzburg herself is largely absent from these pages. And as in that book, here, too, the emotional heart of the text is presented in an almost throwaway fashion, when she makes fleeting reference to her husband's death only in the abrupt shift in tone that characterises the last paragraph of the text. After a meditation on the immutability of the human condition, the last paragraph begins not with the theme of stasis and permanence, but with a unique and very specific historical datum, namely the death of her husband in a Roman prison a few months after being released from exile.[25] Thus at the end of the text, we are at once confirmed in our suspicion that the epigraph does indeed refer to Leone and not to the author, and we are forced to reassess its meaning. Where initially the assertion that 'God has given us this tranquillity' appeared to be ironic, the final paragraph of her text replaces that irony with elegy, when, with the wisdom of hindsight, she calls her life in exile the best time of her life.[26] As we will see, the recognition that the period spent in exile was the happiest of her life will become a key trope in many of the texts under examination here, though they are usually written with the fuzzy vision of distance rather than the acute vision of a recent experience. But in either case, there are considerations of class at stake in what would on the surface appear to be a statement free of similar concerns. That those for whom the memory of confinement evokes feelings of nostalgia and longing are generally the authors of our memoirs is not surprising; these are prisoners for whom, as we saw with Pavese's texts, internal exile is as much an existential state as a political one. Besides its comfortable insertion in a genealogy of writers like Verga, Silone, and Levi, Ginzburg's text reminds us that there is a certain kind of memoir of exile that is rarely written, that is, the kind that would be authored by those for whom existential questions were preceded by practical ones of survival.

Carlo Levi, sent into exile in Lucania (Basilicata) in 1935–36 for participating in the foundation of the *Giustizia e Libertà* movement, wrote *Cristo si è fermato a Eboli* between December 1943 and July 1944; the book was published in 1945. From the very first paragraph emerge many of the questions about genre and truth claims that have vexed the reception of this book, commonly viewed as a form of testimony as much as it is a work of literature. On the surface, the opening lines of the book would appear to be concerned primarily with an evocative introduction to the people and places first of Grassano, then of the much smaller Aliano (which he calls Gagliano) and to the latter's unchanging, eternally static nature (a trope in much of the literature written about southern Italy in the long decade after the war):

> [C]hiuso in una stanza, e in un mondo chiuso, mi è grato riandare con la memoria a quell'altro mondo, serrato nel dolore e negli usi, negato alla Storia e allo Stato, eternamente paziente; a quella mia terra senza conforto e dolcezza, dove il contadino vive, nella miseria e nella lontananza, la sua immobile civiltà, su un suolo arido, nella presenza della morte.[27]

> ([C]losed in one room, in a world apart, I am glad to travel in my memory to that other world, hedged in by custom and sorrow, cut off from History and the State, eternally patient; to that land without comfort or solace, where the peasant lives out his motionless civilization on barren ground in remote poverty, and in the presence of death.)[28]

The key concepts in this passage would seem to have to do with suffering: the suffering of poverty, of hopelessness, of historical irrelevance, here further weighted with the blank forever of the future. Of greater interest here, however, is the centrality of references to the passage of time, and to the role of personal memory in the re-evocation of the *confino* experience. It is difficult not to identify within these lines a set of instructions for reading. These memories are written almost ten years after the events they depict. What's more, they are the memories of a subject whose self-positioning first evokes the literary precedent *per eccellenza* of the father of Italian *verismo*, Giovanni Verga. Levi's and Verga's respective uses of the framing device of the narrator who, from his comfortable metaphorical armchair, is able to conjure up the hardships of others as he observed and/or imagined them (think of Verga's 'L'amante di Gramigna' from *La vita dei campi*) suggest more than simply a shared interest in the object of enquiry – southern poverty – their works examine. The invocation of a Verghian stance carries within it implications for the claims of truth-value or testimony that the literary form of the texts seems to espouse. By that, we mean that when we read Levi's self-description as one who remembers the past, 'closed in one room, in a world apart' alongside similar declarations of Verga's poetics, we must also recall the Verghian paradox of literature whose declarations of literariness are frequently disregarded by a reading public that would prefer to endow it with a documentarist freight not easily compatible with the label of fiction.

In addition to Verga, there are numerous other explicit literary references. Chaucer, Stendhal, Dante, D'Annunzio, Victor Hugo, Vittorio Alfieri, and Virgil all make appearances. And yet the point of these references is greater than the sum of their parts. Beyond the information they convey in short hand (so that our presumed familiarity, say, with Julien Sorel, obviates the need for Levi to elaborate on his own position), their quantity alone underscores the distance between the reader and the narrator on the one hand and, on the other, the narrated world, so great that to fathom it requires the support of a separate discursive regime. The material fulcrum of this symbolic distance is in the contrast between the reader's location in a neutral, natural Elsewhere north of here: 'Le cose, quaggiú, sono assai piú complicate di quello che non appaiono alle chiare menti degli uomini giusti e buoni' (Levi, 1990: 79). ('Things in this part of the world are a good deal more complex than they appear to the clear-thinking mind of a good man or woman') (Levi, 1947: 90). The result, like in Ginzburg, is an explicit sense of us and them, that is, of the shared culture of his readers and the alterity of 'his' peasants; even their language, they say, is incomprehensible. Similarly, the early introduction of supernatural presences and romanticising tones (brigands; a band of dead musicians who play at midnight), underscore the narrator's position. Levi's sentence structure, too, aims at certain rhetorical targets, often employing a series of subordinate clauses in quick succession, like a cinematic montage. The text, in other words, supports at a linguistic level the assertions made explicit by the author both in the opening paragraph cited above and in his 1963 premise about immobility. Once the initial flurry of activity surrounding his arrival has subsided, the silence, solitude, and stasis of the 'world ... cut off from History and the State' re-emerges. To consolidate the notion, Levi employs the image of the doorways of almost all of the houses draped in black fabric in various states of decomposition; in a place outside of time, it is fitting that perpetual mourning be observed.

Mostly, though, Levi borrows from Silone: both the Silone of *Fontamara* (written in 1930, published in 1933) and of *Vino e pane* (*Bread and Wine* 1936–37) are very much in evidence. A passage that concludes with the observation that peasants don't sing replicates an identical assertion in Silone's *Fontamara*.[29] Levi depicts a Fascist demonstration in a piazza in the same terms as Silone's peasants in *Vino e pane*, incomprehensible to the locals for whom politics and politicians are analogous to bad weather, earthquakes, and other similar phenomena: they are unfathomable and impervious to outside influence. The story of the Agri river is a variation of the story the Fontamaresi tell about the Torlonia family and their control of the water (Levi, 1990: 97–8). Images of the Madonna and Roosevelt that adorn the walls of the houses recall *Vino e pane*'s juxtaposition of Jesus and Marx. Levi and Silone both attribute to the peasants the imputation of nonhumanity; Levi's nonhumanity ('we are not Christians') finds discursive equivalence in Silone's *Fontamara*, which dehumanises the peasants by placing them at the very bottom of the scale, two steps lower than the prince's guards' dogs. But unlike Silone, whose narrative voice positions itself in sympathetic parity with the protagonists of its story (and indeed *Fontamara* valorises the peasant perspective by allowing a family of contadini to recount the story, rather than be recounted by others), Levi's 'I', as we saw, eschews subaltern ethnographic enfranchisement in order to maintain a vertical gaze (reaffirmed in the letter to the editor with which the reprint begins), that, while sympathetic, makes visible the distance that separates it from its object.

More broadly, Levi's consistent focus on his surroundings, on the people and places of his exile and not necessarily on his experiences of it (outside of his role as observer) sets the terms for what will become seminal representations – almost standards or set pieces – of *l'arretratezza meridionale* (southern backwardness). He speaks of the centuries-old immobility of the peasant world (Levi, 1990: xviii); a centuries-old boredom (Levi, 1990: 7); ceaseless hate and ancient struggle (Levi, 1990: 20); unchanging landscape (Levi, 1990: 26); soporific patience of peasant culture (Levi, 1990: 124); monotony and hopelessness (Levi, 1990: 54); and so on. Even D'Annunzio's *Fiaccola sotto il moggio*, performed in Grassano by a travelling troupe, represents a timeless world full of passions held in eternal check (Levi, 1990: 161).

Eventually, the narrator, too, enacts the immobility of the town and of the region, when during the hottest afternoons, he takes refuge for hours at a time in an empty grave in the cemetery: the site of timeless immobility *par excellence* (Levi, 1990: 58–9). From the grave, he hears a voice of an ancient peasant following a train of thought that seems to emerge from the 'indeterminata antichità di un mondo animalesco' (Levi, 1990: 60) (shadowy, remote reaches of a primitive world) (Levi, 1947: 67). Indeed, the entire town is literally built on the bones of the dead, making it essentially an extension of the cemetery.

Then there is the question of structure. Silone's texts are built around a series of events embedded in a linear, chronological narrative where Levi's, in contrast, though very roughly chronological, moves not causally from one event to its consequence but instead from relatively unrelated episode to episode. Consonant with the ethnographic model continually recalled through the narrator's detached, objective observations, the book is organised around a series of spectacles whose narrative importance lies in their visual effects. The performance of the *Fiaccola sotto il moggio* in this sense acts as a kind of allegory of interpretation (borrowing the term from Millicent Marcus[30]), providing instructions on the proper hermeneutical strategy to implement. The theatrical performance by D'Annunzio's highly stylised, über-literate peasant characters and the ineluctable influence of magic, superstition and ritual on their closely intertwined destinies offers a model with which to grasp the *gaglianesi's* equally predetermined fates, and their own perpetual staging of the inescapability of their collective destiny. From the performance of the cupi-cupi (friction drum) and the bagpipe-driven dance of seduction to the drunken priest's highly theatrical Christmas mass, from the donning of the carnival masks to the highly self-conscious performance of mourning by the female relatives of the dead man, theatrical performance is crucial to Levi's political project.

Consider, too, the genre of Levi's narrative. Just as *Bread and Wine's* Pietro Spina was both hounded and revered by the peasants who desperately wanted him to perform the offices of his alter ego, the priest Paolo Spada, so Levi's narrator encounters groups of villagers desperate for his medical expertise and prepared to sit outside his door for whatever length necessary in order to be seen by him. Starting in the course of the first afternoon in the new town (the book opens with the narrator's move from Grassano to Gagliano), a group of locals appears on his landlady's doorstep and humbly requests that Levi, whom they know to be trained in medicine, tend to their sick, thus introducing the text's second major narrative thread alongside the immobility of the peasant world: Levi's role as its saviour. Though Levi never exalts his abilities as a healer (his first 'patient' dies almost immediately upon Levi's arrival at his bedside), he is, nonetheless, hailed as a hero as the literal embodiment of a northernist rational, scientific humanism in stark contradistinction to the irrational, superstitious brutishness with which the text characterises the *gaglianesi*. Thus, his confinement is equal parts ethnography, denunciation, and hero's journey (à la Joseph Campbell), taking him 'into a region of supernatural wonder: fabulous forces are there encountered and a decisive victory is won: the hero comes back from this mysterious adventure with the power to bestow boons on his fellow man'.[31] Indeed, it is his scientific rationalism that permits him to brave the risk of love philtres which, far from harming him, 'mi hanno … aiutato a penetrare in quel mondo chiuso, velato di veli neri, sanguigno e terrestre, nell'altro mondo dei contadini, dove non si entra senza una chiave di magía' (Levi, 1990: 14) (helped me to penetrate that closed world, shrouded in black veils, bloody and earthy, that other world where the peasants live and which no one can enter without a magic key) (Levi, 1947: 15).

The Silone model and the performance model merge with the hero narrative near the end of the book, when the narrator inadvertently ignites a spark of political awareness after a patient dies because legal wrangling prevented the doctor from arriving in time to save him. The theatrical performance of the peasants centred on Levi's white doctor's coat marks the finale of the hero's travails, with the last minute introduction and successful cure of the *podestà's* small daughter as a kind of diminutive *deus ex machina* whose arrival changes the course of the future (in this case, softening the authorities' attitude and changing the rules so that Levi can tend patients without threat of punishment).

A major structural deviation occurs midway through the text, when Levi's sister arrives. This chapter constitutes a kind of parenthesis in the text, and affords Levi the opportunity to break away from the present of his narration and to return, whether in memory or as embodied by his sister, Luisa, to another place and time. We also hear another voice – Luisa's – in a kind of echo of Levi's own. Luisa can say things about the area that he cannot; she can express an elegantly scandalised northerner's perspective upon seeing the south for the first time, from revulsion at the dirt, poverty, lack of education, civic values, and hygiene to inedible cuisine (Levi, 1990: 73–7). A lengthy uninterrupted monologue describing her descent down spiralling mule tracks in Matera (a description whose poetics anticipate the photographs of interiors that document Ernesto De Martino's work in Lucania in the 1950s) is even likened to Dante's inferno (Levi, 1990: 75). The parenthesis of Luisa's visit, like Pietro Spina's return to Pietrasecca (as well as the mise-en-abyme constituted by the journal in which he records his observations) creates a space for critique from the margins – within the community but not a part of it. Pietro Spina and Luisa Levi are both, in a sense, self-imposed exiles in an*other* Italy. Educated, literate, skilled and dispassionate observers, they bring to *Cristo si è fermato a Eboli* a further gloss on the question of genre and truth claims. The highly constructed literary self-consciousness of the text's bifocal referentiality – using both ethnography and high literature as cognitive tools – finds its apotheosis in the Luisa chapter and, more broadly, in the many references to Silone, which both consolidates the book's ideological content even as it acknowledges its own construction.

## Foundational texts

Though the previous section focused on fictional works and this section is dedicated to non-fiction, the elements of fiction remain central. In fact, it is a peculiarity of non-fictional memoirs of internal exile that they read like popular fiction, in particular the adventure tale, the rocamboleque or *roman-feuilleton*, and the thriller. The authors of the texts that follow – Lussu's *La catena*, Nitti's *Le nostre prigioni e la nostra evasione*, Rosselli's *Fuga in quattro tempi*, and Magri's *Una vita per la libertà* – share a tendency to present themselves as swashbuckling heroes whose physical prowess – whether exceptional like Magri's or dubious like Rosselli's – played a central role in their exile experience. These authors present their political activities as action-oriented rather than thought-based, and evince a strongly authoritative narrative style that suggests that at any given moment it was they, not their captors, who had the upper hand. Put differently, as ground zero for the genre of the internal exile memoir, these texts consolidate and affirm the way writing recuperates the agency and activity deprived by imprisonment.

The assumption of an action hero persona (or any other persona) serves to reassert experiential control through its rendering in narrative.

Emilio Lussu's *La catena* was first published in 1930, with the first Italian version in 1945. Lussu, who arrived on Lipari in November of 1927, begins by devoting two chapters to the events leading up to the creation and implementation of the penalty of *confino*, as well as the various forms of punishment. He also gives a brief history of his own peregrinations within and outside the Fascist legal system subsequent to the implementation of the *Leggi eccezionali* in 1926. His description of Lipari is instructive, often amusing, and the island sounds like the site of historical derring-dos and swashbuckling adventures. Lussu uses the expression 'piccole vessazioni' (little vexations) to describe the day-to-day difficulties of life on Lipari, which seems to consist in large part of walks, books (there was a library for the prisoners, as there was on Ventotene), and conversations with a select group of the 500-plus *confinati*.[32]

This book presents itself as discursive non-fiction. There are frequent moments of metawriting, the effect of which is a certain unstudied or conversational tone. More than that, the tantalising prolepses of the real adventure of the story, namely Lussu's escape from the island, along with Carlo Rosselli and Francesco Fausto Nitti on 27 July 1929, serve to heighten the book's writerly qualities: 'Il giovane lettore, che s'interessi di avventure romanzesche, ha probabilmente saltato le pagine sul Tribunale Speciale, e attende la fuga. Mi perdoni se ne limito il racconto a pochi episodi' (Lussu, 1997: 73). (The young reader, who is interested in adventures, has probably skipped the pages on the Special Tribunal. Forgive me if I limit the story to a few events.)

Note here that Lussu, who seems not to be writing a text that has novelistic aspirations, nonetheless borrows from the novel's kitbag (with the added effect of changing the valence of the metawriting). He addresses his readers as novel readers, and apologises for deviating from novel form – the opposite of what we saw with Robiony and Conte, who structured what is undeniably a *novel* with the scaffolding of *non-fiction*. Capitalising on the international fascination with his escape, along with Nitti and Rosselli, from Lipari, *La catena* deftly historicises the events that led to his confinement, placing them within the broader Italian context and thus shifting the focus from the drama of his personal story, the better to underscore the severity and violence with which Fascism oppressed its opponents. Lussu has a keen eye for detail (and for humour, particularly the absurd, like when he claims Mussolini's cabinet meeting could take place in a phone booth since the Duce himself led most of the ministries), and his description of the assault on his home anticipates the cinemorphic thrill of his battle descriptions in *Un anno sull'Altipiano* (written 1936–37) the book that would follow *La catena*.

Lussu's description of the actual escape from Lipari, in contrast, is a model of telegraphic synthesis, perhaps because the details of the escape had already circulated widely in the international press, to the extent that the English novelist H. G. Wells welcomed Rosselli, Nitti, and Lussu in his Parisian home with the festive spirit of a novelist who wants to greet 'una squadra di pirati a reputazione ben consolidata' (Lussu, 1997: 7) (a band of pirates with a solid reputation):

> Il mare era calmissimo. Ad una tratto, appena percettibile, il palpito di un motore. Un motoscafo si avvicinò. Il segnale era il nostro. Caio era sulla prua. Non una parola all'incontro. Uno dopo l'altro, passammo a bordo. La prua virò rapida in un cerchio strettissimo. E poi, via, per il libero spazio del mare, seguendo la rotta tracciata. (Lussu, 1997: 78)

> (The sea was very calm. Suddenly, barely audible, the pulse of a motor. A motorboat approached. It was our signal. Caio was at the prow. Not a word when we met. One after another we climbed aboard. The bow turned quickly in a very tight circle. And then, away, for the open sea, following the route laid out.)

More than the actual description of the escape, it is the anticipation of its recounting that drives the narrative engine to its political-activist destination: a move that evinces Lussu's rhetorical acumen. Readers who came for the adventure, stayed for the ethics. Lussu's book ends with a theoretical meditation on the need for the *Leggi eccezionali* to change; and it is here, perhaps, that we catch a glimpse of the stakes behind the swashbuckling. Rather than foreground his own thoughts and actions, much of *La catena*'s ethical force emerges through its emphasis on the history of Fascism's moral outrage in the clearest, most unambiguous terms possible.

Francesco Fausto Nitti's tale of exile and escape comes in two forms. The English language version of his book, *Escape: The Personal Narrative of a Political Prisoner Who Was Rescued from Lipari, the Fascist Devil's Island*, which was written in 1929 and published in 1930, and the Italian version, *Le nostre prigioni e la nostra evasione*, released in 1946, evince striking dissimilarities.

The preface to the English version was written by the author's uncle, the former Prime Minister Francesco Saverio Nitti. In it, Saverio Nitti identifies his nephew and fellow escapees Lussu and Rosselli as the products of a marriage of faith (though each with different roots) and of a long tradition of democracy:

> All religions have the same ideal base; all express the same need of elevation to God. All, when they are practised with sincerity, develop the spirit of sacrifice. Lussu belongs to a Catholic family; Nitti is the son of a parson of a Protestant-Methodist family; Rosselli is of a Jewish family.
>
> In the Nitti family the love of liberty and democracy has resisted all persecutions; the great-grandfather of the writer of this book was murdered in a reactionary movement the grandfather was condemned to death in 1848; the father has for thirty years preached the gospel of Christ among the Italian folk poisoned by clericalism. The Rosselli family is rich and respected and has a great democratic tradition. The greatest idealist and thinker of modern Italy, Giuseppe Mazzini, died in the Rosselli house.

> The three young men condemned to imprisonment on the island of Lipari represent therefore the flower of a healthy middle-class educated to reverence, respect and love, the greatest ideals.[33]

No radicals these, but God-fearing political moderates. The English language preface reveals the rhetorical stakes of the text, its project of persuasion. It is perhaps also for this reason that the English version of the book begins like a thriller: 'A man crept stealthily along the narrow jetty that ran out into the sea on the darkest side of the little harbor' (Nitti, 1930: 3). The book adheres to the conventions of literary fiction, referring to the protagonist in the third person, and recounting dialogue that Nitti cannot have heard and that serves to convey the background information necessary for understanding the 'true story of [the] adventures' (Nitti, 1930: 14) that follow. It also closely follows the *confino* memoir model, including the story of his arrest and imprisonment in Regina Coeli and the requisite description of the voyage to Lampedusa, where he has been sentenced to five years' confinement: the rough waters, seasickness, the physical pain of the chains that bind him to the other passengers, the seemingly endless voyage, and acute thirst.

Eventually transferred from Lampedusa to Lipari, Nitti stays true to form:

> Lipari is the largest of the Aeolian Islands. It is about thirty miles in circuit and rises in two prominent volcanic peaks (Monte Chirica and Monte Sant'Angelo) to an altitude of nearly two thousand feet. Hot springs indicate its volcanic origin, and its most important exports are pumice and sulphur. It has about thirteen thousand inhabitants. Among the seven other islands of the group, Vulcano and Stromboli have active volcanoes. (Nitti, 1930: 142)

The geography lesson will become a common element in the majority of the memoirs of internal exile, along with remarks about the regulations, schedules, absurdity of some of the rules, the insufficiency of the small financial subsidies doled out by the government, and the impossibility of finding work. But with the appearance of Lieutenant Francesco Veronica, the book reverts from memoir (whose narrative events are organised by linear chronology) to the realm of popular fiction (organised by cause and effect). Veronica is painted in garish colours. Fiendishly sadistic and shrilly hysterical by turns, he screams orders at high volume like a cartoon madman. Veronica is replaced by the equally risible, but considerably less violent, General Maggiotto, who voices what would become one of the most problematic of the tropes with which the practice of internal exile was described, when he says to the prisoners, 'We are not afraid of you. We are giving you a little vacation here in order that you may come to your senses' (Nitti, 1930: 135). By the following March (1927), the penal colony at Lampedusa had been dissolved and the deportees redistributed among the other islands.

Nitti's tale is low on rhetoric and high on action. The climax of the story is, of course, the successful escape of Nitti, Lussu, and Rosselli. The description of their attempts is told in an entirely different voice from the one with which the book opened. Here, the facts are recounted in the past tense, with very little drama, in chronological order (and not, in other words, with the confounding of story and discourse more typical of the genre of the thriller). What is important here is the way this text serves to establish what will become the standard tropes of the *confino* memoir, including the validity of mixing genres that we observed in Lussu and will see in Jacometti. Part didactic essay, part adventure story, and part personal musing, Nitti and Lussu (especially the Lussu of *La marcia su Roma e dintorni*) marshal their very distinct and personal narrative voices to lend credibility and readability to their tales. Though Nitti divides these tropes over two periods in the book, corresponding to his arrival on the two respective islands, the elements are all in place.

In contrast, the greatly amplified Italian version, which claims to complete the story he started in 1929, evinces stylistic choices quite distinct, at points, from the English version. First, the preface by Francesco Saverio Nitti, which in the 1929 version read, 'Few adventure books are as interesting as this one' (Nitti, 1930: iii), has been altered to begin: 'Questo libro, interessante come un romanzo di avventure e preciso come una cronaca, è la narrazione semplice e vera e senza alcuna pretesa letteraria, di uno degli episodi più temerari compiuti da tre giovani antifascisti ardimentosi durante la tirannia fascista',[34] (This book, as interesting as an adventure novel and as exact as a chronicle, is the simple and truthful story, with no literary pretenses, of one of the most fearless episodes to occur under Fascist tyranny, achieved by three bold young anti-Fascists).

Such an alteration confirms our observation above that the rhetorical success of the adventure or rocambolesque *confino* memoir depends on its admixture of familiar literary qualities (what could be more accessible than an adventure story) and truth claims, both explicit and implicit. Writing about the escape, the author himself confirms this as well when he compares his adventure to those described in his childhood readings (Nitti, 1946: 13). Also new to this edition is a lengthy paragraph on the illustrious Nitti family, including several pages about Francesco Saverio Nitti, giving the sense that this is a story whose success depends not on the collective efforts of the three protagonists, as was the case with the English version and with Lussu's *La catena*, but rather rests heavily on the shoulders of the Nittis as bulwarks of the Italian democratic tradition. This reduction (from three to one) and refocalisation of the protagonists, taken together with the text's repeated reminders that it is to be approached in the spirit of a novel, suggests a high degree of self-consciousness on the part of the author.

We are moving, in other words, towards a conception of the genre as acutely aware that if the bet is political, the stakes are literary. Consider the punning title of Carlo Rosselli's *Fuga in quattro tempi* (1931) (*fuga* means both musical fugue and flight). Much briefer than Lussu's or Nitti's, the text is divided thus: the 'primo tempo' (first phase or first movement, depending on the meaning of *fuga*) takes place at the transit depot at the Palermo prison; the 'secondo tempo' describes meeting Gioacchino Dolci, Paolo Fabbri, and Lussu on Lipari; the 'terzo tempo' recounts a failed attempt by Nitti, Lussu and Rosselli to flee; and the 'quarto tempo', their successful escape. Told in a style that oscillates between the tele-graphic and the cinemorphic, and unencumbered by political, ideological, social or ethical reflections, the focus on the derring-do of the threesome comes more sharply into focus.

Alberto Jacometti's *Ventotene* was written in August–September of 1943, a few weeks after his return from his exile on that island (1941–August 1943). Though Jacometti's *Ventotene* shares with Lussu's *La catena* a similar general reluctance to exalt the author's own activities in favour of a more broadly impersonal focus, the similiarities more or less stop there. Where Lussu begins with the national events that led to the creation of the *Leggi eccezionali*, Jacometti opens with a lengthy, poetically ambitious excursus on the varieties of birdsong: 'Sono note. Sono colori. Sono la stoffa stessa del giorno',[35] (They are notes. They are colours. They are the very stuff of day).

The passage continues for another page, a rhetorical strategy with which to contrast the 'festa dei suoni' (festival of sounds; Jacometti, 2004: 12); the sub-sequent (hetero-) sexualisation of the nature that surrounds him as he writes ('Vien voglia di rotolarsi nel fieno, di toccare, mordere e succhiare' (Jacometti, 2004: 13) – One feels the urge to roll in the hay, to touch, bite, and suck); and, finally, the gendering and sexual possession of his new life of freedom ('la vita tutta mi sta davanti. Vergine. Io posso abbracciarla. Io posso conquistarla. … Entrerò in lei, mi rotolerò con lei, lotteremo … Mi tenta e per tentarmi mi s'offre' (Jacometti, 2004: 13) – all my life stands before me. Virgin. I can embrace it. I can conquer it. I will enter it, roll around with it, we will struggle … It tempts me and to do so it offers itself). Jacometti's narration is at once much more studied and heavy handed in its literary aspirations (alongside the coitus with nature described above, synesthesia abounds, as do apostrophe, rhetorical flourish, and *recherché* poetic references) and, initially, considerably more self-referential in its positioning of the narrative I at the centre of the narration, so that although he himself is rarely placed directly under scrutiny, the narrating voice is aligned with the reader ('In fondo al piazzale, a sinistra, c'è una larga scala di mattoni: saliamola' (Jacometti, 2004: 20) – at the end of the square, to the left, there's a wide brick staircase: let's climb it; 'avviciniamoci di più' (Jacometti, 2004: 31) – let's get closer; 'In una parete si aprono due porte eguali. Spingiamone una' (Jacometti, 2004: 65) – In one of the walls, there are two identical doors. Let's open one), his personal optic, and the literary aspirations with which it is represented, never move out of focus.

The exuberant tone somewhat diminishes in the second chapter, which serves as a traveller's guide to the island (its history, starting from antiquity, its illus-trious visitors, geography and climate). The remainder of the volume balances the whimsy we noted above with a predilection for the quantitative befitting the book's didactic impulses, such as when he outlines the dimensions and qualities of the barracks in minute detail.[36]

He is equally precise in the articulation of political clout among the prisoners. The Communists, for example, are far and away the most powerful: a function of numbers of adherents but also of organisational efficacy. The Socialists, he claims, are fewer but held in higher regard for their seriousness (Jacometti was a Socialist) as well as for the presence of Sandro Pertini. There is lengthy excursus on the origins and practice of individual surveillance. But all in all, for Jacometti, the island of Ventotene emerges as an interesting object of enquiry for this curious observer (he notes, among other things, that the island is fertile and garden-like in the spring, especially when the broom flowers blossom, and that the women are perpetually pregnant). He describes the *confinati*'s activities, which are primarily intellectual – reading (up to nine hours a day), writing, engaging in political discussions, sunbathing, and swimming.[37] There is also some discussion of hunger, especially during the winter of 1941–42, but once the *confinati* are allowed to garden, they manage better, either by eating what they grow, selling it or bartering it. In short, what he is describing is a full life better characterised by irritations than by hardships; and indeed, one of the book's chapters is entitled 'Piccole vessazioni, piccole angherie, dispettucci e brutalità'. He patiently explains the disappearance of sexual desires as a function of the absence of propitious circumstances (Jacometti's account differs from nearly everyone else's on this count). Bedbugs, flies, mosquitoes, and fleas (the title of another chapter) abound. The chief complaints, however, are lack of privacy – something he compares to marriage[38] – and the arbitrariness with which the many (often apparently contradictory) rules are enforced. A gallery of sketches of some of his most prominent fellow *confinati* is at once bemused and full of admiration.

It is here, embedded in these attempts at drollery, that we get a sense of the emotional heart of the text. The real problem is forced passivity – having to sit out the war ('Altrove c'è la guerra. Qui si studia. Attendendo'. (Jacometti, 2004: 59) – Elsewhere there is the war. Here, we study. Waiting). And to the extent that we take that lament seriously, we must understand the otherwise generally bemused tone of the book not as an act of bravado but as a form of apology. Jacometti's text ends not with the urgent appeal to political action with which Lussu's ends, but with a long description of 23–25 July 1943, the events of the following three weeks (especially the loosening of restrictions on prisoner activities) and, eventually, the return by boat to the mainland. As one of the earliest confinement memoirs, it lays the groundwork for the tropes and commonplaces of the genre that will follow. Its hyperbolic literary pretensions, exaggerated performance of masculinity, hyperheteronormativity, ethnographic impulse, and classism place it in a productive dialogue with Lussu's, Rosselli's, and Nitti's books for the ways it provides the details, facts, and figures that were only broadly sketched in *La catena, Le nostre prigioni e la nostra evasione,* and *Fuga in quattro tempi.*

By these lights, also significant is Mario Magri's *Una vita per la libertà: diciassette anni di confino politico di un Martire delle Fosse Ardeatine,* written at Pescopagano (Basilicata) between September 1942 and August 1943, at the tail end of no fewer than seventeen years of prison and confinement. Less renowned for any particular ideological conviction (he's a democrat[39]) than for his boxing skills (he

created a gymnasium on Lipari in which prisoners and their children could prac-
tise sports[40]), his repeated sentences were due to his role as D'Annunzio's *aiutante di campo* during the events of Fiume, which rendered Magri embarrassing, if not dangerous, to the Regime.

His memoir begins with his arrest in Milan in November 1926, and the requisite descriptions of life in prison, the voyage to Lipari (handcuffs, train journey, being chained to the other prisoners; seasickness on the crossing), the island's beauty, swimming and sunbathing. But the real focus of the book, as were the cases of Rosselli and Nitti (and to a slightly lesser extent, Lussu), are Magri's two escape attempts. The book consists of a series of flights, fights, cos-tume changes, and coincidences, and thus cleaves closely to the conventions of the *roman-feuilleton* and does not reveal the high-literary aspirations of, say, Rosselli. Every bit as daring (and then some) as Lussu, Rosselli and Nitti's escape from Lipari, Magri had nothing close to the material resources that Rosselli made available to his companions; he relied, instead, on his own physical strength and on the hope that he could manoeuvre his past association with D'Annunzio into protection in his moment of need.

His escape attempts are often mentioned in passing in other confinement memoirs, frequently as the lamentable failures that delayed and complicated the departure of Rosselli and company. The first attempt took place in 1927, when he acquired a fake identity card and enough of another prisoner's phlegm to be able successfully to fake tuberculosis and thus return to the mainland for medical care. At Potenza, during a transfer, he took a hotel room, shaved, and changed into a suit. Thus attired, he was able to pass unnoticed and continue as far as Benevento, where another prisoner identified him. To his great displeasure, Magri claimed (falsely) that he had been released as the result of a change of political heart. He travelled to Bolzano, where he discovered that the contrabanders' trails he had intended to follow were hidden under snow; he pushed on instead to Fiume where, having purchased a mechanic's jumpsuit, he hoped to pass as a day worker. Waiting in another hotel room, however, he was spotted and arrested. Despite successfully fending off no fewer than four policemen (recall that Magri was an expert boxer), he was imprisoned though, to his great fortune, a former Fiume expeditioner recognised him and thus ensured decent treatment. He was tried and returned to Lipari.

By mid-1928, however, he had already plotted his second escape attempt. Imprisoned for resisting solitary confinement after refusing, along with other prisoners, to comply with a new rule that made it possible for prisoners to be restricted to quarters without justification, Magri and his cellmate cut through the bars of their cell with a file and broke out late one night. They changed into clothes left outside the prison wall by an accomplice: Magri as a woman, his cellmate as a priest. The plan was to join two others (dressed as local peasants) and run to a motorboat that awaited them, boxing their way out if necessary. When the four fugitives encountered two policemen, however, the peasants fled, leaving the priest and the woman to chat with the policemen and then, eventually, to spend an unsuccessful night looking for their co-conspirators. When faced with the choice of being discovered by either by the *Carabinieri* or the militia, they gave themselves up to the former, in hopes of better treatment.

They returned to prison. Over time, sentences were piled upon sentences: six sentences to confinement (spanning one to five years in length), and three years' incarceration, making seventeen years of persecution in all. Magri left Lipari for Ponza, where he spent 1932, then bounced back to Lipari, San Domino (he describes it as desolate and treeless), Cirò (in the province of Catanzaro, green and fertile), Petronà (full of wolves), and, finally, Pescopagano (province of Potenza). After the events of 25 July 1943, Magri left Pescopagano on 12 August 1943 and went into hiding in Rome; he and his wife (who takes over the narration at this point in his life story) changed hotels every five days for fear of arrest. A member of the Fronte Unione Nazionale, Magri was captured on 16 January 1944 and taken to Via Tasso, where he was imprisoned and tortured. He died on 24 March 1944 in the Fosse Ardeatine massacre.

Though Magri's story – full of audacious plans, dastardly villains, fistfights and cross-dressing – is more Rocambolesque that anything attempted by the more famous Rosselli et al., the narrative strategies are similar. Lussu, Nitti, Rosselli and Magri each chose the adventure tale as most effective model onto which to map their confinement experiences. This has to do, in the case of Lussu, Rosselli and Nitti, with the fact that much of the heavy lifting of establishing political credibility had already taken place by the time they started writing. All three had already enjoyed various degrees of celebrity as a function of their political work by the time of their escape, which was covered by the international press; the principal elements of their adventure having been recounted, they were free to elaborate, contextualise, or embroider upon them. Additionally, all three were well enough educated to be able to move confidently among the literary thickets to find a comfortable position from which to write. Magri, who didn't enjoy the same social and material comforts as Rosselli and the others, could nonetheless rely on the exceptionality of the events themselves to provide the outlandish, extravagant elements of the narrative that are typical of the Rocambolesque or *roman-feuilleton* to which Lussu, Nitti and Rosselli nod.

## The diarist

Camilla Ravera's *Diario di trent'anni 1913–1943*, first published in 1972, mines *Vita in carcere e al confino* (edited by Ada Gobetti) for letters written during exile. It conforms to the gender conventions that reveal themselves in other self-representations. Where Amendola or Spinelli privilege bold vision, Ravera writes in the key of kindness. In his *Ventotene*, Jacometti recounts how Ravera and Umberto Terracini, two of the heaviest hitters in the Italian Communist Party, would stroll around the island reciting poetry. Giorgio Braccialarghe waxes rhapsodic about her delicate beauty and caressing voice. To read contemporary accounts of Ravera is to immerse oneself in a kind of courtly love story. But she also offers a potent counternarrative to the ones so firmly consolidated after Silone and Levi. Of particular interest to us here is the way she overturns the positions of Silone and Levi with respect to the politicisation of the local, the possibility of cross-class solidarity, and the question of backwardness.

Ravera spent thirteen years incarcerated: first in the prisons of Varese, Rome, Trani and Perugia, then in internal exile on Montalbano Jonio, San Giorgio Lucano, Ponza, and Ventotene. She was sent from Montalbano, where she gave lessons to the local men nearing the age of military service, to San Giorgio Lucano, where she was completely isolated. And yet she found solidarity there, in forms that ranged from reassurances whispered along the pathways by protective shepherds to surreptitious social events organised in the home of her hosts. In these, the topics of discussion were wide ranging (unemployment, poverty, inequality) and suggestive of a politicisation unthinkable in, say, a similar encounter depicted by Silone or Levi.

She was enchanted by the landscape (calling it a true Arcadia[41]) and the customs of the people. Her terms being vaguely reminiscent of Levi's *Cristo si è fermato a Eboli*. Note, however, that Ravera stresses the antiquity but not the immobility of the locale, nor does she romanticise their worldview by imbuing it with superstition and magical thinking. Ravera's prosaic depiction of San Giorgio Lucano – including a robust paragraph on the subject of its pigs – can be said to serve as a corrective of sorts to Levi's mythicised *gaglianesi*; the people of San Giorgio Lucano are, precisely, people, and the pigs are pigs: no more and no less.[42]

As noted earlier, her character, as she performs it in her letters, is good-natured. Though on Ponza she is followed at all times by no fewer than two agents, we learn of this from Gobetti, not from her, so little space does she give to the lamentations we have come to expect from other *confinati* who suffer the same fate. These instead are replaced by delight in the horticultural contest being waged between Terracini and Pertini on the balconies of their respective apartments, as well as many pages on the events and conversations leading to her and Terracini's ban from organisational politics (though not from the party). It's not that she does not depict those aspects of internal exile that we have come to expect, such as the library on Ponza, the restrictions on correspondence, the *manciuriani*, and so on – and the *Diario* is unusual for the way it places personal events and events from the life of the exiles in broader historical context, with consistent attention to the respective vicissitudes of the PCI (especially in relation to the Communist Party of the Soviet Union) and of Nazi-Fascism in Europe. Rather, it is her affect that is radically different from any of the others we have examined or will examine soon. Hers is neither the braggadocio of a Spinelli, the hale-fellow-well-met of an Amendola, nor the feat of discursive artistry of an Ansaldo. Her letters engaging intensely with the faraway events of her family life give the reader almost as clear a sense of what is happening to her siblings and their children as is happening to her.

Ravera is also appreciative of elements of natural beauty, however humble (she mentions varieties of flowers, the neighbourhood pets, the joys of a sunny day), on offer in the carceral spaces of which she has ample basis for comparison after so much experience. Rather, of interest to the present analysis is the difference between Ravera's and Nitti's descriptions of their surroundings; where Nitti sees a didactic opportunity, Ravera's motives are relational. Ravera's writings make visible what we might have overlooked in our readings of earlier or more celebrated iterations of the genre, namely their highly gendered qualities. The version of femininity here performed by Ravera finds its correlate in the hypermasculinity of Lussu and Magri and in the ethnographic impulse of a Levi or a Nitti. Her writings aim neither to teach us geography nor to seize control of the exile experience through its recounting in the key of mastery (as in, 'here I sit with pen in hand').

She looks ahead to a life of service from the vantage point of her last days on the island: '[A]nche noi donne saremmo state partecipi del grande moto generale di liberazione e di rinascita: vi avremmo avuto i nostri compiti, la nostra funzione; vi avremmo impressi i tratti della nostra personalità di donne, le nostre aspirazioni profonde, la nostra umanità'[43] (We women, too, will have participated in the big, broad movement of liberation and freedom: we will have had our duties, our task, on which we will have impressed the traits of our personalities as women, our deep aspirations, our humanity). The co-existence of her demonstrated awareness of the broader political context in which she moves (Russia; the direction of the PCI; the contribution of women to the nation's rebirth) and her intimist poetics of small graces (a cat, a sunny day, friendships) is striking. While it is in some ways more difficult to draw conclusions about the strategic implementation of a literary model than it was in the case, say, of those texts we likened to the *roman-feuilleton*, it is no less the case that Ravera's work exerts a rhetorical effect. Her concluding words on the role of women make clear the stakes of her intervention, as the assertion of an alternative to the hegemony of the hypermasculine.

Politically and socially conservative, Giovanni Ansaldo was never more than a lukewarm socialist at best. The fact of his slow abjuration of anti-Fascism and eventual adherence to the Regime in 1935 gave rise to accusations of political opportunism, egotism and cynicism, evident among other things in the appeal for exoneration – anathema in many *confino* circles – that he sent to the government in June 1927, barely a month after his arrival on Lipari.[44] Though in his *L'antifascista riluttante: memorie del carcere e del confino 1926–1927* he touches on the usual themes (surveillance, lodgings, finding decent food, bathing in the sea, rules and regulations, and so on) his memoirs are decidedly anomalous, as much for the *sui generis* nature of his personal iteration as for the sophistication of his cultural preparation. His is the story of long-term discomfort with both the methods and the motives of the political left, on the one hand, and on the other, of a deep personal affection for many of its most illustrious members. His biographer Marcello Staglieno underscores the importance of self-understanding over self-justification in his memoirs.[45] It was only partly written for publication, and largely for himself, a fact made visible, for example, in the occasional paragraphs that go on for several pages, suggesting temporary disregard for his professional training in journalism. A journalist for *Il lavoro* when he was sentenced to five years of internal exile for attempting to expatriate (his stay lasted a few months in 1927), he justifies his appeal in decidedly unpolitical terms, citing instead motives to do more closely with his character than his convictions, a sensitivity to beauty over reason chief among them. Ansaldo's memoir ranks among the most unflinching of the texts we have considered thus far, in its assessment of the personalities and politics of the moment. Writing in the months immediately after his release, his descriptions of Carlo Rosselli, for example, are nuanced and insightful, full of affection and admiration for Rosselli's generosity, indomitable good spirits and intelligence, as well as of a keen awareness of the colossal political ambitions behind Rosselli's much vaunted courage and altruism. Ansaldo speculates that:

> [Rosselli] aveva molto bene compreso che il fuoruscitismo era un 'ramo secco', e che ogni fuoruscito sarebbe stato un uomo politicamente morto; perciò, egli non intendeva minimamente fuoruscire, e preferiva vessazioni e confino, in Italia; e d'altra parte, incitava più gente poteva ad espatriare, un po' per accrescere lo scandalo pubblico, la rabbia dei potenti, la esasperazione generale, e un po' – diciamo tutto – per levarsi di torno concorrenti o predecessori, pesi morti della politica di opposizione, com'egli la intendeva. [...] [E]gli, Rosselli, sarebbe rimasto solo e troneggiante in mezzo alla *religio depopulata* del socialismo italiano, e sarebbe stato il primo uomo dell'opposizione militante. (Ansaldo, 1992: 120)

> (Rosselli had understood perfectly that flight from Italy was a dead end, and that everyone who left the country would be a political dead man; consequently, he hadn't the slightest intention to leave, preferring vexations and exile within Italy; besides that, he incited expatriation in as many people as he could, in part to increase the general outrage, and in part – we all agree – to get competitors and predecessors out of the way, since they were the dead weight of opposition politics, as he understood it. ... He, Rosselli alone, would stay on to reign over the *religio depopulata* of Italian socialism, and become the pre-eminent figure of militant opposition.)

It was Rosselli, Ansaldo claims, who understood first and best Ansaldo's uncertain commitment to the anti-Fascist cause, and indeed revelled in the idea that Ansaldo's imprisonment (they were incarcerated together in Como) would deal Ansaldo's ideological tergiversations the *coup de grâce*: 'Non ti resta che accettare *in pieno* la nostra causa ... La prigione ti lega a noi, caro mio, per sempre' (Ansaldo, 1992: 386) (You have no choice but *fully* to accept our cause ... Prison will tie you to us, my dear, forever). Needless to say, Rosselli was wrong.

Illuminating, as well, are his meditations on the dangers of exaggerating the hardship of internal exile (for one thing, it is too easy to disprove) and on the predilection for martyrdom among the prisoners. *Confino*, he opines, is already serious enough that there is no need to exaggerate its hardships, and yet the prisoners on Lipari and those in exile abroad even more so, crave stories of martyrdom for the cause (Ansaldo, 1992: 360).

Unlike the majority of the memoirs we have examined, Ansaldo's is not crafted to reflect favourably upon his actions or behaviour. Instead, he is very blunt about his own shortcomings, such as the way that fear for his own personal safety caused him to imagine a risk greatly exaggerated with respect to the actual risk he ran. He mocks both his own paranoia and its negative impact on his ability to care for his sisters, who, in contrast, are consistently praised for, on the one hand, their emotional and material support of Ansaldo and, on the other, the hardships they were forced to endure as an indirect result of his cowardice. At the same time, compared to other *confino* memoirs, he is uncharacteristically unstinting in his praise, which occasionally takes on near global proportions. He overflows with the milk of human kindness at the mere thought of southern hospitality (Ansaldo, 1992: 290) and of the courage of women (Ansaldo, 1992: 115). Rather than commenting on the pain of the handcuffs during the journey from prison to the island, he waxes poetic (and slightly ironic) about Italian *caritas* towards the outlaw, whatever his stripe (Ansaldo, 1992: 289). A reflection on the effects of exile on the children who experience it – how they will remember it and what impact it will have on their actions as adults, leads to a conclusion about the interconnectedness of all things.

This is not to suggest breathless naiveté on Ansaldo's part; he is capable of great causticity, when the arm of irony is too weak. To give but one example, true to the genre, he provides an *inventario ragionato* of the major political factions on the island (communisti, socialisti, repubblicani, isolati maldefiniti and isolate rispettabili (Ansaldo, 1992: 318), dissidenti fascisti (Ansaldo, 1992: 321)). His views on the Communists are decidedly unsympathetic; he avows that when short on arguments, they would resort to a magic formula, an 'open sesame' as it were (preferably exotic and of Russian origins), which released them from any ideological impasse. (Ansaldo, 1992: 303). A copious eleven pages are devoted to the figure of Domizio Torrigiani, including not very flattering images of the Grand Master propositioning the under-age daughter of the local baker (Ansaldo, 1992: 335).

Ultimately, the realisation that he was suffering for someone else's cause (Ansaldo, 1992: 343) is self-serving in its apparently organic simplicity. And yet precisely because of its inseparability from both broader questions about freedom, solidarity, and what constitutes a meaningful life, and from narrower ones about how his decision rendered more vulnerable his former fellow travellers, such an admission as the one above must be recognised as a deeply unpopular one to make. What is at once vexing and admirable about Ansaldo's memoir is the attitude of sympathetic (and occasionally bemused) acceptance of his own and others' foibles.

Organised chronologically, each section of Emma Turchi's *La felicità è la lotta* (1976) begins with a lengthy recollection by Turchi followed by letters from her husband Giulio. Turchi, herself a Communist, followed her husband to the Tremiti in 1937; he would later be sent to Ponza (1938–39) and to Ventotene (1939–July 1943). Of the eleven years they had been together, he had spent ten of them in prison; consequently, for them, the sentence to a mere five years of internal exile was a relatively joyful affair. It was soon interrupted by his imprisonment – again – along with the other prisoners who, in response to a new order by the Fascist director, refused to give the Roman salute at roll call.

His letters are generally of a personal nature (easy to imagine considering the length of their separation) and speak of love and other domestic phenomena. Indeed, his is a rich compendium of lover's greetings and salutations. He is also clearly concerned with normalising, to the extent possible considering the distance between them, their *vita di coppia*: hence the unemphatic, nonrhetorical tone of his descriptions of daily life in exile, which follows the usual patterns (walks, sunbathing, reading).

The bulk of his letters, however, have to do with practicalities – what he would like her to send (or not to send – a packet containing neckties distresses him greatly); what kind of request for permission to visit should be submitted; questions of health. Chronically malnourished and deprived of proper medical care, Giulio is plagued by a disfiguring dermatological illness that resolves when his living conditions improve. It is partly to that end that he decides to learn a trade in order to make some semblance of a living rather than depending on Emma's modest wages as a seamstress, so he learns tailoring. To complete the chiasmic twist, soon after Giulio's transfer to Ponza, Emma is arrested and imprisoned for having placed Albanian Communists in contact with Italian Communists. Thus it is Giulio who works as a tailor now and Emma who is incarcerated. But theirs is a proverbial happy ending, with the couple's reunion and the birth of a child whom they call, fittingly, Gioia.[46]

The discursive and affective humility of Turchi's correspondence reminds us of another aspect of the pedagogical aims we have seen in many of these texts, namely, the impulse to turn faraway loved ones into informed participants. The finale – trading places, imprisonment, exoneration, reunion, birth – is, rather, befitting an operetta, and refines our reading of these texts as modelled on literary forms by reminding us that sometimes it is life that follows art and not vice versa.

## The poets

Alberto Jacometti, Cesira Fiori, and Giorgio Braccialarghe's works stand out for their pretensions to literary style, evident in the use of recognisable literary models, and an elaborate linguistic apparatus, besides careful attention to rhetorical effect. We have already noted shades of D'Annunzio in Jacometti's self-positioning at the top of the sexual and literary totem poles. Though she writes from a different class position, Fiori, too, has similar literary pretensions, favouring the purple prose of a D'Annunzio but also the dispassionate stance of the Levian ethnography. But Fiori shares neither Jacometti's protagonism nor the performance of his and others' slightly predatorial hyperheteronormativity; instead, she trains her lens onto female desire, same-sex and otherwise.

Writing in 1965, Fiori's *Una donna nelle carceri fasciste* provides a slightly *osé* glimpse at life in women's prisons in the 1930s (the first section in Rome describes the events of 1933 at Le Mantellate): the homoerotic and sentimental attachments among incarcerated prostitutes; thumbnail sketches of the sisters who manage the prison; and of the children of the inmates (they could bring babies up to three years old). She devotes pages to the religious sisters as well as to non-political women prisoners, eschewing discussion of the politicals from whom she was isolated. She approaches their individual stories with a kind of sympathetic distance. The suffocation of multiple babies by one mother; the prostitute's abortion; the arsenic poisoning of a disabled husband (assisted by the husband's brother, the prisoner's lover); a violent recounting of childhood sexual violence: she comes to these stories as a witnessing consciousness, a neutral, non-participant observer.[47] There are spicy stories as well, like the ones about the times workmen come to make repairs, and the libidinous female prisoners assault them (Fiori, 1965, 102 and before).

Speaking about herself, however, she bars no holds with regard to poetic aspirations. Recalling Jacometti, for whom forced inactivity was at once a kind of mental torture (what might be called the lament of the benched athlete) and an alibi for literary experimentation, Fiori describes the seclusion from and the inability to participate in civil and political life in terms reminiscent of heartache. Events such as a full moon or the melancholy hooting of an owl outside her cell inspire reflections in purple prose.

Another literary model emerges in section two of the book, when Fiori is imprisoned in Perugia. There she discovers a kind of Virgil figure, the *suorina* (literally the 'little nun') who guides her through the various circles of the prison, explains the stories of those who live there, lets them speak and then glosses their comments, prevents others from speaking out of turn, and so on. A quotation from Dante stands at the beginning of section one, not section two, providing a kind of intertextual interweaving.

The Ponza portion of her narration adheres closely to the norms of the genre: transfer from prison, first impressions of the island as seen from the boat; the fauna of the island, registration, fingerprinting; the attempt to impose the Fascist salute; the difficulty of finding work; the 'classes' given among *confinati*; the trials and tribulations connected with surveillance, the library; bedbugs; the Manchurians. In this section, she does not demonstrate the same sustained level of literary reference as in the previous section, but fits squarely into the *confino* genre (Fiori, 1965: 131–2). She also tells stories we have not heard so far. From Amendola, among others, we know about the so-called proletarianisation of the intellectuals (which in his case consisted, besides the development of a cross-class relationship in good faith, of his refusal to shave for days on end, and of related aesthetic and sartorial attempts at rapprochement with the great unwashed masses) but she describes the opposite move: the cultural ascent of the working class, which resulted among other things in a more widespread use of the toothbrush and the adoption of pyjamas (these, too, represent culture) – as streetwear (Fiori, 1965: 156). And there are high jinx as well. She starts writing articles for and with the other Communists on the island. One of her pieces wins a 'prize', given by Giorgio Amendola, which consisted of a fake medal that she was required to wear for a week (Fiori, 1965: 152).

Fiori's more famous work, *La confinata*, displays the same impulses to educate as many of the other memoirists (she describes the architecture, trees, flowers, and geography of the region in L'Aquila where she and her husband are reunited after his stint on Ventotene[48]), as well as a taste for dialogue. This is her last book, published posthumously in 1979, and she has absorbed the lessons of her experience writing fiction. Perhaps this is what is most important about this book – with her implementation of the tropes of the South, she joins Levi and Silone, on the one hand; and with her particular admixture of narrative and non-fictional voices she channels author Renata Viganò's concerns with gender, education, and ideology. She also devotes more time to the free inhabitants, particularly the local women, than do the other writers of her ilk, describing the things they wove, canned, cooked, and preserved, providing a valuable view of the living conditions of rural women at the time. Her closest literary kin, however, remains Levi, whose emphasis on southern immobility she shares: 'E la vita continuava, almeno in apparenza, sempre uguale, come quella del bove che si sottomette con tranquilità inalterabile, sicuro della propria possanza, e ti guarda con i grandi occhi acquosi e dolci' (Fiori, 1979: 55) (And life continued unchanging, at least, in appearance, like that of the ox who submits with unchanging tranquillity, sure of his own strength, and looks at you with big eyes, lustrous and mild). By the same Levian logic, she explains why these towns were chosen as *confino* sites: because their inhabitants had little experience with anti-Fascist movements, but more important still, because they did not experience Fascism as a change from the existing power structures, having simply passed from one form of oppression to another (Fiori, 1979: 24). Levi, following Marx and Silone, describes the peasants as apolitical, indeed as unpoliticisable. But where Levi leaves the observation where it lies, Fiori politicises, when she suggests that there exists a kind of solidarity between the political *confinato* and other, so-called outsider, groups.

Also closely aligned with Levi's poetics of mythicisation is the story of the horse Libero who understands his young master Mimino's father Virgilio's refusal to hand him (Libero) over to a German officer. The horse bursts out of his stall, kicks and kills the two Germans who have come to requisition him, then runs straight away to the woods where Mimino is hiding (Fiori, 1979: 150–4). She also recalls Verga, observing the long-lasting feuds within families over questions of inheritance (Fiori, 1979: 50); like Silone, she, too, dedicates pages to the traditions that revolve around the killing of wolves (Fiori, 1979: 140); and her explanation for why there is so little resistance to Fascism in Aquila might have come from the first chapter of *Fontamara* (Fiori, 1979: 122). Fiori's literary pretensions may or may not be successful by aesthetic standards but her literary models are nonetheless coherent for the insistence with which they adhere to her ideological convictions.

Giorgio Braccialarghe's memoir, *Nelle spire di Urlavento. Il confino di Ventotene negli anni dell'agonia del Fascismo* (first edition 1970), is short on specifics and long on poetic generalities about men, freedom, and sunsets. Its egregious literary pretensions ('[L]a notte era un bimbo che mi prendeva per la mano e mi conduceva ... per i sentieri dell'evasione'[49] – Night was a child who took me by the hand and conducted me ... on the paths of escape), reminiscent of Jacometti's birdsong opening, give way to a slightly more prosaic set of portraits of his fellows, especially Ernesto Rossi and Eugenio Colorni, and more general reflections on humanity, dispersed across very brief chapters (many only one page in length, and all under ten), often heavy on irony. Braccialarghe also devotes many pages to the greatness and difficult character of Altiero Spinelli, though Spinelli barely mentions Braccialarghe in his memoir except to quote Braccialarghe's highly flattering description of Spinelli from this book.[50] He presents himself as Spinelli's faithful sidekick, and shares the latter's disdain for the Communists who for Braccialarghe (echoing Silone's remarks on communist certainties) are deluded by blind faith. By the time of the book's composition, many of the debates that took place among the prisoners had been resolved, forgotten, or transcended and thus the book's political discussions feel slightly outmoded, too well digested to have any effect. Nonetheless, more than any others it is in these pages on Spinelli, and particularly on the informal personal correspondence they, like other exiles, exchanged to help clarify their ideas, that Braccialarghe's memoir makes its most original contribution to the genre and teaches the reader something that has not already been explained by other texts of its type. This is not to suggest that Braccialarghe wrote with the intention of revising Spinelli's reputation in a more positive light; but the pages that recount their discussions do effectively add depth and dimension to Spinelli's character, dimensions that will be subsumed, later, in Spinelli's own self-assessments.

## In praise of great men

First published in 1945, Riccardo Gualino's *Solitudine* recounts the experiences of the industrialist and patron of the arts during his 1931–33 stay on Lipari on charges of fraudulent bankruptcy (an opportunity for Mussolini to demonstrate rare impartiality with respect to the economic power of those in disfavour with the Regime). The book's dearth of self-reflection or objective observation and its surfeit of self-praise, often placed in the mouths of others[51] do not prevent it from conforming to generic expectations like the lamentations about forced inactivity or about being followed that are staples of the genre (Gualino, 1997: 20–1). But while Lussu, Nitti, and Rosselli, who though not as rich as Gualino were neither as penurious as the great majority of the prisoners and thus could permit themselves moments of leisure, the latter produced memoirs about action, not about sunsets. Nor did they personalise relations with their minders, whereas Gualino evinces a feeling of *noblesse oblige* towards those whose job it is to watch him, dispensing largesse and eliciting grateful smiles (Gualino, 1996: 20–1).

Gualino need not complain of lack of intimacy because his wife comes regularly to visit, finding the little house he has rented charming after living in so much luxury (Gualino, 1997: 29). In short, this is no Château d'If; Gualino's exile is singularly comfortable, with an adorable house (Gualino, 1997: 30), wife, and money; the wife of another *confinato* provides domestic help, and tells them about life and strife among the inhabitants of the *camerone* (literally, the 'big room' in which the prisoners lived in crowded conditions) when she brings them their warm milk in bed. In short, Gualino's and his wife's lives are radically different from the average *confinato*'s; their financial resources and prestige assure such physical comforts and special treatment (such as permission to live in a house whose entrance is outside the perimeter of space in which the prisoners are allowed to circulate) that his experience might well seem a bit like a holiday at the shore, as Mussolini once famously asserted, with warm, breezy afternoons on the terrace reading the newspaper (Gualino, 1997: 40–1).

Yet Gualino – not in exile for political opposition but rather for business irregularities – nonetheless felt the need for some sort of activity beyond reading the newspaper and chatting with his wife – hence these memoirs, which are his second set.[52] He devotes a chapter of *Solitudine* to *Frammenti di vita*, the autobiography he had already completed in 1931, and he imagines how it will bring tears to the eyes of unknown readers and smiles of comfort to the faces of his beloveds. But *this* book's completion, more or less concomitant with one of his wife's departures, leaves him to reflect on how the mighty have fallen.

It is an easy book to mock, of course. But this maudlin mixture of self-importance, self-pity, flights of poetic fancy and spontaneous, present-tense documentation does beg the question: what manner of text is this – is it memoir, fiction, does it have historical value? If Lussu's and Jacometti's non-fiction borrowed from the world of popular fiction in order, presumably, to render more legible the submerged political content of their works (which are not only didactic but also calls to action), what are we to make of Gualino's intervention? And if we subsumed Lussu and Jacometti's generally cheerful tones as the teaspoon of sugar necessary to render more tolerable the medicine of political engagement, what are we to make of Gualino's complacency? Insofar as this book has value as a document, it requires a careful calibration of the weight of its stylistics against their strategic value: in this case, demonstrating that he held no grudge against a regime that saw fit to condemn him to an exemplary sentence. Seen in this light, the book's pomposity becomes something other than the proof of its creator's character.[53]

An explicit discussion of privilege and sophistication also appears in the memoir of one major Communist figure – and not, as one might expect, in derogatory terms. Written in 1980 after a lengthy career in the public eye, Giorgio

Amendola's *Un'isola* demonstrates the luxuries of hindsight and of old age. The didactic impulses that we observed in the earlier texts have weakened, and by 1980 there is no need to apologise or explain a past infraction (whether real or perceived) in the way that, say, Altiero Spinelli's memoir evinces. Consequently, there is room to expand on themes that have till now been largely sacrificed in the interests of space and urgency in previous texts. This is a function, as said earlier, of the historical moment in which *Un'isola* was composed (1980, which was also the year of Amendola's death) but also of Amendola's particular position as the son of one of the brightest stars in the Liberal anti-Fascist firmament, Giovanni Amendola. Finally, the author's position of relative class privilege with respect to the great majority of the Communist *confinati* with whom he was interned is a constant and innovative theme. Thus, in the section of the book devoted to his bachelor life in Paris, he lists a good dozen of his favourite French and German authors; he describes in some detail his francophilia, his visit to a German prostitute, and Sunday mornings at the Louvre. He is not afraid to step on toes (Togliatti's wife overcooks her risotto; in order to lunch at Montagnari's house on Ponza, you must also tolerate his wife's operatic performances); to scandalise (masturbation merits numerous mentions, and we learn that prison life is enlivened by competitions for the most accurate and the most copious urination); or to wax sentimental (his proposal to future wife Germaine is constructed as a cliff-hanger). In short, by 1980, there is no longer any need to conform precisely to the standard narrative. Consequently, what emerges is a relaxed, confident, ample account full of *bonhomie* and intermittent moments of self-reflection (occasionally ironic, as when he laughs at the pedantry of his letters or at his propensity to gain weight in prison). Nor, significantly, is there much fear of reprisal for his not always complimentary attitude towards the Communist Party. He is critical of its exaggerated collectivism, for example, especially when it interferes with what reads as bourgeois sartorial taste, here infused with a certain tendency to northernist prejudice: in the communist laundry communal, the best laundresses were the northern wives of the *confinati*; the southern wives, he complained, would ruin one's clothes. Unlike some, more hagiographic, memoirs, Amendola does not resist anecdotes that show his colleagues in a less than glowing light, such as the *giellista* whose refusal to return his library books on time resulted in a fist fight, or the anatomical preferences of a fellow traveller.[54] Finally, he admits more than once to his instrumentalisation by the party authorities (whose *centralismo* he critiques as well) as a function of his illustrious family – he is often made to front acts of resistance or even of outright infraction on behalf of his fellows with no explanation, no warning, and no say in the matter – hence the nineteen months of his internment that were spent not on Ponza but in prison at Poggioreale. Paradoxically, as a vanity memoir, *Un'isola* succeeds where *Solitudine* did not: a function of its intended audience and the historical moment of its composition.

And yet, what a difference from another late memoir. As we saw with Giovanni Ansaldo, the goal of Altiero Spinelli's *Come ho tentato di diventare saggio: Io, Ulisse* is no longer to explain, to educate, or to inspire; rather, it is to justify, to boast, and to lay bare one's own deeds and misdeeds. Spinelli's *Io, Ulisse*, volume one of what was envisioned as a two-volume memoir (1984), does not deviate completely from the *confino* memoir genre as we have been describing it. It contains, for example, the usual description of the voyage from prison to the island – in this case, Ponza – complete with the requisite scene of seasickness and its sequelae. The central narrative events of this memoir are the description of his expulsion from the Communist Party and the evolution of his federalist bent, culminating in the drafting of the *Ventotene Manifesto*. Writing with the benefits of historical hindsight and sufficient distance for the details – and the heat of emotion – to have faded from view, he devotes thirteen dense pages in which to recount, explain, justify, and correct the record on his detachment from and eventual expulsion from the party. Evincing little rancour towards his former fellow travellers in spite of their adherence to the convention of ignoring ex-Communists as though they were invisible (Terracini and Ravera are exceptions), Spinelli spins the expulsion as a necessary precursor to the development of his more mature political thought. What is striking about this presentation is thus less its content than its positioning in the narrative for maximum rhetorical impact.

Consider, in this light, the pages he devotes to women on Ponza. His repeated descriptions of Tina Pizzardo anticipate the presentation of more complex erotic adventures in exile. Indeed, as early as three paragraphs into the story of his arrival on Ponza, he suggests the facility with which he attracted the loving attention of the *confinate* whom, however, he rejects in favour of a no-strings arrangement, turning instead to a compliant (and probably economically disadvantaged) local woman.

The 'more beautiful, simpler' local (she is endowed with 'animal innocence' (Spinelli, 1984: 229)) to whom he refers is Emilia, his laundress and lover for a year. She is acquired (his term) at the same time and in the same fashion as his lodgings (Spinelli, 1984: 229).

Immediately following his story about Emilia, as though they were thematically linked, is a minutely detailed, five-page biography of the prostitute Melasecca. She, in turn, is succeeded in the narrative by the *Manciuriani*, non-political *confinati* whose name dated back to the origins of the Ponza prison's repurposing for internal exile under Fascism. The two large rooms where the prisoners were held were dark, draughty, and leaked water during rainstorms, for which reason they were baptised Siberia and Manchuria. Siberia, which had the advantage of a window and a door, was quickly colonised by the political internees, who were much more adept at collective action than the non-political inmates, so that more than representing spatial relations (this room or that room), the term *manciuriano* came to stand as shorthand for a non-political prisoner. It is a common trope of these memoirs that the manchurians were disorganised at best, violent at worst, and in any case of precious little consequence to the political prisoners' lives or work.[55] The drunkard Bertoni, Manchurian of the first order, would be exemplary in this regard were it not for the fact that he was also the writer of short stories, including one about a murderer called Girolamo.

But insofar as Spinelli's interest in them, and in the short story in particular, strikes the reader as anomalous, it allows a pattern to emerge. The choice of his objects of narrative enquiry – the sensual animal Emilia, the prostitute Melasecca, the drunken *manciuriano* – adumbrate the discussion that follows Bertoni, suggesting a kind of continuity between the characters, as it were, who preceded him and those to whom he next turns his attention: the Communists, from whose ranks he will be very publicly (though not necessarily unwillingly) rejected. In other words, the organisation of the Ponza portion of his memoir, though it appears at first blush to be random, is in fact carefully constructed for rhetorical purposes, to underscore the similarities in the relations of each individual or group to the social norm. This is not to say that he is anything but respectful towards his interlocutors or that he paints them with colours equally garish. But what the language does not say, the structure of the narrative does: Communists, it would seem, are as ethically dubious as the whores and the would-be murderer.

The section on his expulsion from the Communist Party ends with the metaphor to which the title of this first volume of his memoirs (*Io, Ulisse*) makes reference: 'Non solo ero ormai in mare aperto, ma anche in un mare sconosciuto e non sapevo né quanto a lungo si sarei rimasto né dove avrei approdato' (Spinelli, 1984: 258) (Not only was I in open sea, but also in uncharted waters and I had no idea how long I [would] remain there or where I would land). The memoir then turns its attentions to Spinelli's years on Ventotene (1939–43). And indeed this section, no less than the ones that precede it, shows evidence of a carefully crafted rhetorical strategy meant to underscore Spinelli's exceptionality. Here, Spinelli's thoughts turn from earthly pleasures and ideological impasses to matters spiritual. Where before, the Ulysses of the title might have been Homeric, he is here aligned more specifically with Dante's iteration of that figure whose hunger for knowledge took him and his followers beyond the limits of the known world. The Ventotene section opens with Spinelli *as* Dante's Pilgrim, on a voyage that would culminate in his own ascension to the realm of the elect:

'Nel mezzo del cammin di nostra vita' mi ritrovai a Ventotene, dove rimasi quattro anni dal luglio del 1939 al 17 agosto 1943, dall'età di 32 anni a quella di 36 anni, dall'inizio della seconda guerra mondiale alla caduta del fascismo. Quegli anni in quell'isola sono ancor oggi presenti in me con la pienezza che hanno solo i momenti ed i luoghi nei quali si compie quella misteriosa cosa che i cristiani chiamano l'elezione. Le *membra disjecta* dei sentimenti, pensieri, speranze e disperazioni si ricomposero allora in un disegno nuovo, per me stesso sorprendente; la mia debolezza si convertí in forza; sentii che una consonanza straordinaria si andava formando fra quello che accadeva nel mondo e quello che accadeva in me; compresi che fino a quel momento ero stato simile a un feto in formazione, in attesa di esser partorito, che in quegli anni in quel luogo nacqui una seconda volta, che il mio destino fu allora segnato, che io assentii ad esso e che la mia vera vita, quella che sto ora portando a termine, cominciò. Con sublime poetica laconicità la Bibbia descrive questo fenomeno cosí: 'Jahvé vide che si era avvicinato per veder, e Dio lo chiamò dal mezzo del roveto e disse: 'Mosé, Mosé!' Rispose: 'Eccomi'. (Spinelli, 1984: 261)

('When I had travelled half our life's way', I found myself on Ventotene, where I remained for four years from July of 1939 until 17 August 1943, from age 32 to 36, from the beginning of World War II until the fall of Fascism. Those years on the island are still alive in me with the fullness produced only in moments and places in which one achieves what the Christians call election. At that time, the scattered fragments of feelings, thoughts, hopes and despair recomposed themselves in a new design, surprising even to me; my weakness transformed into strength; I felt an extraordinary harmony between what was happening in the world and what was happening in me; I understood that until that moment, I had been similar to a developing foetus, waiting to be delivered, that in those years in that place I was born a second time, that my destiny was already written, that I assented and that my true life, which I am now bringing to a close, began. With sublime poetic concisiveness the Bible describes this phenomenon thus: 'Jahweh saw that he had come closer in order to see, and God called him from the midst of the bush and said, 'Moses! Moses!' He answered, 'Here I am'.)

This is the rhetorical apex of the entire volume. After the dark days of the expulsion, his elevation to the ranks of the exalted can only be followed by stories of a considerably more banal nature, such as the pages devoted to raising rabbits and chickens (including an eight-page anecdote about the erotic adventures of one of his roosters), working as a watch repairer, and the perigrinations of the Jehovah's Witnesses interned on Ventotene.

It is a brief respite in the action, however. The enormity of the build up quoted above suggests that the pitch to follow will be earth shattering, and the major event of the Ventotene section of the memoir is indeed significant: the drafting of the *Ventotene Manifesto*. The *Ventotene Manifesto* is one of the founding texts of the European Federalist movement, a text whose significance was only made relevant a generation after its initial circulation and Spinelli's most significant political legacy (significant enough to merit naming one of the European Parliament buildings in Brussels after him). Consequently, though the tone of his memoirs occasionally exceeds the bounds of modesty conventional in the modern iteration of the genre (not to mention the outdatedness of his depictions of women), one must give credit where due. Of all of the political internees described in this study, Spinelli is arguably the best known internationally, a function of the enormous influence of the *Manifesto*.

## Moving forward

Though documented from early on by those who experienced it from its inception, there is no proper genre called the *confino* memoir; nonetheless, we can posit a category based on the many traits shared by these texts, which depict the hero's experience of internal exile from arrest until liberation. The question of taxonomy has broader implications about the way, far from merely *representing* their lives through narrative, these writers *experience* them through narrative. Akin to Paul Ricoeur's observations about the merging of historical and fictional discourses in the formation of narrative identity,[56] the repetition of so many elements in so many of these texts suggests, as Bruce Merry argues for the partisan novel, that, 'the experience ... arrived into literature through a set of known elements which were instinctively *felt* by the writer to constitute its roles of narrative composition. At some point between reality and representation, a canonical literary formula intervened'.[57] Though those 'known elements', in this case, are clearly delineated, this is not to imply that the formal exigencies of literary convention are ironclad or that deviation is tantamount to disqualification from the genre, however provisional. Rather, what we have tried to demonstrate is that *idem* and *ipse* live in precarious equipoise in these texts: that is, that for all that they are ostensibly generated to produce a life of individual singularity, they are also deeply concerned with – and faithful to the unproblematic idea of – the referent, here internal exile in its most concrete, material manifestations.

To this end, there are two things to note. First, these texts produce largely de-nationalised subjects, that is, subjects for whom the nodal point of identity is founded in an ideological position that transcends nationhood (as well as regionalist variants). With very few exceptions (Magri chief among them), these authors place great weight on the nexus between past opposition to Fascism (even in the case of Ansaldo) and present submission to its authority even when they do not explicitly foreground the specificity of their beliefs (as Communists, *giellisti*, Socialists, and so on). Absent too is recourse to a discourse of autochthony; there is little said about local inflection of the pre-arrest political activity beyond the requirement that the physical journey to exile start somewhere (and that somewhere is as often as not from prison in a city already far from home).

The second observation has to do with the relative formal homogeneity of these texts in relation to their generative function. Ricoeur and Merry (not to mention Derrida) remind us of the mutually constitutive nature of life and lifewriting. In a slightly different vein, Paul de Man suggests, 'whatever the writer does is in fact governed by the technical demands of self-potraiture and thus determined, in all its aspects, by the resources of his medium'.[58] We would add that anterior to the predetermination of the product by the medium (and the coercive hermeneutics that follows) is an initial differential diagnosis that determines who can write in the first place. That is, those who have not the assets (economic, intellectual, political or otherwise) to manage the medium will not be able to produce the portrait. No wonder, then, that the collection of texts assembled here was written top-down, as it were. Whether from a position of economic (Gualino, Rosselli), intellectual (Ansaldo), or political exceptionality (understood as a position of conspicuous prominence: Lussu, Nitti, Ravera, Amendola, Spinelli), the authors of these texts were by and large not representative of the typical prisoner population.

Furthermore, in the light of these two factors, the formal qualities of this body of work – whether literary or otherwise – may be understood as functional to three phenomena: rhetorical, biographical, and gender. As a body of work, these texts demonstrate great coherence in their choice of literary models. Giovanni Verga and Ignazio Silone (as well as Carlo Levi who apart from his own Bloomian anxiety of influence with regard to these two will himself become a model of misprision), provide ideologically credible literary examples to Ginzburg, Levi, and Fiori. Literature in this context, far from the province of the ornamentality of the genre of *belles lettres*, takes on an aura of persuasive didactic objectivity. On the other hand, hagiographic impulses, especially with regard to the holy trinity of Lussu, Rosselli and Nitti, lend these lives an aura of sanctity, the apotheosis of a collective image of secular martyrdom. Form reflects and, in DeManian fashion, determines the biographical moment of composition as well. Ravera and Turchi insert historical artefacts into the contemporary cultural matrix of their writing. Rosselli's impressionist style is calibrated for citation by future biographers. The production of Ansaldo's intellectual autobiography, ostensibly writing for his children, is coterminous with his political rehabilitation. And having consolidated their fame and prestige by the time of writing, Spinelli, Amendola, and Braccialarghe assume the mantles of *eminences grises*, dropping pearls of wisdom rendered indisputable through the dual prisms of hindsight and institutional authority (and, on a more personal note, giving, say, Spinelli the impunity to reveal private details such as Sandro Pertini's tendency to post-coital musicality). And more broadly, the conventions of writing gender produce, predictably, highly gendered lives: men governed by the implicit, naturalised values of action, physical endurance, moral courage, reason, and hyperactive libido, and women by compassion, a caretaking impulse and the ideals of romantic love.

Recall our observation that subject formation and party affiliation emerge and become operative simultaneously and inextricably in these texts, over and above local or national identification although in fairly strict adherence to specifically Italian versions of naturalist literary tendencies. Further, recall that the Communists were the largest and best organised of the *confinati*, and that attitudes towards communism in Italy have been historically highly fluid; hence the *when* of writing is a determining factor in the production of a (properly) ideological subject. With this, we begin to understand why this particular stream of confinement narrative more or less dries up in the mid-1980s. Bettino Craxi's ascent to power and his repositioning of the Italian Socialist Party in closer proximity to the Christian Democrats and away from the Italian Communist Party (PCI), and a concomitant broader cultural shift that redimensioned the hitherto very close relationship in the popular mind between anti-Fascist resistance and the PCI (inaugurated, among other things, by a series of debates among Italian historians and symptomatic of the rapprochement with the Centre among Italian intellectuals at the time), blunted the impact of memoirs by writers whose principal claim to fame was as sacrifices to the cause.[59]

This is not to say, however, that the *confino* years faded from view. Instead, starting in the early 1990s, a new wave of works emerged in which ideological and party identifications were replaced with, on the one hand, depersonalised and regional identities (Lipari, Calabria, Sardinia)[60] and on the other, national ones such as the confinement memoir written by Senator of the Republic Piero Montagnani-Marelli (published in 1999). In addition, we see the emergence of collections of strictly personal letters completely devoid of political content written by unknown prisoners to their families and published by small local presses to commemorate their homegrown heroes.[61] Recall the scene from Nanni Moretti's film *Aprile* (1998): when Silvio Berlusconi wins the election, the 25 April memorial celebrations suddenly gain real relevance. The nation, as Emilio Gentile reminds us in *La grande Italia*, only came back into view in the mid-1990s.[62] Berlusconi's ascent to power in 1994 and the subsequent renewed interest in Fascist strategies for suppressing dissent – and their contemporary correlatives – changed the national discourse about internal exile yet again, offering a new declension of the legacy of Fascism and an urgent summons to examine it.

## Notes

1    Cesare Pavese, *Lettere*, 2 vols, Lorenzo Mondo (ed.) (Turin: Einaudi, 1966).

2    For a selection of writings about prisoners of humbler origins, see Pier Vittorio Buffa, *Non volevo morire così. Santo Stefano e Ventotene: Storie di ergastolo e confino* (Milan: Nutrimenti, 2017).

3    See Pavese's letter, dated 25–28 February 1936, to his sister Maria, in which he writes of a mendicant of the same description, also named Ciccio.

4    *The Political Prisoner*, written 1938–39, was published in 1949 together with *La casa in collina* under the title *Prima che il gallo canti*.

5    Cesare Pavese, *Terra d'esilio*, in *Il Carcere* (Turin: Einaudi, 1990a), p. 93.

6    In Pavese's letter to Augusto Monti dated 29 October 1935, he assures Monti that he will read absolutely everything except political literature. Monti, in turn, had occasion to remark upon Pavese's 'sordità a ogni appello politico' (deafness to any political appeal). Monti, cited in Domenico Zuccaro, 'Carcere e confino. Tre memoriali inediti di Cesare Pavese' *Il Ponte*, 30:5 (1974), 542. Monti cites the letter of Pavese's physician in Brancaleone, Romano Gustavo, which requests that Pavese be released on the basis of his poor health (asthma, of nervous origin). He was liberated within the month (p. 547).

7    Pavese, *Terra d'esilio*, 57.

8    Enzo Romeo suggests that Pavese modelled both Concia and Elena on real acquaintances (Enzo Romeo, *La solitudine feconda: Cesare Pavese al confino di Brancaleone 1935–1936* (Cosenza: Editoriale progetto 2000, 1986).

    Moving from the fictional to the historical realm, besides the real-life analogues of Concia and Elena, we might note that the character Gaetano Fenoaltea recalls the figure of Sergio Fenoaltea (1905–95) a former *confinato* politico (later high-profile diplomat), and contributor to *La Cultura*. Of the several minor characters, he is relatively well developed as a (not altogether comfortable) type. As we will see in a letter to his sister that lauds the hospitality of his hosts in Brancaleone Calabro, the general assessment of the narrator's descriptions of the townspeople, particularly of their courtesy, is positive.

9  Pavese, *Terra d'esilio*, 8–9.

10  Cesare Pavese, *The Political Prisoner*, trans. W.J. Strachan (London: Peter Owen, 2008), p. 16.

11  Pavese, *Terra d'esilio*, 9.

12  Pavese, *The Political Prisoner*, 16.

13  Gian-Paolo Biasin, *Smile of the Gods: A Thematic Study of Cesare Pavese's Works* (New York: Cornell University Press, 1968), p. 31.

14  Note, however, his letter to sister Maria dated 2 March 1936: 'Mi trovo troppo stupido ad aver creduto in passato che l'isolamento individuale, anche di un attimo, fosse la felicità'. (I find myself too stupid to have believed in the past that individual isolation, even for a second, was happiness.)

15  This Caienna is not to be confused with Assab, an internment colony in Africa, called 'la Caienna italiana'. See Dal Pont, *I lager di Mussolini*, 33.

16  Carlo Lucarelli, *L'isola dell'angelo caduto* (Turin: Einaudi, 2009), p. 219.

17  Giorgio Bassani, *Gli occhiali d'oro* (Milan: Oscar Classici Moderni, 1996), p. 24.

18  Examples include Paolo Diacono and Molina, see Giorgio Robiony and Rosaria Conte, *Amori al confino* (Lanciano: Carabba Editore, 2004), p. 69.

19  Eric Santner, 'History beyond the Pleasure Principle: Some Thoughts on the Representation of Trauma', in Saul Friedlander (ed.), *Probing the Limits of Representation* (Cambridge, MA: Harvard University Press, 1992), pp. 143–54.

20  Millicent Marcus, *Italian Film in the Shadow of Auschwitz* (Toronto: University of Toronto Press, 2007), p. 11.

21  Marcus, *Italian Film in the Shadow of Auschwitz*, 166–7.

22  Santner, 'History beyond the Pleasure Principle', 144.

23  Natalia Ginzburg, 'Inverno in Abruzzo', in *Opere*. Vol. 1 (Milan: Arnoldo Mondadori Editore, 1986), pp. 787–8.

24  Natalia Ginzburg, *The Little Virtues: Essays*, trans. Dick Davis (New York: Arcade Publishing, 2017).

25  Ginzburg, 'Inverno in Abruzzo', 792.

26  *Ibid.*

27  Carlo Levi, *Cristo si è fermato a Eboli* (Turin: Einaudi, 1990), p. 3. Subsequent references to this work are given in the main text as (Levi, 1990).

28  Carlo Levi, *Christ Stopped at Eboli*, trans. Frances Frenaye (New York: Farrar, Straus and Company, 1947), p. 1. Subsequent references to this work are given in the main text as (Levi, 1947).

29  Ignazio Silone, *Fontamara* (Milan: Mondadori, 1997), p. 11.

30  Millicent Marcus, *Filmmaking by the Book: Italian Cinema and Literary Adaptation* (Baltimore: Johns Hopkins University Press, 1993), p. xi.

31  Joseph Campbell, *The Hero with a Thousand Faces* (New York: Pantheon Books, 1949), p. 23.

32  Since in theory, there could be no conversations of a political nature, the *confinati* often used elaborate and sometimes hilarious metaphors to cover their tracks. See for example Emilio Lussu, *La catena*, ed. Mimmo Franzinelli (Milan: Baldini e Castoldi, 1997), p. 66. Subsequent references to this work are given in the main text as Lussu, 1997.

33  Nitti, *Escape*, v–vi. Subsequent references to this work are given in the main text as (Nitti, 1930).

34  Francesco Fausto Nitti, *Le nostre prigioni e la nostra evasione* (Naples: Edizioni scientifiche italiane, 1946), 5. Subsequent references to this work are given in the main text as (Nitti, 1946).

35  Alberto Jacometti, *Ventotene* (Genoa: Fratelli Frilli, 2004), p. 11. Subsequent references to this work are given in the main text as (Jacometti, 2004).

36   And if we may open a brief parenthesis here: current scholarship uses the word *witness* advisedly, merely nodding in the direction of a discussion about the literature of testimony – this is a term often heard in connection with the literature of extreme or 'limit' experiences, such as literature about genocide or life in concentration camps. We come to these texts armed with certain expectations about claims to truth and about the privileging of documentary-like qualities over the question of a text's 'literary value', which is of secondary importance. We might ask, in the case of both Lussu and Jacometti, whether their structural and tonal similarities authorise us to read them as a sort of sub-sub-genre of the literature of testimony. Neither Lussu nor Jacometti resemble, say, a Primo Levi, but nor does Robert Antelme's meditative *The Human Race*: and yet it, too, is a form of testimonial.

37   Ventotene also had an orchestra.

38   Jacometti's text is clearly addressed to an exclusively male audience, as is made evident by asides such as 'Vi ricordate il vostro servizio militare, la caserma?' (Remember your military service? The barracks?) (p. 93) and 'Se siete ammogliati, mi capirete meglio' (If you are married, you'll understand me better) (p. 93).

39   Mario Magri, *Una vita per la libertà: diciassette anni di confino politico di un martire delle Fosse Ardeatine* (Rome: Editore Ludovico Puglielli, 1956), p. 33.

40   Magri, *Una vita per la libertà*, 27.

41   Camilla Ravera, *Diario di trent'anni 1913–1943* (Rome: Editori Riuniti, 1973), p. 590.

42   Ravera, *Diario di trent'anni*, 591. Pigs are of great interest to Sante Tani, as well. Interned at San Bartolomeo in Galdo (Benevento), the recurring themes of his letters are the hospitality of the people of San Bartolomeo, the beauty of its countryside, and the pigs, which are leashed and walked like dogs (p. 56). Sante Tani, *Lettere dal carcere e dal confino (1942–1943)*, ed. Luca Berti (Milan: Franco Angeli 1999).

43   Ravera, *Diario di trent'anni*, 681.

44   Regarding requests for exoneration, a typical feature of *confino* correspondence is the unequivocal disapproval by a prisoner of a family member's attempt to intervene with the authorities on the prisoner's behalf. In a letter dated 24 September 1935, we read an irate Pavese forbidding his sister Maria to ask for his transfer to another location: 'O a casa o niente.' (It's either home or nothing.) See also 2 October 1935, in which he repeats the injunction against requests for transferral. Interesting are the motives for staying, which would appear to have nothing to do with the place itself. On the other hand, in stark contrast to the political *confinati* who become incensed at the idea that a family member may try to intervene on his or her behalf by asking for a pardon, Pavese himself asks twice (letter 25–28 February 1936).

45   Ansaldo, *L'antifascista riluttante*, p. 10. Subsequent references to this work are given in the main text as (Ansaldo, 1992).

46   See also Giulio Turchi's *Emma: diario d'amore di un comunista al confino* (Rome: Donzelli, 2012).

47   There are happy stories as well, however. Perugia has a beautiful nursery for the small children of the incarcerated – gorgeously painted in the styles of Tre-, Quattro-, and Cinquecento. There is a four-year old here, though the rule is the same as in Rome (up to three years old), but the nuns love him so much that they keep him on as long as they can. Cesira Fiori, *Una donna nelle carceri fasciste* (Rome: Editori Riuniti, 1965), p. 92. Subsequent references to this work are given in the main text as (Fiori, 1965).

48   Cesira Fiori, *La confinata* (Milan: La Pietra, 1979), p. 10. Subsequent references to this work are given in the main text as (Fiori, 1979).

49   Giorgio Braccialarghe, *Nelle spire di Urlavento: Il confino di Ventotene negli anni dell'agonia del Fascismo* (Genoa: Fratelli Frilli, 2005), p. 30.

50   Altiero Spinelli, *Come ho tentato di diventare saggio: Io, Ulisse* (Bologna: Il Mulino, 1984), p. 300. Subsequent references to this work are given in the main text as (Spinelli, 1984).

51   Riccardo Gualino, *Solitudine* (Venice: Marsilio, 1997), p. 13. Subsequent references to this work are given in the main text as (Gualino, 1997).

52   Gualino also wrote an earlier text (composed in 1931: *Frammenti di vita*).

53   We might therefore mention another book cut from the same cloth, Manlio Rossi-Doria's tellingly titled *La gioia tranquilla del ricordo: memorie 1905–1934* (published posthumously in 1991). His recollection of internal confinement in the countryside of San Fele resembles Lussu and Jacometti's in its strategy of 'accentuating the positive', though Rossi-Doria's motives are somewhat different from theirs, as we might expect (it is memoir more than a history lesson or a piece of journalism, it was written late in life and published posthumously, so that it could be inserted as a productive and logical punctuation mark in his retrospectively coherent personal narrative. But it shares Gualino's difficult categorisation.)

54   Giorgio Amendola, *Un'isola* (Milan: Rizzoli, 1981), p, 119.

55   There is no evidence in the memoirs that we have read to support Lorenzo Benadusi's assertion that 'an exchange was set up whereby the anti-Fascists passed on values and knowledge to criminals, leading them to develop an interest in politics and take anti-Fascist positions' in Benadusi, *The Enemy of the New Man*, 121.

56   Paul Ricoeur, 'Narrative Identity' *Philosophy Today*, 35:1 (1991), 73–80.

57   Bruce Merry, 'The Partisan Novel. Theme and Variations', *Mediterranean Review*, 11:4 (Summer 1972), 72.

58   Paul DeMan, 'Autobiography as De-facement', *MLN*, 94 (1979), 920.

59   Our thinking here is indebted to Claudio Fogu ('*Italiani brava gente*'), who performs a similar reading of the political and memorial climate of the 1980s in Italy.

60   See Pagano, *Il confino politico a Lipari* and Ferdinando Cordova and Pantaleone Sergi, *Regione di confino: la Calabria (1927–1943)* (Rome: Bulzoni Editore, 2005).

61   See for example, Tani, *Lettere dal carcere e dal confino*.

62   Emilio Gentile, *La grande Italia* (Bari: Laterza, 2011).

# 4

# Screening internal exile

## Introduction: *Confino as holiday*

Film has received short shrift in studies on internal exile during Fascism. Those who write on it tend to mention only two films on the subject, in most cases quite briefly: Ettore Scola's *Una giornata particolare* (*A Special Day*, 1977) and Francesco Rosi's *Cristo si è fermato a Eboli* (*Christ Stopped at Eboli*, 1979), which narrate the experience in disparate fashions.[1] In the former, internal exile is briefly referenced, while the latter visualises the experience of political confinement. This chapter fills this scholarly gap by exploring these two narrative approaches to the exile experience of *mafiosi*, intellectuals, and those considered politically suspect in approximately sixteen feature films, documentaries, and made-for-television movies released between 1960 and 2012.[2]

In order to unpack the representations of internal exile in these texts, the chapter engages with the critical categories of narrative fetishism and mourning as theorised by Eric Santner as constituting two possible aesthetic representations of trauma. According to Santner:

> Both narrative fetishism and mourning are responses to loss, to a past that refuses to go away due to its traumatic impact. The work of mourning is a process of elaborating the reality of loss by remembering and repeating it in symbolically and dialogically mediated doses. Narrative fetishism, by contrast, is a strategy of undoing, in fantasy, the need for mourning by simulating a condition of intactness … in narrative fetishism the 'post' is indefinitely postponed.[3]

Narrative fetishism displaces traces of the past traumatic event and, in effect, is a mode of denial through a formal narrative structure. The work of mourning, however, involves a complicated process of 'remembering and repeating' trauma in the present within controlled environments (in dream or therapy, for example).[4] Santner addresses how recent events in Europe (the fall of the Berlin wall and the success of Edgar Reitz's film *Heimat*; *Homeland*, 1984) influence what he calls the altering of the 'German historical imagination' regarding the Holocaust.[5] Far from the possibly productive outcome of mourning, narrative fetishism 'directly or indirectly offers reassurances that there was no need for anxiety in the first place'.[6]

Many films that touch upon the internal exile of politicals and anti-Fascists engage fetishism and work well with Santner's thesis regarding a sense of closure and comfort with respect to a painful event. Whereas literary narratives on the experience of internal exile and its traumatic implications abound, analogous cinematographic representations are wanting. This is striking compared to the breadth of Italian films treating contemporaneous atrocities in Italian history, that of Nazism and deportation to the concentration camps. This list is extensive and includes Gillo Pontecorvo's *Kapò* (1959), Luchino Visconti's *La caduta degli dei* (*The Damned*, 1969), Lina Wertmüller's *Pasqualino Settebellezze* (*Pasqualino Seven Beauties*, 1974), Liliana Cavani's *Il portiere di notte* (*The Night Porter*, 1974), Vittorio De Sica's *Il giardino dei Finzi-Contini* (*The Garden of the Finzi-Continis*, 1976), Roberto Benigni's *La vita è bella* (*Life is Beautiful*, 1998) and Ferzan Özpetek's *La finestra di fronte* (*Facing Windows*, 2003), among many others.[7] All of these films, to different extents, focus on the grey areas of survival while reassessing Fascism and Nazism and frequently questioning the values of those who fought against these regimes. Numerous Italian films then look back on the experiences of Fascism and the Holocaust and thus participate in the construction of a trauma narrative that helps the wounded nation make sense of a difficult past.[8]

E. Ann Kaplan argues that cultures may forget or displace a trauma, and wonders, 'how could one discover the strategies by which dominant power groups [develop] mechanisms to engineer a "forgetting" of traumas that they originally inflicted on victims', a question of particular interest to the case of internal exile during Fascism with regard to recent discussions of exile as vacation.[9] Ultimately, however, remnants of the trauma-inducing event return in the guise of symptoms, and Kaplan looks towards the cinema, with a particular eye on melodrama, to investigate ways in which a culture 'can unconsciously address its traumatic hauntings'.[10] Most of the films in the corpus of Italian cinematic works dealing with internal exile, we argue here, engage in the process of performative forgetting discussed by Kaplan through downplaying the horrors of the experience, as is the case of Rosi's film, or quite frequently displacing pain and atrocity onto narratives that are more pleasurable and generally find a neat sense of closure common to the melodramatic mode.

Clearly, the experience of internal exile is unlike that of the concentration camps and the final solution, and many who write on internal exile preface arguments along these lines, thus couching their work with a pre-emptive apologia.[11] Michael R. Ebner, however, notes how the 'Nazi and Fascist regimes … operated in strikingly similar fashions, first "cleansing" the nation of Communists and anti-Fascists, then stepping up their campaign against ethnic and religious minorities, homosexuals, alcoholics, common criminals, and other categories of enemies and "social outsiders"'.[12] Of course, there are obvious reasons (i.e. Nazi Germany's genocidal history) why this distinction might be drawn. Interestingly, however, only fourteen films, documentaries, and made-for-television movies have been made that centre on the experience of internal exile (the majority of which are short documentaries or features that saw a very limited and short-term release, a few only at a festival here or there), a disproportionately low number when considering the number of individuals subjected to the detention strategy over such a large number of years. As Alan O'Leary argues, 'terrorism and political violence ... continue[s] to exercise the national imagination and that of Italian film-makers to a remarkable degree' (and the same can be said for the Holocaust and the Mafia).[13] This is not the case, however, for the legacy of internal exile, an experience that was shared by many, yet that has been repressed on a national level, to the point where in September 2003, Italy's leading political figure Silvio Berlusconi, could declaim with alarming nonchalance that Mussolini never killed anyone, and only sent them on vacation. Acknowledging national culpability for *confino*-related human rights violations would go against a broader national tendency to cast Italy as the victim ('italiani brava gente') rather than the perpetrator with regards to World War II. As Lidia Santarelli argues concerning Italian war crimes in occupied Greece, much work remains to be done for the nation to take responsibility for past wrongdoings so as to move towards ridding itself of the 'syndrome of self-absolution with which, until now, the "good Italian" has been contrasted with the "bad German"',[14] an operation clearly at work in the national memory of the practice of *confino*.

Berlusconi's categorisation of internal exile as holiday raises some interesting questions about what transpired in these loci. For some, the experience of internal exile was infernal, others, including a selection of homosexual men interviewed in Gabriella Romano's documentary *Ricordare: un documentario su fascismo e omosessualità* (*Remember: A Documentary on Fascism and Homosexuality*, 2004), look on their imprisonment with nostalgia (even though as a whole, gay *confinati* were treated much worse overall than politicals).

Most films examined in this chapter follow the generic indicators of melodrama, a genre with a Manichean perspective that 'renders complex psychic and social relations into easily identifiable codes', while simultaneously revealing 'what is repressed in the process'.[15] Melodrama frequently engages with and repeats a series of traumas (individual, say, of the family or home and national, of, for example, war and terrorism) only eventually to reach a comforting (and predictable) sense of closure that, as Kaplan argues, 'reassures the viewer, who leaves the cinema believing she is safe and that all is well in her world'.[16] Rather than foregrounding the complicated and distressing experience of exile shared by tens of thousands of Italian anti-Fascists, homosexuals, Anarchists, Socialists, *mafiosi*, Jehovah's Witnesses, and other suspect groups whose crimes were never proven, in many films, protagonists merely mention internal exile, in several cases quite flippantly. Otherwise, and more frequently, when detainees are visualised on site, or narrate their memories, suffering is downplayed, love stories are foregrounded, and internees seem to be doing relatively well during their detention.

Most films that treat the on-site experience depict victims interned for political motives, while the experiences of homosexuals or *mafiosi* sent to internal exile are merely referenced. Two films on the Mafia allude to the internment of *mafiosi* and Mafia sympathisers quite dismissively, and represent more of an indictment of the Mafia than of internal exile. This is the case with Pasquale Scimeca's *Placido Rizzotto* (2000) and Marco Tullio Giordana's *I cento passi* (*The Hundred Steps*, 2000) where allusions to internal exile and prison inscribe the films within a moral universe that vilifies *mafiosi*. In these and several other films under consideration, to varying degrees, the internal exile affair is channelled, recalling Santner, into a series of culturally acceptable critiques: the Mafia, Fascism in general, the corrupt Italian state, gender construction, or honour and vendetta.

Films that visualise or narrate internal exile are representative of a larger trend that ultimately works to de-malign the practice. In some works, such as *Il confino di Cesare Pavese* (Giuseppe Taffarel, 1962), *La villeggiatura* (*Black Holiday*, Marco Leto, 1973), *Cristo si è fermato a Eboli*, and *Prima che il gallo canti* (*Before the Cock Crows*, Mario Foglietti, 1993), the representation of Fascist officials comes off as rather benign. For example, in Leto's film, a few government functionaries are cast in a positively glowing light as in the case of the commissioner Rizzuto who provides Professor Franco Rossini (a character loosely based on Carlo Rosselli) with the possibility of teaching in a gorgeous villa with stunning views of the ocean. The film implies that the good commissioner allows the professor's wife and daughter to come and live with him. The same might be said for protagonist Carlo Levi's stay in indigenous exile in Gagliano, where he practises medicine, paints, takes long walks, lives in the nicest house in town, establishes friendships and enjoys the companionship of a dog. The mayor, the main authority figure in the town, is much more interested in sharing local gossip than enforcing rules while the commissioner comes off as a womaniser. Similar acknowledgements of normalcy are found in *Libera, amore mio* (*Libera My Love*, Mauro Bolognini, 1975) in which the eponymous protagonist marries while on Ustica, whereas in *Ricordare*, interviewees are nostalgic for the exile islands of Tremiti because, as one survivor explains, 'life was better' under Mussolini.

Although many of these films leave the viewer with fervent messages regarding both the moralities of Fascism and a plea for political engagement across class lines, reading the protagonists' experiences as particularly traumatic is difficult. (Levi goes so far as to state that he finds himself 'benissimo' in Gagliano). At several points then, the films are aligned with Arturo Bocchini's rationale for the system of internal exile that he put forth in 1928 as 'the least possible of evils'. Situating the *confino di polizia* in Edenic spaces or remote friendly villages, Bocchini argued, would help 'sfatare la leggenda tanto cara ai fuoriusciti italiani e alla stampa estera ostile al Regime, circa il presunto inumano trattamento usato ai confini politici (disprove the legend so dear to Italian political exiles and to the foreign press hostile to the Regime about the so-called inhumane treatment of those sent to internal exile)'.[17] Such heartening representations of imprisonment recall Michael Radford's 1994 film *Il postino* (*The Postman*) treating the exile of Chilean poet Pablo Neruda to the island of Procida or Gabriele Salvatores' *Mediterraneo* (1991), which represses issues relating to Fascism. Like with Radford's and Salvatores' films, in the texts treated in this chapter the exile experience serves as a convenient backdrop to narrate stories that are more pleasant and conform to the traditional logic of desire that dominates the classical cinema.[18] Thus, and recalling Santner, in these films the distressing events surrounding the practice of internal exile are disavowed and political confinement is reimagined as holiday.[19]

## Male melodrama: Pavese, Rosselli, Amendola, Levi

We now turn to a series of films, documentaries, and made-for-television movies dedicated primarily to the experience of four intellectuals sent to internal exile: Cesare Pavese, Carlo Rosselli, Giorgio Amendola, and Carlo Levi. By and large, most of the texts discussed follow the conventions of male melodrama, a genre that privileges and celebrates male suffering and creativity at the expense of the feminine.[20] Indeed, the exile experience of writers and political activists who are trapped on prison islands and isolated from their cause in homosocial milieus (save a wife here and there who leaves everything behind so as to be with her husband) where they frequently write of their desolation, express profound angst over their current unjust situation, and dream of the day when they will be finally united with their comrades in the battle against the oppressor is apt material for the generic formula. In the visual texts under consideration, masculinity might initially appear in crisis, but ultimately the crisis is smoothed over, and in the words of Catherine O'Rawe 'the centrality of hegemonic masculinity'[21] is reasserted, and narrative closure is achieved.

Close to 350 women were sentenced to political *confino*,[22] and yet there is a paucity of research engaging with their exile experience. It is striking that only two films have been made focusing on female *confinati*: Bolognini's *Libera, amore mio* and the made-for-television movie *Edda Ciano e il comunista* (*Edda Ciano and the Communist*, Graziano Diana, 2011), both of which are melodramas in which, in keeping with the genre, the female protagonist is ultimately punished for desiring differently. Conversely, in the many visual representations of the exile experience of male *confinati*, protagonists are redeemed and their suffering has meaning, as is the case in male melodrama.

### Cesare Pavese

O'Rawe makes a strong case that 'all Italian cinema is male melodrama, shot through with regret for unlived possibilities and dwelling lovingly in the space of homosocial crisis'.[23] This is certainly the case for representations and discussions of the experience of Cesare Pavese during his year spent in the small seaside village of Brancaleone in Calabria where he was condemned to three years of internal exile (he was released after one year when he petitioned Mussolini for a pardon) as a result of being in possession of letters from an imprisoned anti-Fascist, correspondence that actually belonged to love interest and Communist Tina Pizzardo. Onscreen representations of or narrations about Pavese's time away from his native Turin in the film *Prima che il gallo canti* (*Before the Cock Crows*, Mario Foglietti, 1993) and the documentaries *Terra d'esilio* (*Land of Exile*, Elio Girlanda, 1980) and *Il confino di Cesare Pavese* (*The Internal Exile of Cesare Pavese*, Giuseppe Taffarel, 1962) are melancholic in tone, and highlight the writer's sense of isolation and longing for Pizzardo, 'la donna dalla voce rauca (the woman with the hoarse voice)' who Pavese protected and refused to turn in to save himself.

Politics play a small role in these texts, and like in several of the films discussed in this chapter, Fascist officials are kind to Pavese, who, despite his existential angst, is able to lead a relatively pleasant life in Brancaleone, where he writes, has amorous encounters, develops close friendships, goes hunting, attends local festivals, and sunbathes and enjoys the ocean. In contrast, Lino Del Fra's *Antonio Gramsci: i giorni del carcere* (*Antonio Gramsci: The Days in Prison*, 1977) adopts a different strategy. The engaged focus on the class struggle and fragmentations in the Communist Party overshadows Gramsci's relationship with his wife and sister-in-law who make minor appearances in the film.[24] Narrative in the film and documentaries on Pavese, however, centres upon the women in his life: his sister Maria, Pizzardo, Elena the daughter of his landlord who cleans his house and with whom he has an affair, and Concia, a servant girl who in the short novel *Il carcere* upon which the feature film is based, is described as 'bella come una capra. Qualcosa tra la statua e la capra'[25] (as beautiful as a goat. Something between a statue and a goat). Indeed, each of these women is constructed as a projection of fantasy and represents something different to Pavese. Through their suffering (Elena), objectification (Concia), or denigration (Pizzardo) the viewer is positioned to feel profound sympathy for Pavese. In the texts, Pavese (or at times his alter-ego Stefano) experiences profound crises regarding his creativity, identity, and general sense of direction in life. Yet, ultimately, his suffering leads to greater insight and animates his expressive faculties.

The first minute or so of Foglietti's film and the two documentaries include images of a train, and as we hear the whistle of the locomotive, we are transported into the past, and move with Pavese towards the site of detention. Of the use made of the train in the cinema, Lynne Kirby writes 'the cinema finds an apt metaphor in the train, in its framed, moving image, its construction of a journey as an optical experience, the radical juxtaposition of different places, the "annihilation of space and time." As a machine of vision and an instrument for conquering space and time, the train is a mechanical double for the cinema and for the transport of the spectator into fiction, fantasy, and dream'.[26] The trope of the train in the three texts seamlessly sutures the spectator into the narrative, which is especially the case of the two documentaries, where the train is moving from right to left across the screen, which in the classical cinema denotes movement from the present to the past.

In Girlanda's *Terra d'esilio*, which is the title of one of Pavese's short stories based on his time in Brancaleone, travelling in the train is the documentary's voiceover narrator. He is constructed as Pavese's double and whilst en route to Brancaleone is shown reading a selection of Pavese's fiction including *Il carcere* and a book of short stories. Once he arrives in Brancaleone, a voiceover begins reading out a letter that Pavese wrote to his sister Maria in which he describes his arrival at the station, how the locals are 'cotti dal sole (baked by the sun)', enjoy swimming, and carry jars of water on their heads, notes the large quantity of pigs, and laments the absence of grappa, before asking that a list of books be sent to him immediately. The voiceover is accompanied by images of the narrator walking the streets, entering the Hotel Roma, Pavese's first residence, while women look cautiously outside of doorframes. Here, Pavese's letter reflects an Orientalist viewpoint on Brancaleone that distinguishes him (a man of letters with northern tastes) from those he describes as the carefree townsfolk who are aligned with, and seemingly blend in with, the natural world. Such a supercilious position is echoed in the letter where we hear of the inhabitants' good-natured hospitality.

Pavese's relationship with women, 'the fundamental theme of his work' as Girlanda explains, is central to the documentary. Oreste Politi who is the inspiration for Giannino Catalano, one of the protagonists of *Il carcere*, discusses his friendship with Pavese, their shared political beliefs, and thoughts on women – the narrator asks whether it is true that he was 'libertino, donnaiolo' (a womaniser, a ladies' man). At one point Elena is described through voiceover from *Il carcere* as 'nera come in lutto' (black as if in mourning). Indeed, in *Terra d'esilio* women come off as types (one man with whom Girlanda speaks explains that women in Brancaleone are 'prototypes'). Elena is a 'buona' (good) and 'materna' (maternal) woman who keeps Pavese's house in order; Concia, who 'sa di capra' (smells of goat), is described as a temptress who betrays men. Women, this man explains, lead Pavese towards death in that he is unable to conquer them. Thus, they are represented as castrating projections of male fantasy.

Later, we hear a voiceover of one of Pavese's letters in which he describes how he takes advantage of his 'efebica prestanza fisica' (youthful good looks) and so as to pass the time 'mi denudavo … il candido fiore del corpo sulla riva del mare, a componevo, così ellenici quadri, che i gerani della spiaggia non dimenticheranno tanto presto' (I undressed … the snow white flower of my body on the shore of the ocean, and I composed Hellenic tableaux that the geraniums on the beach will not forget any time soon). The voiceover accompanies images of the narrator swimming in and emerging from the ocean before lying down on the sand, and the segment concludes with a languid pan in extreme close-up of the narrator's foot, leg, torso, and face still wet from the sea, before cutting to a painting of a woman. Hence, Pavese's corpus is transformed into that of the narrator and the documentary ultimately celebrates the male mind and body, and positions suffering as a means to reach the sublime.

*Il confino di Cesare Pavese* immediately sets up the eponymous subject as a victim who makes extreme sacrifices for love. He wasn't a conspirator, we are told, he 'subiva la condanna per salvare la sua donna, la famosa donna "dalla voce rauca" di cui era innamorato' (he suffered his sentence to save his woman, the famous 'woman with the hoarse voice' with whom he was in love). The documentary underscores repeatedly Pavese's anguish. In a sorrowful tone, the voiceover narrator describes his solitude and melancholy, and conveys that he is without roots, and discusses his sad, lonely, and wretched life, and desire for progeny (the documentary is rife with children). Even when he receives the news of his pardon, he is unmoved, as he feels that it is 'impossible that something not sad could happen to him'. Nostalgia saturates the documentary, and is associated with the train's whistle that would take him back to Turin, and to the woman who haunts him, yet never writes to him. Linda Williams notes that 'If emotional and moral registers are sounded, if a work invites us to feel sympathy for the virtues of beset victims, if the narrative trajectory is ultimately concerned with a retrieval and staging of virtue through adversity and suffering, then the operative mode is melodrama',[27] an ethos that certainly resonates in *Il confino di Cesare Pavese*. The documentary positions the viewer to root for Pavese who endures an 'umorismo tragico' (tragic humourism), to feel his desolation as he recalls his native Turin that is pictured frequently, and to identify with him in the locus of his exile.

Hence we see Brancaleone and its residents through his retrospective gaze (as with *Terra d'esilio*, this documentary includes several of Pavese's letters that describe his environs, interactions, and take on the locals). Frequently, the narrator speaks of how various people pictured in 1962 Brancaleone recall characters from Pavese's life and fiction. An enterprising young man brings to mind Don Giannino, an elderly man buying olives reminds us of a character from the novel *La luna e i falò*; an old man walking the streets evokes Barbariccia, the mendicant from *Il carcere* who reminds Pavese that life is a battle and that Pavese must 'impegnarsi' (engage, make an effort); whilst a woman cleaning a small room is reminiscent of the forlorn Elena, Pavese's love interest during his period of detention who, the documentary tells us, suffers due to unrequited love. All of these subjects appear unhappy, their downcast faces stare off into the distance or into the camera, repeatedly in the case of the woman who looks sorrowful and slightly unhinged, as if she perennially awaits the return of her lover. Like in the other documentary, the townspeople are cast as simpletons who live in poverty, and who accept their cruel destiny and who do not understand Pavese when he speaks to them, the implication being his intelligence estranges those around him. At one point, however, a man at the bar is shown reading Pavese's fiction. These people, who the film implies have not changed at all in almost thirty years, were born of Pavese's memory and continue to live for him. In one letter, his attempt at humour disparages the residents of Brancaleone whilst underlining his suffering: 'I think that I will get married here and procure a child who at two years old already says cuckold and slob. That way I will end my life'.

The documentary concludes recounting Pavese's return to Turin after his release; he desires to arrive quickly, 'for her'. Brancaleone will remain a memory of unjustified punishment that will then, the narrator relates, inspire Pavese to become a more active anti-Fascist (in both culture and life). Thus, his suffering has meaning and is translated into political action. Several images of trains, train tracks, and views from train windows are accompanied by a description of Pavese's anguished journey of return. We learn that a friend meets him at the station, and reluctantly responds to Pavese's question 'and her'? with 'don't think about it anymore, she got married yesterday' and the documentary comes to an abrupt end with the screeching sound of a train crash, the camera idle on the tracks. This denouement encapsulates the temporality of the melodrama whereby events happen, citing Williams, 'too late' and 'the quest for connection is always tinged with melancholy'. Williams borrows from Franco Moretti to argue that the tears so common to the melodramatic mode come when the characters finally realise what the audience knew all along, and when their desire is 'recognized as futile'.[28] Mourning for Pavese's lost love (if only he had arrived one day earlier!) takes precedence over the experience of internal exile, which for him, the documentary implies, was fruitful in both politics and prose.

*Prima che il gallo canti*, the only feature film made on Pavese's time spent in Brancaleone, also implies that the experience of displacement was fundamental to Pavese's development as a writer. While at the seaside struggling with his inability to compose poetry, we hear an interior monologue that urges Pavese, in order to survive, to use his skills as a writer to make use of his time, to create a barrier between him and the people and the land, and to create a life, to write about it and become a writer. He must, he is told, invent his future if he wants to change the past. He must remember, however, that he is still in jail, and Brancaleone must remain a 'terra d'esilio' (land of exile). At this point, Pavese invents his alter ego Stefano, an engineer who is the protagonist of *Il carcere*. In the film, which was produced by the region of Calabria, Pavese's experiences of loss and pain are translated into cultural gain.

The film's beginning establishes the melodramatic tone: When the title sequence which is composed of shots of a gloomy Turin concludes, Pavese is arrested and his narrative of suffering begins. Pavese's distress is foregrounded frequently as we see him thrash about in bed unable to sleep, stare desolately at the ocean, which he describes as just 'one more wall' of his prison, battle with another imaginary *confinato* who torments him, have awkward erotic encounters with Elena, frequently come across Concia who vexes him, and nostalgically recall Pizzardo. At the same time, however, Pavese is treated quite well by the authorities. He establishes several friendships, becomes a father figure to young Corrado whom he tutors and eventually converts into a 'Subversive' like himself, and about whom he writes most pertinently. Politics are minimised in the film. The townspeople prefer talking about beautiful women to affairs of the State while Fascism and Fascist spectacle are relegated to the background (a rehearsal of the local Fascist youth group here, a scene of a woman giving up her wedding ring to the dictatorship there) and not connected to the film's larger diegesis. Even the disciplinary warning given to Pavese on the day of his arrival not to leave his residence 'prima che il gallo canti' (before the cock crows) takes on an amorous tone when Elena begins visiting before dawn.

The representation of women in the film is quite conventional and in line with dominant cinematographic models, thus conforming to Laura Mulvey's thesis in her seminal article on film spectatorship and identification, regarding how female characters are frequently punished so as to fend off castration anxiety. Indeed, in *Prima che il gallo canti*, women are represented as either threatening figures who are then fetishised (Pizzardo), are cast as voyeuristic objects of the male gaze (Concia), or appear hysterical and are ultimately desexualised (Elena).[29] Moreover, two women not visualised in the film are positioned as causing the downfall of the men in their lives. First, Barbariccia's madness, Elena tells Pavese, results from his wife's desertion (she is never pictured in the film), and ever since he cannot stand the sight of women. Also, the other *confinato* that Stefano/Pavese imagines inhabits Brancaleone is interned because of a woman. He explains that he received three years' exile for beating up a man who was courting his woman, and later returns to Pavese in a dream to tell him that she was killed and the 'best thing about it' is the method of death: she was shot seven times in the face supposedly by her lover, yet it is clear that the *confinato* is guilty of the crime.[30] Women are positioned as scapegoats who take the blame for male inadequacy.

Interestingly, during the film we only see Elena in Pavese's room where she cleans, rearranges his books (sometimes to his displeasure) and has sexual relations with him. Thus, her storyline foregrounds domestic space, as is frequently the case with melodrama. Often, Elena appears hysterical, convinced that they will be discovered and then later fears that Pavese will leave her. Voiceover conveys that 'Stefano' experiences Elena's body, but has no love for her. When she comes to say goodbye to him as she assumes he is leaving shortly she prepares his suitcase and claims that she will not cry (she has shed tears repeatedly in the past), and before leaving she glances back at him and stoically covers her head in a dark shawl. Here, the film implies that Elena has entered a period of mourning, and will live out her days grief-stricken over a loss that Pavese barely notices.

Indeed, Pavese is much more taken with Concia, whom he regularly runs into at the seaside or in the mountains. Surrounded by goats (a detail absent in the novel), mute except when she sings (songs in dialect about love), and gazing alluringly at Pavese, Concia is aligned with the natural world and seems to exist only for the pleasure of men. In that she never speaks, appears out of the blue, is shown leisurely and seductively eating a melon, juices dripping down her lips and face, and drives Pavese mad with desire, she is a fetishised projection of male fantasy. After he encounters her on the beach for the first time, he races home where he goes into a panic, searching frantically for the pen that Pizzardo gifted him so that he can write, and thereby reassert his threatened masculinity. In her discussion of the look and the gaze in the classical cinema, Kaja Silverman argues that the look is the most typical mode for the male to 'disburden himself of lack'. Woman, the object of the gaze, becomes the 'site at which male insufficiency is deposited'. In this signifying system, woman is a projection of male fantasy that guards against castration anxiety,[31] which is aptly the case with Concia, who Pavese frequently encounters whilst he is lamenting the loss of Pizzardo and his native Turin.

Pizzardo is frequently constructed as a femme fatale character who lures Pavese down the wrong path. She is mysterious, her motives are unclear to us, and we know little about her attraction to Pavese. Also, she wears dark red lipstick, has a dramatic dark haircut, and in flashback and memory frequently appears out of the blue, once on a stairwell, a conceit typical of the film noir, and routinely emerges from or retreats to shadows. Pizzardo is a typical fetish object of the male gaze who creates desire and sets the narrative in motion (without Pavese's handling of the letter there would be no story) but in essence is without a substantive identity. She is frequently shown in close-up and is the object of Pavese's gaze. In her study on the femme fatale, Mary Ann Doane insists on the figure's traumatic potential. In that she 'never really is what she seems to be',[32] she is threatening, unpredictable, ambivalent and therefore apparently unmasterable. She is a 'figure of fascination' and as a projection of male desire, she is an 'articulation of fears surrounding the loss of stability and centrality of the self, the "I," the ego'. As a 'symptom' of male anxiety she is not an empowering symbol. She has no autonomy in herself and is only a 'carrier' of power.[33] She is a 'secret'[34] that must be revealed, which makes her an ideal character for the film noir whose plot is centred on a mystery. Moreover, the classic femme fatale manipulates men through her sexuality, frequently taking advantage of intimate knowledge of the protagonist's secret past and causing his downfall, as is the case with Pavese's attraction to Pizzardo.

The film comes to a close when Pavese leaves Brancaleone. Whilst at the train station, he gazes intensely at Concia, who is distraught as she realises that his departure is imminent. Once returned to Turin, he walks the fogged-in banks of the Po and contemplates his sojourn in the South, noting that his time in Brancaleone was crucial for his development as a writer, concluding, 'it was better to live down there, looking at the ocean, and having hope for the future, instead of entering in this future, and knowing that I would never be able to leave it'. Pavese's nostalgia has led to the creation of his own aesthetics as his loss becomes, recalling Schiesari, 'idealised' as it 'empowers the ego' which focuses not on the lost object per se but on 'the condition of loss *as* loss'.[35] As we have seen, and as with the other documentaries treating Pavese's confinement, *Prima che il gallo canti* legitimates Pavese's '"excessive" suffering' while women remain 'an oppressed and nameless (or generic) other'[36] and the experience of internal exile is sidetracked, like the women whom Pavese left behind.

## Carlo Rosselli (and Emilio Lussu and Francesco Fausto Nitti)

Unlike in the films focusing on Pavese's period of exile which privilege the personal over the political, visual representations of Carlo Rosselli's (and to a lesser extent Emilio Lussu and Francesco Fausto Nitti's) confinement on the Aeolian island of Lipari foreground political engagement. Activist Rosselli became a martyr to the anti-Fascist Resistance when, with his brother Nello, he was murdered in 1937 in Bagnoles-de-l'Orne in Normandy most likely on the orders of Mussolini. Rosselli is considered a heroic figure and intellectual leader.

Indeed, in Leto's film *La villeggiatura* and the documentaries *Fughe e approdi* (*Escapes and Landings*, Giovanna Taviani, 2010), *I fratelli Rosselli* (*The Rosselli Brothers*, Accasfilm, in the series *Eroi dell'antifascismo*) and *I fratelli Rosselli* (*The Rosselli Brothers*, Nelo Risi, 1960) the hero narrative completely overshadows the routine drudgery of life on an island prison experienced by the vast majority of those interned. Rosselli was spared such a menial existence due to his economic privilege that afforded him quite a different sojourn in the volcanic archipelago. Also, in several of the texts, the experience of confinement proves to be beneficial in terms of intellectual development and political activism. These filmic texts all ultimately celebrate Rosselli's life and accomplishments (for example his involvement in the founding of the anti-Fascist Liberal social movement *Giustizia e Libertà*) and wed his hero status (along at times with that of his brother) with the destiny of a post-Fascist, liberated Italy. Case in point: the concluding words of the Risi documentary, spoken by Ferruccio Parri, partisan and Prime Minister of Italy during approximately the last six months of 1945 to a group of similarly minded individuals: 'Carlo and Nello taught us that our fatherland is only our fatherland if it is free. And comrades, you all now understand why the story of the Rosselli brothers does not end at liberation, why it does not end with the constitution. Justice and Liberty (*Giustizia e Libertà*) is the law that must guide our lives'. Ultimately, in these films, the exile experience is downplayed and rechannelled into a nation-building story and Rosselli becomes shorthand for the new Italy imagined as *just* and *free*. Narratives around Rosselli's period of internment participate in, recalling Santner, the construction of a 'condition of [an intact]' Italy that disavows the mourning process for Mussolini's victims, and internal exile is depicted as one of several productive steps that help to construct Rosselli's hero narrative.

As we discuss in Chapter 5, numerous internees attempted to break free of the prison islands, and a few were successful in their efforts. Rosselli's name, however, is most readily associated with escape, and together with his murder in 1937, the famous 'fuga da Lipari' of 27 July 1929 are the pivotal events from Rosselli's biography that support the Rosselli/hero/martyr identikit, even though Nitti and Lussu, also considered national heroes, evaded the island as well on that summer night. As described by Peter Brooks, 'quest, escape, and fall-expulsion-redemption are in fact all structures that can be classed in the general category of romance (in

Northrop Frye's terms); and melodrama – which often takes its subjects from the novel – generally operates in the mode of romance'.[37] The escape motif endows the Rosselli narrative with an exciting twist and makes a good story of confinement.

The films that treat Rosselli (while Nitti and Lussu are mentioned as well in two of the documentaries, Rosselli's narrative takes centre stage) culminate in the escape episode, a denouement frequently imbued with suspense in the form of dramatic music, hand-held camera, and rapid editing. Rosselli's life is cast in melodramatic terms and his virtue is underlined when, as is frequently the case with melodrama, 'the victim-hero of melodrama gains an empathy that is equated with moral virtue through a suffering ... [and] this victim-hero can turn his or her virtuous suffering into action'.[38] Like with Pavese, Rosselli's relative hardship is restorative and, as we will see, plays into grand narratives of the nation state.

Taviani's documentary takes the shape of a homage to the Aeolian islands, and chronicles the many 'escapes and landings' from and to Lipari, Stromboli, Vulcano, Salina, Filicudi, Alicudi, and Panarea in twelve films and documentaries by some of Italy's most canonical filmmakers, foremost of which are the director's father and uncle. The sequence on the experience of internal exile lasts approximately ten minutes, and follows the introductory segment focusing on the large mountain of pumice mined by locals, several of whom in turn developed, the narrator 'Figliodoro' (Golden Sun) tells us, a deadly 'lung illness' that led to a mass emigration. Golden Sun underlines the harsh conditions on the island, stating that while 'there were many reasons to flee', including volcanic eruptions, pestilence, and pumice poisoning, 'others were forced to come here'. In this way, the documentary sets the scene for an arduous and precarious experience of internment. Yes, one resident recalls that the prisoners arrived in chains and were lined up four by four, and a script onscreen recounting one of Rosselli's letters to his mother tells us that 'exile on an island is crueller than prison. Open spaces, the sky, the sea, but I cannot move, it fills me with anxiety'.

However, the documentary transforms the exile experience into an adventurous escape narrative. Foremost, a script conveys that political prisoners of Lipari are like 'far west heroes', thus mythologising those many who temporarily were constrained to call the island home. Also, the aforementioned resident describes the trio as an amalgam of The Three Musketeers meets Laurel and Hardy: Lussu is small, bearded, and incredibly nervous and agitated, Nitti is calm and robust, while Rosselli is incredibly good looking. Later, as the camera captures dramatic shots of the present-day Lipari coastline, Taviani through voiceover recounts the stringent surveillance on the island during Fascism, and recalls 'in our childhood imagination those coasts seemed like scenes of legendary battles and daring adventures', before the island resident describes the escape as a memorable event that everyone talked about for years to come. *Fughe e approdi* recasts exile as a melodramatic adventure tale befitting the pirate genre.

Montage situates the characters and narrators from Leto's film and Risi's documentary into contemporary Lipari. Images of Professor Rossini's arrival on the island in *La villeggiatura* as he looks earnestly at the shore while he is rowed into the harbour for the first time alternate three times with what are constructed to resemble eyeline matches of the present-day coastline in vivid colour from what would seem to be Rossini's perspective. And the same technique is utilised during the escape sequence from the film: Rossini swimming into the open sea is followed by a shot of the ocean in 2010, from what would approximate Rossini's line of sight. The documentary works to create a neat sense of unity between present and past, an effect that is furthered by the choice to only include scenes of Rossini's arrival at and departure from the island. What happened in between is less consequential than what will be gained by the escape, or 'regaining our people's freedom!' as Rosselli writes to his mother in the Risi documentary.

A similar narrative of elision takes place with the editing of Risi's *I fratelli Rosselli*, which focuses principally on these bookend moments. Nitti chronicles the arrival of the ferry carrying Rosselli, who is swiftly set apart from the group of handcuffed men. Nitti remembers laying his eyes upon 'a tall, powerful man, with sky blue eyes behind his glasses and the dark face of someone who had spent time in prison'. Nitti identifies the man as Carlo Rosselli before noting that a month later Lussu, World War I hero, deputy, and founder of the Sardinian Action Party, arrived on the island. During the segment of the documentary focusing on the escape we again hear Nitti's description of the dramatic enterprise, and the segment arrives at a conclusion with nocturnal shots of the island from the back of a boat departing from the island. We also read a script of verses from Rosselli's *Fuga in quattro tempi* on the screen accompanied by a histrionic score: 'Ora sfiliamo lungo Vulcano, sotto il faro viriamo, i suoi equi raggi investono a intermittenza noi pure. Sorge la luna: gialla, immensa, beffarda. Accompagnerà noi e gli inseguitori tutta la notte' (Past Vulcano we go, under the lighthouse we veer, its fair rays intermittently light us. The moon rises: yellow, immense, scornful. It will accompany us and our pursuers all night long). The narrative of exile concludes on a note that highlights adventure, pursuit, and new beginnings off the island. In *Fughe e approdi*, the trio stands in and speaks for those not fortunate enough to evade the squalid conditions of the barracks, and the documentary suggests that the future is brimming with possibility for political renewal.

Risi's documentary centres on four narrators who recount details about the Rosselli brothers' childhood and family life (Maria Agostini), Carlo's stay on Lipari (Nitti), and the brothers' (particularly Carlo's) involvement in the Spanish Civil War, activism in Paris, and the infamous double murder (Lussu), and concludes with a eulogy that positions the pair as martyrs and intellectual and political leaders (Parri). *I fratelli Rosselli* lasts just over seventeen minutes, five of which are devoted to recounting the events of Carlo Rosselli, Lussu, and Nitti's period of confinement. Interestingly, Nello was sent into internal exile as well, condemned to spend five years on Ustica, although he was released after seven months, yet the documentary does not touch on Nello's island experience. A similar process is at work in the Accas film short *I fratelli Rosselli*, where the narrator states, 'the brothers quickly became acquainted with prison and internal exile on Ustica and Lipari. From Lipari, Carlo was able to escape to Paris where he was to be one of the organisers of the revolutionary movement *Giustizia e Libertà*'. Like with the Risi documentary, Nello's experience of confinement is of less interest than Carlo's.

In the Risi documentary, Nitti is filmed on site on Lipari as he recounts, as we partially discussed earlier in terms of the mise-en-abyme in *Fughe e approdi*, the arrival of Rosselli and Lussu, the homosocial environment created by confinement, Rosselli's lodging arrangements, the trio's desire to escape the island, and the famous escape. Indeed, three of the five minutes of Nitti's voiceover narration are dedicated to the *fuga*, which he narrates in a melodramatic tone that stresses the suspense, adventure, and risk of the endeavour.

'Noi pensavamo alla fuga' (we thought about escape), Nitti declares before describing Rosselli's domicile, a stately villa with terraces and views of the ocean, replete with his books and a piano. The night of the escape is described in detail: Nitti was the first to arrive at the meeting place, he was 'alone, anxious, cold [and he] swam with all of his force' to arrive at the boat. Once aboard, he wonders 'and Rosselli? and Lussu?' as we see an image of a large clock, underlining Nitti's apprehension, before a member of the group spies the pair swimming towards the vessel. The segment concludes as a man (possibly Nitti, his back is turned to the camera) looks towards the island while standing on a boat that speeds away from the shore and we hear in voiceover, 'at dawn we saw Italy disappear, the fatherland that Carlo Rosselli would never see again' and a wipe brings Nitti's testimony to a conclusion.

Here, as with *Fughe and approdi*, the experience of internal exile is translated into an intrepid undertaking that results, for Rosselli, in the loss of his country. The following segment focuses on Rosselli's triumphs in war and activism, sacrifices that he undertakes for the good of the Italian nation. While Nello is briefly described by Lussu as an intellectual, Carlo 'instead is the militant, a political activist with an exceptional character. On Lipari, like in Paris, I always saw him without rest and without exhaustion. Only a man of that temperament and with so much moral enthusiasm could lend such prestige to anti-Fascism and to a movement like *Giustizia e Libertà*'. In the documentary, Rosselli's narrative conforms to that of the hero of the classical cinema theorised by Teresa de Lauretis who 'commands at once the action and the landscape, and … occupies the position of subject of vision, which he relays to the spectator'.[39] Rosselli's heroism and his sacrifices for the country make a good story and greatly overshadow the experiences of all others sent into internal exile on Lipari.

*La villeggiatura* is very loosely based on the exile experience of Carlo Rosselli, and focuses on university professor Franco Rossini who is sent into confinement for refusing to swear loyalty to the Regime. Similarities between the pair (aside from the surname alliteration) mainly consist in details surrounding Rossini's internment (his year of arrival, lodging and familial arrangements, method of escape) and involvement in the Spanish Civil War. Correspondences stop there, however, especially in terms of the level of Rosselli/Rossini's engaged politics before and during internment. Yet, the insertion in particular of the 'escape' episode codes Rossini as Rosselli and, as we will discuss, confers upon the fictional character a hero status that sets him apart from the other prisoners who are in reality much more politically engaged and socially aware.

The initial voiceover of Leto's film lists all of the ordinances that political prisoners must follow during their sentence: they cannot possess scissors, corkscrews, can openers, penknives; they cannot frequent religious ceremonies, restaurants, the cinema, the theatre, public gatherings, brothels; they cannot dine with companions outside of the cafeteria or outside of cafeteria hours, talk about politics, read newspapers out loud, comment about news on the radio, receive books, newspapers, magazines, manuscripts; send correspondence that is not controlled by the authorities; the *confinato* must have a stable job. Rossini is not obliged to follow any of these edicts (although he does not frequent a brothel).

When the commissioner discovers that Rossini is the son of his revered law professor, Rossini receives special privileges and the commissioner moves him into a well-appointed hilltop home with ocean views, the delivery of his beloved books and the church's piano, uncensored correspondence (although the commissioner does at times peek at his mail), and the company of his wife and daughter. He roams freely about town, attends a puppet show and religious rituals, discusses politics regularly, and attempts to educate the other political prisoners on Giolittian politics and the Liberal State. And, although he is at times frustrated with, for example, the ideological approach of the other more radical *confinati* or the commissioner's politics (with whom he strikes up a friendship and the pair bond over classical music, among other things) he appears relatively serene on the island, especially whilst at the seaside, at home with his wife, when playing the piano or conversing with the commissioner and other locals.

This is not the case, however, for the group of prisoners who are not privileged economically, who live in the barracks, and must endure all of the aforementioned ordinances. Theirs is certainly not the 'villeggiatura' of the film's title to which Rossini ironically refers when toasting his arrival on the island at a local bar with the group of well-dressed, advantaged political prisoners (coded as 'intellectuals' with beards, glasses, and wearing white suits), who purposefully set themselves apart from the 'troublemakers' who live below and have plans to flee the island so as to combat the Regime. Instead, the narrative focuses almost wholly on Rossini's coming of age story where he learns political engagement at the expense of those much more politically active than he.

Indeed, Rossini must ultimately choose between his biological father and a new symbolic father in the form of the revolutionary politics of Marx and Lenin. The former is passive and non-interventionist, and urges that his son swear allegiance to the Regime, a gesture as he explains in an uncensored letter that is a pure formality. In the missive, father admonishes son that 'contaminating literature and politics, politics and science is a huge mistake [and that] true culture exists above all factions', a laissez-faire mentality shared by the commissioner.

Pam Cook argues that 'male oedipal problems are the mainspring of the action in tragic melodrama. The hero's incestuous desire to challenge the power of the father and take his place drives the narrative forward along a linear trajectory, though ironic twists of Fate can complicate the narrative', and a similar process of ascension is at work in *La villeggiatura*. Like the tragic hero of melodrama, Rossini too is 'brought low' and redeemed through 'a new-found humility. He becomes aware of his guilt, and the reasons for his suffering'[40] when he comes to understand the plight of the oppressed group of *confinati* on the island after Scagnetti, the most outspoken and radical of the lot, is murdered by the local Fascists and the commissioner refuses to investigate the incident and prohibits a funeral.

At this point, Rossini knows that he must act, and although the commissioner has arranged for him to return to his post without swearing allegiance to the Regime, he becomes loyal to the cause of the proletariat group, declaring to a new comrade as they defiantly carry Scagnetti's coffin through the island during a night-time vigil, 'revolutions are always headed by traitors', thus solidifying his defection from his privileged lineage. With Scagnetti's death he has finally come to understand, as he cites Marx and then Lenin, that 'the substitution of a bourgeois state with a proletariat state is not possible without violent revolution'. The film concludes with Rossini's dramatic escape from the island, which is accompanied by a voiceover of a letter written to his wife explaining his new-found dedication to the armed struggle. 'La villeggiatura è finita' (the vacation is over), he tells her. A final script, which deviates broadly from Rosselli's biography, informs us that 'Professor Rossini has two dates for his death, the first in Spain, with the Democratic Republic in 1936, and the second in Italy, after the Partisan Resistance, on April 18, 1948', cementing his martyr status (were he to die in the Spanish Civil War) and underlining his heroism and ties to a resistance ethos (were he to symbolically die when the overwhelming win of the Christian Democratic party eclipsed all hope for political renewal). And, while the group of *confinati* has spent much of the film plotting and training for their escape, Rossini is the one who evades the island in a melodramatic and unexplained denouement. In the end, Rossini's new-found class-consciousness comes at the literal expense (taking into consideration Scagnetti's death) of the class he is catalysed by and will purportedly fight for.

We conclude this section on Carlo Rosselli noting the relative absence of women (in particular Marion Cave, Rosselli's wife) in the films and documentaries under consideration. Cave is completely omitted in the three documentaries and recast as a traditional wife and mother concerned primarily with cooking and cleaning the Lipari home in Leto's film, and is ultimately abandoned by her husband after his escape. The story of Cave's anti-Fascist resistance, mental illness, and imprisonment after her husband's escape from Lipari is eclipsed from visual representations of Rosselli's period of internment.[41] Cave's story is sacrificed to a larger homosocial narrative that works to forward 'the interests of civilization, law, and culture'[42] for which, the opus suggests, Rosselli dedicated, and subsequently lost, his life.

## Giorgio Amendola

Carlo Lizzani's made-for-television movie *Un'isola* (*An Island*, 1986) is the only screen text to treat writer, intellectual, anti-Fascist, and politician Giorgio Amendola's five-year stay on the Pontine island of Ponza from 1932 to 1937. Based on Amendola's homonymous autobiography, the three-hour television drama narrates, through a flashback from the consequential Turin strike of 18 April 1945 (which created much momentum for Italy's liberation from Nazi rule on 25 April), Amendola's exile to Paris where he met his life partner and later wife Germaine Lecocq, involvement with the anti-Fascist resistance, arrest, imprisonment on Ponza, liberation from the island, and eventual return to Paris. *Un'isola* is a coming-of-age story where, similarly to *La villeggiatura*, the island experience is pivotal for the development and solidification of Amendola's political consciousness.

Part love story and part political drama, *Un'isola* suggests that Giorgio Amendola's involvement with the Communist Party during the *ventennio* is initially motivated by a desire to fill his father's shoes. His father, the politician Giovanni Amendola, was brutally beaten by Fascists in 1925 and perished as a result of his injuries the following year, and he haunts the film. Indeed, when young Giorgio meets Germaine at a dance hall in Paris for the first time, the pair bond over the loss of their fathers (hers was a Socialist) and later, Giorgio tells Germaine that his father was an 'important' man, not because he was a minister, but, he explains, 'because of his culture, and his character, and the courage of his ideas which were very different from mine, but I think he would have understood me'. A fellow *confinato* declares 'not all of us are called Amendola' when Giorgio departs the island after his sentence was converted into *ammonizione*, and frequently, Giorgio is offered special privileges as a result of his father's status (an extra bit of soup, for example) which he generally refuses as he wants to make his own name for himself.

Giorgio desires to prove himself worthy of his father's legacy, and like with many melodramas, *Un'isola* 'stages crises of role fulfilment and [as we will see in the mini-series' conclusion] fantasy resolutions to the often insoluble contradictions of gender roles'.[43] Although in the series Giorgio positions himself as an engaged and courageous freedom fighter willing to risk life and limb for the cause, the programme instead suggests that Giorgio's activism is fuelled primarily by a desire for acceptance from his Communist peer group. He agrees to every mission asked of him even when he is not given specifics as to the larger machination of the assignment. When confined on Ponza he works tirelessly cleaning the barracks (he even is assigned toilet duty) so as to please his would-be comrades who treat him as a lackey.

However, throughout the first part of the mini-series, and in particular before his confinement on Ponza, Giorgio is distracted from the cause by his relationship with Germaine, and their love story is ultimately the driving force of the narrative, as is the case with melodrama. Although he purports to be primarily interested in the anti-Fascist struggle, his voiceovers betray his greater commitment to love. To cite a few examples, the series opens with Giorgio discussing the upcoming strike, but his thoughts move quickly to Germaine; when describing his movements around Paris so as to maintain his cover he realises that he is just moving closer to her; while contemplating the party he is chiefly concerned with how his disappearance will affect her.

This all changes, however, when he, as he claims 'becomes a man' on Ponza. Giorgio's period of internment begins towards the end of the first half of the series and lasts, albeit broken up by a few trips to the Poggioreale prison in Naples, for just over one third of the series. Initially, Giorgio seems content to adopt the internal exile as vacation mentality, asserting just before his arrival on Ponza that he will 'pretend that he is on vacation on Capri'. Also, after Germaine joins him on Ponza, she cheers Giorgio up by telling him that they can imagine that they escaped to the island so as to be alone together. Giorgio even seems unconvinced early on in his stay by his comrade's assertion that 'they are not there on vacation' after they order Giorgio to write a letter to Mussolini that will surely land him in prison.

Slowly, however, he attempts to learn true political engagement and to adopt the party line, and admonishes Germaine in anger (and later her mother who came to Ponza to help her daughter through her difficult pregnancy) that they cannot forget that the island is indeed a prison. Thus, his impotence and isolation motivates him to request the transfer of his sentence (he claims that he wants to change the world), and as they sail towards the mainland, through voiceover he evaluates his formative stay on the island, stating 'On that island we got married, we had unforgettable experiences, Ada was born, I studied, we suffered but we were also happy. Overall it was a positive experience. I was thirty years old, and I had become a man'. It is interesting, however, that his narrative is devoid of a sense of political commitment. He has 'become a man' primarily due to his new-found experience as husband and father.

Nowell-Smith explains that castration is generally 'at issue in the melodrama', a genre that is interested in 'answering of the question: whose child am I (or would I like to be)? ... [Melodrama] is also fundamentally concerned with the child's problems of growing up into sexual identity within the family, under the aegis of a symbolic law which the father incarnates'. Fundamentally, Nowell-Smith asserts that what is at stake in the genre 'is the survival of the family unit and the possibility for individuals of acquiring an identity which is also a place within' the symbolic order, which is not an easy process and 'does not happen without sacrifice'.[44] Accordingly, the island experience, during which the pair did 'struggle' has allowed Giorgio to establish an identity within the family and under the law of the father and therefore to secure a stronghold in the symbolic. Once Giorgio has found his place in the world, Germaine follows suit and experiences a dramatic transformation in character during the remaining twenty minutes or so of the mini-series after the pair depart Ponza. Initially Germaine is uninterested in politics. She tells the female operative with whom Giorgio works early on in the series that 'it is strange for a woman to be involved in politics. What do we women have to do with it?' She urges Giorgio to withdraw from the struggle and tells him that she wishes to lead a normal life. When Giorgio remains in Italy and Germaine returns to Paris she has a series of experiences, including attending the funeral of the Rosselli brothers, that change her, and she announces that while in the past Mussolini and Hitler seemed so distant, she now understands that men like Giorgio are needed to fight, and that she will try to do her part as well, and promises not to bother him any more.

Once Giorgio has educated Germaine to proper politics, the series draws to a conclusion with a flashforward to the eve of the Turin strike during which Giorgio is represented as wholly committed to the anti-Fascist struggle. The series positions him as the sole architect and leader of the uprising, and when we see a large group of women marching in the street, the series implies that Giorgio's sway over his wife extends to all women who have stood on the right side of history. Documentary footage of the strike (notably the only occasion documentary footage appears in the film) then transitions to images of Germaine and Giorgio dancing when they first met before *Un'isola* concludes with Germaine's voice-over recounting the couple's life post-bellum. He wrote, she painted, and their friends felt their love story appropriate to a film by René Clair. As Germaine calls to mind all those who have passed away – her mother, their daughter, and, just the previous night, Giorgio – the camera zooms into a painting of Ponza before transitioning to a shot of the island from a boat. Then, images of the couple's happy time on the island alternate with a shot of Germaine's hand working on the painting of Giorgio she was never able to finish before she too takes her last breath and the series concludes. In this way, *Un'isola* articulates history in melo-dramatic terms and ultimately, returning to Kaplan's work on melodrama, trauma, and cinema, 'seals over the traumatic ruptures and breaks' of the experience of internal exile in Italy.[45]

## Carlo Levi

We conclude this section treating onscreen representations of historical anti-Fascists and intellectuals sent into internal exile with a discussion of Francesco Rosi's *Cristo si è fermato a Eboli*, which was originally made for television but later released in theatres. Based on Carlo Levi's eponymous fictionalised memoir treating the author's 1935–36 exile to the fictional village of Gagliano (Levi was in fact exiled to the Lucanian towns of Grassano and later Aliano), the film positions Carlo as a salvific figure for the locals who are represented as ignorant and superstitious. Like the films and television series discussed in this section, *Cristo si è fermato a Eboli* is a male melodrama that dramatises Carlo's transformation from detached painter to engaged medic who stands up to the local Fascist officer (albeit somewhat lackadaisically) so as to fight to provide 'his' peasants with much needed medical care. Also akin to representations of the exile experience of Pavese, Rosselli, and Amendola, Carlo's stay in Gagliano proves useful as the sojourn allows him to mature as a man and an artist. What's more, and similar to the process at work in the Pavese narratives, the suffering of an oppressed class ultimately leads to greater insight and bolsters Carlo's creativity. As we will see, and recalling Modleski, this film is like 'many male weepies (or male melodramas), [where] real men do not cry, or at best they shed only a few hard-wrung tears; others do the crying for them – usually women and people of color'[46] – think, for example of the cries of mourning by women recurrent in the film.

*Cristo si è fermato a Eboli* is often discussed in terms of its lugubrious style.[47] Rosi repeats techniques such as pans (of dried-out fields, near-empty piazze, the washed-out village), long shots, and tracking shots that go on for some time (case in point: the three-minute continuous shot of the desolate countryside accompanied by a voiceover of Mussolini announcing victory in Addis Ababa). All of these techniques underline the impoverished, neglected condition of southern Italy, a situation that benefits from the doctor's presence. The townspeople with whom Carlo interacts are entrenched in local custom, believing for example in the healing powers of a coin and the bewitching properties of menstrual blood, and making sure to avoid upsetting guardian angels. Women are adorned in black, wail in chorus after the death of a family member (a mourning ritual common in Rosi's opus) and the town is replete with mourning banners. Villages are represented as detached from history, made clear in Carlo's voiceover a version of which we hear both towards the beginning and the end of the film:

> Christ never arrived here, nor did time, the individual soul, hope, the relationship between cause and effect, reason or history. No one has come to this land if not as a conqueror, an enemy, or an uncomprehending visitor. The seasons pass over peasant toil today as they did 3000 years before Christ. To this dark land without sin and without redemption where evil is not moral but is an earthy pain residing in things, Christ did not descend. Christ stopped at Eboli.

Millicent Marcus argues that the film 'represents a kind of summation … of the southern question' for a filmmaker whose 'constant preoccupation has been "the problem of the South"'.[48] Indeed, the film is much more interested in exploring the 'two Italies' problematic announced in the title of Marcus' chapter on the film ('Rosi's *Christ Stopped at Eboli*: A Tale of Two Italies')[49] than pointing the finger at the practice of forced residence during Fascism. *Cristo si è fermato a Eboli*'s ideological stance is quite obvious, for example when Carlo writes in a letter, 'for the peasants, the State is farther away and more malicious than the sky because it never sides with them', when townsfolk complain that money wasted on the war in Africa could be better spent locally, or after a young man enlists to fight in Africa a man comments 'why would he voluntarily go to Africa when he has an "Africa" right here'. During his stay, Carlo comes to understand that the North desires to keep the proletariat 'eternally enslaved' and begins practising medicine. Especially akin to the representation of Pavese in *Prima che il gallo canti*, in Rosi's film, internal exile provides a privileged northerner with the opportunity for cultural understanding and personal enrichment.

Indeed, and even more so than what we have seen with Levi's intellectual contemporaries, Carlo seems somewhat happy in Gagliano, where he lives a life of relative leisure, has a house with a terrace that is tended by a cleaning woman and potential paramour Giulia, practises medicine, paints, takes long walks with the company of his loyal dog Barone, befriends the local priest who is also exiled for suspect behaviour, partakes in local gatherings and events, and receives a visit from his beloved sister. Only two *confinati* in the area – the two Communists who are shunned by the town and are denied the general amnesty granted to Carlo and the other *confinati* at the end of the film – seem to suffer during their internment. The mayor calls Carlo a 'gentleman' who is not deserving of his punishment and assures Carlo he must only sign the register each morning and respect the curfew and will otherwise find his stay in Gagliano quite enjoyable.

The film provides Carlo with a potential love interest in Giulia, who, in addition to cleaning his house and cooking his meals, will assist him in his curative endeavours. Described as a hard worker and a 'strega' (witch) who gives the evil eye, she is the only woman in Gagliano who would enter the house of an unmarried man. She has had seventeen pregnancies, apparently with different men who have since abandoned her, a selection of whom absconded with the children she bore. She is denigrated by the townspeople (one man tells Carlo that she had an affair with the previous priest) and aligned with the women in town who put spells on men with their menstrual blood. Carlo desires to control her, and insists while she is bathing him whilst he is naked that she pose for him so that he might paint her. When she refuses as she is convinced she will become the prisoner of the artist, he becomes angry, demands that she will do what he says before slapping her in front of her young son who watches from the doorway. Rather than demonstrate rage, she appears aroused, and laughs maniacally before consoling her child who Carlo will later paint. In this way, the film normalises and justifies Carlo's violence in the service of aesthetic creativity.

Carlo is constructed as a Christ figure and saviour to the inhabitants of Gagliano. One man exclaims that only Dr Levi can save his brother and the townspeople rally outside of the mayor's office shouting that they 'need Don Carlo' to practise and that he is a good man unlike the other doctors. However, when he receives amnesty he departs for the North and will never return. After a touching goodbye in the rain during which children stare sorrowfully at him through the car window, we see a flashforward to Carlo's artist's studio where the film began. The film opens with an aged Carlo looking nostalgically at paintings of a series of inhabitants of Gagliano while we hear through voiceover:

> Many years have gone by, years of war and of what men call History. Pushed here and there by chance, I was unable to keep the promise I made to *my* peasants [ai miei contadini] upon leaving that I would return to them and I do not know when, if ever, I will keep my promise. But shut off in a room, in a closed world, I am happy to travel in my memory to that other world, shut off by sorrow and custom, denied by History and the State, eternally patient. To *my* land [a quella mia terra] without comfort or kindness, where the peasant lives out his motionless civilisation in misery and distance, on a barren soil and in the presence of death. (My italics)

Levi's words are imbued with a paternalistic sentimentality and suggest that, were he to return, he would indeed take the place of Christ, the saviour who had forsaken *his* peasants. In her study of Clint Eastwood films, Modleski argues that Eastwood's sentimentality, 'his sacrifice, suffering, mourning' is dangerous 'because it *passes itself off as a "socially transformative" act*'[50] and a similar process is at work in *Cristo si è fermato a Eboli*. Carlo has taken on board the suffering of an oppressed group (which expands beyond the residents of Gagliano as Carlo frequently talks in the film about the plight of Italy's peasantry) and makes it his own. He now speaks for 'his' peasants and 'his' land from a position of northern privilege and images of the paintings of the forlorn faces of the children and workers whom Carlo left behind represent, again citing Modleski, 'a supreme instance of man's loss turning into a gain'.[51] Christ might have stopped at Eboli, but Carlo Levi continues the journey inland and acts in his stead.

## The woman's film?

Mauro Bolognini's fiction film *Libera, amore mio* is the only onscreen representation to focus on the experience of a woman sent into internal exile. Unlike the previous films, documentaries, and made-for-television movies discussed in this chapter that by and large focus on historical figures, the eponymous character of Bolognini's film is invented, although screenplay collaborator Luciano Vincenzoni maintains that the film was inspired by his mother's experiences during Fascism.[52] The film focuses on Libera, a self-declared Anarchist, who, following in her father's footsteps, publicly denounces the Regime. These outbursts land her family in trouble as her partner Matteo loses his job and the family is forced to relocate.

Libera, played by Claudia Cardinale, frequently wears red dresses that accentuate her figure (even when fighting alongside the partisans her legs are for the most part bare). In many ways, Libera is a typical fetish object of the male gaze who creates desire and sets the narrative investigation in motion. She is frequently shown in close-up and medium shot in soft focus as she looks out windows or in mirrors. As the object of the spectator's gaze, she is, in Mulvey's words, 'the perfect [stylised] product' who reassures rather than threatens.[53] Yet, at the same time she frequently challenges authority, even killing a Nazi towards the film's close. Earlier in the film, she hides anti-Fascist Sandro Poggi in her attic after he escapes from Ustica and then attempts to aid in his escape from Italy by providing him with false documents. When she is caught, she too is sentenced to five years of internal exile on Ustica where she joins her father.

Mulvey contends that melodramas that privilege a female point of view appeal to the female spectator because they offer 'a fantasy escape for the identifying women in the audience'. Melodramas hinge upon a discernable contradiction, which is, in this case, the incompatibility of female desire and agency in Italian patriarchal culture.[54] *Libera, amore mio* is unique in that it treats the experience of a woman sent to internal exile. However, in that the film is recounted within the generic conventions of the woman's film, unlike her male counterparts, Libera must pay dearly for her transgressions.

*Libera, amore mio* relates the period of Fascism in melodramatic terms, and is ultimately interested in narrating Libera's relationships with the various men in her life (her father Felice, partner Matteo, son Carlo, and love interest Poggi) against the backdrop of several key moments of historical Fascism, such as the colonial campaign in North Africa, the practice of internal exile, war, and resistance. Most apposite, throughout the film documentary footage of significant moments during the *ventennio* (such as Italy's entrance into Addis Ababa, Italy's declaration of war, footage of air raids, the allied entering of Italy, the fall of Mussolini, and the end of World War II) is interposed with events from Libera's life, such as discussions with her son, her marriage to Matteo on Ustica, or arguments between the couple. In this way, the film fetishises history and is in line with *Heimat* (a response to the 1978 American mini-series *Holocaust*) in which, as Santner argues, the national trauma of the destruction of the European Jewry is sublimated to a sentimental love story.[55]

Cases in point are Libera's two experiences on Ustica, which take up about nine minutes of screen time. When she initially makes the trip to the island with her son to visit Felice, they dine in a restaurant and talk politics and Libera bonds with her absent father and falls for Poggi. Indeed, all interned seem relatively cheerful and do not suffer under their sentences. Later, when she learns that she must return to the island as a political prisoner, she is initially happy, telling Matteo that '*confino* will be my university'. Even her father is pleased with her sentence, exclaiming to his friends that Libera was sentenced to 'five years, just like a man. She really is my daughter!' And akin to her earlier visit to the island, the narration of the period of her confinement privileges the emotional over the political, and focuses on the love letters exchanged between Libera and Matteo and the couple's wedding on site.

Throughout the film, Libera is punished for her actions; first she is sent to internal exile, and later she is imprisoned and tortured when she kills the Nazi officer. It becomes clear, however, that more problematic than her militant behaviour is her unwillingness to conform to the normative model demanded by Fascist gender politics and Italian culture more broadly. Her husband, for example, is regularly depicted as emasculated; he is shown cooking and shopping (he even buys a dress for Libera), spends time primarily with his daughter (Carlo is much more drawn to Libera), and regularly gives in to his partner's demands (frequently exclaiming the titular 'Libera, amore mio' in resigned exasperation). Libera is depicted as a castrating and powerful woman who, according to the logic of the classical cinema, will be punished for both her excessive desire and her transvestitism while acting as a man and while being active in the anti-Fascist resistance, a plot-twist in line with Mulvey's reading of castration anxiety and film spectatorship whereby film is a medium that creates and reinforces desire through objectifying the threatening female characters.[56] Mulvey discusses scopophilia in cinema as a system of repression and projection on the part of the audience that allows for a redirection of our 'voyeuristic fantasies' onto the actors while simultaneously identifying with the 'male' image and fetishising or punishing the female protagonist.[57] In *Libera, amore mio*, however, a woman, and not a man, is on centre stage. This focus on a female protagonist troubles traditional notions of film spectatorship and identification and problematises the logic of theories of castration anxiety.

The treatment of female spectatorship offered by Mulvey in her follow-up article is helpful to understand this quandary where she looks at 'films in which a woman central protagonist is shown to be unable to achieve a stable identity, torn between the deep blue sea of passive femininity and the devil of regressive masculinity',[58] and Libera lives this dichotomy, as while active in the resistance and venturing outside of the household, she is the persistent object of the male gaze. Mulvey argues that in the western or the melodrama, the mechanics of Oedipal nostalgia are laid bare. Women protagonists accept masculinisation at a very high price (punishment or death, for example) and 'masculine identification' is unworkable and ultimately fails.[59]

The impossible place of an active desiring woman protagonist is played out at the film's conclusion when Libera is incensed to discover that her Fascist tormentor Dr Testa has secured a position in city government after liberation, and then proceeds to party headquarters to denounce him. Rather than share in her outrage, she is told: 'the place of a woman like you who fought, who suffered, is at home. Now you can finally enjoy your family'. Libera then unmasks for the group the process of political transformism at work following the fall of Fascism before announcing that she must depart and review how to make minestrone (Matteo repeatedly admonished Libera about her preparation of the dish). When returning home from shopping for proper ingredients, whilst crossing a bridge Libera is shot down and killed by a disgruntled Fascist firing a rifle randomly from a rooftop. This finale is shocking as it is completely unmotivated. Indeed, Libera placed herself in harm's way time and again throughout the film and always survived, yet here her death is constructed as an afterthought entirely dissociated from narrative action. In the film's concluding moments, the camera pans from the group of partisans attempting to floor the attacker to Libera's lifeless body slumped on the ground, her face hidden by her hair. 'What am I doing here on the ground? I had to do something [dovevo fa' 'na cosa…]' we hear through voiceover before the camera leaves Libera behind to zoom out to the left to rest on a large building, and the film concludes. Like Pearl, the protagonist of *Duel in the Sun* discussed by Mulvey, Libera is unable to 'become a "lady"' and like the title character of *Stella Dallas*, Libera is also unable to 'accept correct, married "femininity" on the one hand, or find a place in a macho world on the other'.[60] Accordingly, the finale of *Libera, amore mio* dramatises the limits of female empowerment in a war setting. Unlike Libera's historical male counterparts whose (relative) hardships during exile lead to inspiration, insight, creativity, and political awareness, Libera's suffering necessitates her death which, keeping in mind the mise-en-scène of the film's final moments, places her firmly outside of history. In this way, *Libera, amore mio* foregrounds how the feminine is almost entirely excluded historically from cinematic representations of the exile experience.

## The film noir

Carlo Lucarelli's *L'isola dell'angelo caduto* (*The Island of the Fallen Angel*, 2012) is the only fiction film treating internal exile that takes place entirely on the locus of banishment, an anonymous and potentially haunted island populated by, among others, the melancholy commissioner and his depressed wife Hana, a band of tyrannical Fascists led by the diabolical Mazzerino, a couple involved in Dionysian rituals perpetually awaiting the arrival of Aleister Crowley, and Dr Valenza, a pathologist and anti-Fascist sentenced to internal exile on the cursed island. Lucarelli notes that the film is inspired by both Martin Scorsese's *Shutter Island* (2010), which also depicts 'un'isola che non esiste' (an island that does not exist) and Leto's *La villeggiatura*.[61] Rather than focusing on the perspective of the political prisoner and narrating his coming-of-age story as is the case in Leto's film, *L'isola dell'angelo caduto* unfolds from the point of view of the commissioner who was transferred to the island as punishment for arresting a group of drunken Fascists.

Part science-fiction and part murder mystery or *giallo*, *L'isola dell'angelo caduto* is principally a film noir that narrates the commissioner's growing fixation with solving the series of murders on the island (it is made clear that if he accepts that the deaths are a result of suicide, he will be forgiven for his earlier transgression and will be called back to the mainland). The title of the film obviously refers to the Lucifer myth (at one point we hear that Lucifer fell to the island after rebelling against God), but also quite aptly applies to the commissioner, who, borrowing from Janet Staiger's formulation of 'Film Noir as Male Melodrama' is a 'fallen man' who is 'lured into [the] wayward pat[h]' of opposing the status quo. Indeed, the commissioner lacks self control and narrative focuses on his 'lack of self-mastery' and his 'fall from proper manhood' after his expulsion (for example his wife refuses to sleep with him).[62]

Women in the film are represented in bleak terms. Hana is possessed by the island, and forlornly stares into the mirror repeatedly listening to the same song ('Lodovico' by Vittorio Mascheroni and Luciano Ramo, which was not released until 1931). Blonde, innocent, and melancholic, she is the antithesis of Wanda (the wife of the Federale) and the 'wife of the inglese', two women who are constructed as alluring femme fatale characters who 'trick' and 'seduce' the commissioner during his investigations, and are ultimately murdered.[63] Faring no better is Martina, the mute young servant who works in the commissioner's house and is ogled and caressed by Fascists and used by 'l'inglese' and his wife in Dionysian rituals. The commissioner is represented as distinct from the Fascists who are cast in Manichean terms as sadists, abusers of women, and sexually suspect (one Fascist sniffs Hana's undergarments while they dry in her house). The commissioner is also weaker than these men, and sleeps with the wife of 'l'inglese' despite repeated declarations of true love and constancy, and we later learn that she seduced him at her husband's bidding. Women in the film are either desexualised (Hana) or sexualised objects of exchange between men on opposite sides of the law.

The representation of internal exile in *L'isola dell'angelo caduto* is unique with respect to the corpus of films considered in this chapter. Although Valenza is politically coded as opposed to the Regime and abhors Mussolini (clear in his many discussions with the commissioner) he ultimately decides, after nearly losing his life, to write to his mother to ask her to beseech Mussolini for a pardon. He is depicted as weak and recalls Pavese who is motivated by his desire for Pizzardo and not political engagement. He also plays the Watson to the commissioner's Holmes, and serves as his sidekick and is cast in a supporting (yet essential when considering his career as a pathologist) role and ultimately serves to promote the commissioner's hero narrative. In addition, like many of the political exiles discussed in this chapter, he follows very few of the rules mandated by the Regime: he is allowed to read the newspaper, travels around freely after curfew (although at times encountering surreal visions), and forms a deep bond with the commissioner. The film also sidelines the plight of the political prisoners on the island. The one time that the group of *confinati* discusses politics in the barracks, the potential critique of their conversation in minimised as the scene is cross-cut with the discovery of another victim in the woods, and Valenza is again involved in solving the case, which foregrounds the investigative narrative.

Towards the end of the film, the commissioner discovers that almost a year earlier, Mazzerino, so as to not have to leave the island, falsely reported that all of the *confinati* perished in a boating accident and has since murdered all those who stand in his way of never leaving the island. Then the commissioner, with the help of a group of officials dressed in white who have suddenly appeared on site, fatally wounds Mazzerino and the narrative concludes with Valenza departing the island (the reasons why he is freed are unexplained in the film) and the commissioner is left, citing Valenza, the true '*confinato*'. With *Isola dell'angela caduto* we see a role reversal with respect to other films discussed in this chapter whereby the commissioner, and not the political prisoner, is positioned as suffering and constructed as worthy of the spectator's sympathy.

Lucarelli's film qualifies as a 'male suspense thriller' a subgenre of the noir 'tough' thriller theorised by Frank Krutnik where 'the hero is in a position of marked inferiority, in regard to both the criminal conspirators and the police, and seeks to restore himself to a position of security be eradicating the enigma'.[64] Akin to the genre, in *L'isola dell'angelo caduto* we note a 'sense of strain in the narrative resolution' and a 'series of ludicrous and grotesque coincidences' (such as the improbable denouement of the film) prohibit the commissioner from returning to a place of proper manhood. It is clear in the film that the commissioner suffers the plight of the protagonist discussed by Krutnik who ultimately will 'remain outside masculine identification'[65] as he will neither return to the mainland and take up his proper place in government nor will he, the film implies, fulfil the Oedipal trajectory through raising children.

He has 'ruined' things yet again (earlier in the film Hana tells him 'promise me that this time you will not ruin everything) and although he has solved the crime, eradicated the bad guys, and Valenza is set free, he is not rewarded for his actions. Instead, like the private-eye discussed by Krutnik, the commissioner's 'punishment seems far in excess of the transgression', and the narrative of the film is figured 'as an instrument of grotesquely exaggerated (self-)persecution'.[66] At the film's close, the commissioner approaches Hana, who looks despairingly in the mirror, touches her shoulder and says with resignation 'you'll see, Hana, you'll see' which recalls how he confidently assures her just after their arrival on the island, 'you'll see, it wont be long'. In the end, and in line with the resolution of the cycle theorised by Staiger, while the commissioner is able to redeem himself through solving the mystery, he is ultimately rewarded 'in moral heaven' as he will sacrifice himself (and his wife) to suffer in perpetuity for the sins of others on the island-purgatory.[67]

## The Mafia and laws of silence

This section looks at the small number of films, documentaries, and made-for-television movies that either reference the internal exile of *mafiosi* (*La camorra*, Giuseppe Ferrara, 1965 and Giordana's *I cento passi*) or centre on Cesare Mori, 'The Iron Prefect' who descended upon Sicily in 1925 to 'solve' the Mafia problem during Mussolini's dictatorship (*Il prefetto di ferro*, *The Iron Prefect*, Pasquale Squitieri, 1977 and *Cesare Mori – Il prefetto di ferro*, *Cesare Mori – The Iron Prefect*, Gianni Lepre, 2012). The feature film and television programmes represent the Mafia in Manichean terms as is frequently the case with melodrama, centring on a hero's impossible battle against the organisation and not the *mafiosi* sent to prison and into exile. We also consider how the scarcity of primary and secondary texts relating to or engaging with the confinement of numerous *mafiosi* during Fascism speaks to larger questions regarding justice. Ultimately, certain categories of prisoners (intellectuals, anti-Fascists, and more recently homosexuals) merit critical enquiry and are proper subjects for the big and small screen while *mafiosi*, considered in the popular imaginary as deserving of punishment and thus not warranting celebration, remain largely absent from the annals of history, and their narratives of internment remain for the most part untold.

Mori used harsh measures, and sent over 11,000 people suspected of Mafia activity to prison and many into internal exile in accordance with law 1254 from 15 July 1926. In response to the urgent need for public security in the Mafia-dominated Sicilian provinces of Catania, Caltanissetta, Agrigento, Messina, Palermo, Siracusa, and Trapani, the decree sanctioned that 'le persone desig-nate dalla pubblica voce come capeggiatori partecipi, complici o favoreggiatori di associazioni venti carattere criminoso o comunque pericolose alla sicurezza pubblica possono essere ... denunziate, in stato di arresto, per essere assegnate al confino di polizia' (those designated as leaders, members, accomplices, or acces-sories of associations that are criminal in nature or in any case a threat to public security can be ... denounced, arrested, and then assigned to internal exile) for a period of one to five years.[68]

It is interesting that no statistics are locatable for the number of those sent to internal exile suspected of Mafia activity and that Mafia historians only briefly mention the practice. John Dickie notes that 'it was much easier and less con-spicuous' to skip trials and 'just to send suspects into internal exile without proper legal process',[69] while Salvatore Lupo briefly mentions the 1926 law.[70] Christopher Duggan's Ur-text *Fascism and the Mafia* cursorily alludes to internal exile three times, noting for example that the 'Sicilian problem' of the Mafia 'vindicated the frequent recourse to *ammonizione*, *domicilio coatto*, and its equivalent in the fas-cist period, *confino*',[71] What's more, those writing about internal exile as tied to the Mafia are incredibly vague in terms of the number of those sentenced: Ezio Costanzo notes 'many' were sent into exile,[72] while Vittorio Coco writes in *La mafia, il fascismo, la polizia*, a text that by its title would seem an authority on the practice, of 'un massiccio invio al confino di polizia dei sospetti di mafia' (a massive amount of those suspected of Mafia activity were sent into internal exile).[73]

Italy's four mafias (the Sicilian *Cosa Nostra*, the Campanian *Camorra*, the 'Ndrangheta of Calabria, and the *Sacra Corona Unita* from Puglia) are governed by the code of *omertà*, or silence before the law, and it would seem that scholarship on the relationship between organised crime in Italy and the practice of internal exile is steeped in silence as well, an ethos recalled in the title of Camilla Poesio's study on internal exile, *Il confino fascista: l'arma silenziosa del regime*.[74] While historical studies on internal exile are gradually increasing, none of these texts engage with the experience of those sentenced for Mafia activity. Corvisieri makes no mention of the Mafia, while Ebner only references the State's 'brutal' campaign against the Mafia and notes that Fascists place *mafiosi* in the 'confinement colonies'.[75]

Indeed, *mafiosi* have not received critical attention as have other classifications of exiles, in particular political prisoners, who after the fall of Mussolini were considered innocent of their crimes.[76] These lives, discussed in detail in the following section, make much better stories that play into grand narratives regarding the suffering of the just, a mainstay of the melodramatic formula.[77] In the post-Mussolini era, *mafiosi* are still considered part of the ongoing (and seemingly unending) Mafia problem. In that they are considered perpetrators, we suspect that this unknown number of individual lives is of little interest to scholars, novelists, and filmmakers, even though, we must recall, Mori's cruel and decisive tactics while on the island led to the imprisonment and confinement of abundant innocent subjects.

Ferrara's documentary short *La camorra*, the only documentary we could locate that mentions internal exile, attempts to mythologise the criminal organisation, initially aligning Mafia values with those of the Regime: 'La violenza fascista si allea naturalmente con i miti della camorra e molti guappi sono utilizzati contro il movimento popolare. Tutti i camorristi possono iscriversi al partito, qualunque sia il loro passato' (Fascist violence naturally united with the myths surrounding the Camorra, and many thugs were made use of to fight the popular movement. All camorristi can belong to the party, regardless of their past). In the end, however, the voiceover conveys incorrect information, stating, 'Una volta al potere il fascismo però manda in carcere o al confino i guappi che non accettano completamente il regime' (Once in power however Fascism sent those thugs who did not completely accept the Regime to prison or internal exile). Here, Mafia malfeasance is eclipsed from history and is replaced with another, more familiar, narrative foregrounding the punitive consequences of anti-Fascist activity.

A similar process of displacement occurs in Giordana's melodramatic biopic *I cento passi* that centres on anti-Mafia martyr Giuseppe (Peppino) Impastato, born in Cinisi into a family with ties to Cosa Nostra and murdered on the order of local boss Gaetano (Tano) Badalamenti on 9 May 1978 as a result of his outspoken anti-Mafia activity. At one point in the film, a young Peppino approaches local artist and Socialist Stefano Venuti whom he asks to commission a painting of his uncle Cesare Manzella, a *mafioso* recently murdered by Badalamenti's men. When Venuti tells Peppino that his uncle was killed by those 'who wanted to take his place', Peppino queries as to whether the two were friends and had spent time in prison together, to which Venuti responds 'yes, many years ago. Mussolini sent us to *confino*, your uncle because he was a *mafioso*, and me because I was a Communist. But friends, no, we couldn't have been friends'. In the following moments, Peppino and Venuti discuss the several paintings that adorn the artist's studio, and when the boy asks Venuti to tell him all about Soviet poet Vladimir Mayakovsky, the film flashes forward some twenty years to a protest against illegal building contracts (the Mafia was involved in expanding the airport) organised by Venuti and Peppino. The mention of internal exile serves to neatly wed Peppino's inauguration into communism and activism with his anti-Mafia stance, and helps to reinforce what is, as some have argued, the film's overt and uncomplicated anti-Mafia message.[78] It is interesting that the historical Luigi Impastato (Peppino's father) was a *mafioso* sent to internal exile for Mafia-related activity in Ustica for three years and later was a tyrant in the home. This detail is absent from *I cento passi*, where Luigi is recast as a stern, if loving father with minimal ties to the Mafia. In this way, the erasure of internal exile together with several other details that render Luigi much more likable than his historical counterpart privilege the family drama and foreground the Oedipal scenario, which broadens the film's reach. As an aside, early on in Scimeca's *Placido Rizzotto*, another anti-Mafia martyr biopic, when the title character's father Carmelo Rizzotto is arrested by Mori's men for 'associazione a delinquere' (belonging to a criminal organisation) we are immediately shown young Placido's emotional response. Although the film omits Carmelo's jail time (he spent just over four years in the Ucciardone prison in Palermo) it is implied that the father's absence and ill deeds compelled the son to action and initiated his quest for social justice.

One feature film (*Il prefetto di ferro*) and one made-for-television movie (*Cesare Mori – Il prefetto di ferro*) focus on Cesare Mori's campaign to eradicate the Mafia during Fascism. Although both include scenes of various arrests and devote screen time to the infamous siege of the village of Gangi, no mention at all is made of internal exile as these films are much more interested in celebrating the career of Mori, and insinuating that the Mafia has infiltrated politics. *Il prefetto di ferro* and *Cesare Mori – Il prefetto di ferro* are simply not interested in what happens to those thousands who were victim to Mori's aggressive strategies after their arrests. Such a digression would surely alter the melodramatic thrust of the made-for-television movie, which sets up Mori as a just man and loyal husband (yet once tempted by a scantily clad Baroness) to an infirm wife whose motivation to battle the Mafia, the programme suggests, stems from lacking a paternal model as Mori was abandoned as a baby. In their focus on family drama and hero narratives, these films fail to engage with the exile experience of *mafiosi*.

Antonino Calderone was underboss of the Mafia of Catania before he broke omertà and began collaborating with the Italian justice system and in 1992 published a book together with Pino Arlacchi in which he revealed the inner workings of Cosa Nostra, a few brief paragraphs of which are dedicated to discussing his uncle's confinement on one of the prison islands during Fascism. In that he never met his uncle, all of his knowledge is third-hand, passed down through various relatives who spoke of, for example, the facility with which five-year sentences were summarily repeated without cause. He also recounts one episode of rebellion when a group of *confinati* refused to enter the barracks to which they were confined, and in response, Mussolini apparently sent a ship to the unnamed island and threatened to bomb the island from a loudspeaker if the insurgents did not obey orders.[79] This is a rare and circuitous example of a testament to the exile experience of *mafiosi* that speaks to the many gaps and holes of knowledge regarding a condemned group of people who as of yet have not been the subject of the kind of historical memory that would elicit an empathetic response. The omissions discussed in this section underscore that cinematic treatments of the internal exile of anti-Fascists, intellectuals, and *mafiosi* are concerned with questions of romance, heroism, and nation building and not experiences of injustice.

## Conclusion

We conclude by briefly discussing the melodrama *Edda Ciano e il comunista* (*Edda Ciano and the Communist*, Graziano Diana, 2011), a made-for-television movie based on Marcello Sorgi's 2009 book of the same name, that engages the experience of internal exile after the fall of Fascism and end of World War II and focuses on Edda Ciano, daughter of Mussolini, who in 1945 was sentenced to two-years confinement on Lipari yet was released after ten months following a general amnesty (Taviani's documentary *Fughe e approdi* also contains a segment focusing on Ciano's stay on the island). *Edda Ciano e il comunista* serves as a counter example to the texts discussed thus far in this chapter in that it treats the sanctioning of a woman apparently loyal to the Regime – rather than, as we have seen in the majority of films under consideration, men who oppose it – and works to celebrate the Partisan Resistance by focusing on Edda's affair with war hero Leonida Bongiorno, the Communist of the programme's title.

Similar to several of the films discussed in this chapter, internal exile takes a backseat to a narrative focused on heroism and love and although she is initially treated poorly by the commissioner, Edda's experiences on the island are relatively pleasant – she lives in a lovely house overlooking the sea, makes friends, finds true love, and is eventually accepted by the island community, despite her ties to Mussolini. The experience of war is downplayed in the film and functions primarily to highlight the hero narrative and love story. Leonida appears to suffer from the effects of post-traumatic stress disorder: he is haunted by nightmares of being captured by the SS and expresses guilt at having survived when others were not as fortunate. The classical representation of these episodes, however, downplays the trauma of the war and Leonida's internment. For one, an aural projection of SS officers capturing Leonida and his comrades is overlaid with a shot of Edda newly arrived to her lodging on the island, looking bereft. The sound of a machine gun is followed by a cut to Leonida waking up in bed before walking over to the window where he watches his father track down his infirm mother who is apparently suffering from dementia and the sequence concludes with Leonida looking on concerned as the non-diegetic melodramatic score escalates. In this way, Leonida is not 'portrayed as a man haunted by images that slice into his daily existence against his will and outside of this control', as is the case of 'piercing depictions of memory flashes' in films that work to evoke 'a representation of trauma'.[80] Instead, this flashback is melodramatic and classical as it shifts the focus from the trauma-inducing experience of the war to the personal romance and familial narrative and 'works to promote spectator mastery over the time shift' through cues, music, and editing that are far from jarring.[81]

What's more, later in the film at a Communist Party meeting in Messina, Leonida explains that he will be haunted by a sense of guilt for having survived when others did not. He urges his companions to be better than the oppressor because 'otherwise what is the point of surviving, of being alive, otherwise we would no longer be able to look one another in the eye and recognise one another not only as comrades, but as men'. Unlike Primo Levi's writings on survivors' remorse which position culpability in ambiguous terms, in Leonida's survivor narrative, guilt and shame are redemptive and can be productively used so that the wounded resistance fighter can become a man.

*Edda Ciano e il comunista* is about growing up, and foregrounds the sacrifices required to be a man (and a woman) in normative society. In typical melodramatic mode, towards the end of the film just when Leonida and Edda decide that they will risk being ostracised socially so as to be together, Edda receives news that her two children will finally be able to join her. She then must choose between love for her children and love for Leonida, and the film concludes with a flashforward from Edda's perspective, as the two make love for the final time, to the only choice possible for the transgressive woman: she must renounce Leonida to return to her children which allows him to assume the role of patriarch by marrying his childhood sweetheart on Lipari. In this way, the programme dramatises the double bind of the desirous woman in melodrama as the transgressive female 'puts on display the conflicts at the heart of feminine identity between female desire and socially sanctioned femininity'. And 'socially sanctioned femininity – that is, motherhood, and integration into the family – means that she has in the end to resume that position or disappear'.[82] Akin to all of the texts treated in this chapter, the experience of exile in *Edda Ciana e il comunista* is subordinate to a narrative that is more familiar.

It might be argued that a desire to forget or leave behind the years of internal exile is so ingrained in the national imaginary that Ventotene, one of the most notorious *confino* islands, hosted in June 2014 the third annual festival called 'Gita al faro – scrittori al confino' (A Trip to the Lighthouse – Writers in *Confino/* Internal Exile)', where a group of writers are 'condannati' (condemned) to be 'confinati per sei giorni sull'isola di Ventotene a scontare il loro privilegio: essere scrittrici, essere scrittori' (confined for six days on the island of Ventotene to atone for their privilege of being writers). In a publicity video for the 2012 edition of the event, one writer discusses the 'splendid restaurant' where they dine and another comments that he is not in need of libraries or other comforts as reality, what exists around them, is excluded from the creative process, before the short cuts to capture the same man enjoying a televised soccer match with his fellow '*confinati*'.[83] Thus, the memory of internal exile on a prison islands that 'hosted' so many detainees is officially translated, recast, and sanctioned as holiday.

This chapter has investigated how cinema has contributed to this process of displacement and has shown the prevalence of melodrama as a mode to screen representations of internal exile. To conclude, we recall Modleski's work on the male weepie, which is fruitful to help us understand the mechanics of identification at work in the texts focusing on Pavese, Rosselli, Amendola, and Levi. In particular, she looks at how melancholia functions in Clint Eastwood films so as to privilege the male subject position and perpetuate patriarchy[84]. The male weepie genre features stoic characters who, contrary to the protagonist of the woman's film, rarely externalise their grief. The suffering of the melancholic (male) artist is restorative: what was lost (here freedom, home towns, love interests) is recuperated during exile through writing or political activism. Ultimately, the painful implications of the practice of *confino* is denied or dispersed at the national level as the experience does not seem to be ingrained in collective memory. Instead, in the on-screen island and inland excursions here, internal exile is time and again sanctioned as holiday.

## Notes

1    See, for example, Corvisieri, *La villeggiatura di Mussolini*, 33; Goretti and Giartosio, *La città e l'isola*, 3 and 252; Lorenzo Benadusi, 'Private Life and Public Morals: Fascism and the "Problem" of Homosexuality', *Totalitarian Movements and Political Religions*, 5:2 (2004), 173; Benadusi, *The Enemy of the New Man*, 289–90; and Andrea Pini, *Quando eravamo froci: gli omosessuali nell'Italia di una volta* (Milan: Il Saggiatore, 2011), pp. 45–6.

2    Onscreen engagements with those condemned for suspected homosexuality are treated in depth in the following chapter.

3    Santner, 'History beyond the Pleasure Principle', 144.

4    *Ibid.*

5    Santner, 'History beyond the Pleasure Principle', 143.

6    Santner, 'History beyond the Pleasure Principle', 147.

7    For a discussion of these and several other films that engage the Holocaust in the light of the critical categories of narrative fetishism and mourning, see Millicent Marcus, *Italian Film in the Shadow of Auschwitz* (Toronto: Toronto University Press, 2007).

8    As Dana Renga has argued elsewhere, only through the creation of such narratives can the trauma become a part of collective identity, and only then can communities begin the healing process so as to eventually be rebuilt. See the introduction to Dana Renga, *Unfinished Business: Screening the Italian Mafia in the New Millennium* (Toronto, Buffalo, and London: University of Toronto Press, 2013).

9    E. Ann Kaplan, *Trauma Culture: The Politics of Terror and Loss in Media and Literature* (New Brunswick: Rutgers University Press, 2005), p. 67.

10    Kaplan, *Trauma Culture*, 69.

11    For example, although Lutz Klinkhammer identifies many 'striking similarities' between Fascist Italy and Nazi Germany in terms of repressive practices in the penal system, he concludes, 'the fascist dictatorship was always less radical that its German equivalent and the differences became increasingly evident after 1939'. 'Was There a Fascist Revolution? The Function of Penal Law in Fascist Italy and in Nazi Germany', *Journal of Modern Italian Studies*, 15:3 (2010), 390.

12    Ebner, *Ordinary Violence in Mussolini's Italy*, 8.

13    Alan O'Leary, 'Italian Cinema and the 'anni di piombo', *Journal of European Studies*, 40:3 (2010), 244.

14    Lidia Santarelli, 'Muted violence: Italian War Crimes in Occupied Greece', *Journal of Modern Italian Studies*, 9:3 (2004), 294–5.

15    Anke Pinkert, *Film and Memory in East Germany* (Bloomington: Indiana University Press, 2008), p. 23. For a study of Manicheanism in melodrama, see Peter Brooks, *The Melodramatic Imagination: Balzac, Henry James, Melodrama, and the Mode of Excess* (New Haven: Yale University Press, 1995), in particular the introduction.

16    E. Ann Kaplan, 'Melodrama, Cinema and Trauma', *Screen*, 42:2 (2001), 203.

17    Arturo Bocchini as cited in Corvisieri, *La villeggiatura di Mussolini*, 20.

18    See Galt who discusses how films such as *Il Postino* set in beautiful seaside locations present southern Italy in nostalgic terms that preclude any sort of political activism or potential for historical awakening (2002: 172). Rosalind Galt, 'Italy's Landscapes of Loss: Historical Mourning and the Dialectical Image in *Cinema Paradiso, Mediterraneo* and *Il Postino*', *Screen*, 43:2 (2002), 160–73.

19    Santner argues that a key difference between narrative fetishism and mourning 'has to do with the willingness or capacity to include the traumatic event in one's efforts to reformulate and reconstitute identity' ('History beyond the Pleasure Principle', 152).

20    The films, documentaries, and television movies treated in this section stand in opposition to the comedy *Gli anni ruggenti* (*Roaring Years*, Luigi Zampa, 1962) that focuses on a case of mistaken identity in a small town in Puglia and includes a brief scene in which an unnamed political *confinato* is scolded by the local authorities for entering a private club. This episode, the only one in the film where the *confinato* is present, serves as comic relief and functions primarily to make the local officials come off as buffoons.

21    Catherine O'Rawe, 'Stars and Masculinities in Italian Cinema', in Peter Bondanella (ed.), *The Italian Cinema Book* (London and New York: BFI and Palgrave Macmillan, 2014), pp. 268–74, p. 273.

22    Gissi, 'Un percorso a ritroso', 31–59.

23    Catherine O'Rawe, *Stars and Masculinities in Italian Cinema* (New York: Palgrave Macmillan, 2014), p. 165.

24    Interestingly, no films or documentaries have been made treating Gramsci's forty-four-day period of internal exile on Ustica until the release of the documentary *Gramsci 44* directed by Emiliano Barbucci and produced with Ram Film in 2016.

25    Cesare Pavese, *Il carcere* in *Prima che il gallo canti* (Turin: Einaudi, 1949), p. 41.

26    Lynne Kirby, *Parallel Tracks: The Railroad and Silent Cinema* (Durham: Duke University Press, 1997), p. 2.

27    Linda Williams, *Playing the Race Card: Melodramas of Black and White from Uncle Tom to O. J. Simpson* (Princeton: Princeton University Press, 2001), p. 15.

28    Linda Williams, 'Film Bodies: Gender, Genre, and Excess', in B. Keith Grant (ed.), *Film Genre Reader IV* (Austin: University of Texas Press, 2012), p. 174.

29    Mulvey writes that the female figure 'connotes something that the look circles around but disavows: her lack of a penis implying the threat of castration and hence unpleasure … The male unconscious has two alternatives of escape from this castration anxiety: preoccupation with the re-enactment of original trauma (… demystifying her mystery), counterbalanced by the devaluation, punishment or saving of the guilty object'. Laura Mulvey, 'Visual Pleasure and Narrative Cinema', in *Visual and Other Pleasures* (Bloomington: Indiana University Press, 1989), p. 21.

30    In the book, however, he does not commit the murder and indeed laments the lost opportunity to kill his wife.

31    Kaja Silverman, 'Fassbinder and Lacan: A Reconsideration of Gaze, Look, and Image', *Camera Obscura*, 7:1 (1989), 59–60.

32  Mary Ann Doane, *Femmes Fatales: Feminism, Film Theory, Psychoanalysis* (New York and London: Routledge, 1991), p. 1.

33  Doane, *Femmes Fatales*, 2.

34  Doane, *Femmes Fatales*, 1.

35  Juliana Schiesari, *The Gendering of Melancholia: Feminism, Psychoanalysis, and the Symbolics of Loss in Renaissance Literature* (Ithaca: Cornell University Press, 1992), p. 43, original italics.

36  Schiesari, *The Gendering of Melancholia*, 14.

37  Brooks, *The Melodramatic Imagination*, 30.

38  Linda Williams, 'Melodrama Revised', in Nick Brown (ed.), *Refiguring American Film Genres: Theory and History* (Berkeley and Los Angeles: University of California Press, 1998), p. 66.

39  Teresa de Lauretis, *Technologies of Gender: Essays on Film, Theory, Fiction* (Bloomington: Indiana University Press, 1987), p. 44.

40  Pam Cook, 'Melodrama and the Woman's Picture', in Marcia Landy (ed.), *Imitations of Life: A Reader on Film and Television Melodrama* (Detroit: Wayne State University Press, 1991), p. 253.

41  For more on Marion Cave's activism and arrest see Isabelle Richet, 'Marion Cave Rosselli and the Transnational Women's Antifascist Networks', *Journal of Women's History*, 24:3 (2012), 117–39.

42  Mulvey, 'Visual Pleasure and Narrative Cinema', 40.

43  Tom Lutz, 'Men's Tears and the Roles of Melodrama', in Milette Shamir and Jennifer Travis (eds), *Boy Don't Cry? Rethinking Narratives of Masculinity and Emotion in the U.S.* (New York: Columbia University Press, 2002), p. 190.

44  Geoffrey Nowell-Smith, 'Minnelli and Melodrama', in Marcia Landy (ed.), *Imitations of Life: A Reader on Film and Television Melodrama* (Detroit: Wayne State University Press, 1991), p. 271.

45  Kaplan, 'Melodrama, Cinema and Trauma', 203.

46  Tania Modleski, 'Clint Eastwood and Male Weepies', *American Literary History*, 22:1 (Spring 2010), 136.

47  For example, Bondanella claims, 'In contrast to Rosi's better films, this is a slow-moving, even ponderous work that employs the same kinds of tedious film editing of bad American television and even includes a surprisingly bad performance (one of his last) by Volonté'. *A History of Italian Cinema* (New York and London: Continuum, 2009), p. 248.

48  Millicent Marcus, *Italian Film in the Light of Neorealism* (Princeton: Princeton University Press, 1986), pp. 340–1.

49  Marcus argues that the State is uninterested in the South indicting Italy's colonial pursuits in North Africa.

50  Modleski, 'Clint Eastwood and Male Weepies', 154, original italics.

51  Modleski, 'Clint Eastwood and Male Weepies', 150.

52  In a letter in which he discusses the screenplay, Luciano Vicenzoni remarks, 'La storia di mia madre era un bel film (My mother's story made a good film)', 'Montale: presentazione del film *Libera, amore mio*' www.centromaurobolognini.it/pagine/news2010/news_iniziativamontale_ dettagli.htm (accessed 30 September 2014).

53  Mulvey, 'Visual Pleasure and Narrative Cinema', 22.

54  Mulvey, 'Visual Pleasure and Narrative Cinema', 43.

55  Santner, 'History beyond the Pleasure Principle', 147.

56  Mulvey, 'Visual Pleasure and Narrative Cinema', 21.

57  Mulvey, 'Visual Pleasure and Narrative Cinema', 17.

58  Mulvey, 'Visual Pleasure and Narrative Cinema', 30.

59  In her discussion of *Duel in the Sun*, Mulvey concludes that 'Pearl's position … is similar to that of the female spectator as she temporarily accepts "masculinisation" in memory of her "active" phase. Rather that dramatising the success of masculine identification, Pearl brings out its sadness. Her "tomboy" pleasures, her sexuality, are not fully accepted by Lewt, except in death' ('Visual Pleasure and Narrative Cinema', 37).

60  Mulvey, 'Afterthoughts on "Visual Pleasure and Narrative Cinema"', p. 36.

61  Monica Straniero, 'L'isola dell'angelo caduto' (11 November 2012) www.cinemaitaliano. info/news/15466/festival-roma-lucarelli-debutto-alla-regia.html (accessed 16 October 2014).

62  Janet Staiger, 'Film Noir as Male Melodrama: The Politics of Film Genre Labeling', in Lincoln Geraghty and Mark Jancovich (eds), *The Shifting Definitions of Genre: Essays on Labeling Films, Television Shows, and Media* (Jefferson: McFarland, 2008), p. 73.

63  Staiger, 'Film Noir as Male Melodrama', 73.

64  Frank Krutnik, *In a Lonely Street: Film Noir, Genre, Masculinity* (New York and London: Routledge, 1991), p. 86.

65  Krutnik, *In a Lonely Street*, 125–7.

66  Krutnik, *In a Lonely Street*, 135.

67  Staiger, 'Film Noir as Male Melodrama', 73.

68  RDL 1254 (15 July 1926), *Gazzetta ufficiale del regno d'italia*, 127 (27 July 1926), 3334.

69  Dickie, *Cosa Nostra*, 159.

70  Lupo, *History of the Mafia*, 185 does note that one *mafioso*, Mauro Farinella, was twice sentenced to four years of internal exile and ultimately 'died on a small island' (p. 186).

71  Duggan, *Fascism and the Mafia*, 57.

72  Ezio Costanzo, *The Mafia and the Allies: Sicily 1943 and the return of the Mafia* (New York: Enigma Books, 2007), p. 132.

73  Vittorio Coco, *La mafia, il fascismo, la polizia* (Palermo: Centro di studi ed iniziative culturali Pio La Torre, 2012), p. 7.

74  Poesio, *Il confino fascista*.

75  Ebner, *Ordinary Violence in Mussolini's Italy*, 169.

76  Interestingly, recent scholarship looks at the role of internal exile of *mafiosi* in postwar Italy as it relates to the migration of organised crime to northern Italy and internationally. No mention is made, however, of internal exile during Fascism. Paolo Buonanno and Matteo Pazzona, 'Migrating Mafias', *Region Science and Urban Economics*, 44 (2014), 75–81.

77  In all of the memoirs treated in Chapter 3, only one mention is made of organised crime when Giorgio Amendola, whilst in prison at Poggioreale, meets the 'avvocaticchio' who is a boss of bosses of the Camorra, biding his time in prison and continually postponing his trial so as to let the statute of limitations run out. Amendola, *Un'isola*, 153–4.

78  For example, Pauline Small discusses how *I cento passi* 'narrates a tale of exceptional courage' ('Giordana's *I cento passi*: Renegotiating the Mafia Codes', *New Cinemas: Journal of Contemporary Film*, 3:1 (2005), 44), and George de Stefano states that *I cento passi* is 'a consciousness-raising tool for anti-Mafia forces, as well as a memorial to a fallen leader of the anti-mafia struggle'. 'Marco Tullio Giordana's *The Hundred Steps*: The Biopic as Political Cinema', in Dana Renga (ed.), *Mafia Movies: A Reader* (Toronto, Buffalo and London: University of Toronto Press, 2011), p. 320.

79  Pino Arlacchi and Antonio Calderone, *Gli uomini del disonore. La mafia siciliana nella vita del grande pentito Antonino Calderone* (Milan: Il Saggiatore, 2010), pp. 20–1.

80  Maureen Turim, 'The Trauma of History: Flashbacks upon Flashbacks', *Screen*, 42:2 (Summer, 2001), 209.

81   Joshua Hirsch, *Afterimage: Film, Trauma and the Holocaust* (Philadelphia: Temple University Press, 2004), p. 95.

82   Susan Hayward, *Cinema Studies: The Key Concepts* (New York: Routledge, 2013), p. 233.

83   'Gita al faro' (29 June 2012), http://video.corriere.it/gita-faro-festival-lidia-ravera/13b1b8f2-c1f4–11e1–8b65–125b10ae7983?playlistId=b4589f12-a47b-11e3-8a4e-10b18d687a95 (accessed 8 February 2018).

84   Modleski, 'Clint Eastwood and Male Weepies', 154.

# 5

# Queering internal exile on
# Italian screens

## Introduction

The promotion of internal exile as holiday is particularly interesting when considering the experience of men sent to the islands (most commonly the Tremiti but also to Ustica) for suspicion of 'pederasty', as it was referred to at the time. As Lorenzo Benadusi explains, it is difficult to know exactly 'how many people were sent to *confino* because they were thought to be homosexual'.[1] Police records indicate that 88 political prisoners and 298 common criminals were sent to internal exile for suspected homosexuality,[2] and emerging from testimonies of surviving detainees was a sense that life was quite pleasant on the islands. Ex-*confinato* Giuseppe P. (known as Peppinella) states: 'Ci furono femmenelle che piangevano quando venimmo via dalle Tremiti' (there were 'femmenelle' who cried when we left the Tremiti)[3] as he recalls nostalgically the many parties in the barracks on San Domino complete with theatrical performances where men cross-dressed 'senza che nessuno dicesse niente' (and no one cared).[4] Unlike back at home where gay men lived in fear of being arrested,[5] on the islands they could be open about their sexuality and romantic involvements between prisoners, and between prisoners and guards, were common. As Peppinella states 'in fondo, si stava meglio là che qua' (in the end, we were better off there than here).

It is in fact 'ironic', as a BBC article points out,[6] that gay men could find a certain amount of freedom on an island prison where conditions were grim, barracks were overcrowded, illness was rampant, jobs were unavailable, and the average stipend was only four lire per day.[7] Further, according to Benedusi gay *confinati* were treated worse than other prisoners, and were 'derisi e emarginati dagli altri prigionieri e dalla gente del posto' (mocked and marginalised by the other prisoners and by those who lived on the island).[8] Nonetheless, many gay men remember their period of confinement positively as they, for the first time in their lives, were part of a community where they could be open about their sexuality. The island collective for these men approximates a 'queer counterpublic' as theorised by Berlant and Warner, as the space allows for 'the development of kinds of intimacy that bear no necessary relation to domestic space, to kinship, to the couple form, to property, or to the nation' while still establishing 'a public world of belonging and transformation'. While these spaces are inventive and accessible, they are also fragile, 'indefinite', and 'conscious of [their] subordinate relation',[9] which was made clear when the island colonies were emptied out and men were sent home where speaking about the experience was most likely not an option. As the narrator of the documentary *L'albero rosso* (*The Red Tree*, Paul Rowley, 2017) tells us, all the gay exiles sobbed when they were forced to leave the internment island of San Domino in the Tremiti. Why did they cry? As he explains, because they had to go home, because they had to leave, and because they would never be together again.

A photograph from a dance hall in Catania in the 1950s is the most iconic image associated with queer *confino*, most likely because the majority of gay *confinati* were taken prisoner in Catania – it is used on blogs, to advertise documentaries, and is associated with commemorative events. Yet, the photograph dates to after the conclusion of World War II and most likely does not feature any ex-*confinati*. The look on the faces of the men in the photograph is striking: they appear taken surprise by the photographer and are frozen in time: None of them are smiling, and their faces reveal a mixture of fear, apprehension, and shock, a reaction that speaks to the precarious status of counterpublics and those who engage with them.

The experience of many gay men sent into internal exile is cloaked in silence, an attitude apparent in two of the films that engage the experience. In Ettore Scola's *Una giornata particolare* (*A Special Day*, 1977), main protagonist Giovanni's internal exile (and the reasons for it) emerge ambiguously in the closing moments of the film. More to the point, Gabriella Romano's documentary, *Ricordare* (2004) opens with a warning: 'Ogni narrazione storica è un fascio di silenzi' (Every historical narration is a bundle of silences).[10] Romano is playing on the etymology for Fascism, the bundle of wheat ('fascio') held together by an axe rod. Furthermore, Romano alludes to the veil of silence that surrounded homosexuality during Fascism, in particular the legislation against it. Article 528 of the penal code which criminalised 'pederasty' was proposed and then cancelled as 'la previsione di questo reato non [è] affatto necessaria perché per fortuna ed orgoglio dell'Italia il vizio abominevole che vi darebbe vita non è così diffuso tra noi, da giustificare l'intervento del legislatore' (the anticipation of this crime is not really necessary because for luck and pride, the abominable vice that would give it life is not diffused enough amongst us to justify the intervention of the legislature),[11] a position which would respond affirmatively to Foucault's query regarding how prohibition and censorship allow for power to be exercised: '[a]re prohibition, censorship, and denial truly the forms through which power is exercised in a general way'?[12] As activist Massimo Consoli notes during an interview in *Ricordare*, 'si faceva ma non si parlava' (It was done but not discussed). In short, the article was not necessary since homosexuals did not exist in Italy, as gay rights activist Franco Grillini explains in *Ricordare*:

> Italian gay men ... including some famous intellectuals, say that it was better when it was worse. Because at the time homosexuality didn't have a name, didn't have an identity and the homosexual act was confined on the sexual sphere. In this way, there were lots of men who had homosexual relationships, a relevant part of the population, without any particular problems. As long as it wasn't visible. In our country it is visible homosexuality that has been persecuted, not the invisible one. There is a peculiar hypocrisy, absorbed by the legal system, by which we say 'If this is not seen, if it isn't explicit, we don't consider it a crime'.

This is clear in the discussions around penal code 528, 'il silenzio intorno all'omosessualità funziona meglio di una repressione aperta. ... La censura e la negazione hanno il significato di impedire la discussione e la conoscenza' [Not talking about homosexuality works better than open repression ... censorship and negation are capable of impeding discussion and knowledge].[13]

This chapter interrogates this silence by looking at two feature films, four documentaries, and one graphic novel that give voice to experiences of gay men sent into internal exile. In the films *Una giornata particolare* (*A Special Day*, 1977) and *Gli occhiali d'oro* (*The Gold Rimmed Glasses*, 1987), exile is a minor narrative thread. The documentaries and graphic novel, however, are explicit in treating the exile experience of gay men, and evince a clear memorialising tendency surrounding gay *confino*. These five texts are different from the majority of the films discussed in the previous chapter that smooth over the cultural trauma of internal exile. Thus we saw that the stories of *mafiosi*, anti-Fascists, and intellectuals sent to internal exile are recast in a melodramatic light and the suffering of male protagonists is productive. Instead, the queer affect that is rife in the documentaries and graphic novel discussed in this chapter can be read, borrowing from the work of Dijana Jelaca, as a 'productively affirmative response to national trauma'.[14] This is because these works engage in a process of 'queering the public archive', which has a double effect: for the first time, the men who are the focus of the documentaries and graphic novel are positioned within national memory. But also, as Jelaca underlines, queer responses to cultural trauma are not linear and as such might push back against cultural tendencies to heal and to get over the past, which are measures of a healthy nation (thus, being sick 'is OK').[15] Three of the documentaries and the graphic novel position melancholia as productive. Unlike in the films discussed in the previous chapter, however, melancholia is not redemptive as the real and fictional men discussed in this chapter fight to hold on 'to aspects of their history that are constantly devalued or denied'.[16] In this way, these texts aid in the project of recuperating submerged histories without subsuming individual narratives into larger restorative narratives.

## 'Strategies of containment' in *Una giornata particolare* and *Gli occhiali d'oro*

Only two feature films make mention of the internal exile experience for gay men, Ettore Scola's *Una giornata particolare* and Giuliano Montaldo's *Gli occhiali d'oro*. Interestingly, and unlike several of the films treating political prisoners discussed in the previous chapter, neither of these films foregrounds the internal exile experience or depicts detainees on the islands. In *Una giornata particolare*, internal exile assumes a subordinate position with respect to a series of other narrative threads and in *Gli occhiali d'oro* internal exile is only referenced as a threat to curb perceived lascivious behaviour (the main character is gay). These two films only briefly reference internal exile or show glimpses of the detainee in transit before banishment, and not on the scene of detention. Both films do, however, thematise the sense of shame that gay men lived with during Fascism when homosexuality had to remain invisible and any behaviours that diverged from the heterocentrist gender model promoted by the Regime were met with oppressive measures.

In 2014 the newly restored *Una giornata particolare* was awarded the honorary 'Queer Lion' prize. Inaugurated in 2007, the award is presented annually at the Venice film festival for 'the best film with LBGT themes and queer culture'. And more recently, *Una giornata particolare* is receiving critical attention as a queer film, in particular by Sergio Rigoletto who looks at how it is representative of numerous Italian films read by critics who impose 'ideal masculinities – heterosexual, heroic, virile, predatory and aggressive' as the standard against which all masculinities are meant to be read. As a result, when Gabriele (who is gay) has sex with Antonietta and she is on top, he is read as unmasculine because, as Rigoletto argues, he is gay.[17] And Rigoletto's book adeptly challenges what he describes as a 'masculine–unmasculine' binary.[18] Alternatively, Szymon Pietrzykowski offers a socio-cultural-political look at how homosexuality was policed during Fascism while forwarding an intriguing reading of how *Una giornata particolare* represents a gay man as a stranger, someone without a concrete identity yet who embodies a distinct threat.[19]

*Una giornata particolare* is about two encounters: one historical between Mussolini and Hitler that took place in Rome on 6 May 1938 and one emotional involving Fascist housewife and mother of six Antonietta and anti-Fascist Gabriele, who was fired from his job as a radio announcer because, as he explains to Antonietta, he is 'antifascist, useless, and tending towards depravity'. 1938 is an important year because when Italy passed the racial laws, gay men became classified as political prisoners, a more serious sentence than the previous common criminal, because those condemned for the crime of pederasty were viewed as a threat to the newly invented Italian race.[20]

Throughout much of the film, Gabriele is downcast in his apartment, where he packs his books and prepares for a long absence. However, the implications regarding his exile take a back seat to the film's main narrative thrust, which is interrogating Fascist gender policy, in particular exploring the female condition as chained to the home and hearth. While Giovanni mentions the reasons for which he was expelled from the party or fired from his job (he cites more than once his anti-Fascism), he never makes explicit the causes of his exile, which is interesting as Giovanni 'qualifies' to be sent into internal exile for several reasons: he is an intellectual, anti-Fascist, possibly a socialist, *and* gay. Most who write on the film mention that Giovanni is sent into internal exile because he is gay.[21] Moreover, as Benadusi points out, many of those sentenced to internal exile for pederasty were prostitutes and were more public regarding their sexuality. Arrest files reveal that detainees were poor, illiterate, overtly effeminate, and of 'lower social classes with a life of hardship and difficulty behind them', and all were registered as Apolitical.[22] Essentially, it appears that if one were private with regards to sexual orientation, then people tended to look the other way.

Gabriele ambiguously mentions internal exile to Antonietta when discussing a friend who was sentenced to hard labour in the Sardinian mining town of Carbonia. When she queries the reason for his sentence Gabriele answers that, yes, his friend was a Subversive like himself. The second and most explicit reference to internal exile in *Una giornata particolare* occurs at the film's conclusion when two members of the police escort Gabriele from his apartment. As Antonietta watches Gabriele's forced departure from her window above the courtyard, the film's two recurring soundtracks (the diegetic political diatribe and the extra-diegetic romantic theme music) are intermingled for the last time. The shot of Gabriele walking towards the camera is from a low angle in low-key tonality, flanked on each side by a Fascist guard. He has become a shadow, and his face is invisible. Two shots later, a cut to a slow zoom-in on Antonietta framed by her window underlines her imprisonment and forwards the film's message: both protagonists are prisoners, Antonietta is captive in her own home, chained to the Fascist ideal of 'sposa e madre esemplare' while Gabriele must face a more literal incarceration. The film however concludes on Antonietta, and, as the camera literally enters her apartment (mirroring the film's opening sequence), the military song fades away and the sentimental score remains, and the camera tracks Antonietta as she shuts off the lights and adjourns to bed. Gabriele's journey to and internment at an exile island are not visualised as the film is not really about that. We have no information about where he is headed or the length of or specific reason for his sentence. Instead, the film condemns political systems and associated gender policies, and Gabriele's exile provides for a further critique of totalitarianism. In *Una giornata particolare* the *confinato* is only seen in passing and the remainder of his journey and internment is left to the viewer's imagination.

As discussed in Chapter 4, Scola is not alone in his adoption of the event of internal exile for a more expansive assessment of Italian politics, as we see, for example, with *Cristo si è fermato ad Eboli*'s indictment of Italian economic disparity or the selection of films that deal with the Mafia and conclude on a moralising message that stresses Cosa Nostra's pervasiveness into politics. *Gli occhiali d'oro* focuses on the challenges faced by Dr Athos Fadigati when he comes out in 1938 Ferrara. However, his suffering is minimised by the film's foregrounding of anti-Semitism. Fadigati commits suicide because, the film implies, of his sense of shame. The film comes to a close however by memorialising the 151 Jews of Ferrara who were deported to the lager (prison camp) in 1943.

Deportation to Carbonia is mentioned when Fadigati is spied upon through binoculars whilst with his young lover Eraldo in a rowboat in the Adriatic. Signora Lavezzoli, a member of the upper echelons of Ferrarese society, exclaims that the 'spectacle' makes her sick and that Fadigati should feel shame and that he no longer possesses modesty. 'In Rome those like Fadigati would be sent to work in the coal mines', remarks a man seated nearby and Signora Lavezzoli responds 'How so? With all of those pretty young shirtless men'?

William Van Watson argues that 'Montaldo deploys Signora Lavezzoli as the policing Fascist gaze in the film',[23] who aims to enforce 'gender normativity' but also desires to punish Fadigati for repeatedly ignoring her advances. And her character recalls the doorwoman in *Una giornata particolare* whose penetrative gaze monitors the building's tenants and warns Antonietta to stay away from Gabriele whom she considers a 'son of a bitch'. In Giorgio Bassani's 1958 novella, *Gli occhiali d'oro*, the mention of internal exile foregrounds Fadigati's isolation, as the narrator says about Fadigati 'pareva poco meno che un recluso: un confinato di riguardo, in viaggio di trasferimento a Ponza o alle Tremiti per restarci chissà quanto'[24] (he seemed like a recluse: a respectable *confinato*, travelling to Ponza or to the Tremiti to stay there for who knows how long). In the film of the same name, however, discussion of forced labour in Sardinia establishes Fadigati's difference from those like Signora Lavezzoli who view him as deviant and through whose disapproving gaze viewers surveil the couple (we look with her through the binoculars from her position of superiority). Fadigati takes his own life because, as he explains to his friend Davide, he feels too much shame to face anyone. The film implies that once he is out of the closet, Fadigati can no longer conceal that he is gay and has no community to accept him. In this way, Montaldo's film engages in a 'strategy of containment' that, as Van Watson argues, constructs homosexuality as an 'unliveable condition' and suggests, as is the case with Scola's film, that the only 'good' gay man is dead or invisible.[25]

### Difficult memory in *Ricordare*

In *Ricordare* painful experiences from the past bleed into the present when the director attempts to bring the confinement experience for gay men into the public domain. Interviewees however are quite resistant to Romano, made clear in the first five minutes of the film in a voiceover composed of Romano's phone calls to various people who have connections to surviving *confinati* and who tell her that these men do not want to talk to her as they are terrified. For example, the director is told that they 'either do not want to compromise themselves, they have a thousand fears, old fears, many years spent hiding, spent in fear of going public, of the police, of data that can circulate, of having their face seen. It can be many things, or maybe they simply do not want to talk about it'. One man states these men are 'scared to reveal their identities as they grew up during the years of Fascism'. The few men whom Romano succeeds in interviewing attest to several aspects of delayed response to painful experiences as they hide, misremember, or refuse to speak. Borrowing from Dina Georgis, queer affect in the documentary 'haunts and disquiets and refuses endings'[26] and thus works to unsettle history.

Romano acts as director-therapist, and, as the few men with whom she succeeds to speak are pushed back into their memories, she asks them to repeat intricate details of their experiences. Remembering is challenging, particularly as interviewees are asked to bespeak their sexual orientation in a country where, as Giovanni Dall'Orto argues, in Italy homosexuality was repressed for so long that, until recently, it simply did not exist on the national level.[27] One activist interviewed by Romano explains that many older gay men feel that they have no right to national history or collective memory, and therefore cannot process their pain. Unlike the call to arms present in so many of the films engaging with political *confinati*, the past-made-present gets these men nowhere: they miss appointments, do not answer the director's phone calls, or shut the door on her. Thus, we are back at Santner's second category for aesthetic representations of trauma discussed in the previous chapter: that of mourning, which is a process where the subject remembers and relives traumatic experiences in a safe environment.[28]

Cathy Caruth identifies an inscrutable aspect of the association between memory, trauma, and survival: 'for those who undergo trauma, it is not only the moment of the event, but of the passing out of it that is traumatic; that *survival itself can be a crisis*'.[29] The crisis of survival is played out in Romano's film in that men only agree to be interviewed out of fear, as they believe that the director is planning to blackmail them. Most who do speak to Romano are nervous and agitated and end interviews abruptly. Some seventy years later, they, as one interviewee attests, 'think they are still living at that time' and he believes that they cannot let go of their identity as homosexual detainee. Narrative metamorphoses of potentially pain-inducing experiences are central to a larger exploration of onscreen engagements with internal exile for gay man, clear in an interview in *Ricordare* that emphasises the fungiblity of discourses of trauma in the cinematic construction of a single, unified experience of confinement among this population and brings us back to Berlusconi's problematic statement:

Romano: What did you do on Ustica?
'Giovanni': We got up early in the morning because they woke us up and they unlocked us. In the evening they locked us in at six in summer, at four in winter. Sometimes we put up a theatre performance, we sang, danced, because there were also some artists, real famous ones, and we acted on stage, in Ustica, we would dress up as women, we staged variety shows and operettas.

R: Were you watched by some carabinieri?

G: No, they weren't interested.

R: How do you remember the period you stayed in Ustica?

G: I remember that Ustica was beautiful because I love the sea. And it was full of dogs, and that made me happy and I didn't care about anything, so much so that when I had to leave, I was really sorry, I would have liked to stay longer. But then we left, the Americans let us free and I went back to my town, Naples, and with my partner we opened the boutique in via Chiaia.

R: Careful, I am leaning against the door!

G: But we have finished, haven't we? Now I am old, I have a quiet life, I am respected …

R: Was there a scandal when you were arrested …

G: No, scandals never! Goodbye.

Two elements stand out here: One, the sense of nostalgia that pervades 'Giovanni's' narrative. He is not alone as many gay men interviewed say that things were better during Fascism, even though historical studies on the practice attest to the deplorable conditions for those in exile and the public scandal met by gay *confinati* upon their release. One man interviewed attests: 'Look, Fascism was atrocious for everybody, I agree, but I know that during Fascism one lived better than nowadays. There wasn't all the delinquency that we have now!' This response conforms to the psychological definition of 'splitting', defined as a '[s]imultaneous experience within the ego of two contradictory responses to reality, acceptance and *denial*, without the ego needing to produce a compromise between the two or to repress the one or the other'.[30] It is as though these two men integrated experiences under Fascism into the present without acknowledging their painful implications. Second, when Giovanni is pushed to say more about the 'scandal' of his past, he, like others, conveys that he relives the difficulties of his internment daily, and he feels that he is still in danger and he risks deportation, and, when prompted to say more about his arrest, he responds by politely kicking the director out of his flat. Romano is the first in a series of filmmakers treating gay *confino* to open doors that many would prefer remained shut.

## Divided memory in *Isola nuda*

In Debora Inguglia's documentary *Isola nuda* (*Naked Island*, 2007), six residents of the Sicilian island of Ustica recount their memories regarding the large number of gay men confined to the island. Frequently in the documentary internal exile is rewritten in benign terms. At one point a woman confidently claims, 'Il confino è stato una villeggiatura veramente per loro' (*confino* was truly a holiday for them). 'We treated them well, and they were good to us. There were important people here. Professors … even Gramsci came here, and some really powerful people. Because not all of them were "maruschi"' – pejorative slang for gay men. She goes on to explain that it was a 'meraviglia' (wonder) to see people like 'them' for the first time and reiterates that *confinati* were well off while in residence on the island and did not suffer whilst locked in the barracks as they could run around and have fun. While this unnamed woman (and this anonymity applies to all those who speak in *Isola nuda*) recollects fondly the period of internal exile and insists that the islanders have a good memory of the *confinati*, two other men are severe in their reminisces. An elderly man calls gay *confinati* unrepentant sinners and claims that he was filled with disgust upon seeing gay men in the streets of Milan. Another man describes all *confinati* as rapists, thieves, and abusers of power who ate raw cow's livers and cut themselves with broken glass whilst inebriated. A third man is much more sympathetic to the plight of *confinati*, and discusses the deplorable living conditions, inhumane treatment by the police, regular beatings (especially for gay *confinati*), lack of food, and speaks without judgement about love stories between gay *confinati* and male islanders. Finally, a man who works on a farm claims that *confinati* wanted to escape but did not as the island is surrounded by sharks, and then remarks that they really did not want to flee after all as they were quite content on the island.

John Foot argues that since unification 'Italian history is marked by divided memories' and describes divided memory as 'the tendency for divergent or contradictory narratives to emerge after events, and to be elaborated and interpreted in private stories as well as through forms of public commemoration and ritual'. He claims that such recollections are often 'incompatible' but 'survive in parallel' and when reconciliation takes place these memories might 'merge'.[31] In *Isola nuda* the memory of internment on Ustica is indeed divided, and there is no sense that memory will be reconciled. The tone of the documentary *Vladimir Luxuria: L'isola degli omosessuali. Storia di un confino dimenticato alle Tremiti (Vladimir Luxuria: The Island of Homosexuals. History of a Forgotten confino in the Tremiti*, Radiobici, 2013) is redemptive and the narration foregrounds a process of commemoration with regards to gay men interned on the Tremiti. This is not the case in *Isola nuda*.

Most interviewees are on screen for a relatively short time, from about two to six minutes total. An older gay man, however, has twenty-eight minutes of screen time in the fifty-two minute documentary. Mostly, he recounts memories of his lovers or discusses the first time that he had sex, the disappearance of 'real men', closeted actors, and his various ailments, or distractedly cleans his house, looks through photos, dances in slow-motion, or speaks to people in nonsense sentences as they pass on the street. Frequently, the camera lingers inside of his claustrophobic house, or centres on doorways and windows. Although the suggestion is that this man suffered internal exile, he never speaks of his personal experiences. It is striking that the island of the documentary's title is absent, and the ocean is glimpsed only once for a few seconds, and the island never emerges as a unified space. Instead, the island is a 'non luogo'[32] (non space). *Isola nuda*, in particular the treatment of the unnamed man, disrupts 'chrononormativity', or, as Elizabeth Freeman explains, time that is used as an organising principal that guides subjects towards production and procreation. Instead, the documentary foregrounds queer time, which Freeman notes is marked by 'compulsive returns, movements back-wards to reenter prior historical moments'.[33] In *Isola nuda*, space and time are fragmented and repetitive, and domestic time is fraught, especially in the insist-ence on this man's scarred and infirm body which positions, citing Freeman, 'The corporeal event ... outside of heteronormative timing'.[34]

This man's narration is disjointed as is the case with the entire documentary. For example, the documentary lacks both the director's voice and a disembodied voiceover, which traditionally is used as 'the filmmaker's ultimate tool for telling people what to think'.[35] Also, editing is elliptical and the documentary shifts from one subject to another without warning, and the camera frequently pauses on unidentified streets, empty gaping doorways, windows with views obscured, and the film returns frequently to a rundown plot of land resembling a farm occa-sionally traversed by unidentified persons. In many ways, *Isola nuda* embodies trauma cinema as theorised by Joshua Hirsch. In particular, in its clear rejecting of 'the classical realist forms of film narration traditionally used to provide a sense of mastery over the past, and adopting instead modernist forms of narration that formally repeat the traumatic structure of the experience of witnessing the events themselves'.[36] The documentary also deals with the event of deportation in a 'nonrealist mode characterised by disturbance and fragmentation of the film's narrative and stylistic regimes', which is a key component to trauma cinema as discussed by Janet Walker. Rather than positioning viewers to align with characters and showing 'the world as it is', *Isola nuda* engages in a process of 'disremembering' the past by 'drawing on innovative strategies for representing reality obliquely'[37] a strategy that points towards deficiencies and divergences of memory. *Isola nuda* reveals how human, qualified, political life (bios) is transformed into bare life (zoe) 'vita nuda' at the whim of the State.[38]

Towards the end of the documentary, the gay man remarks that although *confinati* lacked freedom, they spent time outside in the fresh air. A friend talks over him, saying 'they were not like the people in Alcatraz' and then the pair debates whether Alcatraz is still an operating penitentiary. While the gay man is convinced that Alcatraz has been closed down for a year and a half, his friend insists that this is not the case, and that US President Bush declared that it must stay open and claims that he saw a news report just fifteen days previously stating that 'they' sent terrorists too dangerous to go anywhere else to the prison island. The pair then discusses a film that was made on the locale starring Clint Eastwood. In this way, the internal exile experience is downplayed as the pair misremember and misin-terpret history (Alcatraz stands in for, most likely, the other detention island space of Guantanamo Bay). Frequently in the documentary imprisonment is rewritten as sojourn. Now, as the woman tells us, tourism is the main activity on the island, and one man explains the history of the term 'confinato': at first, he says, they were called 'stirrati' which he explains are 'wild and bad people, thieves, killers', then 'coatti' (person under house arrest), then after a few years, *confinati*, then, 'arresto domiciliario' (under house arrest) and then finally he notes that now they are called 'soggiornati' (vacationers). In all three cases, the exile experience is displaced onto other narratives that are in most cases more pleasant, or, in the case of Alcatraz, mythical.[39]

Inguglia presents six different 'witnesses' to a past that remains murky and indistinct, much like the final image of the film which is a slow pan to the right to a silhouette of an unrecognisable man enveloped in shadow whilst facing the camera and standing outside of a gaping hole in a building as the camera fades to black. One reviewer argues that the island in the documentary is transformed from a 'spazio di prigionia in uno spazio di libertà' (a prison space to a space of freedom).[40] Another claims that *Isola nuda* is a redemptive film that pushes viewers to forgive and lay the past to rest.[41] Instead, *Isola nuda* does not articulate history in redemptive terms and presents space as claustrophobic, time as monotonous and repetitive, foregrounds melancholia as productive, and suggests that the wounds of deportation for the victims of internal exile are by no means healed.

### Vladimir Luxuria: L'isola degli omosessuali. Storia di un confino dimenticato alle Tremiti: 'In order to stop being a victim, one must become a witness'

The thirteen-minute documentary *Vladimir Luxuria: L'isola degli omosessuali. Storia di un confino dimenticato alle Tremiti* can be viewed for free online and was produced by Radiobici, an organisation that traverses the peninsula on bicycle and produces multimedia programmes on topics to include politics, sustainability, and music (www.radiobici.it/). Such a non-mainstream production and distribution model recalls Derek Duncan's point that 'queer cinema exists in its most robust form outside commercial circuits of distribution'.[42] *Vladimir Luxuria* was shot in the wake of a ceremony on 8 June 2013 honouring the memory of the fifty-three men sentenced to internal exile on the island of San Domino in the Tremiti in 1938 for suspected homosexuality. Organised on the site of deportation by the transgender politician and activist Vladimir Luxuria, the ceremony involved unveiling a plaque stating 'Le isole Tremiti non dimenticano. In memoria degli omosessuali confinati durante il fascismo' (The community of the Tremiti Islands do not forget. In memory of the homosexuals sent into internal exile during Fascism) in front of a group of islanders and activists. On the plaque hangs a bell, which Luxuria explains serves a double purpose: during the period of confinement, a bell was rung at 8:00 pm to alert detainees that their moment of freedom was over and that they were to enter the barracks where they would be locked up until the morning. Instead now, she explains, 'we ring it to say that we will not forget, we will not forget all of the victims of prejudice'. In the commemorative documentary five people speak about topics that include the period of confinement on San Domino, legislation surrounding homosexuality during Fascism, the plight of men who returned home after their period of confinement, continued homophobia in Italy, and the role of testimony and attempts to restore voice to the victims of internal exile. With the exception of one elderly woman, all interviewees are on bicycles. In addition to Luxuria, we also hear from Gianfranco Goretti, co-author with Tommaso Giartusio of *La città e l'isola: Omosessuali al confine nell'Italia fascista*, Luca de Santis, co-author of the graphic novel *In Italia sono tutti maschi* (*In Italy, They Are All Males*, 2008) that focuses on a group of men deported to the Tremiti, and two locals who communicate their memories about the gay detainees.

While Luxuria, Goretti, and de Santis speak principally about topics such as the difficult conditions that men were forced to endure whilst in captivity, repression of historical memory, silence surrounding homosexuality, the complicated re-entry and shame felt by detainees once returned home, issues of survival, and the imperative to memorialise victims, the two islanders instead present a much more tempered version of the exile experience. A woman named Carmela Santoro states that detainees were treated very well, that they were all pretty ('belle') and elegant, and that they all left when the war was over (which is not the case as they were sent home in 1940). When asked what the men did on the island, Attilio Carducci responds 'nothing, they worked' before explaining that they had several parties where they cross-dressed, danced, and ate, and underlines that they were always happy and very 'brave persone' (nice people). Luxuria, however, puts forward that the parties might be more productively thought of as a mechanism to survive the experience of confinement, and reminds viewers that the Tremiti are only beautiful when one has free will and decides to visit them. Like Romano and Inguglia's documentaries, *Vladimir Luxuria* creates a counter memory to the deportation experience by debunking the exile as sabbatical equation.

As we have seen, Romano in *Ricordare* is concerned with the maintenance of a singular, unified, authoritative discourse that Inguglia's *Isola nuda* interrogates through the production of divergent narratives. In contrast, *Vladimir Luxuria* presents a kaleidoscope of narratives at odds with each other not only in content (about how the *confinati* experienced the island and their state of mind during detention) but also in terms of the relative discursive distance of these declarations (the different speaking positions of the academic, first-hand 'witnesses', and political activists).

The documentary suggests, borrowing from Rousso's study *The Haunting Past*, that we might begin to be 'living in the "age of memory", that is, in a sensitive, affective, even painful relationship with the [memory of deportation]',[43] which is indeed a new phenomenon. Goretti notes that when he began work on his book in 1998, only one islander would talk about memories of the exile experience, all others replied 'I do not remember' which he reads as sign of repression and a will not to discuss the past. This willed ignorance recalls the legislation (or lack thereof) surrounding homosexuality during Fascism as explained by de Santis while discussing the inspiration for the title of the graphic novel: 'when a law needed to be created in the Codice Rocco against sodomy in Italy, Mussolini said we do not need this type of law because in Italy they are all "maschi" [manly], virile, and heterosexual, therefore we do not need this law, which left the government free to enforce a very open repression'. As Foucault argues, the homosexual emerged as an individual in the nineteenth century: the 'homosexual became a personage, a past, a case history, and a childhood, in addition to being a type of life, a life form, and a morphology, with an indiscreet anatomy and possibly a mysterious morphology … The sodomite had been a temporary aberration; the homosexual was now a species'.[44] Creating a law against homosexuality, as Goretti explains, would require the enactment of a body of laws, and with legislation comes arrests, trials, and publicity.

Gay men were granted a very controlled sexual freedom while on the Tremiti or on Ustica as they were removed from 'civil' society and were no longer considered a threat. However, once these men returned home, they had to, in the words of de Santis, repress ('rimuovere') their experiences during internal exile. In June 1940, the Tremiti were needed for other internment purposes once Italy entered the war[45] and internees were sent home and sentenced to two years of 'ammonizione' or house arrest. This homecoming, as Goretti and de Santis explain, was quite complicated as men were said to have created a public scandal. It must be imagined that many men had to disavow what might have been the best time of their lives, and tuck away from friends and family the only period where they could be openly gay. Thus, being forced back into the closet works not to conceal homosexuals per se, but, in the words of David M. Halperin, conceals '*homosexuality as queer affect, sensibility, subjectivity, identification, pleasure, habitus, gender style*'.[46]

Discussing the mechanics of surviving traumatic experiences, de Santis paraphrases Primo Levi: 'In order to stop being a victim, one must become a witness'. De Santis also suggests that the graphic novel, documentary, and island commemoration all work to 'return the voice to the victim', an outlook shared by Goretti who states 'indeed, memory works when it is activated, reactivated, and then narrated to create other memories, so I welcome therefore all that we did recently, I think it is important. Now there is a place where it is written that this island was also a *confino* island for homosexuals'. It is clear that *Vladimir Luxuria* engages in a process of commemoration. The voice of the victim, however, is absent. Instead, others stand in for and speak for these men, and negotiate their victim status.

### *In Italia sono tutti maschi* and *L'albero rosso*: 'History is made of pain'

*In Italia sono tutti maschi*, a widely translated 2008 graphic novel by Luca de Santis and Sara Colaone and the short documentary *L'albero rosso* (with de Santis collaborating on the script) engage with gay exile on the island of San Domino. Based in part on historical figures, for example 'Peppinella', who is interviewed in Romano's documentary, *In Italia sono tutti maschi* unfolds along two temporal planes, the first in 1987 when director Rocco and cameraman Nico transport Angelicola Antonio, known as Ninella, from Salerno to San Domino to make a documentary on his experience of exile of almost fifty years earlier. The second is the years 1938–39, and chronicles Ninella's arrest, period of confinement, and eventual release and return home. *L'albero rosso* focuses on an unidentified narrator, possibly based upon Peppinella, who guides viewers through his arrest, internment, and release.

Like several of the men discussed in Romano and Inguglia's documentaries, Ninella from the graphic novel is reluctant to relive the past and is resistant to return to the island; he tries to delay the trip so that he might miss the ferry and attempts to escape while en route, and before boarding the ferry tearfully exclaims that he has not returned to San Domino for forty years. Remembering is too painful, as Peppinella notes in the afterword to the graphic novel: 'dopo quarant'anni non ti viene più la voglia di parlare di queste cose … ti viene da ricordare i processi, i dolori … perché lì ci sono stati grossi scandali, famiglie che hanno avuto un disonore grandissimo'[47] (after forty years, you do not want to talk about these things … you have to remember the trials, the pain … because there were huge scandals, families that were completely disgraced). Peppinella's words are included in the graphic novel when Rocco pushes Ninella to discuss his close friend Mimì, who perished after his release most likely because of complications of ill health due to his forced stay on the Tremiti. Captions of Ninella expressing his desire to forget are accompanied by images of Fascist eagles, which underlines that Ninella feels trapped in the past. History 'è fatta di dolore'[48] (is made of pain) Ninella exclaims whilst on the ferry. Ninella's anguish is most likely confounded by the government not recognising the suffering of men suspected of homosexuality under the classification of *confinato politico*. As Peppinella explains in the afterword, the Italian State refused to give men sentenced for pederasty the same pension provided to political detainees: 'E quando ritornammo a casa, dopo due anni di ammonizione, abbiamo chiesto tutti la riabilitazione allo Stato. Nessuno è riuscito ad ottenerla'[49] (and when we returned home, after two years of 'house arrest', we all asked the State for compensation. No one received it). Such a commemorative gesture would deny the Regime's stance regarding the heterocentricity of the populace, or, 'in Italia sono tutti maschi'.

In the preface to the graphic novel, Tommaso Giartosio and Gianfranco Goretti underscore that de Santis and Colaone help readers to reflect upon the ethical implications (as they say, the 'possibilities', 'responsibilities', and 'dangers') of resurrecting the past through recounting the story of gay men persecuted during Fascism.[50] They note that the relationship between the present and the past is complex because 'il presente tende a fabbricarsi un'immagine semplificata e rassicurante del passato' (the present tends to fabricate a simplified and reassuring image of the past), which recalls Santner's theorisation of narrative fetishism which involves 'the construction and deployment of a narrative consciously or unconsciously designed to expunge the traces of the trauma or loss that called that narrative into being in the first place' and results in an 'inability to mourn'.[51] Ninella notes that although many want to forget arrests, the deportation, and the period of confinement, memories creep and the pain remains.[52]

Before his return to the island, Ninella had yet to confront and narrate his grief. Freud notes that *Trauerarbeit* is painful and requires that the subject undergo a process carried out 'bit by bit' to the point that the mourner can declare the object dead and live again.[53] Ninella's encounter with Rocco and Nico and his return to the island allow him to confront his past and tell his story to empathetic listeners (although Rocco is initially reluctant). According to Dori Laub, the listener is crucial in the construction of a trauma narrative: 'bearing witness to trauma is, in fact, a process that includes a listener. For the testimonial process to take place, there needs to be a bonding, the intimate and total presence of an *other* – in the position of one who hears'.[54] Ninella's story, unlike that of the *confinati* interviewed by Romano, is far from reassuring. Although he does mention the dinners and cross-dressing parties, his narration is not nostalgic and instead is fearful and anxious when he discusses invasive and humiliating medical inspections, inhumane weather conditions, ill health of detainees, nearly non-existent rations, and he compares life in the barracks to living in a prison.

However, sharing his pain helps Ninella heal as the graphic novel concludes with Ninella looking directly into the camera while declaring 'Mi chiamano Ninella' (They call me Ninella). Thus, he has recovered his voice and has begun to 'reclaim [his] world', a crucial step in the process of recovery as theorised by Judith Herman.[55] Towards the end of the novel, he is able to cry, laugh, and form friendships. Others, however, are not that lucky. In Mimì's death throes he returns to the island and Mimì's experiences are akin to that of other men discussed in this chapter who feel that they have no home to which they can return. For example, at the news of his release, rather than expressing relief and happiness, Ninella is lost and confused: 'Oggi il mio regno è quella terra di nessuno dove casa è una parola che non so più pronunciare … Si torna, sì, ma dove?'[56] (Now my kingdom is a no-mans-land where home is a word I can no longer pronounce … yes, we return, but where?). *In Italia sono tutti maschi* narrates the painful return to a home that is indelibly altered for a group of men whose grief has been, until recently, denied on the national level.

The twenty-two-minute documentary *L'albero rosso*, however, is not redemptive as voiceover narration foregrounds the humiliation, pain, fear, and abject loneliness of exile, and the documentary concludes without a commemorative gesture. Early on the narrator queries 'do you want to hear a story? Will you be able to forget it?' and then details his painful experience of arrest, torture, the journey to and arrival at the island, the period of confinement, and eventual release. Regularly the narrator foregrounds his (and others') isolation, not only during exile, but also in the present. Events, names, and descriptions are highly detailed, yet narrative is circular, which implies that the narrator is intensely connected with the past. 'I can still smell the wet leaves of that climb', and 'how young we all are' he notes. Or, 'even the fear [as he is narrating] is the same as before'. This disruption of linear memory that is replete in the documentary helps to create a queer cultural memory with respect to the exile experience (i.e. in the holding on to the past, and in bringing the past into the present). Also, the frequent direct address to the viewer (the experience is 'more than you would be able to endure' we are told) prompts audience alignment with the narrator.

*L'albero rosso* is the only text discussed in this chapter that explicitly discusses the brutal murders of gay men (by the State, by hate groups, by the family unit). Further, here only is sexual intercourse between guards and prisoners communicated as overt sexual violence. For example, the narrator notes that guards only had sex with prisoners as they are 'scum, lowest of scum' and 'were there to be forgotten' and therefore would not be capable of remembering or being remembered. These memories of violence bleed into the mise-en-scène as frequently the island and the ocean are cast in a scarlet-red.

For the most part, the documentary foregrounds loss as the narrator's grief is interminable. The red tree of the title, however, is discussed as a locus of both passion and pain: the 'arvulo rossu' by the port in Catania was historically a gay hookup spot (the narrator describes 'grazed skin, lips opening, panting, his breath in my throat, the red tree embracing you with its branches') until the arrests began. Also, a recurring scene heightens pleasure and nostalgia for an unobtainable past: the narrator's recollections of Mimì – whom he calls 'my Mimì' even though he is deceased – who wears makeup and cross-dresses while appearing ghostlike. This haunting image foregrounds the documentary's queerness as past and present exist in a complementary relationship. Further, the documentary's persistent intermingling of desire and sorrow across temporal planes recalls the ethical imperative of queer historiography as discussed by Carla Freccero:

> Insofar as queer historicism registers the affective investments of the present in the past, however, it harbours within itself not only pleasure, but also pain, a traumatic pain whose ethical insistence is to 'live to tell' through complex and circuitous processes of working through.[57]

In the regular nostalgic returns to the islands this and the other texts under consideration in this chapter disclose a 'stubborn lingering of pastness' that is 'a hallmark of queer affect: … as a turning back'.[58] Towards the end of the documentary, the narrator challenges the trope of internal exile as vacation when he states that detainees could never have imagined that one day tourists would visit San Domino. Thus, unlike with the melodramas discussed in the previous chapter, this documentary is not heartening, and instead underlines that memory is complex.

In conclusion, we note that Romano, Inguglia, and Rowley graciously shared with us otherwise unavailable films. These exchanges point towards a more recent and collaborative openness regarding the circulation of memories of the internal exile experience of gay men, and a willingness for filmmakers in and outside of Italy to engage with these memories and to bring such negotiations with the past into the public domain.

## Notes

1    Benadusi, *The Enemy of the New Man*, 127.
2    Benadusi, *The Enemy of the New Man*, 127–9. Benadusi notes, however, that 'the repression suffered by homosexuals during the Fascist Ventennio was much more widespread than what emerges from the relatively small number of detainees' (p. 131). According to Ebner, *Ordinary Violence in Mussolini's Italy* (p. 171), one should not underestimate the level of repression inflicted on men suspected of being gay during the entirety of Fascist rule.
3    De Santis and Colaone, *In Italia sono tutti maschi*, 171.
4    *Ibid.*
5    Interview with Giuseppe P. in de Santis and Colaone, *In Italia sono tutti maschi*, 170.
6    Alan Johnston, 'A Gay Island Community Created by Italy's Fascists', *BBC News Magazine* (12 June 2013). www.bbc.co.uk/news/magazine-22856586 (accessed 12 February 2018).
7    Benadusi, 'Private Life and Public Morals', 36. For more on the exile conditions for gay *confinati* see Benadusi, *The Enemy of the New Man*, 133 and the chapter 'Vite al confino' in Goretti and Giartosio, *La città e l'isola*, 125–67.
8    Benadusi, 'Private Life and Public Morals', 36.
9    Lauren Berlant and Michael Warner, 'Sex in Public', in Donald Hall, Annamarie Jagose, Andrea Bebell, and Susan Potter (eds), *The Routledge Queer Studies Reader* (London and New York: Routledge, 2013), p. 171.
10   Michel-Rolph Trouillot as cited in the documentary *Ricordare* 'Il suo silenzio è una testimonianza importante'.
11   Cited in Marco Dell'Utri, *Diritto, politica, e cultura* (Rome: Aracne editrice, 2012), p. 149.
12   Michel Foucault, *The History of Sexuality: Vol. 1 An Introduction* (New York: Random House, 1990), p. 10.
13   Cited in Dell'Utri, *Diritto, politica, e cultura*, 149.
14   Dijana Jelaca, *Dislocated Screen Memory: Narrating Trauma in Post-Yugoslav Cinema* (New York: Palgrave Macmillan, 2015), p. 106.
15   Jelaca, *Dislocated Screen Memory*, 106.
16   Modleski, 'Clint Eastwood and Male Weepies', 141.
17   Sergio Rigoletto, *Masculinity and Italian Cinema: Sexual Politics, Social Conflict, and Male Crisis in the 1970s* (Edinburgh: Edinburgh University Press, 2014), p. 6.
18   Rigoletto, *Masculinity and Italian Cinema*, 6.
19   Szymon Pietrzykowski, 'Gay as a Stranger: Homosexuality During Fascism in Ettore Scola's *Una giornata particolare*', *Maska*, 24 (2014), 75–88.
20   Benadusi, however, finds it 'unconvincing to maintain that homosexuality took on political significance precisely in 1938' (*The Enemy of the New Man*, 131).
21   See, for example, Pini, *Quando eravamo froci*, 45, Benadusi, *The Enemy of the New Man*, 289–90, and Goretti and Giartosio, *La città e l'isola*, 3.
22   Benadusi, *The Enemy of the New Man*, 127.
23   William Van Watson, 'Adaptation as Heterocentralization: Giuliano Montaldo's Film Version of Giorgio Bassani's *Gli occhiali d'oro*', in Roberta Antognini and Rodica Diaconescu Blumenfeld (eds), *Poscritto a Giorgio Bassani: Saggi in memoria del decimo anniversario della morte* (Milan: LED Edizioni Universitarie, 2012), p. 546.
24   Giorgio Bassani, *Il romanzo di Ferrara* (Milan: Feltrinelli, 2012), p. 199.
25   Van Watson, 'Adaptation as Heterocentralization', 555.
26   Dina Georgis, *The Better Story: Queer Affects from the Middle East* (Albany: SUNY Press, 2013), p. 11.

27   See Giovanni Dall'Orto, 'La "tolleranza repressiva" dell'omosessualità: Quando un atteggiamento legale diviene tradizione', in ARCI GAY nazionale (ed.), *Omosessuali e stato* (Bologna: Centro di documentazione il cassero, 1987), pp. 37–57. Dall'Orto is borrowing from Herbert Marcuse's thesis of 'repressive tolerance'.

28   Santner argues that the 'dosing out of a certain negative – a thanatotic – element as a strategy of mastering a real and traumatic loss is a fundamentally homeopathic procedure ... the work of mourning is the way human beings restore the regime of the pleasure principle in the wake of trauma or loss' ('History beyond the Pleasure Principle', 146).

29   Cathy Caruth, 'Trauma and Experience', in Cathy Caruth (ed.), *Trauma: Explorations in Memory* (Baltimore: Johns Hopkins University Press, 1995), p. 9, original italics.

30   Sue Walrond-Skinner, *A Dictionary of Psychotherapy* (London and New York: Routledge, 2013), p. 324.

31   Foot, *Italy's Divided Memory*, 10–11.

32   Antonella Lombardi, '*Isola nuda*, una palermitana racconta la condanna dei gay' (24 April 2009), http://livesicilia.it/2009/04/24/isola-nuda-una-palermitanaracconta-la-condanna-dei-gay_4362/ (accessed 8 February 2018).

33   Elizabeth Freeman, *Time Binds: Queer Temporalities, Queer Histories* (Durham: Duke University Press, 2010), p. 23.

34   Freeman, *Time Binds*, 45.

35   Stella Bruzzi, *New Documentary: A Critical Introduction* (London and New York: Routledge, 2000), p. 43.

36   Hirsch, *Afterimage*, 10.

37   Janet Walker, *Trauma Cinema: Documenting Incest and the Holocaust* (Berkeley and Los Angeles: University of California Press, 2005), p. 19.

38   The caged or tethered farm animals rife in the documentary evoke the plight of the men imprisoned on the island, and add a more nuanced reading to the titular 'nuda [naked]' in that the condition of the men exiled approaches Giorgio Agamben's definition of *Homo Sacer*, or someone who is excluded from the State yet is at its mercy as he or she may be done away with without penalty. See Agamben, *Homo Sacer*, 8. *Isola nuda* reveals how human, qualified, political life (bios) is transformed into bare life (zoe) 'vita nuda' at the whim of the state. For more on biopolitics in the documentary see Lorenzo Bernini, 'Luoghi di confino, linee di confine' (30 March 2009), www.nazioneindiana.com/2009/03/30/ luoghi-di-confino-linee-di-confine/ (accessed 9 February 2018).

39   Inguglia's documentary is in line with the films of Claude Lanzmann who presents, according to Linda Williams:

> [the] awareness of the final inaccessibility of a moment of crime, violence, trauma, irretrievably located in the past ... [they] do not so much represent this past as they reactivate it in images of the present ... For in revealing the fabrications, the myths, the frequent moments of scapegoating when easy fictional explanations of trauma, violence, crime were substituted for more difficult ones, these documentaries do not simply play off truth against lie, nor do they play off one fabrication against another; rather, they show how lies function as partial truths to both the agents and witnesses of history's trauma.

Linda Williams 'Mirrors without Memory: Truth, History, and the New Documentary', in Brian Henderson and Ann Martin (eds), *Film Quarterly: Forty Years Selection* (Berkeley and Los Angeles: University of California Press, 1999), p. 319.

40   Lombardi, '*Isola nuda*'.

41    A. Barbiero, 'L'*isola nuda* dell'omosessualità nel cinema italiano. Il documentario di Debora Inguglia', www.coolhunteritaly.it/site/oa/lisola-nuda-dellomosessualita-nel-cinema-italiano-il-documentario-di-debora-inguglia/ (accessed 12 December 2014).

42    Derek Duncan, 'The Geopolitics of Spectatorship and Screen Identification: What's Queer About Italian Cinema?', *The Italianist* 33:2 (2013), 257.

43    Henry Rousso, *The Haunting Past: History, Memory and Justice in Contemporary France* (Philadelphia: University of Pennsylvania Press, 2002), p. 1.

44    Foucault, *The History of Sexuality: Vol. 1*, 43.

45    Goretti and Giartosio write that in September of 1940 San Domino became a '*campo di concentramento*' (*La città e l'isola*, 203), original italics.

46    David Halperin, *How to Be Gay* (Cambridge, MA: Harvard University Press, 2012), p. 86, original italics.

47    De Santis and Colaone, *In Italia sono tutti maschi*, 173.

48    De Santis and Colaone, *In Italia sono tutti maschi*, 129.

49    De Santis and Colaone, *In Italia sono tutti maschi*, 172–3.

50    De Santis and Colaone, *In Italia sono tutti maschi*, 7.

51    Santner, 'History Beyond the Pleasure Principle', 144.

52    De Santis and Colaone, *In Italia sono tutti maschi*, 156.

53    Sigmund Freud, 'Mourning and Melancholia', in J. Strachey (ed. and trans.), *The Complete Psychological Works of Sigmund Freud*, Vol. 14 (London: The Hogarth Press, 1975), pp. 243–58. Specifically, '[e]ach single one of the memories and expectations in which the libido is bound to the object is brought up and hypercathected, and detachment of the libido is accomplished in respect to it', (p. 245).

54    Dori Laub, 'Bearing Witness or the Vicissitudes of Listening', in Shoshana Felman and Dori Laub (eds), *Testimony: Crises of Witnessing in Literature, Psychoanalysis and History* (New York: Routledge, 2013), p. 70.

55    Judith Lewis Herman, *Trauma and Recovery: The Aftermath of Violence – From Domestic Abuse to Political Terror* (New York: Basic Books, 1997), p. 196.

56    De Santis and Colaone, *In Italia sono tutti maschi*, 146.

57    Carla Freccero, 'Queer Spectrality: Haunting the Past', in George Haggerty and Molly McGarry (eds), *A Companion to Lesbian, Gay, Transgender, and Queer Studies* (Malden and Oxford: Blackwell Publishing, 2007), p. 171. Also, see D. Duncan who argues, 'queer critical analysis needs to remain historically grounded in order to contribute to culturally sensitive interpretations of queer lives and their intelligibility'. Derek Duncan, 'The Queerness of Italian Cinema', in Frank Burke (ed.), *A Companion to Italian Cinema* (Malden and Oxford: Wiley Blackwell, 2017), p. 481.

58    Freeman, *Time Binds*, 8.

# Conclusion

## Beyond *confino*

'Britannia waives the rules', and similar cringe-worthy japes proclaimed the results of the United Kingdom European Union membership referendum on 23 June 2016. The vote underscored the depth of anti-European populism and threatened the viability of supra-nationalism as a paradigm for addressing the political challenges of the twenty-first century. In response to this crisis, Angela Merkel, François Hollande, and Matteo Renzi, the leaders of the euro area's three largest economies, met on Ventotene on 22 August 2016. Although the summit itself took place on the aircraft carrier *Garibaldi*, the meeting had a symbolic purpose as well: to honour a vision of a unified Europe. They visited the Pontine Island to lay yellow and blue flowers, three bouquets in the colours of the European Union, at the tomb of Altiero Spinelli, a leading advocate for the European federalist movement and co-author of the so-called *Ventotene Manifesto*.

This aspirational proclamation for a free and united Europe sprang from the raging global war and from the injustice of *confino*. Its authors – Spinelli, Ernesto Rossi, Eugenio Colorni, and Ursula Hirschmann – conceived, drafted, and published this vision of European federalism, between 1941 and 1943, while confined to Ventotene. Like several of the other political colonies, the island's penal history harked back to Imperial Rome.

Numerous emperors had favoured Ventotene as a site for banishing uncomfortable women: Augustus, invoking the *Lex Iulia de Adulteriis Coercendis*, exiled his only child, Julia the Elder; Tiberius exiled Julia's daughter, Agrippina the Elder; Caligula exiled his sisters Julia Livilla and Agrippina the Younger; Nero exiled his wife, Claudia Octavia; and Domitian exiled Vespasian's granddaughter, St Flavia Domitilla. Under Fascism, the undesirables sentenced to the Pontines far outnumbered their imperial counterparts and included such future political leaders as Sandro Pertini, Giorgio Amendola, Luigi Longo, Pietro Secchia, and Umberto Terracini. Indeed, with the shuttering of the Lipari colony, Ventotene had become the Ministry of the Interior's preferred site for political prisoners because its size (1.75 km²), small population (some 700 inhabitants), and coastline (relatively inaccessible) made escape difficult thereby reducing the risk of another Lipari fiasco. By 1940, over 900 *confinati* were on the island. To facilitate management of the prisoners, the authorities utilised the formidable prison on neighbouring Santo Stefano, a 27-ha island 2 km east of Ventotene. Here too, the Ministry of the Interior benefited from the repressive measures of past regimes. Commissioned by the Bourbons, Major Antonio Winspeare of the Engineer Corps and the architect Francesco Carpi designed, according to Enlightenment precepts, a horseshoe-shaped penitentiary that bore a striking resemblance to Jeremy Bentham's Panopticon. Completed in 1797 (and in active use until 1965), the prison was an imposing symbol of surveillance and oppression. Much like Ventotene was a site for the origin of the European Union, so Santo Stefano, where both Pertini and Terracini were imprisoned, was an inspirational site for the constitution of Italy.

Regarding the *Manifesto*, a confluence of political and personal factors led to its publication. Spinelli, Rossi, and Colorni were on Ventotene because they had all been charged with anti-Fascist activities under the TULPS. Arrested on 3 June 1927, Spinelli received a prison sentence of sixteen years and eight months. After ten years, he was transferred to *confino* in Ponza, and then, from 1939 until August 1943, to Ventotene. The Special Tribunal sentenced Rossi, who was arrested on 30 October 1930, to twenty years in prison. On 6 November 1939, Rome's Provincial Commission ordered his transfer to Ventotene.[1] The OVRA seized Colorni, who was Jewish, in Trieste, on 8 September 1938. The arrest fed Fascism's anti-Semitic campaign with the press hurling accusations of a 'Jewish plot' in anticipation of the promulgation of the racial laws.[2] Lacking evidence for a conviction, the Special Tribunal sentenced him to five years *confino*. From January 1939 to October 1941, he served his detention in Ventotene where he participated in those preliminary discussions that would give form to the *Manifesto*. Colorni's spouse, Ursula Hirschmann, accompanied him in *confino* and maintained contact with Spinelli and Rossi even after Colorni's transfer to Melfi (Potenza). She smuggled the *Manifesto* from the island to the mainland, where Colorni oversaw its clandestine publication in Rome on 22 January 1944.[3] Murdered by the Banda Koch[4] on 30 May 1944, he never saw Rome's liberation or the profound influence the *Manifesto* would have on Europe's future.

A foundational document for European federalism, *Per un' Europa libera e unita. Progetto d'un manifesto* (*For a Free and United Europe. A Draft Manifesto*), called for a change from national to transnational governance models so that Europe might never bear witness again to such horrors and abuses as those wrought by nationalistic fervour.[5] Fascism's divisive strategy to solidify its own power was to foment ethnic, social, cultural, religious, and ideological polarisation to fracture the opposition. Its military defeat, however, did not produce *Stunde Null*. The *Manifesto*'s authors presciently recognised that the impulse to assert the primacy of national identity could well lead modern nation-states: 'to play on the most widespread feeling among the population, a feeling so damaged by recent events and so easily manipulated to reactionary ends: patriotism'.[6] They understood that the very ubiquity and virtuosity of the sentiment made it vulnerable to demagoguery; patriotism could act as a sleeper agent that, when aroused, would incite dissension towards all those who were perceived as different. Such virtues needed to be controlled. Today they are severely challenged.

The testaments of *confinati*, however, resided not only in the grandiose statements of Rosselli's *Liberal Socialism*, the *Ventotene Manifesto*, and the emerging constitution, but also in the everyday records of those who suffered. Yet, these personal recollections are all too readily dismissed as self-serving, subjective memoirs. In reviewing Emilio Lussu's *Road to Exile*, the *New York Times'* book critic Ralph Thompson opined, perhaps cynically, perhaps pragmatically:

> [E]xiles' narratives prove one thing, and one thing only. As objective accounts of a form of government, or a dictator's personality, or a national state of mind, they are generally of little value. The disaffected authors are, for altogether obvious reasons, unfit to pass judgment upon the very matters they attempt to judge. As personal interpretations, moreover, they are usually far from ideal, so harrowing and unsettling has been the experience behind them. These stories of men without a country serve one useful purpose only – they show that under any sort of absolutism the penalty for independent thinking is severe, and that those who want continued freedom of thought had better see to it that it is their side that comes out on top.[7]

Their own testimony does not suffice; in fact, it is suspect. To concede that the value of these narratives resides exclusively, as Thompson asserts, in their imperative call to arms, is to acknowledge their potential pragmatic import. Nevertheless, the numerous testimonials (e.g., Giorgio Amendola, Jaurès Busoni, Cesira Fiori, Natalia Ginzburg, Carlo Levi, Emilio Lussu, Mario Magri, Francesco Fausto Nitti, Camilla Ravera, Carlo Rosselli, Ernesto Rossi, Altiero Spinelli, Emma Turchi) whether public or private, literary or historical, are potent reminders that Fascism is deeply personal. Filmic representations complement the written record by visually substantiating these experiences of displacement and trauma. Together these texts expose the complexities, contradictions, and ambiguities of the exile experience. For those sentenced to *confino*, the time served cannot be reduced to the acquisition of political consciousness. Subscribing to the writings of an elite few distorts the collective memory by neglecting opposing voices, indifferent voices, and the vast majority of possible voices, which are silent, whether because of illiteracy, poverty, motivation, or opportunity. Today, *confino* is a contested memory.

Writing from Bari's Turi prison, Antonio Gramsci observed the dire status of the world order: 'The crisis consists precisely in the fact that the old is dying and the new cannot be born; in this interregnum a great variety of morbid symptoms appear'.[8] The transition has degenerated into an impasse from which there is no release. In assessing the political landscape, Gramsci ascribed to 'interregnum' a specific meaning that drew on social, political, and legal structures. In the words of Zygmunt Bauman:

> The term 'interregnum' was originally used to denote a time-lag separating the death of one royal sovereign from the enthronement of the successor … Gramsci detached the idea of 'interregnum' from its habitual association with the interlude of (routine) transmission of hereditary or electable power. He attached it to the extraordinary situations in which the extant legal frame of social order loses its grip and can no longer hold, whereas a new frame, made to the measure of newly emerged conditions responsible for making the old frame useless, is still at the designing stage, has not yet been fully assembled, or is not strong enough to be put in its place.[9]

The exceptional laws establishing *confino* brought to a close what amounted to Fascism's interregnum. The TULPS dissolved many of the legal tensions between Liberal and Fascist Italy by proclaiming legislatively the latter's definitive triumph.

Mussolini declared as much in his 'Viatico per il 1926', in which he essentially administered last rites to the previous political order to announce his new Regime founded on faith in Fascism and in Fascism's new legal codes all for the greater glory of Italy:

> Fede nella vitalità del Fascismo che sta cambiando la faccia fisica all'Italia e i connotati morali agli italiani; fede nella rivoluzione fascista che avrà nel 1926 il suo anno napoleonico, anche perché entreranno in vigore i nuovi codici penale, commerciale, marittimo, di procedura civile e di procedura penale, e sarà questa una delle più grandi realizzazioni del regime.[10]

> (Faith in the vitality of Fascism, which is changing the physical face of Italy and the moral profile of Italians; faith in the Fascist revolution, which will have in 1926 its Napoleonic year, also because the new penal, commercial, maritime, civil procedural, and penal procedural codes will go into effect. This will be one of the regime's greatest accomplishments.)

*Confino* was a foundational aspect of this 'extraordinary' year that would inaugurate a new hegemonic order. Gramsci was a prominent victim of these exceptional measures, which suspended, rather than implemented, the rule of law. The law no longer governed political power, but rather, as Thomas Hobbes had imagined, 'auctoritas facit legem', power made the law. Yet, what Gramsci postulated is precisely what innumerable *confinati* foresaw as well: the need to imagine new social, political, and legal structures to replace the inevitable collapse of Fascism. After the war, the Allies' military triumph produced a new interregnum, one that would eventually cede though never completely concede the national and international orders conceptualised by the internally exiled.

What this book has argued in Part I is that the Fascist Regime expanded upon a pre-existing practice of political repression to surveil Italians to an unprecedented

extent. Surveillance based on economic class, political affiliations, social associations, religious communities, ethnic groups, and public and private behaviours to
consolidate power, to define a new Italian identity, and to exert political and social
control. The texts discussed in Part II bear witness to a coercive past and portents
of possible futures. As such, this study also speaks to how personal memories
shape popular memory. The collective memory of *confino* tends to be presented
as inextricably linked to the Resistance, but the literature surveyed resists such a
neat identification. These stories, memoirs, and testimonies explain and describe
divided memories through experiences that must be interpreted, remembered,
and contested. Competing narratives call for a nuanced appreciation for the complexities of remembrance that are not fixed and cannot be reduced to a single
moment, but instead are in constant flux and span two decades. Furthermore, in
making these materials accessible to an English language audience, we hope to
encourage comparative studies with other totalitarian regimes in terms of both
precautionary punishments and everyday life.

Today, new geo-political and socio-economic challenges threaten the ideals
of justice and freedom at the root of both the Italian constitution and European
integration. Bauman, taking a cue from Keith Tester, has proposed 'the present-day
planetary condition as a case of interregnum'.[11] The current system is unsustain-
able. Although more prosaic than Yeatsian, the conclusion is the same: the centre
cannot hold. Today, a new spectre haunts Europe: one that spews out the old
sectarian hates of nationalism, racism, and intolerance, one that divides in order
to conquer. A possible response resides in the advice of another Action Party
founder, Piero Calamandrei, who reminded university students in Milan, on 26
January 1955, of how the Resistance begat Italy's constitution:

> Se voi volete andare in pellegrinaggio nel luogo dove è nata la nostra costituzione,
> andate nelle montagne dove caddero i partigiani, nelle carceri dove furono
> imprigionati, nei campi dove furono impiccati. Dovunque è morto un Italiano per
> riscattare la libertà e la dignità della nazione, andate là, o giovani, col pensiero, perché
> lì è nata la nostra costituzione.[12]

> (If you wish to make a pilgrimage to those places where our constitution was born,
> go to the mountains where partisans fell, to the gaols where they were imprisoned,
> to the fields where they were killed. Wherever an Italian died to redeem the freedom
> and dignity of the nation, go there, with your mind, because that is where our con-
> stitution was born.)

From *confino*, an instrument of oppression, emerged the imperfect blueprints for
a new society. *Confinati* endured sufferings and hardships for not conforming,
whether politically, ethnically, sexually, religiously, or socially, to an imaginary
Italian identity in the service of the State. The sites of detention and the people
imprisoned are public memorials to Fascism's private identity. We would do well
to remember lest, to appropriate Yeats, there be a second coming.

## Notes

1   Dal Pont and Carolini, *L'Italia al confino*, 1437. See also Giuseppe Fiori, *Una storia italiana. Vita di Ernesto Rossi* (Turin: Einaudi, 1997).

2   See, for example, 'Ebrei antifascisti deferiti al Tribunale Speciale' *Corriere della Sera* (17 October 1938), p. 6; 'La trama giudaico-antifascista stroncata dalla vigile azione della polizia' *Corriere della Sera* (18 October 1938), p. 5; 'Fatti e persone del complotto giudaico antifascista' *Corriere della Sera* (19 October 1938), p. 2. The Gran Consiglio del Fascismo approved the first of the racial laws, *Provvedimenti per la difesa della razza italiana* (Regio Decreto-Legge 1728 of 17 November 1938).

3   Ugo Intini, 'L'unità europea e i pericoli del post fascismo' *Il mattino* (23 March 2017), p. 55.

4   The Banda Koch was a special police task force established by Pietro Koch, see Massimiliano Griner, *La Banda Koch: il reparto speciale di polizia, 1943–44* (Turin: Bollati Boringhieri, 2000).

5   For the genesis of the *Manifesto*, see Nello Ajello, 'L'Europa che nacque a Ventotene', *La Repubblica* (21 July 2001), p. 38.

6   Altiero Spinelli and Ernesto Rossi, *Per un'Europa libera e unita. Il manifesto di Ventotene. Le manifeste de Ventotene. The Ventotene Manifesto* (Rome: Senato della Repubblica, 2017), p. 46.

7   Ralph Thompson, 'Books of the Times' *New York Times* (25 July 1936), p. 11.

8   Antonio Gramsci, *Selections from the Prison Notebooks*, ed. and trans. Quintin Hoare and Geoffrey Nowell-Smith (London: Lawrence & Wishart, 1971), p. 276. This quotation has also been rendered, with extreme poetic licence, as 'the old world is dying, and the new world struggles to be born: now is the time of monsters'. See by way of example, Slavoj Žižek, 'A Permanent Economic Emergency', *New Left Review* 64 (July–August 2010), p. 95.

9   Zygmunt Bauman, 'Times of Interregnum', *Ethics & Global Politics* 5:1 (2012), 49.

10  Benito Mussolini, 'Viatico per il 1926', *Gerarchia* 5:1 (January 1926).

11  Bauman, 'Times of Interregnum', 49; Keith Tester, 'Pleasure, Reality, the Novel and Pathology', *Journal of Anthropological Psychology* 21 (2009), 23–6.

12  *Piero Calamandrei, Discorso ai giovani sulla Costituzione nata dalla Resistenza (Milan, 26 January 1955).* www.napoliassise.it/costituzione/discorsosullacostituzione.pdf (accessed 7 February 2018).

# Select bibliography

## Archives

*Archivio Centrale dello Stato*
Ministero dell'Interno
Direzione Generale della Pubblica Sicurezza
Direzione Affari Generali e Riservati
Ufficio Confino Politico
Casellario Politico Centrale
*Centro Studi e Ricerche di Storia e Problemi Eoliani*
*Istituto Storico della Resistenza in Toscana*
Archivio Domizio Torrigiani

## Newspapers and magazines

*Ames Daily Tribune-Times*
*Atlanta Constitution*
*Avanti!*
*Boston Globe*
*Chicago Tribune*
*Christian Science Monitor*
*Corriere della Sera*
*Gazzetta Ufficiale della Repubblica Italiana* (1946–2005)
*Gazzetta Ufficiale del Regno d'Italia* (1861–1946)
*Il mattino*
*La Repubblica*
*La Stampa*
*La Voce di Rimini*
*Los Angeles Times*
*Manchester Guardian*
*New York Times*
*Spectator*
*Sun*
*Syracuse Herald*
*The Times*

*Time*
*Washington Post*

## Published Works

Agamben, Giorgio, *Homo Sacer: Sovereign Power and Bare Life* (Stanford: Stanford University Press, 1998).

——. *Stato di eccezione. Homo Sacer II, 1* (Turin: Bollati Boringhieri, 2003).

Albertazzi, Alessandro, Luigi Arbizzani, and Nazario Sauro Onofri (eds), *Gli antifascisti, i partigiani e le vittime del fascismo nel bolognese (1919–1945). Vol. III. Dizionario biografico: D-L* (Bologna: Istituto per la Storia di Bologna, 1986).

Allegretti, Umberto, 'Dissenso, opposizione politica, disordine sociale: le risposte dello stato liberale', in Luciano Violante (ed.), *Storia d'Italia. Annali 12. La criminalità* (Turin: Einaudi, 1997), pp. 719–56.

Amendola, Giorgio, *Un'isola* (Milan: Rizzoli, 1981).

Ansaldo, Giovanni, *L'antifascista riluttante: memorie del carcere e del confino 1926–1927* (Bologna: Il Mulino, 1992).

——. *Il giornalista di Ciano. Diari, 1932–1943* (Bologna: Il Mulino, 2000).

Aquarone, Alberto, *L'organizzazione dello stato totalitario* (Turin: Einaudi, 1965).

Arthurs, Joshua, Michael Ebner, and Kate Ferris (eds), *The Politics of Everyday Life in Fascist Italy* (New York: Palgrave Macmillan, 2017).

Barile, Paolo (ed.), *La pubblica sicurezza* (Vicenza: Neri Pozza, 1967).

Bartolini, Stefano, *Fascismo antislavo: il tentativo di «bonifica etnica» al confine nord orientale* (Pistoia: Istituto storico della Resistenza e della società contemporanea, 2006).

Bassani, Giorgio, *Gli occhiali d'oro* (Milan: Oscar Classici Moderni, 1996).

——. *Il giardino dei Finzi-Contini* (Turin: Einaudi, 1999).

——. *Il romanzo di Ferrara* (Milan: Feltrinelli, 2012).

Benadusi, Lorenzo, 'Gli omosessuali al confino', *Rivista storica dell'anarchismo*, 11:1 (2004), 24–41.

——. *The Enemy of the New Man: Homosexuality in Fascist Italy* (Madison: University of Wisconsin Press, 2012).

Bosworth, Richard J. B., *Mussolini's Italy: Life under the Fascist Dictatorship, 1915–1945* (New York: Penguin, 2005).

Boursier, Giovanna, 'Gli zingari nell'Italia fascista', in Leonardo Piasere (ed.), *Italia romaní*, vol. 1 (Rome: CISU, 1996).

——. 'La persecuzione degli zingari nell'Italia fascista', *Studi storici*, 37:4 (1996), 1065–82.

Braccialarghe, Giorgio, *Nelle spire di Urlavento: il confino di Ventotene negli anni dell'agonia del Fascismo* (Genoa: Fratelli Frilli, 2005).

Bravi, Luca, 'Lo sterminio degli zingari', in Alessandra Chiappano and Fabio Minazzi (eds), *Il paradigma nazista dell'annientamento. La Shoah e gli altri stermini* (Florence: Editrice La Giuntina, 2006), pp. 109–22.

——. *Rom e non-zingari. Vicende storiche e pratiche rieducative sotto il regime fascista* (Rome: CISU, 2007).

Brezzi, Camillo and Luigi Ganapini (eds), *Cultura e società negli anni del fascismo* (Milan: Cordani, 1987).

Bricarelli, Stefano, 'Fai vedere come vivevano: dall'archivio di un grande fotografo degli anni Trenta un inedito reportage sui confinati del regime a Ponza', *Storia illustrata*, 30:359 (October 1987), 24–33.

Buffa, Pier Vittorio, *Non volevo morire così. Santo Stefano e Ventotene: storie di ergastolo e confino* (Milan: Nutrimenti, 2017).

Burgio, Alberto (ed.), *Nel nome della razza: il razzismo nella storia d'Italia, 1870–1945* (Bologna: Il Mulino, 2000).

Busoni, Jaurès, *Nel tempo del fascismo* (Rome: Editori Riuniti, 1975).

——. *Confinati a Lipari* (Milan: Vangelista editore, 1980).

Canali, Mauro, *Le spie del regime* (Bologna: Il Mulino, 2004).

——. *La scoperta dell'Italia: il fascismo raccontato dai corrispondenti americani* (Venice: Marsilio Editori, 2017).

Cantor, Nathaniel, 'Fascist Political Prisoners', *Journal of Criminal Law and Criminology*, 27:2 (1936–37), 169–79.

Capogreco, Carlo Spartaco, *I campi del duce: l'internamento civile nell'Italia fascista (1940–43)* (Turin: Einaudi, 2004).

Caràfoli, Domizia and Gustavo Bocchini Padiglione, *Il viceduce: storia di Arturo Bocchini capo della Polizia fascista* (Milan: Rusconi, 1987).

Carbone, Donatella, *Il popolo al confino: la persecuzione fascista in Basilicata* (Rome: Ministero per i beni culturalie e ambientali, 1994).

Carbone, Salvatore, *Il popolo al confino: la persecuzione fascista in Calabria* (Cosenza: Lerici, 1977).

Carbone, Salvatore and Laura Grimaldi, *Il popolo al confino: la persecuzione fascista in Sicilia* (Rome: Ministero per i beni culturali e ambientali, 1989).

Carucci, Paola, 'L'organizzazione dei servizi di polizia dopo l'approvazione del Testo Unico delle leggi di PS del 1926', *Rassegna degli archivi di stato*, 26:1 (1976), 82–114.

——. 'Arturo Bocchini', in Ferdinando Cordova (ed.), *Uomini e volti del fascismo* (Rome: Bulzoni, 1980), pp. 63–103.

Ceva, Lucio, *Storia delle Forze Armate in Italia* (Turin: UTET Libreria, 1999).

Checchia, Giuseppe, *Misure di polizia e misure di sicurezza* (Naples: Tipomeccanica, 1934).

Coco, Vittorio, *La mafia, il fascismo, la polizia* (Palermo: Centro di studi ed iniziative culturali Pio La Torre, 2012).

Coletti, Alessandro, *Il governo di Ventotene: stalinismo e lotta politica tra i dirigenti del PCI al confino* (Milan: La Pietra, 1978).

Cordova, Antonino, *Commento al Testo Unico delle leggi di Pubblica Sicurezza 6 novembre 1926 n. 1848 e al Regolamento 21 gennaio 1929 n. 62* (Palermo: Orazio Fiorenza, 1929).

Cordova, Ferdinando and Pantaleone Sergi, *Regione di confino: la Calabria (1927–1943)* (Rome: Bulzoni Editore, 2005).

Corner, Paul, 'Everyday Fascism in the 1930s: Centre and Periphery in the Decline of Mussolini's Dictatorship', *Contemporary European History*, 15 (2006), 195–222.

——. 'Italian Fascism: Whatever Happened to Dictatorship?', *Journal of Modern History*, 74 (June 2002), 325–51.

Corvisieri, Silverio, *La villeggiatura di Mussolini: il confino da Bocchini a Berlusconi* (Milan: Baldini Castoldi Dalai, 2004).

Crispino, Michele, *Storie di confino in Lucania* (Venosa: Edizioni Osanna, 1990).

Crociani, Piero and Pier Paolo Battistelli, *Italian Blackshirt, 1935–1945* (Oxford: Osprey Publishing, 2010).

Dalla Casa, Brunella, *Attentato al Duce: le molte storie del caso Zamboni* (Bologna: Il Mulino, 2000).

Dal Pont, Adriano, *I lager di Mussolini. L'altra faccia del confino nei documenti della polizia fascista* (Milan: La Pietra, 1975).

Dal Pont, Adriano and Simonetta Carolini, *L'Italia dissidente e antifascista* (Milan: La Pietra, 1980).

——. *L'Italia al confino: le ordinanze di assegnazione al confino emesse dalle Commissioni provinciali dal novembre 1926 al luglio 1943*, 4 vols (Milan: La Pietra, 1983).

Dal Pont, Adriano, Alfonso Leonetti, Pasquale Maiello, and Lino Zocchi, *Aula IV. Tutti i processi del Tribunale Speciale fascista* (Milan: La Pietra, 1976).

De Felice, Renzo, *Intervista sul fascismo* (Bari, Laterza, 1975).

——. *Mussolini il fascista. Vol. 1. La conquista del potere, 1921–1925* (Turin: Einaudi, 1995).

De Felice, Renzo, Ettore Lucas and Giorgio De Vecchi, *Storia delle unità combattenti della MVSN 1923–1943* (Rome: Giovanni Volpe Editore, 1976).

De Grazia, Victoria, *How Fascism Ruled Women: Italy, 1922–1945* (Berkeley: University of California Press, 1992).

De Grazia, Victoria and Sergio Luzzato (eds), *Dizionario del Fascismo*, 2 vols (Turin: Einaudi, 2002).

Del Boca, Angelo, *Italiani, brava gente? Un mito duro a morire* (Vicenza: Neri Pozza Editore, 2005).

Dell'Utri, Marco, *Diritto, politica, e cultura* (Rome: Aracne, 2012).

De Luna, Giovanni, *Donne in oggetto: l'antifascismo nella società italiana, 1922–1939* (Turin: Bollati Boringhieri, 1995).

De Luttis, Giuseppe, *I servizi segreti in Italia: dal fascismo all'intelligence del XXI secolo* (Milan: Sperling & Kupfer, 2010).

De Santis, Luca and Sara Colaone, *In Italia sono tutti maschi* (Bologna: Kappa Edizioni, 2008).

Detragiache, Denise, 'Un aspect de la politique démographique de l'Italie fasciste: la répression de l'avortement', *Mélanges de l'École française de Rome*, 92:2 (1980), 691–735.

Dickie, John, *Cosa Nostra: A History of the Sicilian Mafia* (New York: Palgrave Macmillan, 2005).

Di Nucci, Loreto, 'Podestà', in Victoria De Grazia and Sergio Luzzatto (eds), *Dizionario del fascismo. II: L-Z* (Turin: Einaudi, 2003).

——. 'Il podestà fascista. Un momento della costruzione dello stato totalitario', *Ricerche di Storia Politica*, 1:1 (1998), 12–21.

Di Sante, Costantino (ed.), *I campi di concentramento in Italia: dall'internamento alla deportazione (1940–1945)* (Milan: Franco Angeli, 2001).

Di Vito, Luca and Michele Gialdroni, *Lipari 1929. Fuga dal confino* (Rome-Bari: Editori Laterza, 2009).

Dogliani, Patrizia, *L'Italia fascista, 1922–1940* (Milan: Sansoni, 1999).

Duggan, Christopher, *Fascism and the Mafia* (New Haven: Yale University Press, 1989).

——. *Fascist Voices: An Intimate History of Mussolini's Italy* (London: Bodley Head, 2012).

Dunnage, Jonathan, *The Italian Police and the Rise of Fascism: A Case Study of the Province of Bologna, 1897–1925* (Westport: Praeger, 1997).

——. *Mussolini's Policemen: Behaviour, Ideology and Institutional Culture in Representation and Practice* (Manchester: Manchester University Press, 2012).

Ebner, Michael R., 'Dalla repressione dell'antifascismo al controllo sociale. Il confino di polizia, 1926–1943', *Storia e problemi contemporanei*, 43 (2006), 81–104.

——. *Ordinary Violence in Mussolini's Italy* (Cambridge: Cambridge University Press, 2011).

Fabei, Stefano, *I neri e i rossi: tentativi di conciliazione tra fascisti e socialisti nella Repubblica di Mussolini* (Milan: Mursia, 2011).

Faggi, Vico (ed.), *Sandro Pertini: sei condanne, due evasioni* (Milan: Mondadori, 1970).

Fedele, Santi, *La massoneria nell'esilio e nella clandestinità, 1927–1939* (Milan: Franco Angeli, 2005).

Ferrari, Chiara, *The Rhetoric of Violence and Sacrifice in Fascist Italy: Mussolini, Gadda, Vittorini* (Toronto: University of Toronto Press, 2013).

Fiori, Cesira, *La confinata* (Milan: La Pietra, 1979).

——. *Una donna nelle carceri fasciste* (Rome: Editori Riuniti, 1965).

Fiori, Giuseppe, *Il cavaliere dei rossomori. Vita di Emilio Lussu* (Turin: Einaudi, 1978).

——. *Una storia italiana: vita di Ernesto Rossi* (Turin: Einaudi, 1997).

Florian, Eugenio, Alfredo Niceforo, and Nicola Pende (eds), *Dizionario di criminologia* (Milan: Francesco Vallardi, 1943).

Foa, Anna. *Andare per i luoghi di confino* (Bologna: Il Mulino, 2018).

Fogu, Claudio, '*Italiani brava gente*: The Legacy of Fascist Historical Cultures on Italian Politics and Memory', in Richard Ned Lebow, Wulf Kansteiner, and Claudio Fogu (eds), *The Politics of Memory in Postwar Europe* (Durham and London: Duke University Press, 2006), pp. 147–76.

Fonio, Chiara, 'Surveillance under Mussolini's Regime', *Surveillance & Society*, 9:1/2 (2011), 80–92.

Fonio, Chiara and Stefano Agnoletto, 'Surveillance, Repression and the Welfare State: Aspects of Continuity and Discontinuity in Post-Fascist Italy', *Surveillance & Society*, 11:1/2 (2013), 74–86.

Foot, John, *Italy's Divided Memory* (New York: Palgrave Macmillan, 2009).

Forsdyke, Sara, *Exile, Ostracism, and Democracy* (Princeton: Princeton University Press, 2005).

Fozzi, Daniela. *Tra prevenzione e repressione: il domicilio coatto nell'Italia liberale* (Rome: Carocci, 2011).

Franceschini, Ettore, *Il domicilio coatto (Il cosidetto 'confino di polizia') come l'hò visto io* (Rome: Luigi Morara, 1956).

Francini, Marco and Gian Paolo Balli, *Il gran maestro Domizio Torrigiani (1876–1932)* (Pistoia: CRT Il Tempio, 2004).

Franzinelli, Mimmo, *I tentacoli dell'OVRA: agenti, collaboratori e vittime della polizia politica fascista* (Turin: Bollati Boringhieri, 1999).

——. *Delatori. Spie e confidenti anonimi: l'arma segreta del regime fascista* (Milan: Mondadori, 2001).

——. *L'amnistia Togliatti, 22 giugno 1946: colpo di spugna sui crimini fascisti* (Milan: Mondadori, 2006).

——. *Il tribunale del Duce: la giustizia fascista e le sue vittime (1927–1945)* (Milan: Mondadori, 2017).

Fucci, Franco, *Le polizie di Mussolini* (Milan: Mursia, 1985).

Gabrielli, Gloria, *Carlo Silvestri socialista, antifascista, mussoliniano* (Milan: Franco Angeli, 1992).

Gabrielli, Patrizia, *Mondi di carta: lettere, autobiografie, memorie* (Siena: Protagon, 2000).

Garosi, Alcide, *Il dottore e il maestro: al confino di polizia con Domizio Torrigiani* (Siena: Primamedia editore, 2008).

Gentile, Emilio, *Fascismo: storia e interpretazione* (Bari: Laterza, 2002).

——. *Il mito dello Stato nuovo: dal radicalismo nazionale al fascismo* (Bari: Laterza, 2002).

Ghini, Celso and Adriano Dal Pont, *Gli antifascisti al confino: 1926–1943* (Rome: Editori Riuniti, 1971).

Gillette, Aaron, 'Guido Landra and the Office of Racial Studies in Fascist Italy', *Holocaust Genocide Studies*, 16:3 (Winter 2002), 357–75.

Ginzburg, Natalia, *Opere*. Vol. 1 (Milan: Arnoldo Mondadori Editore, 1986).

——. *The Little Virtues. Essays*, trans. Dick Davis (New York: Arcade Publishing, 2017).

——. *Lessico famigliare* (Turin: Einaudi, 2010).

Gissi, Alessandra, 'Un percorso a ritroso: le donne al confino politico 1926–1943', *Italia Contemporanea*, 226 (March 2002), 31–59.

Goretti, Gianfranco, 'Il periodo fascista e gli omosessuali: il confino di polizia', in Circolo Pink, *Le ragioni di un silenzio: la persecuzione degli omosessuali durante il nazismo e il fascismo* (Verona: Ombre Corte, 2002), pp. 64–74.

Goretti, Gianfranco and Tommaso Giartosio, *La città e l'isola: omossessuali al confino nell'Italia fascista* (Rome: Donzelli Editore, 2006).

Gramsci, Antonio, *Selections from the Prison Notebooks*, eds Quintin Hoare and Geoffrey Nowell-Smith (London: Lawrence & Wishart, 1971).

———. *Sul fascismo* (Rome: Editori Riuniti, 1973).

Gualino, Riccardo, *Solitudine* (Venice: Marsilio, 1997).

Horn, David G., *Social Bodies: Science, Reproduction and Italian Modernity* (Princeton: Princeton University Press, 1994).

Iaquinta, Mario, *Mezzogiorno, emigrazione di massa e sottosviluppo* (Cosenza: Luigi Pellegrini Editore, 2002).

Ipsen, Carl, *Dictating Demography: The Problem of Population in Fascist Italy* (Cambridge: Cambridge University Press, 1996).

Italy. Ministero della Difesa, *Tribunale Speciale per la difesa dello stato: decisioni emesse* [1927–43], 17 vols (Rome: Stato Maggiore dell'Esercito – Ufficio Storico, 1980–99).

Iuso, Pasquale, *Il fascismo e gli ustascia, 1929–1941: il separatismo croato in Italia* (Rome: Gengini Editore, 1998).

Jacometti, Alberto, *Ventotene* (Genoa: Fratelli Frilli, 2004).

Klinkhammer, Lutz, 'Was There a Fascist Revolution? The Function of Penal Law in Fascist Italy and in Nazi Germany', *Journal of Modern Italian Studies*, 15:3 (2010), 390–409.

La Greca, Giuseppe, *La lunga notte di Lipari: anarchici e socializti al confino coatto* (Lipari: Edizioni del Centro Studi Eoliano, 2010).

———. *Curzio Malaparte alle Isole Eolie* (Lipari: Edizioni del Centro Studi Eoliano, 2012).

———. *Voci dal Confino: antifascisti a Lipari. Anno 1926 – L'arrivo* (Lipari: Edizioni del Centro Studi Eoliano, 2014).

———. *Voci dal Confino: antifascisti a Lipari. 1927 – Il Primo Anno* (Lipari: Edizioni del Centro Studi Eoliano, 2016).

Landra, Guido, 'Il problema dei meticci in Europa', *La difesa della razza*, 4:1 (1940), 11–15.

Lazzero, Ricciotti, *Il Partito nazionale fascista* (Milan: Rizzoli, 1985).

Leto, Guido, *OVRA: fascismo e antifascismo* (Bologna: Cappelli, 1952).

Levi, Carlo, *Christ Stopped at Eboli*, trans. Frances Frenaye (New York: Farrar, Straus and Company, 1947).

———. *Cristo si è fermato a Eboli* (Turin: Einaudi, 1990).

Longhitano, Claudio, *Il Tribunale di Mussolini (Storia del Tribunale Speciale 1926–1943)* (Rome: ANPPIA, 1994).

Lucarelli, Carlo, *L'isola dell'angelo caduto* (Turin: Einaudi, 1999).

Lucarini, Federico, 'Breve viaggio attraverso una presunta continuità? Per un riesame dell'assetto istituzionale e amministrativo del comune italiano durante il fascismo (1926–1941)', *Quaderni fiorentini per la storia del pensiero giuridico moderno*, 39 (2010), 437–64.

Lupo, Salvatore, *History of the Mafia* (New York: Columbia University Press, 2009).

———. *L'unificazione italiana: mezzogiorno, rivoluzione, guerra civile* (Rome: Donzelli Editore, 2011).

Lussu, Emilio, *La catena,* 1930 (Rome: Edizioni U, 1945).

Lyttelton, Adrian, *The Seizure of Power: Fascism in Italy, 1919–1929* (Princeton: Princeton University Press, 1987).

Maccari, Mino, *Visita al confino (a Ponza e a Lipari nel 1929)* (Marina di Belvedere: Cultura Calabrese Editrice, 1985).

Magistro, Cristoforo 'Storie di confino: gli zingari nel Materano', *Basilicata regione notizie*, 127–8 (20 October 2011), 216–25.

Magri, Mario, *Una vita per la libertà: diciassette anni di confino politico di un Martire delle Fosse Ardeatine* (Rome: Ludovico Puglielli, 1956).

Mariani, Laura, *Quelle dell'idea: storia di detenute politiche, 1927–1948* (Bari: De Donato, 1982).

Marini, Marina, *Gino Lucetti: lettere dal carcere dell'attentatore di Mussolini (1930–1943)* (Salerno: Galzerano Editore, 2010).

Martucci, Roberto, *Emergenza e tutela dell'ordine pubblico nell'Italia liberale* (Bologna: Il Mulino, 1980).

Mascaro, Pietro (ed.), *Le ali della memoria: confinati a Cortale durante il regime fascista* (Lamezia Terme: Centro-stampa Dal Margine, 2000).

Massara, Katia, *Il popolo al confino: la persecuzione fascista in Puglia*, 2 vols (Rome: Ufficio centrale per i beni archivistici, 1991).

Masserini, Annamaria, *Storia dei nomadi: la persecuzione degli Zingari nel XX secolo* (Padua: Edizioni GB, 1990).

Maugeri, Franco, *Mussolini mi ha detto: confessioni di Mussolini durante il confino a Ponza e alla Maddalena* (Rome: Quaderni di politica estera, 1944).

Mazzonis, Filippo, 'Confinati politici a Lipari nei documenti inediti del Presidente generale della CRI 1', *Trimestre*, 9:3–4 (July–December 1976), 463–96.

——. 'Confinati politici a Lipari nei documenti inediti del Presidente generale della CRI 1', *Trimestre*, 10:1–2 (January-June 1977), 320–61.

Meneghini, Adele Rita, 'L'antifascismo nella provincia di Matera (1926–1943)', (Thesis, Università degli Studi di Roma 'La Sapienza', 1990–91).

Meoli, Claudio, *Il prefetto nell'ordinamento italiano* (Florence: R. Nocciolo, 1984).

Milletti, Nerina, 'Accuse innominabili: lesbiche e confino di polizia durante il fascismo', in Nerina Milletti and Luisa Passerini (eds), *Fuori della norma: storie lesbiche nell'Italia della prima metà del Novecento* (Turin: Rosenberg & Sellier, 2007), pp. 135–69.

Mola, Aldo, *Storia della massoneria italiana dalle origini ai giorni nostri* (Milan: Bompiani, 2001).

Montagnani-Marelli, Piero, *Lettere dal confino* (Viareggio: Mauro Baroni, 1999).

Montanelli, Indro, *L'Italia in camicia nera* (Milan: Rizzoli, 1976).

Musci, Leonardo. 'Il confino fascista di polizia: l'apparato statale di fronte al dissenso politico e sociale', in Adriano Dal Pont and Simonetta Carolini, *L'Italia al confino*. Vol. 1 (Milan: La Pietra, 1983), XXI–CI.

Mussolini, Benito, 'Viatico per il 1926', *Gerarchia*, 5:1 (1926).

——. *Discorso dell'Ascensione: il regime Fascista per la grandezza dell'Italia. Pronunciato il 26 maggio 1927 alla Camera dei Deputati* (Rome: Libreria del Littorio, 1927a).

——. *Opera omnia*, 36 vols, eds Edoardo Susmel and Duilio Susmel (Florence: La Fenice, 1951–62).

——. *Opera omnia. Appendici I–VIII*. Vols 37–44, eds Edoardo Susmel and Duilio Susmel (Rome: Giovanni Volpe Editore, 1978–80).

Nitti, Francesco Fausto, *Escape: The Personal Narrative of a Political Prisoner Who Was Rescued from Lipari, The Fascist Devil's Island* (New York: Putnam and Sons, 1930).

——. *Le nostre prigioni e la nostra evasione* (Naples: Edizioni Scientifiche Italiane, 1946).

Oliva, Gianni, *Storia dei Carabinieri: dal 1814 a oggi.* (Milan: Mondadori, 2002).

Osti Guerrazzi, Amedeo, *Poliziotti: i direttori dei campi di concentramento italiani 1940–1943* (Rome: Cooper, 2004).

Ottolenghi, Salvatore, *Trattato di polizia scientifica* (Milan: Società editrice libraria, 1932).

Pagano, Alessandra, *Il confino politico a Lipari* (Milan: Franco Angeli, 2003).

Paterlini, Roberto, *Cani randagi* (Rome: Rai Eri, 2012).

Pavese, Cesare, *Prima che il gallo canti* (Turin: Einaudi, 1949).

——. *Lettere*, 2 vols, ed. Lorenzo Mondo (Turin: Einaudi, 1966).

——. *Il carcere* (Turin: Einaudi, 1990a).

——. *La casa in collina* (Turin: Einaudi, 1990b).

——. *La luna e i falò* (Turin: Einaudi, 1995).

——. *Paesi tuoi* (Turin: Einaudi, 2001).

Persichilli, Gina Antoniani, 'Le misure di pubblica sicurezza: dal domicilio coatto al confino di polizia', *Temi ciociaria*, 5:4 (1978), 107–21.

Pescarolo, Loris, *Il lungo cammino* (Suzzara: Edizioni Bottazzi, 1984).

Petacco, Arrigo, *L'uomo della provvidenza: Mussolini, ascesa e caduta di un mito* (Milan: Mondadori, 2004).

Petrini, Davide, *La prevenzione inutile: illegitimità delle misure praeter delictum* (Naples: Jovene, 1996).

Peyrot, Giorgio, *La circolare Buffarini-Guidi e i Pentecostali* (Rome: Associazione Italiana per la Libertà della Cultura, 1955).

——. *Gli evangelici nei loro rapporti con lo Stato del fasicsmo ad oggi* (Torre Pellice: Società di studi valdesi, 1977).

Piccioli, Paolo, 'I testimoni di Geova durante il regime fascista', *Studi Storici*, 41:1 (2000), 191–229.

Pini, Andrea, *Quando eravamo froci: gli omosessuali nell'Italia di una volta* (Milan: Il Saggiatore, 2011).

Pirastu, Salvatore, *I confinati antifascisti in Sardegna: 1926–1943* (Cagliari: Anippia, 1997).

Pitamitz, Antonio, 'Silvestri: L'ultimo amico di Mussolini', *Storia Illustrata*, 271 (June 1980), 13.

Poerio, Ilaria, *A scuola di dissenso: storie di resistenza al confino di polizia (1926–1943)* (Rome: Carocci, 2016).

Poesio, Camilla, *Il confino fascista: l'arma silenziosa del regime* (Bari: Laterza, 2011).

Pratolini, Vasco, *Cronache di poveri amanti* (Florence: Vallecchi, 1947).

Previato, Luciano, *L'altra Italia. Carceri, colonie di confino, campi di concentramento durante il ventennio fascista* (Bologna: Consiglio regionale dell'Emilia-Romagna, 1995).

Procacci, Giovanna, 'L'internamento di civili in Italia durante la prima guerra Mondiale: normativa e conflitti di competenza', *DEP: Deporate, esuli, profughe. Rivista telematica di studi sulla memoria femminile*, 5–6 (2006), 33–66.

Pugliese, Stanislao, *Carlo Rosselli: Socialist Heretic and Antifascist Exile* (Cambridge, MA: Harvard University Press, 199).

Ravera, Camilla, *Vita in carcere e al confino: con lettere e documenti*, ed. Ada Gobetti (Parma: Editore Guanda, 1969).

——. *Diario di trent'anni 1913–1943* (Rome: Editori Riuniti, 1973).

Rigoletto, Sergio, *Masculinity and Italian Cinema: Sexual Politics, Social Conflict, and Male Crisis in the 1970s* (Edinburgh: Edinburgh University Press, 2014).

Robiony, Giorgio and Rosaria Conte, *Amori al confino* (Lanciano: Carabba Editore, 2004).

Rochat, Giorgio, *Regime fascista e chiese evangeliche: direttive e articolazioni del controllo e della repressione* (Turin: Claudiana, 1990).

Rocco, Alfredo, *Scritti e discorsi politici di Alfredo Rocco. Vol. 3. La formazione dello Stato fascista (1925–1934)* (Milan: Giuffrè editore, 1938).

Romeo, Enzo, *La solitudine feconda: Cesare Pavese al confino di Brancaleone 1935–1936* (Cosenza: Editoriale progetto 2000, 1986).

Rosselli, Carlo, 'Fuga in quattro tempi', *Almanacco socialista 1931* (Paris: PSI, 1931), pp. 76–89.

Rossi, Cesare, *Il Tribunale Speciale: storia documentata* (Milan: Ceschina, 1952).

Rossi, Ernesto, *Miserie e splendori del confino di polizia: lettere da Ventotene, 1939–1943* (Milan: Feltrinelli, 1981).

——. *Una spia del regime. Carlo Del Re e la provocazione contro Giustizia e Libertà* (Turin: Bollati Boringhieri, 2000).

Rossi-Doria, Manlio, *La gioia tranquilla del ricordo: memorie 1905–1934* (Bologna: Il Mulino, 1991).

Salvatorelli, Luigi and Giovanni Mira, *Storia d'Italia nel periodo fascista* (Turin: Einaudi, 1964).

Salvatori, Luigi, *Al confino e in carcere* (Milan: Feltrinelli, 1958).

Sannino, Antonio, *Il fantasma dell'OVRA* (Milan: Greco & Greco, 2011).

Scoppola, Pietro, *La chiesa e il fascismo: documenti e interpretazioni* (Bari: Laterza, 1973).

Secchia, Pietro and Enzo Nizza (eds), *Enciclopedia dell'antifascismo e della Resistenza*, 6 vols (Milan: La Pietra, 1968–89).

Semizzi, Roberto, 'Gli Zingari', *Rassegna di clinica, terapia e scienze affini*, 38:1 (1939).

Silone, Ignazio, *Vino e pane* (Milan: Mondadori, 1989).

———. *Fontamara* (Milan: Mondadori, 1997).

Simonini, Augusto, *Il linguaggio di Mussolini* (Milan: Bompiani, 1978).

Sorgi, Marcello, *Edda Ciano e il comunista: l'inconfessabile passione della figlia del Duce* (Milan: Rizzoli, 2009).

Sorgoni, Angelo, *Ricordi di un ex-confinato: un socialista recanatese dal 1898 alla liberazione* (Urbino: Argalìa, 1975).

Spackman, Barbara, *Fascist Virilities: Rhetoric, Ideology, and Social Fantasy in Italy* (Minneapolis: University of Minnesota Press, 1996).

Spadafora, Rosa, *Il popolo al confino: la persecuzione fascista in Campania*, 2 vols (Naples: Athena, 1989).

Spinelli, Altiero, *Come ho tentato di diventare saggio: Io, Ulisse* (Bologna: Il Mulino, 1984).

Spinelli, Altiero and Ernesto Rossi, *Per un'Europa libera e unita. Il manifesto di Ventotene. Le manifeste de Ventotene. The Ventotene Manifesto* (Rome: Senato della Repubblica, 2017).

Spini, Giorgio, *Italia di Mussolini e protestanti* (Turin: Claudiana, 2007).

Spinosa, Antonio, *Edda: una tragedia italiana* (Milan: Mondadori, 1993).

Tabori, Paul, *The Anatomy of Exile: A Semantic and Historical Study* (London: Harrap, 1972).

Tani, Sante, *Lettere dal carcere e dal confino (1942–1943)*, ed. Luca Berti (Milan: Franco Angeli, 1999).

Teruzzi, Attilio, *La milizia delle camicie nere* (Milan: Mondadori, 1939).

Tosatti, Giovanna, 'La repressione del dissenso politico tra l'età liberale e il fascismo: l'organizzazione della polizia', *Studi storici*, 38:1 (1997), 217–55.

Trentin, Silvio, *Les transformations récentes du Droit public Italien: de la Charte de Charles-Albert à la creation de l'État fasciste* (Paris: Marcel Giard, 1929).

Treves, Anna, *Le nascite e la politica nell'Italia del Novecento* (Milan: LED, 2001).

Turchi, Emma, *La felicità è la lotta* (Venice: Marsilio Editore, 1976).

Turchi, Giulio, *Emma. Diario d'amore di un comunista al confino* (Rome: Donzelli, 2012).

Turchi, Emma and Giulio Turchi, *Se potessi scriverti ogni giorno: lettere 1927–1943*, ed. Gianfranco Porta (Rome: Donzelli, 2013).

Vecchiato, Giorgio, *Con romana volontà* (Venice: Marsilio, 2005).

Vecchini, Silvia, 'Leggere al confino di polizia: fonti e studi', *TECA. Testimonianze, editoria, cultura, arte*, 0 (September 2011), 1–19.

Ventura, Angelo (ed.), *Sulla crisi del regime fascista 1938–1943: la società italiana dal 'consenso' alla Resistenza* (Venice: Marsilio, 1996).

Venzi, Fabio, *Massoneria e fascismo: dall'intesa cordiale alla distruzione delle logge: come nasce una 'guerra di religione', 1921–1925* (Rome: Castelvecchi Editore, 2008).

Violante, Luciano, 'La repressione del dissenso politico nell'Italia liberale: stati d'assedio e giustizia militare', *Rivista di storia contemporanea*, 5:4 (1976), 481–524.

Woller, Hans, *I conti con il fascismo: l'epurazione in Italia 1943–1948* (Bologna: Il Mulino, 1997).

Zuccaro, Domenico, 'Carcere e confino: tre memoriali inediti di Cesare Pavese', *Il Ponte*, 30:5 (1974), 530–47.

# Index

EU authorised representative for GPSR:
Easy Access System Europe, Mustamäe tee 50,
10621 Tallinn, Estonia
gpsr.requests@easproject.com

www.ingramcontent.com/pod-product-compliance
Lightning Source LLC
Chambersburg PA
CBHW052003270326
41929CB00015B/2771